GLOBAL STRATEGIC MANAGEMENT

GLOBAL STRATEGIC MANAGEMENT

Kamel Mellahi

Jedrzej George Frynas

Paul Finlay

OXFORD

UNIVERSITY PRESS

OXFORD
UNIVERSITY PRESS

Great Clarendon Street, Oxford OX2 6DP

Oxford University Press is a department of the University of Oxford.
It furthers the University's objective of excellence in research, scholarship,
and education by publishing worldwide in

Oxford New York

Auckland Cape Town Dar es Salaam Hong Kong Karachi
Kuala Lumpur Madrid Melbourne Mexico City Nairobi
New Delhi Shanghai Taipei Toronto

With offices in

Argentina Austria Brazil Chile Czech Republic France Greece
Guatemala Hungary Italy Japan Poland Portugal
Singapore South Korea Switzerland Thailand Turkey Ukraine Vietnam

Oxford is a registered trademark of Oxford University Press
in the UK and in certain other countries

Published in the United States
by Oxford University Press Inc., New York

British Library Cataloguing in Publication Data

Data available

Library of Congress Cataloging in Publication Data

Data available

Typeset by Laserwords Private Limited, Chennai, India

Printed in Great Britain
on acid-free paper by
Ashford Colour Press Limited, Gosport, Hampshire

ISBN 0-19-926615-8   978-0-19-926615-9

10 9 8 7 6 5 4 3 2 1

PREFACE

Some time ago, we realized that strategic management books no longer reflected the world we live in. Globalization had arrived on the doorstep of many industries and books on global competition were mushrooming. But strategic management textbooks did not reflect that change. Most of them started including case studies of multinational companies and sometimes mentioned international competition, but they continued to use the same old frameworks and provided the same prescriptions as before.

We felt that a new type of textbook was needed, which combined the tools of strategic management with insights from international business studies. We were encouraged by our enthusiastic OUP editor and colleagues who thought that this was a book waiting to be written.

We also found that existing textbooks concentrated mainly on large US companies, which did not reflect the new global markets where US, European, Asian or Latin American companies vie for success. So we put a lot of emphasis in our book to include case studies of firms from emerging economies such as India and Brazil alongside US and European firms, and we also tried to keep in mind the needs of small and medium sized firms, which only started to internationalize recently. We hope that, in the age of globalization, this book feels much more inclusive than previous books.

We have written the book in a user-friendly style and we have designed it so that it can be used by students who did not previously study strategic management. An important feature of the book is the inclusion of opening and closing mini cases at the beginning and end of each chapter and full-length case studies at the end of each part. These are designed to enable students to analyse global strategic issues in real business situations. The book is organized in four parts. Part I, Introduction, provides a big-picture approach and introduces the field of global strategic management. Part II, Global Strategic Analysis, deals with the external macro environment, the industry environment, corporate social responsibility and stakeholders and the internal business environment within which multinational firms operate. Part III, Global Strategic Development, covers the internationalization process, international strategic alliances and subsidiary and headquarter level strategies. Part IV, Global Strategic Implementation, focuses on structures and designs of multinational firms, global management of change and issues surrounding global strategic control.

Kamel Mellahi was the lead author on Chapters 1, 6, 7, 8, and 9. Jedrzej George Frynas was the lead author on Chapters 2, 3, 4, and 5. Paul Finlay was the lead author on chapters 10, 11, and 12. However, the book is a product of a collaborative effort between the authors, who contributed to each others' chapters.

Kamel Mellahi
Jedrzej George Frynas
Paul Finlay
2005

ACKNOWLEDGEMENTS

We would like to take this opportunity to thank all of those individuals whose insight, time, and hard work have contributed to this book. First and foremost, we want to thank the editor Sacha Cook. Sacha's professionalism, unflagging patience, good humour (especially when things were not going very well) and superb support for the project made this book possible. A special thanks goes to Ross Bowmaker for organizing the review process and dealing with copyright permissions. We also want to thank our copy editor Sarah Barrett. The manuscript was reviewed by a number of global strategic management professors. We appreciate the time and efforts that those reviewers put into the reading of the chapters as well as their many useful suggestions for improvement.

Publisher's Acknowledgement

We are grateful to the following for permission to reproduce copyright material:

Exhibit 1.6, Global firms: National regulation & Global firms investment 1991–1997, used by permission of UNCTAD; Exhibit 1.5, Number of Regional Trade Agreements 1948–2002, http://www.globalpolicy.org/globaliz/charts/tradecomp.htm, reprinted by permission of Global Policy Forum, Tom Hale, and WTO; Exhibit 2.3, Diamond Model, Michael Porter, *The Competitive Advantage of Nations*, 1990, reprinted by permission of MacMillan; Exhibit 3.1, Strategic Groups, McGee, John and Segal-Horn, S. (1990). 'Strategic Space and Industry Dynamics', *J. Marketing Management* (3): 173–93, pp. 181+183, reprinted by permission of Westburn Publishers Ltd.; Exhibit 3.2, Five Forces Model, Michael Porter, 'How competitive forces shape strategy', *Harvard Business Review*, March–April 1979, reprinted by permission of Harvard Business School; Exhibit 3.4, Product Life Cycle, Louis T. Wells, Jr. 'A Product Life Cycle for International Trade?' *Journal of Marketing*, July 1968, (32): 1–6, reprinted by permission of The American Marketing Association; Exhibit 4.1, Views of CSR, Richard Holme & Phil Watts, *Corporate Social Responsibility: Making Good Business Sense* (World Business Council for Sustainable Development, Jan. 2000, pp. 8–9), reprinted by permission of WBCSD; Exhibit 4.3, NGO–Business Partnerships, Elkington, John and Fennel, Shelly (2000). 'Partners for Sustainability' in Jem Bendell (ed.), Terms for Endearment—Business, NGOs and Sustainable Development, reprinted by permission of Greenleaf Publishing Ltd; Exhibit 4.7, Cross-Impact Analysis, Steger, Ulrich, from *Corporate Diplomacy*, 2003 reprinted by permission of John Wiley & Sons Ltd.; Exhibit 4.8, 6 Step Process 'FOSTERing', reprinted by permission of Ann Svendsen at CoreRelation Consulting at http://www.corerelation.com.

Chapter 4, Suncor case, WBCSD website, reprinted by permission of SUNCOR/Dianne Humphries; Exhibit 5.1, Core Competencies, Prahalad, C. K. and Gary Hamel, 'The Core Competence of the Corporation', *Harvard Business Review*, May–June 1990, 68(3): 79–93, reprinted by permission of Harvard Business School Publishing Corporation; Exhibit 5.2, VRIO model, Barney, Jay B. (1997). *Gaining and Sustaining Competitive Advantage*. Addison Wesley, reprinted by permission of Pearson Education; Exhibit 5.3, Subsidiary Resources,

Birkinshaw et al. (1998). 'Building Firm-Specific Advantages in Multinational Corporations', *Strategic Management Journal* 19(3): 221–41, reprinted by permission of John Wiley & Sons Ltd.; Exhibit 5.4, Clothing Industry, Frynas J. G. 'The Transnational Garment Industry in South and South-East Asia', in Frynas/Pegg *Transnational Corporations & Human Rights*, Palgrave 2003, pp. 164–6, reprinted by permission of Palgrave; Exhibit 5.5, South African Peaches, Kaplan, D. & R. Kaplinsky (1999). 'Trade and Industrial Policy on an Uneven Playing Field: The case of the Deciduous Fruit Canning...', *World Development* 27(10): 1787–1801, reprinted with permission from Elsevier.

Exhibit 5.6, Value Chain, Porter, M. (1985). *Competitive Advantage: Creating and Sustaining Superior Performance*, adapted by permission of Free Press, Simon & Schuster Inc; Exhibit 5.7, Value System, Porter, M. (1985). *Competitive Advantage: Creating and Sustaining Superior Performance*, adapted by permission of Free Press, Simon & Schuster Inc; Exhibit 5.8, Value added in four industries, 'Globalisation and unequalisation: What can be learned from value chain analysis?' (2000) *Journal of Development Studies* 37(2): 117–46, reprinted by permission of Frank Cass; Exhibit 5.9, Value added chain/competitive advantage, Kogut, Bruce. (1985). 'Designing Global Strategies', *Sloan Management Review* (Summer): 15–28, p. 19, reprinted by permission of *Sloan Management Review*; Exhibit 5.10, Intelligence Onion, O'Guin, M. C. & T. Ogilvie. (2001). 'The Science, *Not Art*, of Bus Intelligence', *Competitive Intelligence Review* 12(4): 15–24, reprinted by permission of John Wiley & Sons Limited; Exhibit 5.11, 10 Step Benchmarking, Cox, A. & I. Thompson. (1998). 'On Appropriateness of Benchmarking', *J. of General Mgmt* 23(3): 1–19, reprinted by permission of Braybrook Press; Chapter 5, Case Study: F&C management, FT (FT Report), 30 June 2004, reprinted by permission of Financial Times; Chapter 7, Case study: 'Hands across the sea', (1998) *International Business*, 11(4): 12–13, Richard Zelade; Chapter 8: Case Study: Vive la difference, *Management Today*, October 1996, p. 101, Laura Mazur, Haymarket Reprints; Chapter 9, Exhibit 9.7, A global market portfolio matrix, in Harrell, D. G and Kiefer, O. R. 'Multinational market portfolios in Global Strategy Development', (1993) *International Marketing Review* 10(1), Emerald Group Publishing Limited; Exhibit 12.3, with permission of Pearson Education; Exhibit 12.4, The Tavistock Institute; Exhibit 12.5, with permission of The British Council; Professors Gupta and Prashanth for using the material in their case *Restructuring Sony*; and Palgrave for using the material in the case *Lessons in 'cross-vengeance': Restructuring the Thai subsidiary*.

In some instances we have been unable to trace the owners of copyright material and we would appreciate any information that would enable us to do so.

CONTENTS

LIST OF EXHIBITS

LIST OF CASES

PART I
Introduction

Introduction to global strategic management

Learning outcomes

After reading this chapter you should be able to:

- understand the characteristics of the strategic management process;
- list and describe the key phases of global strategy;
- understand the differences between international strategy and global strategy;
- examine the national, sector and firm level drivers for global strategy.

Established in the 1940s in a small village in Sweden by Ingvar Kamprad, IKEA has become one of the world's leading retailers of home furnishings. In 2002 it was ranked 44th out of the top 100 brands by Interbrand, topping other known brands such as Pepsi. In 2002, it had more than 160 stores in 30 countries.

IKEA's strategy is based on selling high-quality, Swedish designed, self-assembly furniture products at low price. The IKEA business idea is: 'We shall offer a wide range of well-designed, functional home furnishing products at prices so low that as many people as possible will be able to afford them.' IKEA targets price-conscious young couples and families who are willing and able to transport and assemble furniture kits.

By the early 1960s the Swedish market was saturated and IKEA decided to expand its business formula outside Sweden. IKEA's CEO, Anders Dehlvin, noted: 'Sweden is a very small country. It's pretty logical: in a country like this, if you have a very strong and successful business, you're bound to go international at some point. The reason is simple—you cannot grow any more.'

IKEA opened its first store outside Sweden in 1963 in Norway. In 1969 it opened its second international store, in Denmark. It moved outside the Scandinavian countries when it opened its store in Switzerland in 1973, and then entered a new country every couple of years. Under IKEA's global strategy, suppliers are usually located in low-cost nations, with close proximity to raw materials and reliable access to distribution channels. IKEA has over 2,500 suppliers scattered in over sixty countries. IKEA works closely with its suppliers by helping them to reduce costs, and sharing technical advice and managerial know-how with them. In return IKEA has exclusive contracts with its suppliers. These suppliers produce highly standardized products intended for the global market.

IKEA's internationalization strategy in Scandinavian countries and the rest of Europe has not paid significant attention to local tastes and preferences in the different European countries. Only necessary changes were allowed, to keep costs under control. IKEA's business formula is based on low cost and affordability. Adaptation to each country's local requirement would lead to higher cost of production and subsequently put pressure on the company to increase its prices. IKEA applied its initial vision—to sell a basic product range that is 'typically Swedish' wherever it ventures. To emphasize its Swedish roots, it often uses a Swedish theme in its advertising campaign, and has a Swedish blue and gold colour scheme for its stores. The firm reaps huge economies of scale from the size of each store, and the big production runs made possible by selling the same products all over the world. IKEA's low responsiveness to local needs strategy seems to work. In 1997 its international sales represented around 89 per cent of its total sales. IKEA sales in Germany (42.5 per cent) were much higher than its sales in Sweden (11 per cent).

IKEA's strategy of not paying attention to local market peculiarities has worked well in Europe. The company has been able to sell its standardized products across Europe, and as a result was able to build considerable economies of scale into its operations and maintain a price advantage over its competitors. The first challenge came when IKEA entered the US market in 1985. Although between 1985 and 1996 IKEA opened twenty-six stores in North America, these stores were not as successful as their counterparts in Europe. IKEA faced several problems in the US market. The root of most of these problems was the company's lack of attention to local needs and wants. US customers preferred large furniture kits and household items. For example, Swedish beds were five inches narrower than those US customers were used to, IKEA's kitchen cupboards were too narrow for the large dinner plates typically used in the US, IKEA's glasses were too small for US customers who typically add ice to their drink and hence require large glasses—it is said that US customers bought flower vases thinking they were drinking glasses—and bedroom chests of drawers were too shallow for US consumers, who tend to store sweaters in them. In addition, IKEA Swedish-sized curtains did not fit American windows, a mistake about which a senior IKEA manager joked, 'Americans just wouldn't lower their ceilings to fit our curtains.'

As a result of initial poor performance in the US market, IKEA's management realized that a standardized product strategy should be flexible enough to respond to local markets. The company has recently adopted a more balanced strategic focus (giving weight to global and domestic concerns). The current approach puts greater emphasis on global market coordination to limit duplication of activities and capture synergies or economies of scale and scope. In the early 1990s IKEA redesigned its strategy and adapted its products to the US market. While overall its subsidiaries are still no more than extensions of the corporate head office in Sweden, following instructions provided from the centre, subsidiaries in the US are given more autonomy, to respond effectively to the local business environment. A greater customization in the US is made possible by the large size of the US market, which enables IKEA's subsidiaries in the US to produce kits designed specifically for the US market in large quantities and hence keep cost under control. During the 1990–94 period, IKEA's sales in the US increased threefold to $480 million, and rose to $900 million in 1997. By 2002 the US market accounted for 19 per cent of IKEA's revenue.

Sources: IKEA's website: **www.ikea.com**; 'Furnishing the world', *Economist* (19 Nov. 1994), 79–80; H. Carnegy, 'Struggle to save the soul of IKEA', *Financial Times*, (27 Mar. 1995), 12; J. Flynn and L. Bongiorno, 'IKEA's new game plan', *Business Week* (6 Oct. 1997), 99–102; 'Ikea has designs to furnish the world', *European* (19 Nov. 1994), 32; Barbara Solomon, 'A Swedish company corners the business: worldwide', *Management Review* (Apr. 1991); Katarina Kling and Ingela Gofeman, 'Ikea CEO Anders Dahlving on international growth and Ikea's unique corporate culture and brand identity', *Academy of Management Executive* (Feb. 2003).

1.1 **Introduction**

Many young people in most parts of the world take for granted the mobile phones, internet access, e-mails, and cheap travel abroad that were unavailable or very expensive a few decades ago. These products and services permeate all aspects of our lives, and they have radically changed the way organizations are managed. For example, while the international manager of yesterday spent hours on the phone talking to regional or country managers, the international manager of today enters an internet or a videophone conference room or uses e-mails and instant messaging to communicate with his or her subsidiaries at all hours and around the world. International managers are now, by using mobile phones and laptop computers, able to connect with their organization and access information on any of their subsidiaries whenever they want, wherever they are.

It is fair to assume that such technological innovations will continue to flourish and to play an ever more significant role in the way organizations are managed in the future. As they do so, the meaning of physical presence at a particular space or location will become increasingly blurred, and will never be as important as it was in the past. Make a 'local' phone call from London to inquire about your train, plane, or coach or your phone bill, and it is more likely that the person dealing with your inquiry is located in India than in the United Kingdom. We are not suggesting that location does not matter any more. But we are suggesting that geographical distance has become far less of a hindrance to managing globally.

In addition to the recent technological advancements in several industries, products, customer tastes, and managerial practices are converging across countries. A converged global market permits a standardized product across countries that minimizes complexity and the cost of adapting the product to local market peculiarities, thereby achieving higher performance. While the global convergence of markets offers multinational firms (also known as multinationals) the opportunity to standardize their products across countries, the technological revolution makes the execution of the strategy possible.

As the opening case study illustrates, in several industries firms with effective strategy do not have to change their core strategy significantly when they move beyond their home market. IKEA does not significantly change its corporate strategy and operations to adapt to local markets unless there is a compelling reason for doing so. By so doing, it reaps the benefits of economies of scale and scope. Economies of scale are cost savings that accrue from increases in volume of production. Economies of scope are savings that accrue from cross-business cost-saving activities.

This should not be taken to mean that nothing will ever have to be changed. IKEA's strategy in the US during the 1980s demonstrates that even the most successful formula in the home market can fail if multinationals do not respond effectively to local business realities. While IKEA's strategy worked well in Sweden, Scandinavian countries, and the rest of Europe, it failed initially in the US. The company had to reconsider the perceived universal appeal of its products, and adjusted its activities to local markets without compromising the huge benefits gained from sourcing and selling standardized products. IKEA's example shows that some form of adaptation to local markets does not always require the complete and radical change of the core strategy. A key challenge for managers is to be able to determine the extent to which adaptation to local markets is achieved without compromising the core strategy. Differently put, to be successful firms must strike a balance between the benefits and costs of providing subsidiaries with the flexibility to react to local business realities they encounter, and the benefits and costs of coordinating a global strategy from the centre.

1.2 Defining the strategic management field

In this book, we take it that global strategic management is a subcategory—albeit different and distinct—of domestic or single-country strategic management (henceforward referred to as strategic management). Therefore, we expect our readers to be familiar with a number of core concepts of strategic management, so as to be able fully to understand the process and content of global strategic management. Whenever necessary, these prerequisite core concepts of strategic management will be presented and explained in this book.

Before we proceed to discuss the field of global strategic management, it would be beneficial to define strategic management. What, then, is strategic management? We start with a fairly simple definition of strategic management so that we may bring attention to its important characteristics. Strategic management is *the process of setting long-term direction for the organization.* The central thrust of strategic management is achieving a sustainable competitive advantage. The term 'advantage' refers to the superior benefit, or superior position or condition, resulting from a course of action taken by the firm. 'Competitive' refers to a position in relation to an actual or potential rival. Finally, 'sustain' means to keep up a position over a long period of time. A sustainable competitive advantage is therefore the prolonged benefit gained from developing and implementing some unique value-adding strategy that is not simultaneously (or shortly thereafter) being imitated by current or potential rivals (Bharadwaj et al. 1993).

The above definition of strategic management suggests that strategic management is the process of strategic decision-making. A *process* is a systematic way of carrying out interrelated activities in order to obtain desired goals and objectives. Strategy-making process involves 'key decisions' made for and on behalf of the entire organization. For firms operating in several countries, the strategy process consists of the *analysis, development,* and *implementation* steps taken by firms in order to manage the global network of subsidiaries in different parts of the world. These three steps form the framework used in this book (see Exhibit 1.1).

We offer this framework with some reservations, since any framework simplifies reality. However, we believe that a successful strategy involves each of these steps.

Although, in practice, the above three phases—analysis, development, and implementation—take place simultaneously, in this book, for reasons of clarity, we are going to examine them sequentially. This may give the false impression that managers should first analyse the environment and that only after completing this activity should they develop the appropriate strategy and finally implement it. In a fast-changing and turbulent global competitive environment, by the time managers complete the analysis of the environment and start the development stage, a new competitive environment emerges and may render the first analysis absolute. Imagine what would have happened to a meticulous analysis of the global airline industry just before September 11, 2001. The September 11 attack on the World Trade Center would have rendered the analysis useless. Or imagine a multinational with a well-developed strategy to enter the Chinese market just before the outbreak of Severe Acute Respiratory Syndrome (SARS) in 2003. The multinational would have been forced to change the implementation plan or delay its entry altogether.

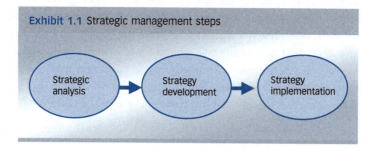

Exhibit 1.1 Strategic management steps

Strategic analysis → Strategy development → Strategy implementation

> **KEY CONCEPT**
>
> Strategic management is the process of strategic decision-making that sets the long-term direc-
> tion for the organization. The central thrust of strategic management is achieving a sustainable
> competitive advantage. The strategy process consists of the *analysis*, *development*, and *imple-
> mentation* steps.

1.3 Phases of global strategy

The term 'global strategy' has been in use only since the late 1970s, and began to assume widespread use in the 1990s. Prior to the 1990s, 'international strategy' was the term
most often used, and it is still in use now, to describe the strategic activities of firms operating across borders. In fact, for many, 'global' is just a new replacement for the term
'international', and hence 'international strategy' and 'global strategy' are sometimes used
interchangeably. We take global strategy to mean something new and different from international strategy. As you will see in this chapter and throughout this book, there are real
differences between international strategic management and global strategic management
(see Exhibit 1.2). However, before we explain in detail what global strategic management
is, let us first look at the most likely phases firms go through before they adopt a global
strategy. These phases will be explored further in Chapters 6 and 10; by way of introductory
summary, however, we group them into four main phases.

1.3.1 Single-country strategy

Most firms operating around the world at one time operated in a single country. Firms that
are now household names around the world started as small ventures in a single country. Firms operating strictly within the confines of their home country use single-country
strategies to compete in their home market, where they face only one set of business factors
and one set of customers.

In the past, so long as the firm's home market kept growing and remained profitable,
there was no urgent need to expand into foreign markets. Internationalization was often
considered when the firm's home market became unprofitable or the prospect for growth
started to diminish, and attractive opportunities to expand internationally were available.
Given the recent acceleration of the globalization process, successful firms operating in
global industries cannot afford to wait until the home market becomes unattractive or unprofitable, but must take proactive actions to capture the benefits of operating around the
globe. Even for firms that do not operate internationally, formulating and implementing
a strategy that focuses solely on local competitors and customers may not guarantee their
strategic competitiveness. Robert Lutz, General Motors' vice-chairman, noted: 'We can no
longer afford the luxury of telling ourselves we're going after the domestic buyer ... That's

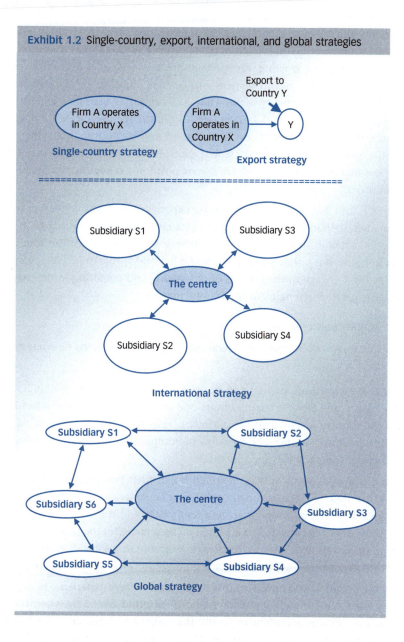

Exhibit 1.2 Single-country, export, international, and global strategies

just looking for a bigger piece of a shrinking pie' (quoted in Fahey 2002: 82). The benefits and risks of a single-country strategy are discussed below.

Benefits of a single-country strategy

It should be noted that extending a firm's business scope from a single country to several countries is not always the best strategy. Some firms are better off staying at home:

- First, despite the pressure to globalize, some firms can still achieve high returns on investment without relying on foreign markets. Solberg (1997) argues that there is no need for firms operating in a growing non-global industry—such as construction, primary and secondary education, or health services—to operate globally. He suggests that the best strategy in this case is to stay at home. That is, if a firm has a strong competitive strength at home and the pressure for global competition in the sector in which it operates is low, then concentration on the home market is a good strategy option. By staying in the home market the firm is able to capitalize astutely on its local identity; and its strong familiarity to local customers puts it in an advantageous position vis-à-vis firms operating from far away countries.

- Second, if a firm has limited international experience and has a weak position in the home market, it should try first to improve its competitive position at home before expanding its activities to foreign markets (Solberg 1997; Yip 2002). Without an effective strategy at home, it is unlikely that IKEA would have been able to succeed outside Sweden. Firms like IKEA engage in the process of competing and operating in different countries to capitalize on their strengths in their home market.

Risks of a single-country strategy

Operating in a single country entails several risks, especially when the business environment in that country is unstable.

- First, since the organization is dependent on one market, it is putting all of its eggs in one country basket, and adverse changes in its one and only market could affect its performance. If the country where the organization operates becomes unattractive due to market saturation, political instability, or erosion of competitive advantage by rivals, then the survival of the company becomes doubtful.

- Second, if managers focus only on competitors in their home market, they run the risk of being surprised by global competitors offering far superior products or technology that could make their firm uncompetitive. As a result, they will at best be forced to reduce their market share or be relegated to serve a small niche segment of the market. At worst, if they engage in price wars with large multinational firms offering superior-quality products and services at lower prices, they might be forced to withdraw from the marketplace.

- Third, since organizations operating in a single country have experience in only one country, they have limited ability to move quickly to other countries when times become tough in the home market; consequently they may hurt their performance further by moving outside their home country hurriedly, without proper planning.

1.3.2 Export strategy

Before a firm establishes subsidiaries outside its home market and becomes directly involved in their management, it may start by exporting its products and services outside its home market. This stage will be fully covered in Chapters 6 and 10. In most exporting firms the domestic strategy remains of primary importance. While an exporting firm makes strategic decisions to select appropriate countries to export to, determines the appropriate level of product modification to meet local market peculiarities, and sets and manages export channels, the thrust of its strategy deals with the management of the firm in the home country. For this reason, this phase could be considered as a domestic strategy with an export strategy attached to it.

1.3.3 International strategy

When firms first establish subsidiaries outside their home market, they move from a domestic strategy phase to an international strategy phase. Firms that manufacture and market products or services in several countries are called 'multinational firms'. During this phase, each subsidiary is likely to have its own strategy, and will analyse, develop, and implement that strategy by tailoring it to its particular local market. At this phase, adaptation of products to fit local market peculiarities becomes the main concern for multinational firms. Internationally scattered subsidiaries act independently and operate as if they were local companies, with minimum coordination from the parent company. This approach leads to a wide variety of business strategies, and a high level of adaptation to the local business environment.

1.3.4 Global strategy

As multinationals mature and move through the first three stages, they become aware of the opportunities to be gained from integrating and creating a single strategy on a global scale. A global strategy involves a carefully crafted single strategy for the entire network of subsidiaries and partners, encompassing many countries simultaneously and leveraging synergies across many countries. The term 'simultaneous' is used here to indicate that most of the activities of the different subsidiaries are coordinated from headquarters in order to maximize global efficiency, which allows multinational firms to achieve the economies of scale and scope that are critical for global competitiveness (Ghoshal 1987; Bartlett and Ghoshal 1989; Prahalad and Doz 1987; Doz 1980).

Moving from a domestic or international strategy to a global strategy is not an easy process, and creates various strategic challenges. The challenge here is to develop one single strategy that can be applied throughout the world while at the same time maintaining the flexibility to adapt that strategy to the local business environment when necessary.

KEY CONCEPT

A *global strategy* involves the carefully crafted single strategy for the entire network of subsidiaries and partners, encompassing many countries simultaneously and leveraging synergies across many countries. This stands in contrast to an *international strategy*, which involves a wide variety of business strategies across countries, and a high level of adaptation to the local business environment.

1.4 International strategy and global strategy: what is the difference?

What differences are there between the global strategy and international strategy? There are three key differences. The first relates to the degree of involvement and coordination from the centre. Coordination of strategic activities is the extent to which a firm's strategic activities in different country locations are planned and executed interdependently on a global scale to exploit the synergies that exist across different countries. International strategy does not require strong coordination from the centre. Global strategy, on the other hand, requires significant coordination between the activities of the centre and those of subsidiaries.

The second difference relates to the degree of product standardization and responsiveness to local business environment. Product standardization is the degree to which a product, service, or process is standardized across countries (Zou and Çavusgil 2002). An international strategy assumes that the subsidiary should respond to local business needs unless there is a good reason for not doing so. In contrast, the global strategy assumes that the centre should standardize its operations and products in all the different countries, unless there is a compelling reason for not doing so.

The third difference has to do with strategy integration and competitive moves. 'Integration' and 'competitive move' refer to the extent to which a firm's competitive moves in major markets are interdependent. For example, a multinational firm subsidizes operations or subsidiaries in countries where the market is growing with resources gained from other subsidiaries where the market is declining, or responds to competitive moves by rivals in one market by counter-attacking in others (Yip 2002). The international strategy gives subsidiaries the independence to plan and execute competitive moves independently—that is, competitive moves are based solely on the analysis of local rivals (this issue will be discussed in Chapter 3). In contrast, the global strategy plans and executes competitive battles on a global scale. Firms adopting a global strategy, however, compete as a collection of a globally integrated single firms. Yip (2002: 7) notes that international strategy treats competition in each country on a 'stand-alone basis', while a global strategy takes 'an integrated approach' across different countries.

1.5 Defining global strategic management

Having examined the broad field of global strategic management, we are now able to define it more accurately. Because (as stated earlier) global strategic management is a subset of strategic management, any definition of global strategic management has to be built on basic definitions of strategic management, with an added explanation of the global dimensions. So what are these global dimensions? We use the three differences between international strategy and global strategy to define global strategic management. Section 1.4 suggested that global strategy dimensions can be categorized into three main dimensions: the

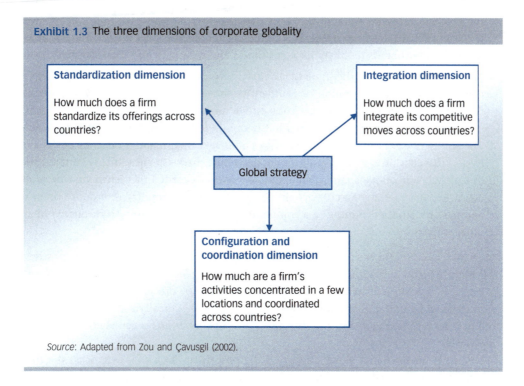

Exhibit 1.3 The three dimensions of corporate globality

Standardization dimension

How much does a firm standardize its offerings across countries?

Integration dimension

How much does a firm integrate its competitive moves across countries?

Global strategy

Configuration and coordination dimension

How much are a firm's activities concentrated in a few locations and coordinated across countries?

Source: Adapted from Zou and Çavusgil (2002).

configuration and coordination, standardization, and integration dimensions (see Exhibit 1.3). The discussion that follows describes the three sets of dimensions in more detail.

- The first major dimension of global strategy is *coordination* and *configuration* of the multinational firm's activities across countries. According to this view, global strategy is the process of exploiting the synergies that exist across different countries, as well as the comparative advantages offered by different countries (Zou and Çavusgil 2002). Comparative advantages offered by different countries include resources that are inherited—such as a country's location, climate, size, or stock of natural deposits—and resources that are the subject of sustained investment over a considerable period of time—such as a country's education system and specific skills, its technological and organizational capabilities, its communication and marketing infrastructures and its levels of labour productivity. According to the *configuration and coordination* perspective, multinational firms must configure their operations to exploit the benefits offered by different country locations, and coordinate their activities across countries to capture synergies derived from economies of scale and scope (Zou and Çavusgil 2002).

- The *standardization* dimension expressed by Levitt (1983) defines global strategic management as the process of offering products across countries. According to this view, multinational firms pursuing a standardization strategy have a *global strategy*, while multinational firms pursuing an adaptation strategy should be referred to as implementing an *international strategy*. It is important to note that for strategy to be global absolute standardization across countries is not necessary. Rather, it suffices if core elements of the product or service are applied consistently across countries with minor adaptations to local peculiarities. For example, IKEA offers its standard products worldwide but makes necessary adjustments to satisfy local customers and meet different legal standards.

- The third perspective is the *integrations* view. According to this view, global strategy is concerned with the integration of competitive moves across country markets (Zou and Çavusgil 2002). Here, a firm makes competitive moves not because they are best for the particular country or region involved but because they are best for the firm as a whole. The ability of a firm to coordinate activities globally across markets depends on its ability to cross-subsidize, explicitly or implicitly, across markets. Yip (2002: 15) noted that in a global competitive strategy, competitive moves are made in a systematic way across countries, and that a competitor could be 'attacked in one country in order to drain its resources for another country, or a competitive attack in one country is countered in another country'.

Each of the above dimensions offers a partial explanation of global strategy. In this book we adopt a broad definition of global strategy that integrates the above three dimensions. We take it that the pursuance of one dimension does not preclude a multinational firm from pursuing another. A multinational firm may provide globally standard products, coordinate its activities globally, and integrate its competitive moves across countries simultaneously.

It must be noted that a global strategy is the process towards one, two, or all the three dimensions, as opposed to the extreme points of the perspective (Zou and Çavusgil 2002). For a strategy to be global does not require absolute standardization across countries, complete coordination between countries, and fully integrated competitive moves. Rather, as the IKEA case study shows, it suffices for the main elements of the core strategy to be standardized, coordinated, and integrated consistently across countries, with varying degrees of adaptation to local market peculiarities when required. That is, multinational firms look for the appropriate level at which each dimension or all dimensions can be pursued. In addition, one cannot pigeonhole multinational firms into global and non-global firms. Rather, as Govindarajan and Gupta (2000) noted, 'globality is a continuous variable along a spectrum', with some firms highly global and others less so.

On the basis of the above analysis, a global strategic management definition must take into consideration all three dimensions. Thus, we define global strategic management as a process of crafting a coherent, coordinated, integrated, and unified strategy that sets the degree to which a firm globalizes its strategic behaviours in different countries through standardization of offerings, configuration and coordination of activities in different countries, and integration of competitive moves across countries.

For the purpose of this book, we will occasionally use the term 'global strategic management' to refer to the broad field of managing across countries. This is because the term 'global strategic management' has become the preferred term of academics and managers. For example, both the Academy of International Business and the Strategic Management Society have 'global strategic management' research tracks which deal with strategic management issues across countries. In fact, the term 'global strategic management' was chosen as the title for this book not to neglect international strategies (or even single-country strategies) but to indicate that a significant part of the book deals specifically with global strategies.

While we restrict the use of the term 'global strategy' to strategies that relate to the specific phenomenon of global strategy, we use the term 'multinational firm' (or 'multinational' for short) to refer to any firm that has extensive operations outside the home market, including producing and marketing in at least two different countries.

KEY CONCEPT

Global strategic management is the process of crafting a coherent, coordinated, integrated, and unified strategy that sets the degree to which a firm globalizes its strategic behaviours in different countries through standardization of offerings, configuration and coordination of activities in different countries, and integration of competitive moves across countries.

1.6 Drivers for a global strategic perspective

The extent to which a multinational firm adopts a global strategy is determined by three broad factors: *macro globalizing drivers*, namely globalization and information and communication technology; *industry globalizing drivers*, namely market drivers, cost drivers, government drivers, and competitive drivers; and *internal globalizing drivers*, namely global orientation and international experience. The macro globalizing drivers have an overall impact and are not specific to certain industries or organizations. The industry globalizing drivers determine the globality of a sector, industry, or market. The internal globalizing drivers determine how a firm responds to its globalizing business environment. The combination of these drivers will be unique for each sector and more unique for each multinational firm (see Exhibit 1.4).

1.6.1 Macro globalizing drivers

As Exhibit 1.4 shows, there are two key macro globalizing drivers: globalization and information communication technology.

Globalization

Globalization is inescapably a multi-faceted process. There is fundamental disagreement about what globalization is and, indeed, what it is not. For the purpose of this book, we see globalization as being a composite of three interrelated elements: the creation of a global economy, political globalization, and a globalization of ideas and values. Globalization is simultaneously accelerating and deepening these three elements.

Global Economic integration   For the last few decades we have been witnessing a dramatic increase in the density and depth of economic interdependence. The number of regional trade agreements, which has increased from very few in the late 1950s to over 180 in 2002, is good evidence of the interconnectedness of the global economy (see Exhibit 1.5). Other

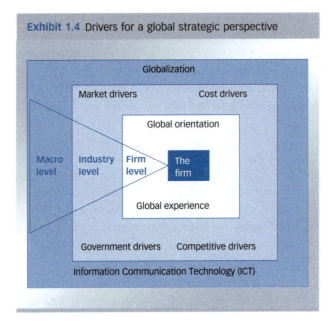

Exhibit 1.4 Drivers for a global strategic perspective

indications include the increase in national regulations in favour of foreign direct invest-ment (FDI) and other types of foreign investment. Exhibit 1.6 shows that the changes coun-tries are making in favour of FDI and other forms of international investment far exceed the changes that are not in favour.

However, on the basis of analysis of FDI flow across borders, Alan Rugman argues that there is no such thing as globalization (Rugman 2001; Rugman and Hodgetts 2001). What there is instead, he argues, is an economy based on a regional triad. Rugman and associ-ates studied the activities of a large number of the Fortune 500 companies, and measured their activities against the flow of FDI. Rugman's work shows that most of what is called globalization activity is, in fact, based within a triad of Europe, Japan, and the US. He ar-gues that most FDI is largely intra-firm and industry, and that the key driver is regional- and local-based economic activity, not a global one.

The degree of global integration varies from one national economy to another. For instance, in terms of economic integration the Netherlands is more global than Switzerland. Further, within countries some sectors are more global than others. A study by OECD (2001: 13) showed that in 1998, the percentage of industrial production generated by firms under foreign control varied from 70% in Ireland and Hungary to less than 2% in Japan. In most other European countries this was between 25% and 30%, while in the United States it was 18%.

Political globalization Globalization is also believed to be leading to an unprecedented and growing consciousness of so-called global problems which require global political systems. As a result, globalization is leading to the end of strong nation-states. The interconnectedness of the global economy has significantly reduced national governments' ability to control their social, economic, and even political policy, and as a result, slowly but surely, the role of national governments in economic development is becoming considerably weaker. For

Exhibit 1.5 Number of regional trade agreements 1948–2002

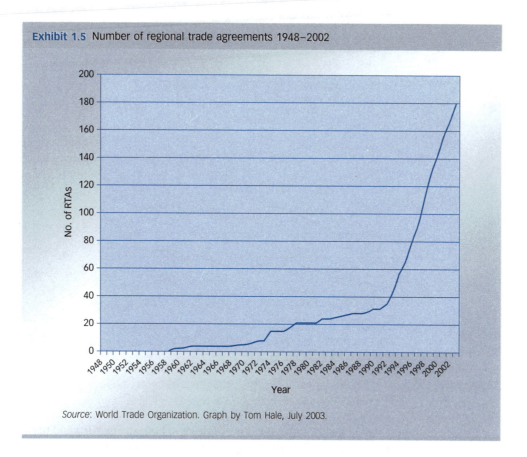

Source: World Trade Organization. Graph by Tom Hale, July 2003.

example, in recent decades there has been a major delinking of financial activities from their mother countries and the emergence of supra-territorial financial systems which, some argue, have largely undermined the capacity of nation-states to regulate financial transactions.

Globalization of ideas and values   Several studies suggest that the increasing globalization of economic transactions, coupled with global electronic mass media, is generating new sets of managerial values, especially among young managers (Ralston et al. 1997; Mellahi and Guermat 2004). For example, cross-border music channels such as MTV, greater travel, and better global communication have encouraged the notion of a 'global teenager', that is, the notion that teenagers possess similar values regardless of their country of origin (Assael 1998). Take for instance an experiment conducted by BSB Worldwide, a New York City advertising agency, which videotaped teenagers' rooms in twenty-five countries. They reported that the rooms looked strikingly similar: it was hard to tell the country of the teenager from the belongings and posters on display in his or her room.

On the basis of the above discussion, we define globalization as a diverse process embracing economic, political, and cultural change which is deepening the integration of the world economy, strengthening political interdependence between countries, and causing values to converge across countries.

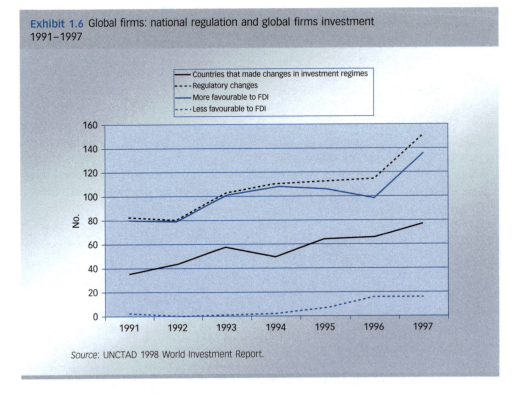

Exhibit 1.6 Global firms: national regulation and global firms investment 1991–1997

Source: UNCTAD 1998 World Investment Report.

Also, we must note that globalization denotes movements in both the *intensity* and the *extent* of the above three elements. It is intensifying cross-border business activities by making governments and economic policies more integrated, and interdependent on each other; and to some degree social and cultural policies are interpenetrating each other. The extent of globalization refers to the geographical spread of these intensifying tendencies. The two movements—intensity and extent—are leading to the compression of the world, universalization of managerial values and practices, and homogenization of customers' needs, wants, and behaviours.

KEY CONCEPT

Globalization is a diverse process embracing economic, political, and cultural change which is deepening the integration of the world economy, strengthening political interdependence between countries, and causing values to converge across countries.

Information communication technology (ICT)

Both popular and academic literature claims that, as a result of the ICT revolution, the 'conduct of global business will be changed in fundamental ways' (de la Torre and Maxon 2001: 617). The ICT revolution, it is believed, is shrinking distances, eliminating intermediaries between producers and consumers, and bringing about closer integration of the world economy. For instance, thanks to ICT, geographical distance is not significant for the transportation of information, and hence global firms are able to collect information about their global activities faster and cheaper. In the past, exchange of information among the global firm's partners was done through paperwork, such as paper documents and faxes. This often caused delays in information-sharing and mis-communications among the different partners. This was an enormous problem for firms operating on a worldwide scale, because out-of-date and/or incomplete data could translate into a poor understanding of what customers actually needed and what suppliers actually had in their warehouses.

ICT makes the information flow more complete, and makes the information more accurate, timely, and accessible. It helps multinational firms to reduce uncertainties, such as demand, delivery times, quality, and competition in the global supply chain. For instance, ICT has helped Dell Computers eliminate inventory from its manufacturing plants, and has been a key in establishing ultra-close ties with its suppliers (Hagel and Brown 2001). As a result, Dell has been able to cut inventory to just three to five hours. The reduction has been so profound that Dell has been able to turn factory storage space into production lines. Additionally, the company now uses ICT to link suppliers with manufacturers so that suppliers can eliminate excess inventory.

The Dell example shows that ICT enables managers to develop and analyse new and effective ways to improve competitiveness through successful management of global supply chains—through, for example, instant access to information—and information-sharing between different supply-chain parties in order to meet increasing global customer demands for responsiveness, quality, and low prices. It is believed that, thanks to ICT, managers are now able to coordinate their entire global business, including procurement, inventory, manufacturing, logistic, distribution, sales, and after-sales service, to reduce costs, and to achieve high speed and precision in delivering their products and services. Multinational firms are doing this through, for example, having one data entry form for all partners in the network, one data structure for all partners, and a common means of access, often via a tightly secured and controlled intranet. This is enabling firms to collect necessary information to trace in 'real time' the history of every single part in the transformation process. By so doing, ICT provides firms with greater assurance of product quality and specifications, and enables quick identification of problems throughout the global network.

1.6.2 Industry globalizing drivers

There are four industry globalization drivers: market globalization drivers, cost globalization drivers, government globalization drivers, and competitive drivers.

Market globalization drivers

There is a general belief that several markets are converging around the world. There are several reasons for this (Yip 2002). First, the convergence of Gross National Product (GNP) per capita in the developed world is leading to a convergence in markets sensitive to wealth and level of income such as passenger cars, television sets, and computers.

Second, there is evidence to suggest that in some industries, customers' tastes, perceptions, and buying behaviours are converging, and that the world is moving towards a single global market that is basically Western and, more specifically, North American. In a landmark article titled 'The globalization of markets' Levitt (1983) predicted that globalization drivers such as new technology would lead to homogenization of consumer desires and needs across the world. He argued that this would happen because generally consumers would prefer standard products of high quality and low price to more customized but higher-priced products.

Third, in the quest to build a global brand and company image, multinational firms are increasingly favouring a global standardization of marketing and advertising efforts (Zou and Çavusgil, 2002). This does not mean identical marketing and advertising campaigns, but the use of similar themes that send the same message across the world. Recent developments in broadcast media, particularly direct-broadcast satellite and international media, are making this more possible. CNN, for example, broadcasts standard adverts around the world.

Cost globalization drivers

Several key cost drivers may come into play in determining an industry globalization level. One key factor is global scale economies. That is, the costs of producing a particular product or service are often subject to economies or dis-economies of scale. Generally, economies of scale arise when a product or a process can be performed more cheaply at greater volume than at lesser volume. This is often the case when the product or service is standardized; hence it becomes hard for multinational firms to differentiate themselves, and cost becomes key in achieving and sustaining a competitive advantage. Producing different products for different countries leads to higher cost per unit. This is because multinational firms serving countries with separate products may not be able to reach the most economic scale of production for each country's unique product. Multinational firms could reduce the cost by using common parts and components produced in different countries.

Another factor is sourcing efficiencies. Global sourcing efficiencies may push multinational firms towards a global strategy. The prices of key resources used in the production process have a strong impact on the cost of the product or service. As will be discussed in Chapter 3 (section 3.3.2), the cost of inputs depends on the bargaining power of the firm vis-à-vis suppliers. For example, large firms purchasing large volumes have more clout with their suppliers than their small rivals. Hewlett-Packard (HP) is a good example. In the past, country-level subsidiaries used to solicit bids for insurance coverage independently. Each subsidiary chose the local provider who bid less than the competition. However, HP now belongs to a global insurer–insured pool which provides rebates based on business volume.

In addition, as noted earlier, some countries provide a cost advantage because of low cost of raw material, low cost of labour, or low cost of transport because of location. Thus multinational firms locate their activities in different countries to benefit from these advantages. Further, in sectors where transportation cost is low, closeness to customers is not important, and urgency to distribute the product is low, multinational firms tend to concentrate their production in large plants producing large-scale products. Finally, high cost of product development drives multinational firms to focus on core products that have universal appeal to control cost.

Government globalization drivers

The impact of government drivers on industries will be fully examined in Chapters 2 and 3. Governments have different policies for different industries. While (as discussed above) the general trend is lower trade barriers and less regulation, for a few sectors trade barriers are prohibitive and highly regulated by governments.

In addition to trade barriers and regulations, technical standards are becoming similar around the world. For example, several countries have accepted new international accounting norms and standards. In Europe, the International Accounting Standards (IAS) are quickly becoming the norm. This will allow direct cross-border comparison of financial statements, and facilitate communication between subsidiaries and the centre. Companies like Nokia, the Allianz group, and Novartis are working to bring about a convergence of US accounting standards with IAS.

Competitive drivers

Because of tight interlinks between key world markets, intense competition across countries, and the continuous increase in the number of global competitors, multinational firms are adopting a 'globally centred' rather than 'nationally centred' strategy (Yip 2002). According to George Yip, the increase in interactions between competitors from different countries requires a globally integrated strategy to monitor moves by competitors in different countries. He notes that by pursuing a global strategy, competitors create competitive interdependence among countries (Yip 2002: 57). This interdependence forces multinational firms to engage in competitive battles and to subsidize attacks in different countries. Cross-subsidization is only possible if the multinational firm has a global strategy that monitors competitors centrally rather than on a country-by-country basis.

Globalized competitors drive industries to adopt a global strategy. Yip noted that when major competitors, especially first movers, use a global strategy to introduce customers to global products, late movers adopt the same strategy so as to achieve economies of scale or scope and other benefits associated with adopting a global strategy.

Last, the ability to transfer competitive advantage globally drives multinationals to adopt a global strategy. For example, IKEA succeeded in transferring its locally developed advantage to a global market. Conversely, sectors where the competitive advantage is 'locally rooted' and hard to transfer across countries, multinationals tend to adopt an international strategy rather than a global one.

1.6.3 Internal globalizing drivers

Two key internal factors significantly influence the extent to which a multinational firm adopts a global strategy: global orientation and international experience.

Global orientation

Global orientation is a part of a multinational firm's culture, and is essentially the belief that success comes from a worldwide globally integrated strategy rather than from one operated on a country-by-country-basis. Multinational firms with worldwide orientations look for similarity between markets and synergies across countries, and make globally integrated moves. In these multinationals, managers have a global mindset and tend not to tolerate differences across countries. For example, the global orientation of Lotus is articulated by the vice-president's question: 'How can I manage an organization in which I am getting different answers to the same question depending on location?' These multinationals have the desire to raise corporate strategy above subsidiary strategy. This illustrated by a Hewlett-Packard manager's comment: 'We want one solution for the world rather than fifty-four country solutions. We optimize at the company rather than the country level.'

International experience

There is evidence to suggest that the most experienced multinationals are likely to adopt a global strategy, whereas the less experienced are unlikely to do so (Douglas and Craig 1989). Experience gained over the years enables the multinational to take advantage of the comparative advantages of various countries, to spot and capitalize on synergies between subsidiaries in different countries, and to establish common needs among the customer segments worldwide so that core product features are kept intact (Hill 1996). While the multinational may depart from total standardization, as shown in the case of IKEA in the US, it will keep the core product features to simplify global operations, develop consistent image globally, and achieve scale economies, synergies, and efficiencies.

KEY CONCEPT

The extent to which a multinational firm adopts a global strategy is determined by three broad factors: *macro globalizing drivers*, namely globalization and information communication technology; *industry globalizing drivers*, namely market drivers, cost drivers, government drivers, and competitive drivers; and *internal globalizing drivers*, namely global orientation and international experience.

The macro drivers have an overall impact, and are not specific to particular industries or organizations. The industry globalizing drivers determine the globality of a sector, industry, or market. The internal globalizing drivers determine the globality of a firm.

1.7 Organization of the book

The book is structured around the three key strategic management phases: strategic analysis, strategy development, and strategy implementation. It is divided into four parts.

In Part II we deal with the analysis of the environment within which a multinational firm operates. To be able to craft and implement an effective global strategy, the firm must master the three phases. That is, global strategic management is concerned with conducting a global situation analysis by analysing the external (Chapters 2, 3, and 4) and internal (Chapter 5) business environment of the firm and its subsidiaries to identify the key factors that have, or could have, an influence on the multinational firm's competitive advantage.

This phase forms the basis for developing and selecting the most appropriate strategy, and proposing actions to implement it.

In Part III we deal with the strategy development phase. Once the internal and external environments have been analysed, managers then turn their attention to developing and selecting the appropriate strategy for the firm. Managers need to choose the mode of entry and location in different countries (Chapter 6), to establish and manage relationships with global partners (Chapter 7), to develop a subsidiary-level strategy (Chapter 8), and to develop a headquarter-level strategy (Chapter 9).

In Part IV we deal with the implementation phase. To be able to implement the strategy successfully, managers must design a structure that fits the selected strategy (Chapter 10), implement change (Chapter 11), and monitor and control the new strategy (Chapter 12).

KEY READINGS

- For further discussion of the phases of global strategy, see Bartlett and Ghoshal (1989), Doz (1980), and Ghoshal (1987).
- For an extensive discussion of industry globalizing drivers, see Yip (2002).
- For further insight into the three dimensions of global strategy, see Zou and Çavusgil (2002).

DISCUSSION QUESTIONS

1 Discuss the differences between global strategic management and strategic management in the domestic context.

2 List and discuss the main differences between international strategy and global strategy.

3 Select a multinational firm that follows a global strategy and discuss the key phases of its global strategy.

4 Which do you think would be the most relevant factors driving the globalization of mobile phones, automobiles, and pop music?

5 Explain why some industries are more global than others.

6 Explain why, in the same industry, some firms are more global than others.

Closing case study
The Starbucks experience—going global

Most analysts who follow Starbucks are bullish on the stock, despite the current general market woes. After all, a share purchased in 1992 at the IPO is now worth more than sixteen times its original value, taking into account stock splits. As Schultz points out, a contemplative moment of relaxation over a Starbucks latte is an affordable luxury even during a recession. 'I have a strong buy recommendation on the stock', says John Glass of Deutsche Bank Alex Brown. 'This is the best long-term play in the restaurant/retail field I've ever seen.' As long as the company sticks to its core expertise, Glass is confident that the firm can continue to expand successfully. Schultz clearly tried to spread the Starbucks brand image too thin, particularly with forays into various internet companies that made the share price tumble severely in the summer of 1999. But when the brand sticks close to its identifiable product—the cold coffee drink Frappuccino, sold in a venture with Pepsi, or coffee-flavoured ice cream with Breyer's—it may succeed.

The major unanswered question is how Starbucks will fare in continental Europe over the next few years, particularly when it goes back to Italy, where Schultz had his epiphany in 1983. It is likely that Starbucks will do well in Germany, where there are already Starbucks clones. But what about Scandinavia, which already prides itself on its fine coffee heritage and the world's highest per capita coffee consumption? And what about France, which has a long history of anti-American sentiment and which already hosts a vibrant cafe culture? Finally, of course, what about Italy, with its 121,000 existing neighbourhood espresso bars?

Peter Maslen, the president of Starbucks Coffee International, is cautiously optimistic. 'We know that Europe has a long coffee tradition, so it's with humility and respect that we come back to Europe.' On the other hand, he says that 'so far, we've been very fortunate; we've been embraced everywhere we've gone without exception, but it still surprises us.'

That isn't quite true, however. When Starbucks opened an outlet in Beijing's Forbidden City in 2000, it provoked protests from Chinese nationalists such as Duan Fei, a middle-aged officer in the People's Liberation Army. 'This is an American product', he complained. 'It's imperialism. We should kick it out.' On the other hand, Huang Bing, a young part-time model, bubbled, 'It's fantastic. Coffee is cool now. The Forbidden City can be cool, too.'

That attitude is likely to be the key to Starbucks' success in Europe over the next few years as well. With minimal advertising, Starbucks already has phenomenal brand recognition around the world, through word of mouth, movie placements, and the like. With its saturation placement, Starbucks acts as its own advertisement, analyst John Glass points out. 'Almost anywhere in the world, even in Beijing, you can see one Starbucks outlet after another. They've raised store density to a level I've never seen before. Their secret is to put outlets in suburban markets, with a second and third in each town.'

In Europe, while older people may remain faithful to their neighbourhood cafe, it is likely that younger consumers will flood the new Starbucks. If the company is wise, it will open its first Italian franchise in Milan, which is a fast, trend-setting city. Since that is where Schultz had his first espresso, it would be a sweet full circle as well.

Dan Cox, owner of Coffee Enterprises, thinks that the fate of Starbucks in Europe depends on its cultural savvy. 'If they go in with the attitude, "We're Starbucks and know it all, we're bringing good coffee to the heathens", then I think they'll be in for a surprise.' But he points out that if Starbucks is more astute, it could do quite well, offering its 100% fine Arabica blend, since the trend in Europe has been to increase the amount of inferior Robusta used in blends. Norwegian Alf Kramer, the co-founder of the Specialty Coffee Association of Europe, is cautious in his forecast. 'Europe is a continent with a huge variety of coffee cultures, and Starbucks will have to adapt to all of them. When all that is said, however, coffee as a product is probably not that important to Starbucks. People will go to them for the fifteen minutes of relaxation.'

Ted Lingle, the executive director of the Specialty Coffee Association of America (SCAA), says that Starbucks has a 'strong potential to do well in Europe, in part because its proven retail concept, established management team, substantial financial resources, and a good game plan'. His only caution is that 'one approach does not fit all countries. While the Starbucks Experience is their signature, that may not call for the same execution in every country or city. That could apply to the menu mix, the availability of chairs or just walk-away tables, and hours of operation.'

At the moment, the Starbucks rollout appears to be advancing like a well-oiled machine. It may vary its food offerings somewhat to fit local tastes, but Peter Maslen says that it has no plans to alter its coffee. People can choose milk-based drinks, drip coffee or espresso, light or dark roasts. 'We want to elicit the same emotional response all over the world', he emphasizes. Before going into a country, Starbucks conducts extensive focus groups and quantitative research.

The company also seeks a strong local business partner, which shares its values and aggressive growth strategy. 'We have no debt and we're spinning a lot of cash, so we could go on our own', he says. But Starbucks wants to rely to some extent on a business partner's local knowledge and enterprise, and this strategy also allows the company to expand more rapidly with the same resources.

Despite occasional protests by activists, Starbucks has managed to maintain a squeaky-clean image, working with Conservation International to promote shade-grown, ecologically friendly coffee. It sells Fair Trade certified coffee and encourages local employees to volunteer in orphanages and other worthy causes. In the midst of the disastrously low prices coffee growers are getting for their green beans, Starbucks gave a one-time shot in the arm of $1 million to the Calvert Social Investment Foundations to help coffee farmers. At the same time, the company announced that it would expand its fair trade programme, promising to buy at least a million pounds over the next year and a half.

And the bright-eyed coffee evangelists who serve up Starbucks blends throughout the world are all trained in the Starbucks Experience that some have likened to a cult. 'Starbucks is a brand built on passion,' Maslen says, 'and you can easily feel the passion of our partners in any of our international stores.' To instil this attitude in its first Swiss employees, Starbucks flies its new foreign managers to Seattle for thirteen weeks of rigorous education and indoctrination.

Will Starbucks approach a saturation point in places like the United States and, eventually, elsewhere in the world? Will it face increasingly stiff competition as imitators spring up to feed on its success? Amazingly, there is no real Pepsi to Starbucks' Coke, anywhere in the world. Tully's and Seattle's Best Coffee (SBC, now owned by AFC Inc.) also have international profiles, but they are so far behind Starbucks that they pose no real threat.

And saturation? That's not likely to be an issue for the next few years. Look at all those coffee bars in Italy. What if Starbucks could convince the Chinese to drink coffee like Italians? Also recall lessons from history: in London, back in 1700, there were 2,000 coffeehouses. Even in the US and Canada, there still appears to be room for growth. In the province of Quebec, for instance, Starbucks teamed up in 2001 with a Quebec pizza franchiser to open some seventy-five retail outlets. And in [the] state of Vermont, Starbucks has recently opened one lonely outlet in Burlington, the hip college town. There is obviously room for growth. They don't seem to be feeling the success wind down; Starbucks has just opened its third US roasting plant in Nevada, a 300,000-square-foot facility scheduled to begin operations in 2003.

And what happens if an emergency arose and leader Howard Schultz had to leave the company tomorrow? Analyst Glass isn't worried. 'Schultz is important, one of the great entrepreneurs of our time, but he has already taken on more of an ambassador role with a concentration on international development. He leaves the day-to-day operations to CEO Orin Smith and CFO Michael Casey. Starbucks has a wonderful, deep management team. It is not dependent on one person.' On the other hand, he notes that Schultz 'embodies the passion, the human side' of the company, and as a symbolic leader of the loyal troops he is unparalleled.

Source: Mark Pendergrast (Feb. and Mar. 2002), 'The Starbuck experience: going global, tea and coffee', www.teaand-coffee.net/0202/coffee2.htm, 176(2).

Discussion questions

1 Discuss the forces for and against the globalization of the coffee shop industry.

2 Discuss the advantages and drawbacks of Starbucks' global strategy.

3 If you were Starbucks' global manager, what would you do differently?
   And what would you stop doing?

REFERENCES

Assael, H. (1998). *Consumer Behavior and Marketing Action*, 6th edn. (Cincinnati: South Western College Publishing).

Bartlett, C. A., and Ghoshal, S. (1989). *Managing across Borders: The Transnational Solution* (Cambridge, Mass.: Harvard Business School Press).

Bharadwaj, S. G., Varadarajan, R. P., and Fahy, J. (1993). 'Sustainable competitive advantage in service industries: a conceptual model and research propositions', *Journal of Marketing* 57: 83–99.

de la Torre, J., and Maxon, R. W. (2001). 'Introduction to the Symposium. E-commerce and global business: the impact of the information and communication technology revolution on the conduct of international business', *Journal of International Business Studies* 32: 617–39.

Douglas, S. P., and Craig, S. C. (1989). 'Evolution of global marketing strategy: scale, scope, and synergy', *Columbia Journal of World Business* 24(3): 47–58.

Doz, Y. L. (1980). 'Strategic management and multinational corporations', *Sloan Management Review* 21: 27–46.

Fahey, J. (9 Dec. 2002). 'Would you buy a ChevySaab?', *Forbes* 170(12): 82.

Ghoshal, S. (1987). 'Global strategy: an organising framework', *Strategic Management Journal* 8(5): 425–40.

Govindarajan, V., and Gupta, A. (2000). 'Analysis of the emerging global arena', *European Management Journal* 18(3): 274–84.

Hagel, J. III, and Brown, S. J. (2001). 'Your next IT strategy', *Harvard Business Review* (Oct.): 105–13.

Hill, C. W. L. (1996). *International Business: Competing in the Global Marketplace* (Chicago: Richard D. Irwin).

Levitt, T. (1983). 'The globalisation of markets', *Harvard Business Review* 61(3): 92–102.

Mellahi, K., and Guermat, G. (2004). 'Does age matter? An empirical investigation of the effect of age on managerial values and practices in India', *Journal of World Business* 39(3): 199–215.

OECD (2001). *'Measuring globalisation: the role of multinationals in OECD economies'* (Paris: OECD).

Prahalad, C. K., and Doz, Y. L. (1987). *The Multinational Mission: Balancing Local Demands and Global Vision* (New York: Free Press).

Ralston, D. A., Holt, D. H., Terpstra, R. H., and Yu, K. C. (1997). 'The impact of national culture and economic ideology on managerial work values: a study of the US, Russia, Japan, and China', *Journal of International Business Studies* 27(1): 177–207.

Rugman, A. (2001). *The End of Globalization* (New York: McGraw-Hill/Ryerson).

___and Hodgetts, R. (2001). 'The end of global strategy', *European Management Journal* 19: 333–43.

Solberg, C. A. (1997). 'A framework for analysis of strategy development in globalizing markets', *Journal of International Marketing* 5: 9–30.

Yip, G. (2002). *Total Global Strategy* (London: Prentice-Hall).

Zou, S., and Çavusgil, S. T. (2002). 'The GMS: a broad conceptualization of global marketing strategy and its effect on firm performance', *Journal of Marketing* 66: 40–57.

PART II
Global strategic analysis

2

Global business environment: the external macro environment

Learning outcomes

After reading this chapter you should be able to:

- understand the significance of the external business environment for the strategies of multinational firms;

- understand the influence of the political, economic, social, and technological business environment on global and international strategy;

- conduct a PEST analysis;

- Apply Michael Porter's Diamond Model to an industry.

The Brazilian aircraft manufacturer Embraer is one of Brazil's leading high-technology firms and the largest single Brazilian exporter. Founded in 1969 as a government initiative, Embraer has become the fourth largest commercial aircraft manufacturer in the world behind Boeing, Airbus, and Bombardier. Unlike Boeing and Airbus, Embraer focuses on smaller aircraft with up to 110 seats, which can serve regional airlines. Operating globally, the company has sold thousands of planes to airlines as diverse as American Eagle, South African Airlink, and Air Caraibes in Guadaloupe.

Throughout its history, the state-owned Embraer has had a friendly relationship with the Brazilian government, and the firm was only privatized in 1994. The Brazilian government's support was crucial for Embraer's expansion. The government not only provided financial assistance when the company needed funds, it also assisted Embraer's exports. Under an exchange rate subsidy scheme called Proex, the Brazilian government provided funds for the purchase of Brazilian aircraft. If a foreign airline wanted to buy an Embraer plane by taking out a loan from a commercial bank, the Brazilian government would subsidize the loan. As a result, the airline would pay a much lower interest rate on the loan, which made Brazilian aircraft more attractive to foreign buyers.

The Brazilian government subsidies helped Embraer quickly to gain a large market share in the global market for regional aircraft in the 1990s. Embraer's quick expansion was not welcomed by its main rival, Canada's Bombardier, which complained to the Canadian government about Embraer's 'unfair' advantage. The Canadian government subsequently filed a complaint against Brazil to the World Trade Organization (WTO), the world's most important settlement body for trade disputes. In 2000 the WTO ruled that the Proex-assisted sales of Embraer aircraft were unlawful and could not proceed. The WTO then gave Canada permission to impose trade sanctions worth US$1.4 billion on Brazilian products. Canada never imposed the sanctions, instead negotiating with Brazil while matching the export assistance offered to Embraer.

But the WTO ruling was a big setback for Embraer, as the Proex scheme helped to sell some 900 aircraft. An end to the Brazilian government subsidies and the continuation of Canadian subsidies to Bombardier would make it more difficult for Embraer to survive in the global aircraft market.

The Brazilian government launched a counter-offensive against the Canadian government, accusing the Canadians of illegally subsiding Bombardier's aircraft sales. It called on the WTO to prevent Bombardier from receiving Canadian government subsidies. In 2002 the WTO ruled that the Canadian government's financing of Bombardier exports violated WTO rules and had to withdraw any such assistance. In early 2003 the WTO officially announced its decision to allow Brazil to impose US$248 million in counter-trade measures against Canada. The dispute has not yet been resolved. Both Embraer and Bombardier managers are wary as to how the strategic direction of their companies would be affected by the WTO rulings.

While the WTO dispute continued, Embraer managers cautiously watched global developments, which led to a dramatic decline in the demand for aircraft. The attacks on the World Trade Center in September 2001 were followed by a marked decline in global air travel. Faced with fewer air travellers, airlines either cancelled or delayed orders for new aircraft, hitting the sales of aircraft manufacturers. Within only one month after the events of September 11, Embraer announced that about US$1 billion worth of tentative orders (known as options) have been cancelled.

While managers were hoping for a rise in air travel, the war in Iraq in 2003 further worsened the business prospects for airlines and aircraft manufacturers. After the war broke out, the International Air

Transport Association (IATA) estimated that the war in Iraq alone could add US$10 billion to airline losses worldwide in 2003. As a result of the events of September 11 and the Iraq war, important Embraer clients such as the US carrier ExpressJet (a regional carrier for Continental Airlines) and Swiss International Air Lines deferred or cancelled the delivery of aircraft that they previously ordered, forcing Embraer to revise its business plans.

Embraer had world-class products on offer, but the WTO dispute and the decline in air travel were major challenges to the company. Embraer's president and chief executive, Mauricio Botelho, could not predict how the global aircraft market would be affected by political and social forces outside his control.

Sources: Embraer website at **www.embraer.com/english/**; T. C. Lawton and S. M. McGuire, 'Supranational governance and corporate strategy: the emerging role of the World Trade Organization', *International Business Review* 10 (2001): 217–33; various newspapers and magazines.

2.1 Introduction

The Embraer case shows how a firm's strategic direction may be influenced by global developments outside the managers' control. The events of September 11 and decisions of the World Trade Organization are two examples of global developments which could determine a firm's success or failure. Other examples could be the introduction of a new technology, a financial crisis, an armed conflict, or international migration of people. A business firm is not isolated from the environment in which it operates. Its future development, the results it can achieve and the constraints within which it operates are all functions of the business environment.

The business environment consists of all factors inside and outside the company which influence the firm's competitive success. It is often divided into the external macro environment, the external industry environment, and the internal firm environment (see Exhibit 2.1).

The macro environment consists of political, social, economic, and technological factors in the broader society, which are discussed in this chapter. These factors can be specific to an industry or a firm (e.g. the WTO ruling on Embraer) or, more typically, they can influence many different industries (e.g. the events of September 11). The industry environment consists of all factors stemming from actions within a specific industry by buyers, suppliers, competitors, and others which directly influence competitive success within the industry and for the firm (see Chapter 3). The internal firm environment consists of all resources and capabilities found within the firm which influence the firm's ability to act (see Chapter 5). In recent years, there has been increasing pressure on firms to take on new roles in promoting social and ecological objectives, and the notion of the business environment has further broadened to encompass new external forces such as non-governmental organizations (see Chapter 4). The analysis of these different parts of the business environment allows the firm to understand the context within which strategy needs to be developed and implemented.

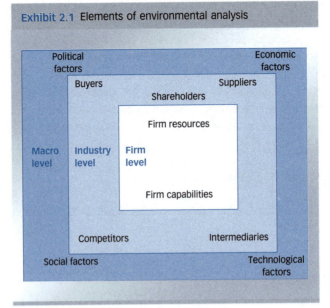

Exhibit 2.1 Elements of environmental analysis

2.2 The external business environment

The external business environment of the multinational firm can provide both opportunities and threats to firms, so managers must pay adequate attention to them. Opportunities
refer to events or processes in the external business environment, which may help the company to achieve competitive success. Threats refer to events or processes in the external business environment, which may prevent the company from achieving competitive success.

For the most part, the external business environment cannot be easily changed by the multinational firm (although Chapter 5 suggests that this can sometimes be done). Multinational
firms usually have little control over demographic changes, cultural norms, or government
policy, so they need to adapt the organization to the external environment. The task of the
strategic decision-maker is to develop strategies based on what the multinational firm can do
to exploit opportunities and counter threats in the external business environment. Successful
strategy is, then, about matching the resources and activities of a firm to the external environment in which it operates—which is known as 'strategic fit'. Organizations which do not
possess a minimum degree of 'strategic fit' are bound to fail (Galbraith and Kazanjian 1986).

An organization must achieve a strategic fit with both the macro environment and the industry environment. In this chapter, we deal with the macro environment. But we need to remember that the macro environment should only be considered if it is likely to affect the specific industry and the specific firm. For instance, a new government policy will be of little interest to you if it does not affect your industry or your firm. The ability of a manager to recognize the relevant macro environmental factors, understand their implications, and adapt the firm's products and operating methods to the demands of the business environment will influence a firm's success or failure. A common way of studying the macro environment is through the analysis of PEST (Political, Economic, Social, and Technological) factors.

KEY CONCEPT

Strategic fit is about matching the resources and activities of a firm to the external environment in which the firm operates. Organizations which do not possess a minimum degree of strategic fit are bound to fail.

2.3 **PEST analysis**

Firms which are skilful at monitoring and analysing the business environment are said to perform better than those firms which are not (Norburn 1974). Business textbooks often advise managers to conduct an external audit, which surveys all key opportunities and threats faced by the firm. The aim of an external audit is to draw up a list of different types of external forces, which can present either opportunities or threats to the firm. But analysing the macro environment is not easy in practice, for several reasons:

- The macro environment is highly complex, with a vast number of potentially relevant external influences on the firm.

- The macro environment changes over time, which requires an analysis of today's PEST factors and a forecast of future PEST factors.

- A firm's decision to go international entails a movement into new economic, political, and cultural environments, which makes any analysis even more challenging.

- Too much information may lead to an information overload: more information is available than the management of the firm can cope with.

- It is difficult and expensive to monitor constantly the macro environment.

Therefore, we do not suggest that there is a magic formula for making sense of the external business environment. In this chapter we do not provide detailed advice on how managers should monitor, analyse, or forecast changes in the macro environment. Every firm must decide how far it wants to take systematic analysis, and every firm needs to find its own approach. In particular, small- and medium-sized firms frequently do not have the resources for regular and comprehensive analyses. But it is useful for managers to have a checklist of potential external macro influences. PEST analysis can be used as such a checklist. PEST analysis is not a rigorous management tool but instead a broad framework to help managers understand the macro environment. Managers can simply use this framework as a checklist to ask themselves questions as to how political, economic, social, or technological developments can influence their industry and their company.

The importance of political, economic, social, and technological factors differs considerably from one industry to another. Political factors can be crucial for success in industries where governments play an important role, such as the defence industry, which depends on government contracts. Technological factors can be crucial for success in industries where the rate of technological innovation is fast, for instance the electronics industry. So every industry and every firm will need to focus more attention on those factors which are most relevant to it.

Before the rise of global competition PEST analysis was more straightforward, as the manager simply had to scan the business environment in his/her own country. For firms operating internationally, the scope of PEST analysis will depend on the location of their operations. A small Indian firm with exports primarily to the United States may want to focus its analysis on the domestic macro environment in that country. A large German firm which operates primarily in the European Union (EU) will want to conduct primarily an EU-wide PEST analysis. A large global firm must scan the entire world for new developments and trends. At the same time, subsidiaries of a multinational firm may still want to conduct a PEST analysis for a specific country or a geographical region. This chapter merely shows what types of external influences firms could encounter in the international marketplace. Exhibit 2.2 summarizes a number of key PEST factors to be considered by international managers; but many other factors could be added to this list.

KEY CONCEPT

PEST analysis (Political, Economic, Social, and Technological factors) is a broad framework to help managers understand the environment in which their business operates. Managers can simply use this framework as a checklist to ask themselves questions as to how political, economic, social, or technological developments can influence their industry and their company.

Exhibit 2.2 Summary of key PEST factors in global strategic management

Political factors	Economic factors
Global political institutions Regional integration Government legislation Political risk	Cost of production Currency exchange rates Cost of capital
Social factors	**Technological factors**
Social change Global convergence	Global technology scanning and technology clusters The knowledge-based economy The spread of the internet

2.4 The political environment

Governments can have a major impact on business by imposing regulations on multinational firms. The government can change the levels of taxation or import duties, provide subsidies to certain firms, or impose regulations which require multinational firms to change how they operate (e.g. through anti-pollution regulations). At the same time, business strategies are now also affected by the emergence of new global institutions such as the World Trade Organization and regional economic blocks such as the European Union. In the global economy, therefore, the multinational firm must pay special attention to a complex set of important political issues: global institutions, regional economic integration, government legislation, and political risk.

2.4.1 Global political institutions

There are many different global political institutions which affect business operations. The most important ones include the International Monetary Fund (IMF), the World Bank, and the WTO (see Exhibit 2.3). Furthermore, many global institutions specialize in dealing with specific trade and investment issues; for example, the International Tribunal for the Law of the Sea was established in 1996 to rule over matters related to disputes over sea matters.

The importance of global institutions varies widely. Some institutions, such as the WTO and the IMF, are very powerful, as they can force countries to change economic policy. The WTO can, for example, impose economic sanctions on member states which violate its rules. Other institutions, such as the International Labour Organization (ILO) or the International Organization for Standardization (ISO), have few or no sanctions to enforce their will. However, governments and companies often find that it is in their self-interest to comply with the rules of global institutions. For example, many firms have adopted ISO quality standards, such as ISO 9000, which specify how firms must comply on quality management and quality assurance. The ISO standards were not initiated by governments but were developed by various groups of professionals. Firms have often sought ISO certification in order to demonstrate that they apply the highest-quality standards or because the customers demanded the introduction of ISO standards (Parker 1998: 429–30).

Global institutions have generally helped to facilitate international business operations. There are fewer barriers to trade between countries today, there is less likelihood of damaging political events than ten or twenty years ago, and there are forums in which to resolve commercial disputes between countries. A more stable global business environment allows multinational firms to expand business operations globally. For instance, when a new country wants to become a member of the WTO or the EU, one condition of membership is tough action against those who infringe intellectual property rights (IPRs) of foreign firms. Until some years ago, IPRs were rarely enforced in countries such as Hungary and Poland, and cheap counterfeit copies of music CDs, computer software, and other goods flooded their markets. But these countries have joined the battle against counterfeit products in recent years, not least because they have become members of the EU and the WTO. Therefore, manufacturers of music firms such as EMI or software firms such as Microsoft find it easier to expand globally.

Exhibit 2.3 The most important global economic institutions

The International Monetary Fund (IMF)

The IMF was established in 1944 by a conference of forty-four governments in Bretton Woods in the United States. Its original aim was to supervize a system of so-called 'fixed' exchange rates between the world's currencies, but this system had collapsed by the 1970s. Today, the IMF's aims are to promote international monetary stabilization and exchange stability, and to help member countries in dealing with temporary balance of payments difficulties. In order to achieve those aims, the IMF provides loans to national governments of member countries to stabilize the national economy. In return for a loan, the IMF imposes a set of conditions on member countries—these conditions have previously included changes to the country's tax policy, changes to monetary policy, privatization of formerly state-owned enterprises, currency devaluation, government spending cuts, and removal of foreign investment restrictions. As of April 2003, the IMF had 184 member countries.

The IMF has played an important role in providing stability to the international financial system. For instance, with the help from the United States and other countries, it was able to stabilize the Mexican economy with US$50 billion after a devastating economic crisis in 1994–5. But the IMF has attracted heavy criticism. Some economists such as Milton Friedman suggested that its assistance to Mexico was counterproductive: the money ended up in the hands of US banks and other institutions, which had foolishly lent money to Mexico. More importantly, the financial aid to Mexico fuelled the East Asian economic crisis in 1997 by encouraging international investors again to make risky investments. Since investors expected that the IMF would bail them out in the case of another financial crisis, they invested major sums in East Asia despite the fact that the Asian markets were very risky. In effect, the IMF encouraged undesirable behaviour amongst investors (Gilpin 2001: 273).

The IMF mostly affects business behaviour indirectly: for instance, a rescue financial package for a specific country will improve the external macro environment in that country and will encourage foreign firms to invest there.

For more information, see the IMF website at www.imf.org and Lee (2002).

World Bank

Like the IMF, the World Bank was established in 1944 by the Bretton Woods conference. Its original aim was to help nations (especially the European ones) recover from the devastation of the Second World War of 1939–45. Today, it is one of the world's largest sources of development assistance, and its work focuses mainly on developing countries. The World Bank consists of several distinct institutions:

- The International Bank for Reconstruction and Development (IBRD) aims to reduce poverty in middle-income and creditworthy poorer countries by promoting sustainable development, through loans, guarantees, and non-lending services to national governments (including analytical and advisory services).

→

→

- The International Development Association (IDA) helps the world's poorest countries reduce poverty by providing loans at zero interest with a ten-year grace period and maturities of thirty-five to forty years.

- The International Finance Corporation (IFC) is responsible for promoting the private sector in developing countries. It funds private-sector projects, helps companies in the developing world to raise capital in international financial markets, and provides advice and technical assistance to businesses and governments.

- The Multilateral Investment Guarantee Agency (MIGA) provides political risk insurance (guarantees) to investors and lenders, and helps developing countries attract and retain private investment.

- The International Centre for Settlement of Investment Disputes (ICSID) provides facilities for the conciliation and arbitration of business disputes between member countries and foreign investors.

The World Bank has played an important role in providing funds for developing countries. But its activities have sometimes been criticized, and it has been stated that many World Bank projects in developing countries were poorly designed and ineffective, and that the Bank's policies were incompatible with its professed goal of helping the poor (George and Sabelli 1994). The World Bank has responded to some of these criticisms by changing its policies in several areas. Membership of World Bank institutions varies. As of April 2003, the IBRD had 184 member countries, while the ICSID had only 134.

The IBRD and the IDA mostly affect business behaviour indirectly: for instance, a loan for a specific country may help to improve the infrastructure in that country (e.g. through a better road system) and will encourage foreign firms to invest there. The IFC, MIGA, and ICSID directly assist many private businesses. For instance, the IFC aims to fund companies in India which have the potential to expand successfully in the global market. One beneficiary was Cosmo Films Limited (Cosmo), India's leading manufacturer of BOPP (biaxially oriented polypropylene) films used for packaging and lamination applications. In 2002 the IFC provided a US$10 million loan to assist Cosmo in expanding its film manufacturing capacity. As a whole, IFC planned to increase its investment in Indian companies to US$1.0 billion in 2003. Money was also available to foreign companies, which invest in India. In early 2003 the IFC pledged $40 million to Niko Resources, a Canadian oil and gas company, for developing two gas fields in Gujarat, India.

For more information, see the World Bank website at www.worldbank.org and Gilbert and Vines (2000).

The World Trade Organization (WTO)

The WTO was created in 1995 out of the General Agreement on Tariffs and Trade (GATT). Launched in 1947, the purpose of GATT was to reduce tariff barriers and to forbid certain types of discrimination in international trade; this took the form of treaties between countries which pledged more

→

→

freedom in conducting international trade. The WTO is a permanent institution which promotes free trade and rules in commercial disputes between countries. As of April 2003, the WTO had 145 member countries.

The WTO incorporated previous GATT provisions for free trade in goods between countries. In addition, it aims to end discriminatory treatment by governments against foreign firms in the services sector (e.g. banking) and to end discrimination against foreign investors. The WTO also aims to protect intellectual property rights globally. A country which violates a WTO principle must remove the cause of the violation or pay compensation for the harm caused. As the opening case on Embraer shows, if the country fails to obey a WTO decision, the WTO has the power to force the country to comply by imposing economic sanctions on that country. But one criticism of the WTO is that it largely forces the application of economic rules of the developed countries on developing countries. While the United States or Sweden can continue to operate most of their old economic policies unchanged, the application of WTO rules forces many developing countries to spend a lot of money on complying with those rules. For instance, Argentina was forced to spend over US$80 million to achieve higher levels of plant and animal sanitation prescribed by the WTO (Finger and Schuler 2000). So, paradoxically, the WTO rules against discrimination may disadvantage some companies from developing countries in the global market.

The WTO affects the business environment indirectly by providing a more stable business environment in which firms can operate globally. Since member governments of the WTO generally try to respect WTO rules, investors have less to fear from discriminatory government regulation against them and political risk. At the same time, WTO rulings can have a major direct impact on specific firms and specific industries, as the opening case study to this chapter shows.

For more information, see the WTO website at www.wto.org and Wilkinson (2002).

2.4.2 Regional integration

In addition to the rise of global institutions, the business environment has changed in the last few decades with the emergence of regional economic blocks. The most far-reaching economic block is the EU; other important ones include NAFTA, AFTA, and MERCOSUR (see Exhibit 2.4). Regional economic blocks differ widely (Dicken 1998: 101–2):

- The *free trade area*, the simplest form of regional economic block, whereby member states abolish some trade restrictions between themselves (an example is NAFTA in North America).

- The *customs union*, whereby member states abolish some trade restrictions between themselves and, in addition, establish a common trade policy towards non-member states (an example is MERCOSUR in South America).

- The *common market*, whereby member states abolish some trade restrictions among themselves, establish a common trade policy towards non-member states, and, in addition,

---

Exhibit 2.4 Important regional economic blocs

AFTA (ASEAN Free Trade Area)

Type of regional bloc: Free Trade Area (established in 2002)

Member countries: Brunei, Cambodia, Indonesia, Laos, Malaysia, Myanmar, Philippines, Singapore, Thailand, Vietnam

CARICOM (Caribbean Community)

Type of regional bloc: Common Market (established in 1973)

Member countries: Antigua and Barbuda, Bahamas, Barbados, Belize, Dominica, Grenada, Guyana, Haiti, Jamaica, Montserrat, St Kitts-Nevis, St Lucia, St Vincent and the Grenadines, Suriname, Trinidad and Tobago.

EU (European Union)

Type of regional bloc: Economic Union (established in 1992; European Common Market from 1957)

Member countries: Austria, Belgium, Cyprus, Czech Republic, Denmark, Estonia, Finland, France, Germany, Greece, Hungary, Ireland, Italy, Latvia, Lithuania, Luxembourg, Malta, Netherlands, Poland, Portugal, Slovak Republic, Slovenia, Spain, Sweden, United Kingdom

MERCOSUR (Southern Cone Common Market)

Type of regional bloc: Customs Union (established in 1995)

Members: Argentina, Brazil, Paraguay, Uruguay

NAFTA (North American Free Trade Agreement)

Type of regional bloc: Free Trade Area (established in 1994)

Members: Canada, Mexico, United States

SADC (Southern African Development Community)

Type of regional bloc: Free Trade Area (to be established by 2008)

Members: Angola, Botswana, Democratic Republic of Congo, Lesotho, Malawi, Mauritius, Mozambique, Namibia, Seychelles, South Africa, Swaziland, Tanzania, Zambia, Zimbabwe

---

allow the free movement of people and capital between member states (an example is CARICOM in the Caribbean).

- The *economic union*, the most complex type of regional integration, with the EU being the prime example. The EU not only has adopted all the policies mentioned earlier, but also harmonizes government policies of member states on many issues such as anti-competitive behaviour by firms. Furthermore, unlike other regional economic blocks, the EU has developed many common institutions, such as the European Court of Justice and the European Parliament, which exercise supranational control over policies of member states.

Regional economic blocs affect the strategies of firms. In order to benefit from lower barriers to trade, some firms invest in a given country in order to be able to sell goods and services to other countries in the same regional bloc. For instance, some foreign firms have invested in countries such as Poland to benefit from its future membership of the EU, while many foreign firms have invested in Mexico in order to be able to export goods to the United States.

Regional integration poses both problems and opportunities in international business. One of the key challenges for managers in the EU is to keep track of the countless regulations which may apply to their firms. For instance, Polish agricultural firms wishing to export goods to other EU countries were forced to obtain an HACCP (Hazard Analysis and Critical Control Point) certificate from May 2004, when Poland joined the EU. The certificate is compulsory for any agricultural firm with over fifty employees, and is aimed at identifying any potential threats to human health during the food production process. Polish firms which failed to obtain such a certificate by the beginning of May 2004 were unable to serve previous export markets such as the Czech Republic (which was not an EU member until 2004, so that HACCP certificates had not previously been compulsory). It can take on average four to ten months to obtain an HACCP certificate, so compliance with regulations must be part of a firm's medium-term planning.

The same regulation can create business opportunities for some firms. For instance, the obligation for Polish agricultural firms to have HACCP certificates opened new business opportunities for international quality assurance firms such as TÜV and Lloyd's Register Quality Assurance, which have set up foreign subsidiaries in Poland. In the EU with its many business regulations, good knowledge of the political business environment can be a distinctive competitive advantage for some firms.

2.4.3 Government legislation

While managers must pay attention to the emergence of global institutions and regional economic blocs, they must continue to pay attention to government regulations which affect business operations. These include regulations on unfair trade practices (e.g. laws against monopolies), financial regulations, tax codes, environmental regulations, and employment laws. In addition to national regulation by different national governments, firms are also affected by new supranational entities such as the EU. The EU imposes its own laws. These laws are superior, for example, to English, Dutch, or Swedish law, so, for example, English courts must apply European law in preference to English law whenever applicable. European laws affect foreign firms, which want to do business in any EU country.

The importance of governments for business is particularly apparent in the 'transition economies', i.e. countries which are experiencing a transition from socialism (where the government made all the important economic decisions) towards capitalism (where market forces determine the direction of economic development). Transition economies include two of the world's largest countries—China and Russia—and other states in Eastern Europe such as Poland, and in Asia such as Vietnam. In those states, the impact of the government on business is still very strong, various large enterprises are state-owned, and good government links can be important for a firm's success (Peng 2000). But political factors are also important in Western Europe or the United States, which continue to impose many regulations and subsidize some sectors of the economy.

Despite globalization, different countries continue to have different rules on the same trade or investment issue. This even applies to the internet, where a company with a website can theoretically reach customers anywhere in the world. The internet knows no boundaries; however, internet firms have to pay attention to regulations in foreign countries. For instance, a new European law in May 2002 required suppliers of digital products from outside the EU to charge value added tax (VAT) on sales of electronically supplied services to private consumers inside the EU. Non-EU suppliers will need to register with a VAT authority in a EU country of their choice, but to levy VAT at the rate applicable in the country where each customer is resident. So, if a US or Canadian firm sells digital music files or downloadable videos to European consumers through a website, it will have to pay VAT, whether it has any physical presence in Europe or not (Frynas 2002).

Regulations can have both positive and negative effects on firms. For instance, anti-pollution regulations may raise the cost of doing business, since a company may need to instal new filters or a waste-treatment facility in order to comply with government legislation. However, anti-pollution regulations can also help certain firms to compete. Porter and van der Linde (1995a; 1995b) suggested that companies based in countries with more stringent environmental laws are able to gain an international competitive advantage over firms in countries with less stringent environmental laws. As more and more countries introduce environmental laws, a firm can gain a headstart by introducing a new environmentally friendly product or service before its rivals in other countries. Therefore, government regulations provide both opportunities and threats for multinational firms.

2.4.4 Political risk

The above example of environmentally friendly products shows that firms can gain from government regulations. But business writers have usually stressed how governments can create potential problems for firms expanding into new countries. Foreign investors have often suffered at the hands of governments: governments have single-handedly expropriated firms and taken their assets, forced firms out of business by increasing tax rates, and imposed restrictions on transferring profits abroad. Many writers therefore focused on 'political risk' in foreign investment, which is defined as 'the likelihood that political forces will cause drastic changes in a country's business environment that affect the profit and other goals of a particular business enterprise' (Robock and Simmonds 1989: 378). Political risks can include changes in government regulations, war, civil unrest, and politically motivated terrorism.

For instance, the tensions over the US-led war against Iraq have harmed US business interests in the Middle East. While some Arab governments supported the US government, many citizens of Arab countries opposed the war and stopped buying American goods. Coca-Cola was amongst the first companies to suffer from these tensions. Amidst growing anti-US sentiment, Middle Eastern-produced 'Islamic' cola gained popularity at the expense of Coca-Cola sales. Coca-Cola's Middle East and North African operations were based in Bahrain, which was officially an ally of the United States and was home to the US Navy's Fifth Fleet. However, in March 2003 Coca-Cola transferred its regional base from Bahrain to Greece and moved the staff to Greece. It also closed its bottling plant in Riyadh, the capital of Saudi Arabia, to re-equip it to produce other drinks including water and fruit juices.

Political risks have often been associated with developing countries in Latin America, Africa, and Asia, but there are plenty of examples of risks in Europe, North America, or Japan. It is nonetheless correct that political risk is more severe in developing countries (Kobrin 1982). Political risk is also more severe for sectors perceived as important to the country, such as the oil industry and the provision of infrastructure (e.g. water and electricity provision or road construction) (Wells and Gleason 1995).

A key point to remember is that political risk can be different for different companies. Certain companies may be much better able to cope with certain political events than others. For instance, South African Breweries (SAB) is an example of a company which has done well in several politically risky African markets that other brewers have avoided, such as Mozambique and Angola. Frynas (1998) and Frynas and Mellahi (2003) have even argued that political risk itself may be beneficial to specific firms and may assist corporate goals under certain circumstances. Certain firms may have good political connections or experience in politically risky markets, which allow them to weather political risk better than other firms.

2.5 The economic environment

Changes in the economic business environment can influence a firm's expansion. For instance, if economic growth increases, the firm may be able to expand production and open new plants; during an economic recession, when economic activity stagnates or even declines, the firm may need to close down plants and reduce production. Firms have to consider other economic factors such as the rate of inflation, disposable income, and rates of unemployment. In the global economy, the firm must pay special attention to three important issues: cost of production, currency exchange rates, and cost of capital.

2.5.1 Cost of production

One of the key global economic issues for companies is the cost of production. Since there are fewer barriers to international trade today and transport costs are not significant for many products, multinational firms can scan the entire world for the cheapest production location. The cost of labour is of key importance. Wage rates can differ significantly between countries. In 2000, the average hourly wage rate was *c*. US$15 in high-cost Germany, less than US$3 in Mexico, and less than US$1 in Sri Lanka (Dicken 2003: 211). Firms in labour-intensive industries (where labour accounts for a large part of the total cost of production) have often found that they had to relocate production or services abroad because this allowed them to reduce labour costs and become more internationally competitive. For instance, many American and European call centres are based in India, where wages are low. Since international telephone calls have become relatively cheap, a telephone inquiry from a British or American customer can be rerouted to India, where the service can be performed at lower cost.

But wage rates are not the only determinant of labour costs. Another important factor is labour productivity, which is defined as the amount of output produced per unit of inputs used to produce it. Labour productivity is much higher in Germany than in Sri Lanka. So the managers have to weigh up the advantages of cheap labour versus other factors such as the necessary skills and efficiency of their workforce, which may not always be available in low-wage countries.

2.5.2 Currency exchange rates

Cost of production is affected by the currency exchange rate, i.e. the rate at which one country's currency can be exchanged for another's. If the value of the euro goes up relative to other currencies, Dutch or German goods become more expensive to buy for foreigners; Dutch and German firms may find it more difficult to export their goods. At the same time, firms outside the euro zone will find it easier to import goods into Germany. Similarly, foreign firms will find it less attractive to invest in the Netherlands or Germany, while Dutch and German firms will find it more attractive to invest outside the euro zone. Multinational firms have to monitor currency exchange rates in the global economy in order to spot threats and opportunities for their existing operations in different countries. Political and social events can influence exchange rates. For instance, the threat of a war against Iraq in early 2003 contributed to the depreciation of the US dollar and an appreciation of European currencies such as the euro and the Swiss franc.

In some cases, a firm may need to shift production away from a country where the exchange rates make it too expensive to produce (Froot and Stein 1991; Dewenter 1995). For instance, various Japanese car manufacturers started constructing car plants in the United States in early 1996, as the Japanese yen had become very expensive relative to the US dollar. However, multinational firms face the problem that it can be very difficult to predict future changes in exchange rates. In late 1996 and throughout 1997, the value of the Japanese yen fell against the US dollar, but Japanese car manufacturers had already committed themselves to building plants in the United States.

Currency exchange rates affect different firms differently. Certain industries, such as electrical equipment or precision machinery, are more affected by changes in currency exchange rates than other industries because they rely heavily on globally sourced inputs and are more dependent on exports than e.g. utilities companies (He and Ng 1998). Firms which operate in many different countries are less affected than others which do not. It has been shown that foreign market participation through direct investment reduces a firm's exposure to exchange rate movements, especially if a firm's investments are widely spread geographically between markets with different currencies (Miller and Reuer 1998).

Currency exchange rates are also less of a problem for firms which resort to 'currency hedging'—the practice of protecting a firm against potential losses resulting from adverse movements in currency exchange rates. For instance, a firm in the Netherlands buys computer equipment from a firm in Singapore at a fixed price and the payment is due in 100 days. If the contract is denominated in Singaporean dollars, the Dutch firm could lose money if the euro were weaker relative to the Singaporean dollar in 100 days. So the firm could buy a 'forward exchange contract' with a bank, which will deliver foreign currency at a specific exchange rate in 100 days. The firm could also buy a 'currency option'—this gives the firm the right to buy or sell a certain amount of currency at a specified date in future (an option is more flexible than a forward contract, as the Dutch firm does not have to exercise the option). A firm with a forward exchange contract or with a currency option will be less affected by changes in currency rates in the short term. In the long term, a sustained appreciation of the Singaporean dollar over many years could make imports from Singapore less internationally competitive. In that case, currency hedging will be of little use.

2.5.3 Cost of capital

In the global economy, a multinational firm can obtain capital in different countries. But different countries may have different rates for borrowing money. This is important for multinational firms, as the cost of borrowing in the home country affects the firm's ability to raise capital. When the lending rates in the UK increase, the cost of raising capital in the UK increases. In the international marketplace, a firm from a country with high lending rates is at a disadvantage in raising capital compared to a firm in a country with low lending rates (Aliber 1970; Grosse and Trevino 1996). If the cost of borrowing increases in the UK relative to other countries, foreign firms will find it easier to compete in the UK market and their investment in the UK will increase. Conversely, if the cost of borrowing decreases in the UK relative to other countries, firms which raise capital in the UK will find it easier to compete in foreign markets.

In the global economy, large multinational firms are able to raise capital in different countries and they are able to deal with the threat of increasing or decreasing cost of borrowing in any one country. These large multinational firms will need to continuously monitor the global business environment for the cost of borrowing in different countries in order to benefit from the best rates available. When you compete on the world stage, you need to obtain capital from the best available source.

However, raising capital outside the firm's home country may not always be possible, so the home base of a multinational firm still influences the cost of borrowing. The national origin of a firm may thus determine how much money you can raise and at what rate. In the most extreme cases, firms decide to change corporate nationality in order to benefit from lower cost of borrowing. For example, several major South African firms including South African Breweries (SAB), the life assurer Old Mutual, and the mining firm Anglo American Corporation strategically switched their stock exchange listing and headquarters from Johannesburg to London. This allowed those firms to raise significantly greater amounts of capital to finance their international operations. When Anglo American and SAB announced their decision to move to London in late 1998, interest rates in Johannesburg were around 22%, while those in London were close to 6%.

2.6 **The social environment**

Social change can have a major influence on firm strategies. Some products and services may become less fashionable, and decline. New social trends may open new business opportunities for multinational firms. In the global market, the firm must pay special attention to two key social issues: social change and global convergence of tastes and needs.

2.6.1 **Social change**

Firms need to pay attention to new global trends in order to strategically exploit new opportunities. For instance, migration of people can open new business opportunities. The presence of a large ethnic Chinese or Indian population in a foreign country opens new international business opportunities for Chinese or Indian firms. Some small and medium-sized firms from China and Hong Kong began their international expansion by strategically locating in foreign countries and cities with a large Chinese population, such as Malaysia or Los Angeles (Child et al. 2002). The presence of a large Chinese minority helped to ensure initial demand for goods and services (ranging from Chinese foodstuffs to banking services), and it also helped to reduce transaction costs of setting up a foreign subsidiary. In turn, early expansion into Malaysia or Los Angeles helped Chinese managers to gain international experience and confidence to expand into more challenging international markets.

Firms also need to pay attention to social issues such as changing relations between age groups of consumers. For example, the rising number of old age pensioners in developed countries opens new markets for multinational firms which provide appropriate goods and services for that age group. In order to benefit from this social change, multinational hotel chains such as Marriott and Hyatt constructed special apartment blocks for the elderly, with meals, transportation, and utilities included in the rent. Some social changes are more subtle. Lindstrom (2003) has shown how the brand-awareness of small children has changed the buying patterns for many goods. His study on children in fourteen countries suggested that almost 80% of all brands purchased by parents are strongly influenced by their offspring. Children as young as eight or even younger may determine which car or computer their parents buy. The rising influence of children on buying decisions is one example of how social change can have major effects on global marketing, and may require a strategic reorientation of some firms. Other important social changes may relate to changes in lifestyle (e.g. more international travel), the levels of education (e.g. more people with higher education), or income distribution (e.g. greater levels of disposable income amongst certain groups in society). Identifying social change early may allow firms to stay ahead of competitors.

2.6.2 **Global convergence**

Some experts claim that the tastes and needs of customers in different countries are becoming increasingly similar, which has been labelled 'global convergence' (Levitt 1983). Thanks to the spread of global communications and transportation, certain social behaviours spread globally. As people travel abroad, watch the same Hollywood-made films, use the same internet websites, and play the same video games, they absorb habits from other countries. According to this view, tastes become more similar globally and this global convergence is most visible in young people. Many young people in developed countries drink Coca-Cola, play the Sony Playstation, and listen to the latest Eminem rap songs. As a result of this convergence, multinational firms with a global strategy are increasingly able to offer identical or very similar products in many different countries. In other words, global convergence of tastes and needs can lead to global market convergence, whereby the world becomes one global market for the same products.

At this point in human history, one should be cautious about the idea of 'global convergence', as some experts claim that there are still huge cultural and other differences between countries (Douglas and Wind 1987). These differences are sometimes major and sometimes minor; seeming similarities between countries may also be superficial. Even if people use the same or similar products in different countries, they may use them at different occasions, under different circumstances, and for different reasons in each country. Where cultural differences play a major role (as with many types of local foodstuff, clothing, or interior design), global business strategies may not be possible. Convergence facilitates global strategies in some industries; conversely, the absence of convergence hinders global strategies in other industries. So managers need to be aware of the impact of global convergence on their specific products and services.

Nonetheless, even if there are differences between countries, firms may often be able to introduce relatively small changes to their global products or global marketing campaigns. For example, McDonald's in India sells two mutton patties as the 'Maharaja Mac', while the taste of Coca-Cola varies between some countries, but the overall marketing strategy of McDonald's and Coca-Cola remains largely the same. Similarly, IKEA (the opening case study in Chapter 1) was forced to change some product features for the US market, but it was able to keep the core product features, which helped to simplify global operations.

2.7 The technological environment

Technological change can have a major impact on business strategies. In the global economy, technological innovation can spread very quickly around the world and the pace of technological pace is increasing. The internet, advances in computer technology, genetic engineering, or laser technology revolutionize the ways in which firms operate. An innovation may render a firm's technology obsolete or it can lead to the creation of entirely new industries. Three important issues to consider are global technology scanning and technology clusters, the rise of the knowledge-based economy, and the spread of the internet.

2.7.1 Global technology scanning and technology clusters

In the global economy, a technological innovation may occur anywhere and it may spread quickly around the globe, so managers must constantly monitor the external business environment for new developments (Granstrand et al. 1992). The process of identifying technologies in the external business environment is called 'technology scanning'. The firm may use different methods to learn about new technologies, from attending scientific conferences to pursuing technical partnerships with other technically advanced companies or research centres.

In a large multinational company, technology scanning can be pursued by locating the company's research centres in countries or regions where relevant cutting-edge research is pursued. Technological advances often occur in high-technology 'clusters' where you find many advanced firms from the same sector, often linked to a high-quality university or research centre. The best-known cluster in information technology is Silicon Valley in California, but smaller ones include India's Silicon Valley near Bangalore, the Multimedia Super Corridor in Malaysia, and Silicon Fen near Cambridge in the UK. One key strategy for a multinational firm is to locate inside a cluster to benefit from its advanced knowledge networks. For example, companies such as Olivetti and Oracle (whose research centre was later taken over by AT&T) located some of their research activities in Silicon Fen, where firms benefited from the proximity to the University of Cambridge, and from advanced research in information technology by other firms located in the region.

As with PEST analysis in general, technology scanning should be as wide-ranging as possible. Relevant technological innovations may often occur outside the firm's industry: achieved by firms in other industries, by universities, or by specialized research centres. The government may be an important source of innovation—often as a result of government research related to the military. For instance, the development of the flat-panel NXT technology for loudspeakers began in the British military by chance. The military conducted research into reducing noise in helicopter cabins, but the material used in the research amplified the noise instead of reducing it. The research was later continued by NXT—a firm based in Silicon Fen—and was commercialized with the help of the British packaging manufacturer DS Smith.

2.7.2 The knowledge-based economy

The introduction of new information technologies such as computers and the internet has generally raised the importance of knowledge in the economy. Some experts talk about the rise of the so-called 'new economy'—businesses based on technological innovation. Rifkin (2000) argues that ownership mattered most in the old economy: physical capital was used to make goods which went to market where they were exchanged. In the new economy, intellectual capital is the driving force and the location of the business activities is much less important. The difference between the 'old' and the 'new' economy can be shown by contrasting the oil industry and the computer software industry. In the oil industry, a company's wealth is largely determined by the physical control of oil fields, oil tankers, and petrol stations. In the software industry, a company's wealth is determined by the intellectual ownership of computer programs and the creativity of its staff. The physical location of oil fields and petrol stations plays a huge role, whereas a software programmer can work anywhere.

Some industries increasingly move from the 'old' towards the 'new' economy, for example, movie-making. American movies were largely made in Hollywood in the past, re-lying on the physical ownership of film studios and proximity to specialized firms which provided stuntmen or film props. But, thanks to technological advancements, computer software can now generate 3D characters who are indistinguishable from live-action film. These technological opportunities were first used extensively by the creators of the movie *Independence Day*, who made much of the movie with computers in warehouses at perhaps half of the cost of a comparable Hollywood movie. The *Lord of the Rings* trilogy and the *Matrix* movies also made extensive use of computer software. As a result of this technolo-gical shift, movie-makers depend less on the physical infrastructure of Hollywood. Many of the leading special-effects companies are based outside Hollywood and indeed outside the United States, so the infrastructure for movie-making is becoming more global. This example shows how technological advances can reshape an industry in the knowledge-based economy.

A key characteristic of the knowledge economy is that knowledge—unlike physical as-sets—can often be transferred and used for different purposes on a global scale. Mental Im-ages, a leading German-based company providing 3D modelling software for movie-making, became famous, winning a special award from the prestigious US Motion Picture Academy (the organization behind the Oscars) for its work on movies such as *Star Wars II: Attack of the Clones*. But Mental Images did not only serve film companies such as Disney and Dream-Works. With only about thirty staff based in Berlin/Germany and San Francisco/United States, the company was able to use the same intellectual property to serve customers in the video games sector (Nintendo and Sega), the car industry (DaimlerChrysler and Honda), and aerospace (Airbus and Boeing).

2.7.3 The spread of the internet

The rise of the knowledge-based economy was greatly helped by the spread of the internet. This made possible new types of product/service (e.g. communications tools and online auc-tions), operational efficiencies (e.g. savings on distribution costs and improved lead times), and better customer service and relationships (e.g. twenty-four-hour service and personal-ized marketing and customer service).

Some experts have argued that the internet has not only brought new products and new distribution channels but also transformed the way we do business in general. Don Tapscott (2001) argued that wealth will be largely created through partnerships in future. Since phys-ical assets are less important in the new economy, companies will no longer have to control all stages of research, production, and marketing as oil companies did in the old economy. At the same time, global partnerships between different firms will spread because the in-ternet can connect people working on the same project in many different countries at a low cost. According to Tapscott, in future managers may simply start with a new idea for a product/service and a blank sheet for the production and delivery system, and then create a network of companies to carry out all necessary activities including research, production, and marketing. One example was the software company Siebel Systems Inc.; this had about 8,000 staff in 2001, but 30,000 people worked for the company as consultants, technology providers, system implementers, suppliers, and vendors. A leading firm in the network will identify discrete activities that create value and will parcel them out to appropriate business web partners. A key ingredient of successful strategy will be web partnerships; ownership of distinct activities and rivalry will be less important.

Michael Porter (2001) disagrees with Dan Tapscott. Porter does not question that the internet has brought many changes such as new types of product/service or huge efficiency gains. But he maintains that the logic of old economy strategies, integration of distinct activities, and rivalry has essentially remained the same. According to Porter, the crash in internet company shares questioned the wisdom of 'new strategies' and ways of assessing the success of online companies (e.g. using click-through rates for websites instead of traditional profitability measures). Porter points out that the big winners of the internet age are not internet-based companies. Some internet businesses such as eBay.com and Amazon.com can claim a huge commercial success. More often, existing companies and industries use the internet to improve their operations, to offer new products or to refocus their business strategies. In commercial banking, for example, established institutions like Wells Fargo, Citibank, and Fleet have many more online accounts than internet banks. Established companies are also gaining dominance over internet activities in such diverse sectors as online retailing and online brokerage (Porter 2001).

Whether you agree with Tapscott or with Porter, it is clear that the internet has the potential to reshape old industries and to create entirely new businesses. One example is online gaming. The introduction of high-speed broadband internet connections has led to a boom in online gaming in many countries, with Germany, France, and the Netherlands in the lead. This was further helped by improvements in gaming technology such as the introduction of Xbox Live. Nearly six million Europeans visited an online games site during January 2003, more than double the figure from the same period in 2002.

2.8 National environmental influences and the Diamond Model

PEST analysis is a useful tool for understanding the external business environment. This understanding can also help to explain why some firms and industries in some countries are more competitive than others. We know that Japanese firms are particularly strong in industries such as cars, consumer electronics, and video games. American firms are particularly strong in sectors such as movie-making, computer software, and defence. Given the existing external business environment in Japan, it would be difficult to develop a world-class movie industry or defence industry there.

Michael Porter (1990) has suggested that there are intrinsic reasons why some nations are more competitive than others and why some industries are very successful in some nations. According to Porter, the national home base of a firm plays a key role in shaping that firm's competitive advantage in global markets. A country's national values, culture, economic structures, institutions, the strength of local rivalry, and challenging local customers all contribute to an industry's economic success. Porter states that the key to global economic success is innovation in the broadest sense—not just technological innovation but also new skills, new knowledge, or the application of old ideas in new areas. A strong

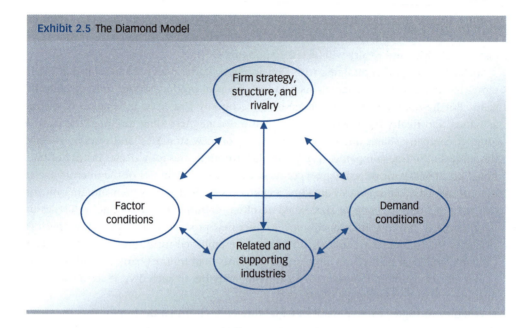

Exhibit 2.5 The Diamond Model

home base of a company often provides the basis for innovation, which in turn can lead to global success.

Porter suggests that four characteristics of the home base help to explain why certain nations are capable of consistent innovation in some sectors: (1) factor conditions, (2) demand conditions, (3) related and supporting industries, and (4) firm strategy, structure, and rivalry. These four conditions form the basis of Porter's 'Diamond Model' (see Exhibit 2.5). The Japanese video game industry provides an example of how the Diamond Model can be used to explain the success of a national industry (see Exhibit 2.6).

KEY CONCEPT

The Diamond Model assumes that the national home base of a firm plays a key role in shaping that firm's competitive advantage in global markets. Four characteristics of the home base help to explain why certain nations are capable of consistent innovation in some industries: (1) factor conditions, (2) demand conditions, (3) related and supporting industries, and (4) firm strategy, structure, and rivalry. The model can be used to analyse the global competitive success of a national industry.

2.8.1 Factor conditions

A country's position in factors of production affects the ability of firms to compete internationally. Basic factors of production include labour, capital, and natural resources, but much more important are advanced factors such as specialized skills of the labour force, a

Exhibit 2.6 The Diamond Model and the Japanese video game industry

The video game industry has become a sizeable industry, with annual sales of about US$20 billion worldwide, bigger than the global film industry. While the industry originated in the United States, industry insiders today agree that it would amount to little without Japanese firms such as Nintendo and Sony Computer Entertainment (SCE). Indeed, after the crash of the American video game industry in 1983 which wiped out demand for video games, Nintendo played the leading role in re-establishing the profitability of the entire sector. How did the Japanese video game industry manage to conquer the global market?

The Diamond Model helps to understand why the home base in Japan was well suited to the birth of a world-class video game industry. The *demand conditions* were favourable: Japanese customers had high expectations of consumer electronics products and role-playing games enjoyed huge popularity in Japan. The *domestic rivalry* was initially low or nonexistent, but Nintendo was challenged by the early 1990s when a number of well-established Japanese consumer electronics firms such as Matsushita attempted to enter the market. In 1994 SCE launched its Playstation consoles, which provided formidable competition for Nintendo's Super Famicon and Game Boy game consoles. There was also strong rivalry from Japan's third video game company, Sega, which later transformed itself into a sub-contractor to Microsoft's Xbox.

Japan also provided favourable *factor conditions* for the video game industry. Nintendo and its rivals benefited from highly educated individuals from Japan's electronics industry and other sectors who worked as game designers or sound programmers. More importantly, they drew artistic creativity from Japan's unique tradition of making cartoons ('manga'). Cartoons had a great influence in Japanese society compared with the US or Europe, and Japanese cartoonists were crucial in introducing characters and story-lines into video games, while their graphic design skills helped to create realistic movement by video game characters. Japan's educational system also helped the industry. By the early 2000s, Japan had roughly 300 vocational programmes offering training specifically designed for video game-related occupations, and some 170 vocational programmes offering training specifically designed for cartoonists, animators, and illustrators.

Above all, Japan's *related and supporting industries* played a key role in the rise of the Japanese video game industry. Nintendo's initial shift from a toy manufacturer to a high-tech video game business was only possible through collaboration with Japanese consumer electronics firms and the sharing of engineering skills with them in areas such as liquid crystal display technology. The presence of firms such as Mitsubishi Electric, Ricoh, and Sharp allowed for frequent communications and experiments at initial stages of console design. The success of the Playstation also depended on partnerships with other firms. A partnership with the software publisher Namco—a Japanese firm which previously worked with Nintendo—greatly helped SCE's entry into the market and helped to showcase the advantages of Playstation's 3D graphics. Japanese video games also benefited from other local industries including innovations from the software industry, multimedia technology from broadcasting and ideas from the cartoon and animation films sectors.

Source: Yuko Aoyama and Hiro Izushi, 'Hardware gimmick or cultural innovation? Technological, cultural and social foundations of the Japanese video game industry', *Research Policy* 1390 (2002), 1–22.

scientific base, and infrastructure. Basic factors are of little importance in the knowledge-based economy—global companies can obtain them through their worldwide operations. An educated workforce in the home country does not necessarily lead to success in global markets—a multinational firm can recruit university graduates anywhere in the world. According to Porter, a factor must be highly specialized to an industry's particular needs—for example, a scientific base specializing in optics, or venture capital to fund computer software firms. These factors are not widely available to every firm, they are more difficult for rivals to imitate and they require sustained investment to create.

Porter suggests that nations are successful in those industries where they are particularly good at factor creation. One example is Denmark, which had two hospitals specialized in studying and treating diabetes and was a global leader in insulin. Another example was the Netherlands, with its high-quality research institutes in the cultivation, packaging, and shipping of flowers, where the country is the global export leader.

2.8.2 Demand conditions

Porter thinks that local demand remains very important despite globalization. The home market affects how companies perceive, interpret, and respond to customer needs. The size of the home market is not so important; what is crucial is the character of demand conditions. A firm can better compete globally if domestic buyers are the world's most sophisticated and demanding buyers for a specific product or service. The presence of a sophisticated home demand provides companies with clearer or earlier signals of emerging global buyer needs. Sophisticated buyers push companies to meet higher standards, and urge them to improve, to innovate, and to enter more advanced market segments. As with factor conditions, strong demand conditions at home help firms to face tough challenges abroad.

Local values and circumstances in the home country are frequently an important stimulus to innovation. For example, Japan's innovations in quiet air-conditioning units with energy-saving rotary compressors were stimulated by the fact that the Japanese lived in small, tightly packed flats and endured hot, humid summers and high-cost electrical energy. As another example, environmentalism of German consumers has greatly helped German-based firms towards success in exporting wind energy products.

2.8.3 Related and supporting industries

Globally competitive related and supporting industries in the home base can greatly help companies to innovate and upgrade. A firm located close to its suppliers or related firms benefits from better communications and the exchange of ideas and innovations with firms in other industries. A firm can influence suppliers' technical efforts and serve as a test site for research and development, which can speed up innovation. At the same time, competition among suppliers can result in lower prices of inputs and higher quality of products. In a global economy, a country does not have to be competitive in all related and supporting industries—a multinational firm with a global strategy can source materials, components, or technologies anywhere in the world. But the local availability of high-quality suppliers and related firms in the home base often strengthens the competitive advantage of home-based industries in global markets.

Close relationships between firms, suppliers, and related industries help firms to attain global market leadership in many industries. For example, Italian leather footwear firms obtained new styles and manufacturing techniques from domestic leather manufacturers, who helped them to learn about new fashion trends and to plan new products.

2.8.4 Firm strategy, structure, and rivalry

Porter noted that there are major differences how firms are created, organized, and managed in different countries, and there are also differences in the nature of domestic rivalry. He found that many globally successful Italian firms were often small in size, privately owned, and operated 'like extended families'. In contrast, many successful German firms had very hierarchical organizations and management practices, and top managers had a technical background. No one country is 'the best' for every industry—some managerial structures are more appropriate for some industries than for others. Globally successful Italian industries such as footwear and packaging machines were compatible with the character of Italian management structures, emphasizing focus, customized products, niche marketing, and flexibility. The Germans typically excelled in technically demanding and engineering-oriented sectors such as chemicals and complicated machinery, which benefited from precision manufacturing and a careful development process.

An important stimulus to innovation is the extent and character of domestic rivalry. When faced with strong local rivals, firms are forced to lower costs, improve quality, raise productivity, and develop new innovative products or production processes. Firms which face such tough competition at home, often develop the necessary skills enabling them to succeed abroad. Porter et al. (2000) found that the global success of many Japanese sectors such as fax machine manufacturing was greatly helped by intense local competition, while government intervention and lack of local competition could help to explain the mediocrity of many Japanese sectors such as chemicals.

2.9 Criticisms of the Diamond Model

The Diamond Model was not intended as a practical management tool to help specific firms compete more successfully; it was designed to help understand why a particular nation is successful in some industries and not in others. The model has been used by governments to consider how government policies can help to foster the competitive advantage of their national industries (e.g. through specific education policies or through high-quality standards for certain products). Some industry leaders and managers have also used the Diamond Model to understand better how they can build on their home base to compete more successfully in global markets.

However, the Diamond Model has come under much criticism. It has been said that there are flaws in Porter's methodology and reasoning, that the Diamond Model cannot explain the success of many global industries, and that Porter provided no reliable guide for governments and managers as to how to formulate effective global strategies (Davies and Ellis 2000). Two important criticisms are related to small nations and globalization.

2.9.1 The Diamond Model for small nations

Several studies suggested that firms from small countries do not rely on a single home base for their success. Large firms in Austria are dependent on the German industrial base, Mexican and Canadian firms depend heavily on the United States, while New Zealand firms rely on the Australian market. A Canadian or a Mexican firm may try out its products in the United States from the start, make intensive use of the US research base, and compete head to head with US-based rivals. Therefore, Rugman and Verbeke (1993) suggested that firms from small nations often depend on a large neighbouring nation to the extent that the distinction between the home base and host nation as a source of economic success becomes blurred.

Regional economic integration has erased many barriers to international trade, so managers in a Canadian firm may perceive the United States as part of their home base and Austrian managers may also think of southern Germany or northern Italy as part of their home market. Rugman and D'Cruz (1991) suggested that we should apply a 'Double Diamond' to explain the success of large firms from small nations. Accordingly, many Canadian firms such as Northern Telecom or Seagram should not be regarded as part of a Canadian diamond but as part of a 'North American diamond'. Canadian managers need to assess the conditions of competitiveness in both Canada and the United States when developing corporate strategies (Rugman and Verbeke 1993).

2.9.2 The Diamond Model and globalization

Another criticism of the Diamond Model is that it pays too little attention to the importance of globalization. By their nature, multinational companies can own or generate new assets in a foreign country. We suggested earlier that large global companies can locate the company's research centres in countries or regions where latest cutting-edge research is pursued such as Silicon Valley or Silicon Fen (section 2.7.1). A global company can also start a strategic alliance with a foreign company (see Chapter 7) or buy a foreign company in order to acquire important resources. In this way, a company can gain innovation from factor conditions in a foreign location (Dunning 1993).

Globalization also affects demand conditions, supporting and related industries and rivalry. We suggested earlier that the tastes of consumers are becoming increasingly similar (section 2.6.2), so the demand conditions become similar across countries. Since global companies pursue global sourcing strategies and can use any supplier from any country, local supporting and related industries are becoming less important. Finally, local rivalry is becoming less important in the global market, as multinational companies have to compete against the best companies in their sector on a global scale. Therefore, some observers have argued that the Diamond Model no longer makes much sense, since national competitive conditions are now not as important for the success of large global businesses.

2.9.3 Response to criticisms

Michael Porter does not deny the importance of international and global strategies. He admits that companies have to compete globally today, but he suggests that the secret of their global success usually lies in the unique mixture of domestic conditions in their home base. At least two further arguments can be made in defence of the Diamond Model.

First, Porter has pointed out that regions are still important despite globalization, and that 'home base' can often refer to a specific region. Technology 'clusters' such as Silicon Valley and Silicon Fen are regional—not national or international—in character. The existence of such clusters shows that, despite globalization and the spread of the internet, the close physical proximity between firms in the same sector helps to create new ideas and technical innovations. The internet cannot fully replace the human interaction between engineers, managers, and others. If a Japanese computer software company wanted to invest in the United States, it would be advised to locate in Silicon Valley—not in Florida or Ohio—to benefit from local factor conditions, local suppliers, and domestic rivals in the software sector. Despite globalization, some locations provide a unique mixture of local factors, which facilitates innovation.

Second, in contrast to the view of a truly global economy, Pauly and Reich (1997) showed that firms from different countries continue to differ in their internal governance and long-term financing structures, in their approaches to research and development as well as in the location of core research facilities, and in their foreign investment and intra-firm trading strategies. German and Japanese firms obtain most of their financing through banks (about 60–70%), while US firms rely more on capital markets (bank loans provide only 25–35% of financial liabilities). Foreign research facilities account for less than 15% of the total research and development spending by large American firms; Japanese and German firms spend even less on research abroad. Furthermore, much of corporate research and development spending abroad is used to customize products for local markets or to gather knowledge for transfer back home, not to generate new knowledge. Firms are still largely dependent on innovation in their home country. Therefore, the local conditions in the home base still shape the global strategies of German, Japanese, or American firms.

2.10 Summary

The competitive success of organizations is determined by the business environment, which consists of the external macro environment, the external industry environment, and the internal firm environment. The external business environment of the firm provides both opportunities and threats to firms, and the task of the strategic decision-maker is to develop strategies based on what the firm can do to exploit external opportunities and counter external threats. In order to be successful, a firm must achieve strategic fit, i.e. it must match its resources and activities to the external environment in which it operates.

There are no simple recipes for monitoring, analysing, and forecasting external factors, which may influence the firm's development. But it is useful to have a checklist of potential external macro influences—PEST analysis—which can serve to ask questions as to how political, economic, social, or technological developments can influence a specific industry and a specific firm. If managers ask the appropriate questions relevant to their business, PEST analysis can help to formulate strategies, which aim to exploit external opportunities.

An understanding of the external business environment can also help us to explain why some firms and industries in some countries are more competitive than others. According to Porter, the national home base of a firm plays a key role in shaping that firm's competitive advantage in global markets. Porter suggests that four characteristics of the home base help to explain why certain nations are capable of consistent innovation in some sectors: (1) factor conditions, (2) demand conditions, (3) related and supporting industries, and (4) firm strategy, structure, and rivalry. The model can be used to analyse the global competitive success of a national industry. It demonstrates how the wider business environment can have a major impact on competitive success in the international marketplace.

KEY READINGS

- On the external business environment, see Dicken (2003).
- On the Diamond Model, see Porter (1990).
- On critique of the Diamond Model, see Davies and Ellis (2000).

DISCUSSION QUESTIONS

1 What problems do managers face in conducting a global PEST analysis and how might they overcome these problems?

2 Do regional economic blocs such as the EU, NAFTA, or AFTA help or obstruct free trade in the world?

3 What is your opinion about the criticisms that have been made against international institutions such as the WTO, the IMF, and the World Bank?

4 To what extent has the world experienced 'global convergence' of tastes and needs?

5 To what extent did the internet change the nature of business activity and business strategy?

6 Take one national industry of your choice. Can the Diamond Model explain the international success or lack of success of your industry?

Closing case study
Lockheed Martin—from conquering Russia to conquering space

In 1995, two companies—the Lockheed Corporation and the Martin Marietta Corporation—merged to form the Lockheed Martin Corporation. Today, Lockheed Martin is a major global company engaged in the research, design, development, manufacture, and integration of advanced technology systems, products, and services. It employs some 125,000 people worldwide and its reported sales were $26.6 billion in 2002. Much of the company's business is in the defence sector, and Lockheed Martin's products include tactical aircraft and naval systems. Nearly 80% of the company's business is with the US Department of Defense and the US federal government agencies.

One of Lockheed Martin's main business lines are Space Systems—space launch, commercial satellites, government satellites, and strategic missiles. In the 1990s, a global market for satellite launch services emerged and Lockheed Martin wanted to share in this market growth. The emergence of commercial launch services was made possible by two developments in the external business environment. On the one hand, there was a rapid growth in telecommunications technologies driving significant acceleration of demand for launches of telecommunications satellites. The growth of satellite television channels and mobile phones was dependent on launching new satellites. On the other hand, the political environment changed.

During the Cold War, global access to satellite launch services was tightly regulated, and in many cases controlled, by governments because of the close linkage between satellites and defence requirements. In the 1980s, a global market in satellite launches began to emerge. In 1980 the European Space Agency created Arianespace, the first real commercial space transportation company, which launched its first commercial satellite payload into orbit in 1984 from the European Space Agency's launch site at Kourou, Guyana. Commercial satellites were also launched by NASA from Cape Kennedy during the 1980s. However, commercial launch services remained subject to government control. Soviet and Chinese launch sites remained entirely state-controlled, and were used predominantly for domestic military, scientific, and state telecommunications needs.

In the early 1990s the global political environment changed radically. The Cold War ended and the Soviet Union disintegrated. The old enemies—the United States and Russia—began to work together on economic and technological issues. In the space sector, NASA and the Russian Space Agency (RSA) cooperated by utilizing the US space shuttle and the ageing Russian Mir space station to prepare for the construction of the International Space Station (ISS). Old barriers to technological transfers in the space sector between Russia and the United States were relaxed.

The US and Russian governments promoted the privatization of Russian firms and commercialization of Russia's space sector to facilitate joint ventures between US and Russian firms. The prospect of joint ventures with Russian firms was attractive for American companies such as Lockheed at a time when the demand for commercial satellite launches had increased. Access to Russia's aerospace assets—launch platforms, rockets, and support services—could help US firms to gain new technology and to increase capacity for a larger number of satellite launches.

In April 1993, Lockheed formed a joint venture with two Russian aerospace firms—RSC Energia and Khrunichev called Lockheed-Energia-Khrunichev International (LEKI). Following the merger in 1995, Lockheed Martin established Lockheed Martin Commercial Launch Services Company (LMCLS) to market launch services using Lockheed Martin's Atlas II and III rocket boosters, to be launched from Cape Canaveral and Vandenberg Air Force Base, California. LMCLS and LKEI then joined forces to form a highly innovative new company, International Launch Services (ILS) to market jointly the commercial launch services of the Russian Proton and American Atlas boosters on a global basis. The first ILS commercial launch using a Proton booster took place in 1996, and business grew steadily.

Lockheed Martin's entry into Russia allowed the company to benefit from the technological base of the country. The company was able to get access to (amongst others) the Proton rocket booster and the RD180 engine, which gave it an advantage in the global market for satellite launches. Most crucially, it benefited from the political situation. The US–Russian cooperation in the space sector gave a privileged position to US companies in Russia. The US and Russian governments actively supported the ILS venture; for instance, the Russian government negotiated with the government of Kazakhstan to allow ILS the use of the Baikonur space facility in Kazakhstan. Political support also helped ILS to cope better with existing government restrictions in the space sector (e.g. pricing restrictions) and to obtain the required government permits (e.g. export licences).

With government support, Lockheed Martin was able to benefit from early market entry in Russia several years before its rivals. Its competitor Arianespace only entered Russia in 1996. The early entry into Russia gave Lockheed Martin time to develop a customer base before its rivals obtained the relevant technology. In other words, the conquest of Russia led to Lockheed Martin's conquest of space.

The ILS venture continues to be very successful. In 2000 alone, ILS launched six Proton and eight Atlas rockets and signed contracts for sixteen future launches worth US$1 billion, bringing their backlog to forty launches worth over US$3 billion. Customers have included Loral, SES, Inmarsat, Iridium, Motorola, PanAmSat, Hughes, ICO Global Communications, and INTELSAT, and ILS has 40–50% of the global market for commercial satellite launches today.

Sources: Lockheed Martin website at www.lockheedmartin.com/ and ILS website at www.ilslaunch.com/; Jedrzej George Frynas, Kamel Mellahi, and Geoffrey Allen Pigman, 'First mover advantages in international business and firm-specific political resources'; interview with a senior ILS manager.

Discussion questions

1 How did the external business environment influence the success of Lockheed Martin in satellite launch services?

2 Michael Porter suggested that a company based in a country with a high level of government intervention will lose out to international competitors. Does the case of Lockheed Martin support his view?

REFERENCES

Aliber, Robert Z. (1970). 'A theory of foreign direct investment', in C. Kindleberger (ed.), The International Corporation (Cambridge, Mass.: MIT Press).

Child, John, Sek Hong, Ng, and Wong, Christine (2002). 'Psychic distance and internationalization', International Studies of Management and Organization 32(1): 36–56.

Davies, H., and Ellis, P. (2000). 'Porter's Competitive Advantage of Nations: time for the final judgement?', Journal of Management Studies 37(8): 1189–1213.

Dewenter, Kathryn L. (1995). 'Do exchange rate changes drive foreign direct investment?', Journal of Business 68(3): 405–33.

Dicken, Peter (2003). Global Shift: Reshaping the Global Economic Map in the 21st Century, 4th edn. (London: Sage).

Douglas, S. P., and Wind, Y. (1987). 'The myth of globalization', Columbia Journal of World Business 22(4): 19–29.

Dunning, J. H. (1993). 'Internationalizing Porter's diamond', Management International Review 33(2): 7–15.

Finger, J. Michael, and Schuler, Philip (2000). 'Implementation of Uruguay Round commitments: the development challenge', *World Economy* 23(4): 511–25.

Froot, Kenneth A., and Stein, Jeremy C. (1991). 'Exchange rates and foreign direct investment: an imperfect capital markets approach', *Quarterly Journal of Economics* 106: 1191–1217.

Frynas, J. G. (1998). 'Political instability and business: focus on Shell in Nigeria', *Third World Quarterly* 19(3): 457–79.

____(2002). 'The limits of globalization: legal and political issues in e-commerce', *Management Decision* 40(9): 871–80.

____and Mellahi, K. (2003). 'Political risks as firm-specific (dis)advantages: evidence on transnational oil firms in Nigeria', *Thunderbird International Business Review* 45(5): 522–41.

____Mellahi, K., and Pigman, A. G. (2003). 'First mover advantage in international business and firm-specific political resources'. *Academy of International Business Conference* (Monterey, Calif., July), 91–2.

Galbraith, J. R., and Kazanjian, R. K. (1986). *Strategy Implementation*, 2nd edn. (St Paul, Minn.: West).

George, Susan, and Sabelli, Fabrizio (1994). *Faith and Credit: The World Bank's Secular Empire* (Harmondsworth: Penguin).

Gilbert, C. L., and Vines, D. (eds.) (2000). *The World Bank: Structure and Policies* (Cambridge: Cambridge University Press).

Gilpin, R. (2001). *Global Political Economy: Understanding the International Economic Order* (Princeton, NJ: Princeton University Press).

Granstrand, Ove, Bohlin, Erik, Oskarsson Christer, and Sjöberg, Niklas (1992). 'External technology acquisition in large multi-technology corporations', *R&D Management* 22(2): 111–33.

Grosse, Robert, and Trevino, Len J. (1996). 'Foreign direct investment in the United States: an analysis by country of origin', *Journal of International Business Studies* 27(1): 139–55.

He, J., and Ng, K. L. (1998). 'The foreign exchange exposure of Japanese multinational corporations', *Journal of Finance* 53(2): 733–53.

Kobrin, Stephen (1982). *Managing Political Risk Assessment*. Berkeley: University of California Press.

Lee, Simon (2002). 'The International Monetary Fund', *New Political Economy* 7(2): 283–98.

Levitt, T. (1983). 'The globalization of markets', *Harvard Business Review* (May–June): 92–102.

Lindstrom, Martin (2003). *BRAND Child*. London: Kogan Page.

Miller, Kent D., and Reuer, Jeffrey J. (1998). 'Firm strategy and economic exposure to foreign exchange rate movements', *Journal of International Business Studies* 29(3): 493–514.

Norburn, D. (1974). 'Directors without direction', *Journal of General Management* 1(2): 37–49.

Parker, Barbara (1998). *Globalization and Business Practice: Managing across Boundaries* (London: Sage).

Pauly, L. W., and Reich, S. (1997). 'National structures and multinational corporate behaviour: enduring differences in the age of globalization', *International Organization* 51(1): 1–30.

Peng, Michael W. (2000). *Business Strategies in Transition Economies* (Thousand Oaks, Calif.: Sage).

Porter, Michael (1990). 'The competitive advantage of nations', *Harvard Business Review* (Mar.–Apr.): 73–93.

____(2001). 'Strategy and the internet', *Harvard Business Review* (Mar.).

____Takeuchi, H., and Sakakibara, M. (2000). *Can Japan Compete?* (London: Macmillan).

____and van der Linde, C. (1995a). 'Green and competitive', *Harvard Business Review* (Sept.–Oct.): 120–34.

____ ____(1995b). 'Toward a new conception of the environment–competitiveness relationship', *Journal of Economic Perspectives* 9(4): 97–118.

Rifkin, Jeremy (2000). *The Age of Access* (New York: Tarcher/Penguin Putnam).

Robock, H. Stefan, and Simmonds, Kenneth (1989). *International Business and Multinational Enterprises*, 4th edn. (Homewood, Ill.: Irwin).

Rugman, Alan M., and D'Cruz, Joseph (1991). *Fast Forward: Improving Canada's International Competitiveness* (Toronto: Kodak Canada).

Rugman, Alan M., and Verbeke, A. (1993). 'Foreign subsidiaries and multinational strategic management: an extension and correction of Porter's single diamond framework', *Management International Review* 33(2): 60–73.

Stubbs, R., and Underhill, G. R. D. (1994). *Political Economy and the Changing Global Order* (London: Macmillan).

Tapscott, D. (2001). 'Rethinking strategy in a networked world', *Strategy+Business* 24(3): 1–8.

Wells, Louis T., and Gleason, S. E. (1995). 'Is foreign infrastructure investment still risky?', *Harvard Business Review* (Sept.–Oct.): 44–55.

Wilkinson, Rorden (2002). 'Global monitor: the World Trade Organization', *New Political Economy* 7(1): 129–41.

3

Global business environment: the industry environment

Learning outcomes

After reading this chapter you should be able to:

- understand the significance of the global industry environment for the strategies of multinational firms;

- apply market segmentation analysis, strategic group analysis, and the Five Forces Model;

- understand the importance of industry evolution and the International Product Life Cycle;

- appreciate differences between forecasting techniques for understanding the future of an industry.

Formed in 1998, Boo.com launched a website in 1999 to sell expensive fashion clothing on the internet. It was a highly international company. The headquarters were in London, with a New York buying office, smaller offices in Paris, Amsterdam, Munich, and Stockholm, and new offices opening in Italy and Spain. The back-end structure at Boo.com was intended to allow premium prices to be maintained in different countries, with sales in different currencies, and for orders to be directed back to a distribution system that could deliver globally within days.

Like many new online businesses, the British-based Boo.com was trying to harness the power of the internet. The Boo.com formula was simple: 'We'll take the experience of a day shopping in glamorous stores and turn it into twenty minutes of bewilderment in front of your PC.' But Boo.com went bankrupt in May 2000, which heralded the fall of many other dot com stocks.

Why did the company fail? Some journalists and former Boo.com managers have said that blunders by the management of Boo.com were responsible. According to one report, Boo.com did not even have a business plan. The website was supposed to be launched in May 1999, but technical problems delayed the launch until November. While Boo.com was not earning any money, millions were spent on advertising, sophisticated technology, and lavish office parties.

The management also made the mistake of launching the website in eighteen different countries at the same time, which created practical problems such as the use of different languages, different foreign currencies, and payment of tax in different countries. Boo.com management had underestimated the infrastructure dilemmas of building—from the ground up—a global system capable of handling and integrating currencies, languages, customers, deliveries, and logistics.

Certainly, many individual mistakes were made. But can individual mistakes explain why so many other internet businesses have failed? The most compelling explanation of the Boo.com failure is that the managers failed to understand their business environment. Most importantly, Boo.com managers failed to understand their customers.

The first version of the Boo.com website totally failed to understand the needs of customers. The website could not be accessed by Macintosh computers, which were frequently used by key customers such as graphics and design companies. It required the Flash plug-in, which was not as widespread as it is today. It used sophisticated graphics, pop-up windows, and 3D images which required high-speed internet connections, so many customers had to wait minutes for web pages to download. The firm's overloaded web servers and its 'over-fancy' images simply could not come through at a reasonable speed. Analysts reported: '99% of European and 98% of US homes lack the high-bandwidth access needed to easily access such animations.' Furthermore, the website was difficult to navigate and the shopping process was cumbersome. In some respects, Boo.com behaved in the opposite manner to successful internet retailers such as Amazon.com, which tried to simplify the website and speed up the shopping experience as much as possible.

Boo.com did not fully understand the needs of its customers. It sought to serve eighteen countries from the start; but it seems that little or no research had been carried out regarding the potential variation between different countries in terms of taste and price. Although several aspects of the fashion sector had converged across countries, variance still existed. Boo.com also failed to understand why people buy online. Most people buy on the internet because goods tend to be cheaper; Boo.com's goods commanded premium prices, so customers could not save money by buying online.

More fundamentally, the internet is not the most suitable distribution channel for selling clothes. Buying clothes is not the same as buying books, films, or CDs online. Buyers like to touch clothes and to try them—things you cannot do on the internet. The target customers of Boo.com were young and trendy women with high spending power, who saw shopping as a social experience. They were unlikely to abandon shopping in their favourite boutique or department store in favour of one hour at the computer screen. They liked the feel of a chase, the sale item being hunted, taken home, taken out of the bag, shown off to friends and family, talked about and worn that night. The Boo.com bosses did not fully appreciate how their industry worked.

Sources: various newspaper articles.

3.1 Introduction

The last chapter demonstrated the importance of political, economic, social, and economic (PEST) factors in the external business environment. But PEST factors are only important if they impact on the industry and the firm. For example, the introduction of a new technology—the internet—may offer major opportunities for some industries and fewer opportunities for others. The example of Boo.com shows that it is important to understand how changes in the external industry environment affect or do not affect your business.

Managers need to understand the industry environment in which they operate, to understand the external opportunities and threats, and to adapt the organization to the industry environment. In order to achieve 'strategic fit' (see Chapter 2, section 2.2), the firm needs to understand the structure of its industry, no matter whether you are a domestic or a multinational firm.

Above all, managers need to understand their customers—their preferences, lifestyles, shopping habits, etc. The firm must also understand competition in the industry—who your competitors are, how much they charge for their products, and how easily new competitors can enter the market. Finally, managers need to understand the suppliers—how to form business relationships with them, or how suppliers deliver their goods. Together, customers, competitors, and suppliers are the main elements of the industry environment. This is the topic of this chapter.

3.2 Understanding and adapting to industry environment

What industry are you in? On the surface, the question seems very simple, but it is not that simple in real life. Mercedes and Ford are both in the car industry. But an increase in the price of Mercedes S class cars does not necessarily mean more sales of the Ford Focus. The customers for the Mercedes S class and for the Ford Focus are different groups. The skills and resources necessary to produce a Mercedes S class car are different from those needed to produce a Ford Focus. The nature of advertising, product development, and pricing policies are different for the two products. Indeed, using the word 'industry' may be unhelpful because it is very broad. A focus on a broad industry may lead to an inaccurate understanding of the market and the nature of competition: it does not tell you who your competitors are and which are the key competing products for your firm. You need to identify your precise market, which can be achieved by conducting a 'market segmentation analysis' and 'strategic group analysis'.

3.2.1 Market segmentation analysis

When identifying the market, the firm should—above all—identify the customers who buy the firm's product or service. In the opening case study, Boo.com failed to understand which customers it served, and the technology used by the company was too advanced for many customers. Several simple questions could have prevented Boo.com from pursuing some inappropriate elements of its strategy.

'Market segmentation analysis' aims to identify similarities and differences between groups of people who buy and use your goods and services. To aid market identification, firms can ask questions such as:

- Which other products with similar perceived attributes do my (current) customers rate as highly as mine?
- How price-sensitive are my customers? How much can we increase the price of our goods without losing customers to another firm?
- How far will my (current) customers travel to buy this or that alternative?
- Why do customers buy the product, and what is its value to them?
- How should it best be produced and distributed, and at what cost? i.e. does it cost more than the value it creates for customers?
- Who is willing to purchase the good or service?

Such a long list may be confusing, so Doyle (1997) suggested that strategists should concentrate on three questions:

- Customer segmentation: which customer segments are to be served by the strategy?
- Customer needs: what is the range of customer needs to be met?
- Technology: which technologies are required in order to pursue customers?

Doyle argued that a focus on these three points helps to identify the relevant market in a way which is relevant to developing strategy. For instance, personal care products could be divided according to customer needs: oral care, grooming, infant hygiene, feminine hygiene, or senior hygiene—all of these would present separate markets for companies.

An added difficulty in global business strategy is that your competitors and customers may differ between countries. So, as part of a market segmentation analysis, a multinational firm may try to identify its main competition by listing all of its main product categories and all of its main geographical markets. For example, Unilever has three principal product categories—foods, personal care, and fabric care—and operates in three main geographical areas—the Americas, Europe, and Asia Pacific–Africa. In most of these product groups and most geographical areas, Unilever's main competitor is the US firm Procter & Gamble (makers of Folgers coffee, Pampers diapers, and Tide laundry detergent). In order to identify the firm's other important international competitors, Unilever could scrutinize each product group (e.g. personal care products according to oral care, grooming, etc.) and list main competitors by geographical region. It could ask simple questions like 'Who is our key competitor for oral care in Europe, in the Americas, in Asia Pacific–Africa?' (MacMillan et al. 2003). Such questions could help the firm to gain a picture of its global competitive position in the broader industry.

KEY CONCEPT

Market segmentation analysis is about identifying similarities and differences between groups of people who buy and use your goods and services.

3.2.2 Strategic group analysis

Market segmentation analysis focuses on understanding customers. But it is not always the perceptions of customers that define the market. Sometimes markets may be defined by the long history of the industry or by the requirements of technology used to manufacture goods. For example, the Japanese steel industry is divided into two main groups: the integrated steel mills and the 'mini-mills', despite the fact that they may share the same customers. The two groups are distinct because of the use of technology: integrated mills use basic-oxygen furnaces and mini-mills use electric-arc furnaces, which require very different inputs in the production of steel. Furthermore, the two groups have been shaped by different histories, different government policies towards them (as Japan's government supported integrated mills), and different economic forces (integrated mills require larger production capacities to become profitable due to the steel-melting technology used) (Nair and Kotha 2001).

The Japanese steel industry is an example of an industry divided into two strategic groups. A strategic group is defined as 'a group of firms within the same industry making similar decisions in key areas' (Porter 1980: 129). Strategic group analysis aims to identify firms with similar strategies or competing on similar bases. Such an analysis helps to understand who your main competitors are and what strategies your main competitors are likely to pursue. It has been suggested that strategic groups differ in profitability: for instance, Japanese integrated steel mills were more profitable than mini-mills in the 1980–87 period but less profitable after 1987 (Nair and Kotha 2001). Strategic group analysis can therefore help us to understand the nature of competition and profitability within an industry sub-group;

Exhibit 3.1 Strategic groups in the food-processing industry

By the 1980s a new strategic group had emerged: multinational food processing companies (e.g. Unilever, BSN, Nestlé), which were distinct from other food-processing firms thanks to product differentiation and distinct brands. This change in industry structure was facilitated by:

- global homogenization of customer demand for food products
- slow growth and saturation of national markets
- rise in the importance of international sourcing
- dismantling of trade barriers

Strategic groups in the food-processing industry in the 1980s

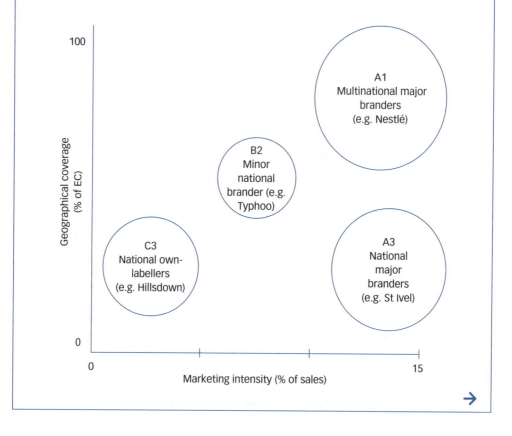

→

Summary of mobility barriers

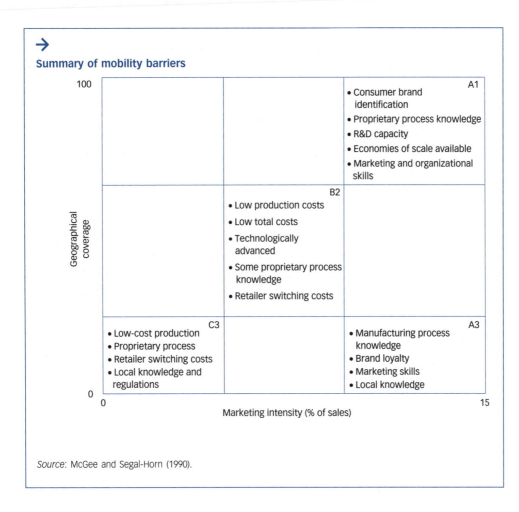

100

Geographical coverage

- Consumer brand identification
- Proprietary process knowledge
- R&D capacity
- Economies of scale available
- Marketing and organizational skills

A1

B2
- Low production costs
- Low total costs
- Technologically advanced
- Some proprietary process knowledge
- Retailer switching costs

C3
- Low-cost production
- Proprietary process
- Retailer switching costs
- Local knowledge and regulations

A3
- Manufacturing process knowledge
- Brand loyalty
- Marketing skills
- Local knowledge

0

0   15

Marketing intensity (% of sales)

Source: McGee and Segal-Horn (1990).

this gives managers better information about where to invest or what type of strategic action to expect from competitors (see McGee and Thomas 1986).

There are no easy prescriptions as to how to identify a strategic group within an industry. As we said earlier, strategic groups are sometimes created because customers perceive certain types of product as distinct, or they can be created as a result of different industry histories, government intervention, or different use of technology. A good predictor of strategic groups is 'mobility barriers', barriers which prevent other firms entering the strategic group and threatening the existing members (McGee and Segal-Horn 1990). In the case of Japanese steel, the key mobility barrier is expensive core-melting technology, which prevents steel firms from switching groups. In the case of the international food-processing industry, the major mobility barriers are brands (see Exhibit 3.1).

A key problem is that the boundaries between strategic groups can be blurred: sometimes a multinational firm can be unique and may not easily fit into any strategic group. Mobility barriers are not always very tight, while the external business environment may change (e.g. technology change). The objective criteria cannot always tell us what constitutes a strategic group. Therefore, the most important determinants of strategic groups are perceptions by the senior managers in the industry. Research shows that managers like to partition the external business environment in order to cope with the demands of an uncertain globalizing world where you cannot follow developments in every conceivable market. Therefore, managers create mental pictures of where the boundaries of strategic groups lie, and these imagined boundaries are often shared with managers of other firms in the same strategic group (Peteraf and Shanley 1997; Greve 1998).

One problem with creating and using mental pictures of strategic groups is that this may lead to 'strategic myopia', a human tendency to reject unfamiliar or negative information. This threat is especially present when industries become more international, while the managers' mental picture of the boundaries of their industry remains rooted in national strategic groups. For instance, Scottish knitwear manufacturers did not recognize Japanese or Italian knitwear firms as competitors for a long time, despite the obvious similarities of the foreign products, as managers had always focused on their domestic competition. A rigid focus on a strategic group reduces opportunities for cooperation with firms outside the strategic group and makes firms vulnerable to surprise competitive attacks from outside the group (Peteraf and Shanley 1997).

KEY CONCEPT

Strategic group analysis is about identifying firms with similar strategies or those competing on similar bases.

3.3 The Five Forces Model

Market segmentation analysis and strategic group analysis are not enough to provide managers with a thorough understanding of their industry. Michael Porter (1980; 1985) suggested that managers must understand the underlying economic and technical characteristics of the industry or strategic group in which their firms operate.

Porter believed that the most fundamental determinant of a firm's profitability was industry attractiveness. As a result of the way a specific industry operates, some industries are inherently more profitable than other industries. For instance, the pharmaceutical and soft drinks industries are much more profitable than steel or rubber. Managers should understand the rules of competition in their industry so that they become aware both of industry attractiveness and of their firm's own competitive position within the industry.

In order to understand these underlying rules of competition in an industry, Porter proposed a technique called the Five Forces Model (see Exhibit 3.2). He suggested that industry attractiveness and the firm's competitive position in an industry are influenced by five competitive forces: the entry of new competitors, the threat of substitutes, the bargaining power of buyers, the bargaining power of suppliers, and the rivalry amongst existing competitors. The strength of these five forces varies from industry to industry and can change as the industry evolves. Exhibit 3.3 applies the model to Amazon.com.

Like PEST analysis in Chapter 2, the Five Forces Model can be used to understand the

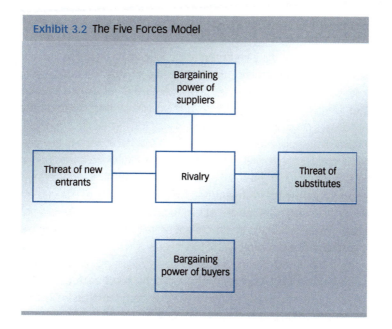

Exhibit 3.2 The Five Forces Model

industry environment within one country, one geographical region, or the entire world. But the competitive forces may be very different in countries and regions, so an international manager may be advised to conduct several Five Forces analyses for different countries or regions and then compare the results. It is also very important that the Five Forces are analysed for a specific market segment or similar market segments, not for an entire industry. It would make little sense for Ford or Volkswagen to analyse the Five Forces for the entire car industry, because the great number of industry factors would be of little use to managers. On the other hand, a car company might find it useful to analyse a specific market, for example, pick-up vans. The following sections discuss the Five Forces in more detail.

KEY CONCEPT

The Five Forces Model assumes that industry attractiveness and the firm's competitive position in an industry are influenced by five competitive forces: the entry of new competitors, the threat of substitutes, the bargaining power of buyers, the bargaining power of suppliers, and the rivalry amongst existing competitors. The model can be used to analyse a firm's competitive position in a specific market segment or similar market segments.

3.3.1 Barriers to entry

Barriers to entry are obstacles which potential newcomers would encounter when entering the market. If there are many barriers to entry, it is less likely that the firm will face new competitors. New entrants could lead to lower sales for the firm, they could force the firm to lower prices, or they could force the firm to spend more money on innovation or new

Exhibit 3.3 The Five Forces Model and Amazon.com

According to Michael Porter, the introduction of the internet has changed industry structure in many industries with the consequence that internet-based firms find it more difficult to make profits. Internet buyers usually buy on the internet because goods tend to be cheaper, so firms compete more intensely to sell their products as cheaply as possible. Rivalry is also higher than in traditional business because the geographical market for internet firms is huge, so there can be many online rivals in many countries. The internet also reduces barriers to entry, as the costs for sales forces, distribution channels, and other physical assets are lower. The internet allows buyers easily to access information about products, and it is relatively easy for buyers to switch suppliers. As a result, while the internet allows firms to save costs or introduce new products, the new industry structures make it more difficult to convert those benefits into profits.

However, the introduction of the internet is not entirely damaging. Applying the Five Forces Model to Amazon.com (the online retailer of books, CDs, and other products) shows how a firm may act to soften the impact of industry forces so that these forces can work in its favour. Amazon.com was able to place itself favourably within the global market for online book retailing. Above all, the threat of new entrants is lower for Amazon.com than for its competition. The company was able to build up an impressive brand which helped to differentiate the firm from other e-retailers and to protect Amazon.com's position.

The five forces which impact on Amazon.com can be summarized as follows:

(+) means that the industry force protects Amazon.com's position.
(–) means that the industry force threatens Amazon.com's position.

Rivalry

- Amazon.com has many rivals worldwide. (–)
- The rivals are very diverse, including: online booksellers and vendors of other products such as CDs or videotapes; indirect competitors such as web portals and web search engines (e.g. Yahoo!), which are involved in e-commerce directly or in partnership with other retailers; publishers, distributors, and retail vendors of books, CDs, and other products (including Bertelsmann and other large speciality booksellers and media firms, many of which possess significant brand awareness, sales volume, and customer bases); traditional retailers who sell through the internet such as Barnes & Noble. (–)
- As customers spend more time on the internet, their expectations increase, which requires more value adding activities by competitors. (+)
- There is large unpredictability in terms of future revenues and wide fluctuations in short-term operating results. Combined with this is a need to develop infrastructure in preparation for future demand. (+)
- While Amazon.com carries a great range of products, it is not the products that differentiate it from its rivals (products are increasingly becoming commodities and customers can easily

→

→

make price comparisons on the net). Its differentiation factors include strong brand name and the firm's ability to use technology to serve customers effectively (e.g. individual and instant recommendations of books). (+)

- Amazon.com has one of the world's best internet brands (it was once rated as the most widely recognized internet brand in the United States and the fifty-seventh most valuable brand worldwide). (+)

Threat of new entrants

- Capital requirements are low in e-commerce (i.e. Amazon.com exceeded sales of $1 billion with only $30 million in inventory and $30 million in net plant and equipment). (−)
- Economies of scale exist in terms of providing high-level customer service, and Amazon.com has been building distribution capacity ahead of expected demand. (+)
- Differentiation plays an important role thanks to Amazon.com's ability to use technology and thanks to its strong brand image. (+)
- Amazon.com developed proprietary software including its patented '1-Click®' online shopping system (Amazon.com sued its rival BarnesandNoble.com in court for using a similar system). (+)
- Amazon.com makes intensive use of technology development in its global strategy and requires very specialized skills. (+)

Power of buyers

- Buyer information is high as buyers can easily compare prices on the internet. (−)
- Buyers have low switching costs when shopping on the internet. (−)
- Amazon.com's focus on using buyer information has focused on value-added activities aimed at reducing the buyer's propensity to switch. Combined with a strong brand image, this has increased the loyalty of Amazon.com customers, resulting in very high repeat purchasing rates. (+)
- Improved customer services and quality levels also aim at reducing customer switching to other products or companies; Amazon.com uses information on prior buyer purchases to predict or prompt additional purchases. (+)

Power of suppliers

- For a long time, Amazon.com's book supplies came from only three vendors; while switching costs in e-commerce are relatively low, switching from one of the suppliers would be costly due to the volumes required. (−)

→

→

- There is little differentiation in terms of products so there is limited power of suppliers in terms of the uniqueness of the product. With the growing range of products offered by Amazon.com, the power of the three book suppliers has diminished. (+)

- The threat of vertical integration is high due to the low capital requirements for traditional firms. (−)

Threat of substitutes

- With very low switching costs, buyers can easily shop elsewhere. (−)

- Amazon.com has tried to mitigate the threat of substitutes by offering new products such as CDs, toys, videos, and gifts. It also helps shoppers to find anything for sale on the internet by providing an easy-to-use online shopping guide, so customers can continue shopping without leaving the Amazon.com website. (+)

- Amazon.com has used information on customer buying habits—the unique Recommendations Centre—to recommend other books and products that the customer might enjoy, which can be bought from its website. (+)

Sources: Michael Porter, 'Strategy and the Internet', *Harvard Business Review* (March 2001), 63–78; David Street and Gary J. Stockport, 'Amazon.com: from startup to the new millennium—teaching note', case study at the Graduate School of Business, University of Cape Town, 2000; J. G. Frynas, 'The Limits of Globalization: legal and political issues in e-commerce', *Management Decision* 40(9) (2002), 871–80.

---

distribution channels. As a result, new entrants could mean lower profits for the established firm, so high barriers to entry help to maintain the firm's profitability. Studies by Bain (1956) and Mann (1966) have shown that profitability is greater in industries with higher entry barriers. There are several different types of barrier to entry, which are discussed below.

Capital requirements

Entry into a new industry requires a firm to have resources to invest in, for example, inventories, advertising, and equipment. The capital requirements of entering a new industry vary between industries. Entry into some markets such as large passenger planes is so prohibitive that it is unlikely that Airbus or Boeing will face any new competitors in the foreseeable future. In other markets such as internet food delivery the costs are much lower and market entry is much more realistic. But the general rule applies: the higher the capital requirements in an industry, the less likely is the entry of new competitors.

However, the barrier of capital requirements can be overcome by new entrants. Research by George Yip (1982) has shown that new entrants can overcome entry barriers. Large multinational firms can use resources from established businesses to fund market entry into new business areas. For instance, large oil companies such as Shell and BP used profits from the oil business to enter the market for solar energy. As many established solar energy firms could not mobilize the same capital resources, Shell and BP quickly became some of the world's largest firms in the solar energy business. Firms may also overcome the barrier of capital requirements by using innovative new strategies. For instance, selling over the internet can allow firms to overcome the capital requirements of setting up traditional distribution channels in every country.

Economies of scale

Economies of scale are 'reductions in the firm's average costs as a result of an increase in the firm's output'. When a firm increases production of a specific good, the cost of producing each good may decrease. Economies of scale may come as a result of: the firm's specialization (e.g. larger outputs may allow greater use of specialist labour or machinery); the cheaper cost of buying raw materials and other supplies in bulk; savings in marketing costs, as the firm can sell more products without increasing advertising and distribution costs; and savings in production costs, as the firm can use the same equipment to manufacture more products. If there are economies of scale in an industry, new entrants have two choices: either they can enter the market on a small scale and face high unit costs, or they can enter on a large scale and face the risk of not being able to sell their products.

Internationalization of markets means that economies of scale increase. If you can sell the same product in many different countries using the same production process, using similar marketing, or benefiting from cheaper raw materials, the firm can produce goods more cheaply. As a result of internationalization, economies of scale have increased considerably in many industries such as the car industry. In order to be a low-cost producer in the car industry today, you need to produce several million cars a year. The only important new entrants in the car industry in the last ten to twenty years were companies which benefited from massive government support, such as Proton of Malaysia.

Product differentiation

A well-known brand name, perceived higher quality of the firm's products, or high-quality after-sales service may foster customer loyalty and prevent customers from buying products of a new entrant. When product differentiation is high in a market, new entrants will have to spend large amounts to overcome customer loyalty to established firms. They may need to spend money on advertising in order to increase brand recognition, or on product development in order to improve product quality. Alternatively, new entrants may need to sell their products at a lower price, leading to lower profits. So product differentiation leads to barriers to entry.

Internationalization of markets compels new entrants to spend more on additional advertising and other costs in order to gain international awareness of their products. For example, many international travellers are often more likely to choose established international brands such as Coca-Cola when they travel abroad on holiday or business. So a firm which wants to enter the international market for soft drinks would have to spend enormous funds to get established in many countries simultaneously, which deters new entrants.

Access to distribution channels

Established firms develop effective ways of distributing their products to customers as time goes on, so access to distribution channels may be restricted for new entrants. Distribution channels may have limited capacity (e.g. retailers have only limited shelf space). Distributors may be reluctant to carry a new product (e.g. there may be additional costs related to distributing a new product) or may be prevented from doing so by a long-term contract or an exclusive dealing agreement. Distributors and customers may also be reluctant to switch suppliers, as they develop close relationships with established firms based on trust (e.g. this may be important when a manufacturer buys components which need to be delivered on time to exact specifications). When expanding internationally, a new entrant may also find that the distribution channels for the same product vary between different countries.

Nonetheless, marketing over the internet may help companies to expand into new countries without having to build up expensive traditional distribution channels. In the case of China, Prahalad and Lieberthal (2003) suggested that restricted access to new markets may indeed help new entrants. Distribution channels in China are largely local and regional, not national. Many foreign companies have started joint ventures with Chinese firms to gain access to regional distribution channels, but their joint-venture partners were often unable and sometimes reluctant to expand beyond their home region. A new entrant with patience and creativity can more easily build a national distribution system in China to suit its needs, and gain the upper hand over firms with local and regional distribution channels. As with other entry barriers, restricted access to distribution channels can sometimes be overcome with creativity and persistence.

Government policy

It has long been recognized that government policy can act as an important—or even the most important—barrier to entry in an industry (Oster 1982). In industries such as radio and TV broadcasting a company usually cannot operate without a government licence, so the entry of new firms is highly restricted. In knowledge-intensive industries such as pharmaceuticals, established firms are protected by government patents on their products, so that only the innovating firm can use the patent for a period of time. Governments can also raise entry barriers more indirectly, for instance, through quality standards or environmental standards. A new environmental law which forces all firms in an industry to instal pollution control technology raises the cost of operating in the industry. Large, established firms tend to be in a better position to comply with environmental legislation, and environmental compliance costs therefore raise barriers to entry for newcomers (Dean and Brown 1995).

As the last chapter discussed, the creation of the World Trade Organization (WTO) and the progress of liberalization has led to fewer direct government interventions in the world economy. So governments have less freedom to raise barriers to entry today than ten to twenty years ago—there are fewer tariffs on imported goods and fewer restrictions on foreign firms entering markets. But the abolition of government barriers to entry has been uneven. Some governments still use protectionist policies such as tariffs (e.g. the US tariffs on steel) or selective government policies to protect local producers (e.g. government policies in emerging economies such as China to encourage manufacturers to use locally made components). At the same time, licences, patents, or environmental policies continue in many industries.

Expected retaliation

Potential new entrants may be discouraged from entering a market if they expect the established firms to retaliate against them. Retaliation against a new entrant can include, for example, aggressive price-cutting, raising expenditure on advertising, or lobbying the government to erect new entry barriers. A potential new entrant can expect vigorous retaliation when the established firm has a strong position in the market, when the established firm has substantial resources which can be used to retaliate, or when industry growth is slow. In order to deter new entrants, established firms need to pose a credible threat of retaliation; this can be achieved, amongst other means, by maintaining excess capacity which can be used to quickly increase production in the case of new market entry (Lieberman, 1987).

3.3.2 Bargaining power of buyers and suppliers

Every firm must satisfy buyer needs in order to be profitable. Unless buyers are prepared to buy a product or service, the industry cannot survive in the long run. At the same time, buyers push firms to sell products at the lowest possible price, with higher quality and higher levels of service, which reduces firm profitability. The bargaining power of buyers influences the extent to which firms can retain the value created by a product: high power of buyers in an industry leads to lower industry profitability; low power of buyers leads to higher industry profitability.

The bargaining power of buyers and suppliers are related to each other, so these two forces can be treated together. The power of the buyer depends on the buyer's bargaining position vis-à-vis the seller/supplier. The average consumer has high buyer power relative to a computer manufacturer (the supplier). In turn, the computer manufacturer has low buyer power relative to its suppliers, such as the computer chip manufacturer Intel. From the perspective of the computer manufacturer, both the buyers (consumers) and the suppliers (e.g. Intel) have high bargaining power, which is a key reason for lower profitability of computer manufacturers. From the perspective of Intel, both the buyers (computer manufacturers) and the suppliers of raw materials have low bargaining power. The use of the terms 'high bargaining power' or 'low bargaining power' depends on your perspective.

Buyers and suppliers can include very different groups. Buyers can include, amongst others, consumers, manufacturers buying components or universities buying equipment. Suppliers include not only firms, providing products and services, but also employees, who supply labour. The bargaining power of buyers and suppliers is determined by several factors.

Buyer/supplier concentration

Buyer power is high when buyers are concentrated and there are few of them, for instance, when supermarkets buy agricultural products from farmers or when national governments buy defence equipment. Buyer concentration has been shown to be a key reason for lower profits in supplying industries (Lustgarten 1975). Conversely, buyer power is low when suppliers are concentrated. High supplier concentration can often be found amongst suppliers of high-technology products; examples include the computer chip maker Intel and the supplier of operating systems Microsoft. When there are many different sources of supply, suppliers may try to increase their bargaining power by forming joint organizations in dealing with the buyers, such as farmers' marketing cooperatives or trade unions.

Buyer switching costs

Buyer power is high when it is easy for the buyer to switch suppliers. In the extreme case, switching costs can be very low and buyer power can be very high. For example, an individual consumer can easily buy air tickets from a different airline for a flight, so airlines introduce loyalty schemes to increase switching costs for consumers. Supplier power is high if buyers would incur high costs in switching to a new type of equipment, breaking existing legal contracts, or retraining their employees. In addition to financial costs, there may also be psychological costs of ending a business relationship or the costs of damaged reputation. The computer operating system Linux (see closing case study to this chapter) is much cheaper than Microsoft Windows, but buyer switching costs deter many potential buyers from using it.

Product differentiation

The less differentiated the products of the supplier, the more likely it is that the buyer will switch suppliers on the basis of price. Supermarkets have much higher buyer power vis-à-vis farmers and manufacturers of unbranded goods than vis-à-vis firms with recognized international brands such as Coca-Cola or Levi's.

Price/total purchases

If a product accounts for a high proportion of the buyer's total purchases, the buyer will be more sensitive about the price of the product. Buyers will be more likely to shop around for the best price and will squeeze suppliers, thereby reducing the power of suppliers. In industries where components make up a high proportion of total costs—such as cars, electronics and data-processing industries—firms occasionally form shared-supply alliances to increase their buyer power and gain economies of scale. In industries where employment costs make up a high proportion of total costs, such as textiles or call centres, American and European firms have been pushed to expand internationally to find cheaper suppliers of labour.

Threat of vertical integration

The alternative to finding a buyer or a supplier is to do it yourself, or vertical integration. For example, European supermarkets have undercut some of their suppliers by introducing their own branded food and cosmetics products. But a firm does not necessarily need to undertake vertical integration; a credible threat may be enough to get greater bargaining power. If a firm can potentially undertake the value-added activities previously provided by a supplier or a buyer (i.e. vertically integrate), it can use the threat of vertical integration to force more profitable business terms on its suppliers and buyers.

Buyer information

If the buyer has full information about product demand, market prices, and actual production costs, he/she knows how much the seller can be pushed to offer lower prices. Partial vertical integration can be an effective method of gaining more information about actual production costs. The production of own-branded products enables supermarkets to gain information about the cost structures of their suppliers and allows them to negotiate more effectively.

Impact on quality/performance

The more important the product of the supplier to the quality of the buyer's own product or service, the less likely it is that the buyer will switch suppliers on the basis of price. The bargaining power of computer manufacturers is low, as the quality of their computers relies heavily on specific products provided by suppliers (Windows operating system, Intel chips, etc.) and the manufacturers cannot switch to other suppliers.

International expansion

While this point was not explicitly mentioned by Michael Porter, a firm's international expansion helps to increase its bargaining power. International presence expands the strategic options of the firm, increasing the number of potential buyers and suppliers.

3.3.3 Threat of substitutes

A substitute product is a good or service which is regarded by buyers as interchangeable. For instance, if a significant rise in the price of beer would prompt consumers to switch to wine, wine would be regarded as a substitute for beer. If there are no readily available substitutes for a product, buyers will be more likely to accept the price for a product. If substitutes are available, buyers will switch to substitutes when the price of the product increases. The existence of substitutes provides a limit on how much the seller can charge for the product; so the threat of substitutes ultimately constrains the profitability of a firm.

The development of substitutes is heavily influenced by technological change. To take one example, the spread of the internet led to the development of many substitutes, such as the use of e-mail instead of fax and postal service, obtaining information online instead of buying a newspaper, or downloading MP3 files instead of buying music CDs. Even if there is no technological change, substitutes can also be created as a result of product innovation and advertising. When Smirnoff's Ice was introduced, its advertising was similar to that for beer in order to create a substitute for beer.

The extent to which substitutes can reduce profitability in an industry depends on three factors (Porter 1985). First, what is the *relative price performance of a substitute*? Even if a substitute is cheaper, to what extent can the substitute perform the same function as the other product? Second, how high are the *switching costs* for the buyer? Third, what is the *buyer's propensity to substitute*? These three basic questions will help to assess the threat of a substitute. Substitutes will present a serious threat to the firm's products if the substitute can perform more or less the same function as the firm's product, the buyer switching costs are low, and the buyer is willing to substitute.

3.3.4 Rivalry

Rivalry between firms encourages innovation, but it also has the effect of depressing firm profitability. The intensity of rivalry differs between industries. In intensely competitive markets, firms may be forced to lower their prices or invest in new research and development, just to keep up with competitors; the result of intense rivalry is therefore lower profits. The intensity of rivalry is influenced by the factors outlined below.

Concentration

Seller concentration refers to the number and size of rivals. When there is only one dominant company (a monopoly) or when there are only a few firms in the market (an oligopoly), price competition may be restrained and the leading firms may be able to safeguard their profits. The presence of many rivals makes it more difficult to coordinate pricing (either through outright collusion or through self-imposed restraint), so one of the rivals is more likely to reduce prices forcing other firms to do the same. Entry barriers often cause seller concentration, as they restrict the number of firms in an industry. However, there is no unambiguous evidence that high concentration leads to high profits (Schmalensee 1988).

Concentration may also affect a firm's international expansion. Research has shown that the international expansion of firms in oligopolistic industries tends to take place in clusters. An oligopoly implies a high interdependence between firms: a strategic move by one firm may trigger a strategic response from another firm, which is most pronounced in industries dominated by two firms (e.g. Coca-Cola vs. PepsiCo). If firms in an industry are highly interdependent, firms may be worried that international expansion will provide their rivals with larger markets or, even worse, will provide their competitors with some key advantage (e.g. a new technology). Therefore, foreign investment by one leading firm in an oligopolistic industry may trigger international expansion of other firms, a move regarded as necessary in order to negate the leading firm's early gains (Knickerbocker 1973; Flowers 1976).

Diversity of rivals

Rivalry is more intense if the competitors have very different strategies, origins, and 'personalities'. If the diversity of rivals is large, firms in the same industry have different ideas about how to compete and often run into each other. Diversity of rivals tends to be greater in international competition, because firms come from different cultural backgrounds, have different sources of capital, and have very different origins.

Product differentiation and switching costs

When a firm's products are highly differentiated (i.e. customers perceive the firm's products as significantly different from competing products), the firm will be under less pressure to lower prices when faced with rivalry. In other words, product differentiation provides some protection from competition (Deephouse 1999). Similarly, when switching costs are high for the buyer, the firm will also be protected to some extent. Conversely, when products are perceived as 'commodities' (i.e. they are regarded as virtually the same), price wars may occur. Even multinational firms with a strong brand name may face intense price competition because their products are seen as commodities (e.g. films made by Kodak and Fuji).

Industry growth

When industry growth is high, firms can expand by winning new customers. When industry growth is slow, firms are under more pressure to fight over the existing customers of their competitors, which increases rivalry. A good predictor of industry growth is the product life cycle model (see section 3.5).

Fixed costs and storage costs

If the firm's fixed costs are high as a proportion of total costs (e.g. aluminium production), or if the product is perishable (and therefore the storage costs are high, e.g. fresh prawns), firms may be tempted to cut prices. For a firm with high fixed costs, it would be expensive to reduce production, so there is a greater pressure to maintain or increase production even if prices decrease. For a firm with high storage costs, products lose value very quickly, so it may be better to sell them cheaply rather than not selling them at all. As a result, both high fixed costs and high storage costs lead to more intense price rivalry.

Exit barriers

Barriers to exit are obstacles which established firms would encounter when leaving the market. If there are many exit barriers, it is less likely that an established firm will leave the market, which may result in more intense rivalry. Exit barriers can include: the presence of specialized assets (assets which are of little value outside the particular business or location); fixed costs of exit (e.g. cost of laying off staff); government restrictions (e.g. environmental clean-up costs); or emotional barriers (e.g. management loyalty to a firm's traditional line of business). Exit barriers can also have an effect on entry into the industry. When exit costs are high, firms will be more cautious about entry into the market, especially if the probability of success is low or uncertain (Rosenbaum and Lamort 1992).

Excess capacity

Excess capacity may result from a fall of demand during a recession, over-investment, or when production capacity in an industry comes in large increments (e.g. bulk chemicals). When faced with over-capacity, firms may be tempted to cut prices (Baden-Fuller 1990).

3.4 Criticisms of the Five Forces Model

Porter's Five Forces Model has come under criticism. It has been said, for example, that the model cannot help firms to cope with the fast-changing business environment; that it cannot be used for analysing the position of charitable organizations or government bodies; and that it disregards the importance of human resource management (Lynch 2000: 131). Two key criticisms relate to the 'static' nature of the model and to the ability of firms to earn profits.

3.4.1 Static vs. dynamic competition

The Five Forces Model has been criticized for being too 'static', leading managers to making wrong assumptions about the business environment. Managers are expected to decide on their firm's strategy based on an analysis of the Five Forces, assuming that these normally change slowly. But it has been said that competition is not 'static' but 'dynamic': the industry environment is constantly changing, so firms cannot make strategic choices by assuming that the threats of entry will not grow or that no new substitutes will be developed.

Some authors even speak of 'hyper-competitive behaviour' today: 'the process of continuously generating new competitive advantages and destroying, obsoleting, or neutralizing the opponent's competitive advantage' (D'Aveni 1994: 217–18). This hyper-competition is said to be driven by globalization, and it is said to be greatest in industries that have moved into the global arena (Harvey et al. 2001). In industries with hyper-competition, it does not necessarily make sense for firms to concentrate on building up strength in specific sectors where higher profits can be made; a firm has constantly to improve and innovate, and cannot hide behind entry barriers or its bargaining power towards existing suppliers. This view would suggest that the Five Forces Model could be of only limited value to managers.

3.4.2 Industry profitability

Porter assumes that a firm's profitability depends on how attractive the industry is. If competition is intense in an industry, firms will earn low profits no matter how skilful the firm's managers are. But business research has suggested otherwise. Several studies have compared the relative significance of industry-specific influences and firm-specific influences on firm profitability, and discovered that only a small proportion of firms' profitability could be ascribed to the industry in which the firm operated (compare section 5.2.3). According to this research, firm profitability seemed to depend primarily on how skilful individual units of the firm were (Rumelt 1991; Mauri and Michaels 1998). By implication, an analysis of the Five Forces cannot provide a good guide to profitability.

3.4.3 Response to criticisms

Firm-specific, rather than industry-specific, influences on firm profitability are becoming more important in the global market (see Chapter 5). But research has suggested that in many industries changes in barriers to entry (Masson and Shaanan 1982; 1987) or changes in seller concentration (Caves and Porter 1980) have been very slow. Therefore, when industry structure changes slowly, the industry's influence on the firm's profitability only changes very slowly.

Certainly, there are some highly visible industries where change is very fast (e.g. certain types of consumer electronics) but—for most industries—the industry environment does not change quickly. Brian Arthur (1996) has argued that firms usually have the ability to influence industry structure in the early stages of a technological wave. But once a specific product, process, or technology wins over the alternatives, the development of the industry becomes locked into a specific path of development and firms can do little to change the Five Forces. Examples here include Microsoft's Windows operating system, when the introduction of the product at an early stage led to an enduring industry structure. As a result of the early domination of the market by Microsoft, other firms could not challenge the superior bargaining power of the company and could not easily overcome the entry barriers in the market for operating systems (see closing case study). The Five Forces Model would have been of relatively little use to managers when computer operating systems were first introduced, but it is very useful to an understanding of that market today.

Ultimately, whether you accept the above criticisms of the Five Forces Model depends on your point of view. What does it mean, for example, that an industry is 'static' or 'dynamic'? Porter recognized a long time ago that industries change, sometimes in fundamental ways which could not have been expected. Firms can also help to change the Five Forces in an industry; for example, a firm's innovations in marketing can raise brand identification and differentiate the product, which in turn will increase the firm's bargaining power.

3.5 Industry evolution

The Five Forces and market conditions change over time as a result of industry evolution, which has important consequences for the formulation of strategy. Industry evolution can make an industry more or less attractive as an investment opportunity, and it often forces firms to adjust their strategies. Industry evolution is only important for strategy if it changes the underlying Five Forces. If these are not modified, the firm needs to change only some day-to-day practices, but the strategy can remain the same. The easiest way to analyse industry evolution is by asking the question: are there any changes occurring in the industry that will affect any element of the Five Forces Model? For instance, do any changes imply a change in entry barriers or a change in the bargaining power of suppliers? If this question is asked systematically for each of the Five Forces and the causes underlying industry change, the most significant issues will emerge (Porter 1980).

The concept of the Product Life Cycle is useful in understanding the course of industry evolution. The basic idea of this cycle is that every product evolves through a cycle of roughly four stages—introduction, growth, maturity, and decline—which correspond to the rate of growth of industry sales. There are few sales in the introduction stage: customers may be reluctant to buy a new product, and sales prices for newly developed products are initially high. Once buyers learn to appreciate the value of a product, sales increase rapidly and prices decline as a result of larger production runs and new competition. After a period of time, the market becomes saturated and rapid growth comes to an end; as demand for a product slows down, firms are under more pressure to fight over the existing customers and rivalry increases. Eventually, demand for a product declines as substitute products emerge (Levitt 1965).

The Product Life Cycle has major implications for international strategies of firms as industry change may force firms to re-locate parts of their business to other countries. Vernon (1966) first argued that advanced countries, which have the necessary financial, technological, and human resources to innovate, and high wages and plenty of disposable income to spend on new products, are the first to introduce new products. However, the innovating country tends to lose its exports initially to other developed countries and subsequently to less developed countries, and eventually could become an importer of these products. According to Vernon, many products go through an international life cycle, during which the United States (and nowadays Japan or other developed countries) is initially an exporter,

Exhibit 3.4 The international product life cycle

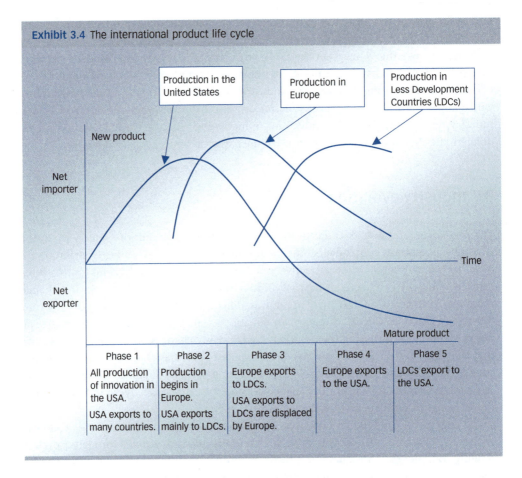

then loses its export markets, and finally could become an importer of the product. Many industrial products such as televisions have conformed to this pattern (see Exhibit 3.5). Advocates of this International Product Life Cycle (IPLC) model argue that although there are certainly exceptions, new products tend to evolve along similar international paths, creating more or less predictably five stages or phases (Vernon 1966; Wells 1968). There are five phases of the IPLC model (see Exhibit 3.4).

3.5.1 The five phases of the International Product Life Cycle (IPLC)

Phase 1: Introduction in the Home Market. According to the IPLC Model, most new products are first introduced in rich developed countries. This is because, it is argued, firms located in such countries have more capability to innovate than firms in poor developing countries. In addition, people in developed countries have more money to spend on newer products than people in developing countries. In this phase the total production of the new product takes place in the country of origin (often the USA) because the speed of adjusting the product to the home market demand is very important for the success of the new product.

Exhibit 3.5 The international product life cycle and TV manufacturing

Electronic television broadcasting began in Britain and Germany in 1936. Three years later, the first American TV sets went on sale, but the Second World War interrupted the worldwide development of television. Before the Second World War, only 7,000 sets were manufactured in the United States and some 20,000 in Britain. After the war, the United States emerged as the unrivalled innovating country. By 1950 there were only 344,000 British homes with a TV set, but the annual sales of TV sets in the United States reached over 7 million. The American TV sets were designed for the US market but some production was exported, mainly to Europe.

Until 1962, the United States was totally self-sufficient in the production of televisions. In that year, the first Japanese black-and-white televisions were imported into the United States; the first colour televisions were imported in 1967. From 1970, foreign imports into the United States rose very quickly despite the introduction of import restrictions by the US government. By 1982, 68% of black and white TV sets and 13% of colour TV sets sold in the United States were imported. In 1965, when US output was approaching 3 million colour TVs, Japan produced less than 100,000. By 1980, Japan produced over 10 million colour TVs per year.

As the product matured, TV production moved from developed to developing countries. In the 1970s the remaining American TV manufacturers relocated production activities to Mexico and Far East Asia, including Korea and Taiwan. But the importance of Japanese TV production also began to decline soon after, as Japanese firms relocated some production activities to Korea and Taiwan to obtain lower labour costs. Until 1978 most US imports came from Japan; thereafter, imports from developing countries such as Korea exceeded Japanese imports.

In the last twenty years, countries such as Korea and Taiwan have become more developed themselves and production has once again been relocated, this time to China and other developing countries. Today, China is reputedly the world's largest supplier of TV sets, with an annual production capacity of some 40 million units in 2003.

The shift of TV manufacturing from the United States to Japan and other Asian countries was accompanied by major shifts in the ownership of the leading TV manufacturing firms. As early as 1971, five of the ten largest consumer electronics producers in the world were Japanese, led by Matsushita. In 1978 the world's ten largest manufacturers of colour TV sets were as follows:

Company	Market share (%)
Matsushita (Japanese)	12.5
Philips (Dutch)	12.1
RCA (US)	6.9
Zenith (US)	6.8
Sanyo (Japanese)	6.8
Sony (Japanese)	5.9
Toshiba (Japanese)	5.2
Grundig (German)	4.8
Hitachi (Japanese)	4.3
GTE-Sylvania (US)	4.2

→

→

Since then, US-owned manufacturers of TVs have vanished completely. Their number declined from sixteen in 1966 to three by 1980; later all three remaining firms disappeared. The last surviving American firm was Zenith, an early pioneer of radio and TV technology. In November 1999 Zenith became a wholly owned subsidiary of a South Korean firm LG Electronics, which had acquired a majority shareholding in Zenith four years earlier.

Sources: International Competitiveness in Electronics (Washington, DC: US Congress, Office of Technology Assessment, OTA-ISC-200, Nov. 1983), ch. 4, pp. 107–62; Peter Dicken, *Global Shift: Transforming the World Economy*, 3rd edn. (London: Sage, 1998); various online resources.

This stage is characterized by high unit production costs, but these costs are less significant because the demand for innovative products is price inelastic (demand does not vary with price) at this phase. The price is inelastic when, with all other factors held constant, the change in the quantity demanded to a change in price is very small or nonexistent. Initially, the new product goes through a slow sales growth and profits are nonexistent because of the heavy expenses in production and marketing. At some point the product becomes well-known in the home market, and customers from other developed and high-income countries start buying the product. This leads to the second phase.

Phase 2: Export to developed countries. The market for the product widens as demand develops in other high-income countries. The production of the product becomes fairly standard, and the widening of the market makes economies of scale possible. As a result, price decreases. This causes the market for the product to widen further, as customers in low- and medium-income countries are able to afford the new product. As the production of the product becomes standard, firms in other developed countries imitate the product and start production in their own countries.

Phase 3: Export by developed countries to developing countries. The low price attracts more customers from developing countries. As the demand for the product increases in developing countries, late movers from developed countries begin to export and even produce the new product in developing countries.

Phase 4: Export by developed countries to the home country. Eventually, the increasing international distribution of the product, and the relatively lower costs of production, will result in developed countries exporting back to the country where the product was originally introduced.

Phase 5: Export by developing countries to developed countries. At this stage, demand for the product declines in the home market and other developed countries as customers demand new products. The standardization of the production process makes it possible to produce the product in developing countries. Because of the cost advantage developing countries have over developed countries due to cheap labour costs, production moves to developing countries. Finally, the country in which the product was first introduced and produced becomes the importer of the product.

KEY CONCEPT

The concept of the 'Product Life Cycle' suggests that every basic product evolves through a cycle of roughly four stages—introduction, growth, maturity, and decline—which correspond to the rate of growth of industry sales. The concept of the 'International Product Life Cycle' suggests that many products go through an international life cycle, during which a developed country is initially an exporter (when innovation is central to product success), then loses its export markets, and finally could become an importer of the product from developing countries (when production costs become central to product success).

3.5.2 Criticisms of the IPLC model

The IPLC model proved most useful in explaining the flows of US foreign direct investment, immediately after the Second World War, in Europe and developing countries. It also helps to explain international trade in the 1950s and 1960s, in that more sophisticated, innovative products such as TV sets and cars tended to be exported from advanced countries. However, there are several criticisms of the model:

Duration of life cycles

The duration of a life cycle varies widely between industries, and the shift from one stage to the next stage may not always be clear. Furthermore, industry growth does not always seem to go through all the stages of the model. Sometimes industry growth resumes after a period of decline (e.g. in the growth of the motorcycle and bicycle industries). So the value of the IPLC model as a planning tool for strategists is limited (Porter 1980).

Applicability of the model in the global economy

The applicability of the model to explain the behaviour of multinational firms in the current global business environment is questionable. As speedy introduction of new products is often important in the global economy, various industries may skip the slow takeoff of the introductory stage altogether (Porter 1980). As discussed in Chapter 2, the current global business environment allows multinational firms to introduce their new products simultaneously in different countries. The introduction of new generation of mobile phones or new computer software is launched simultaneously in the home market, in other developed countries, and in developing countries. For example, on 17 February 2000 Microsoft chairman Bill Gates launched the company's new product, Windows 2000, in more than eighteen countries and fifty-seven cities in the US and Canada via satellite. While Windows 2000 was produced in the United States, it was available the same day in more than sixty countries in ten languages, for immediate purchase from a variety of retail outlets, PC manufacturers, and systems builders, as well as other venues. The first purchase of Windows 2000 did not take place in the United States; most of the first customers who were able to purchase the new product at commercial outlets were in Japan, as computer shops in Tokyo's technology-centred Akihabara district opened their doors at midnight to sell the new product. Therefore, if products no longer move from the innovating country to other developed countries and then to developing countries, the model becomes of little use.

Importance of innovation

The IPLC model focuses on entirely new innovations or products, and does not include products that emerge from a continual process of technological innovation. Even with new innovations and products, firms in developing countries could imitate the products innovated in developed countries very quickly (Grossman and Helpman 1991). When imitation is possible, quick, and cost-effective, firms in other developed countries and in developing countries could charge less than the original innovators, and thus capture the home market before innovators from developed countries start exporting.

Non-standard industrial products

The IPLC model deals with standard products, and may not explain the evolution of certain non-standard industrial products. Luxury products may not follow the IPLC, because demand for them depends on their being associated with rich developed countries. For example, the demand for French perfume or Italian leather depends on being associated with France or Italy. As the price of luxury goods is of little concern to rich customers, it is not so important for production to be relocated to developing countries. Similarly, IPLC may not apply to products which require specialized knowledge to link present output with the training of technical labour and the development of the next generation of technology. For example, medical equipment is still mostly produced in major developed countries. Production is not generally transferred to developing countries because these countries may not have the skills and organization to produce them. Production may also depend on physical proximity to the research centres, where constant improvements are made.

3.6 Forecasting the future

Understanding industry evolution and forecasting future change is crucial, as the cost of changing strategy increases as the need for change becomes more obvious (Porter 1980). For instance, if you are aware that a new technology may become widespread, your firm may be able to reap major profits by introducing the technology before its rivals.

Forecasts are educated assumptions about future trends and events such as future demand for specific products, future changes in currency exchange rates, or future shifts in technology. They may be used by firms in different ways. A firm may, for instance, use weekly or monthly sales forecasts to fine-tune the distribution of products to its affiliates. We are interested in 'strategic' forecasts—forecasts used to understand the future changes in the industry environment which may require major shifts in the firm's operations.

Major surveys of the world's largest multinational firms have shown that the most widely used form of forecasting is 'trend extrapolation' (Klein and Linneman 1984; Reger 2001). Two other important techniques are called 'Delphi survey' and 'scenario analysis'.

> **KEY CONCEPT**
>
> Forecasts are educated assumptions about future trends and events such as future demand for specific products, future changes in currency exchange rates, or future shifts in technology. 'Strategic forecasts' are used to understand the future changes in the industry environment which may require major shifts in the firm's operations.

3.6.1 Trend extrapolation

On the most basic level, trend extrapolation is the extension of present trends into the future. The assumption behind the method is that change occurs relatively slowly, and that there are relatively few major discontinuities in the future. Trend extrapolation typically uses past quantitative data to predict future economic trends. Mathematical techniques such as 'moving averages' and 'exponential smoothing' are used to find an average amongst historical figures to give a prediction of probable future figures. Trend extrapolation can also help managers to understand trend patterns—for instance, that sales have been on average declining or increasing over a period of time, or that sales are cyclical (i.e. they repeatedly move up and down according to some pattern). Making forecasts based on trend extrapolation has become relatively easy, even for small firms: managers can use relatively cheap and user-friendly computer software to analyse a firm's data.

Trend extrapolation can aid strategic decisions about future investments or product development. For instance, forecasts have shown that the demand for chilled drinks is seasonal; above all, warm weather helps to push up sales. Using information about seasonal trends, Bass plc has attempted to smooth out the highs and lows of customer demand for alcopops by introducing different versions of Hooper's Hooch at different times of the year in limited editions: Smooch on Valentine's Day or Ho Ho Hooch at Christmas.

But trend extrapolation has weaknesses: it implicitly assumes that historical relationships will continue into the future, without examining causal relationships between the different factors. Historical trends depend on many different factors: change in one factor could markedly alter the future direction of the trend. According to a survey amongst Japanese (mostly corporate) research and development labs, trend extrapolation was the most frequent method used to forecast future technological developments (39% of the responding labs used it), but it was seen as one of the least effective forecasting methods (Reger 2001).

Trend extrapolation is least useful in external environments which are prone to frequent changes or where little historical data exists. In those instances, the Delphi survey and scenario analysis can be far more useful forecasting tools.

3.6.2 Delphi survey

The basic idea of a Delphi survey is to ask the opinion of experts on the future of a specific subject. Questionnaires are sent out to the chosen experts, and the returned questionnaires are analysed. In the second stage a new, refined questionnaire is sent out to the experts, which takes into consideration the previously collected expert opinions about the future; after the experts have filled in the second questionnaire, the results are once again analysed. A Delphi survey consists of at least two stages, but it can have many more, especially if the experts disagree. One of the key goals of a Delphi survey is to improve the spread of information and communication amongst participants, and to disseminate expert opinions to strategic decision-makers.

Delphi surveys are very expensive and time-consuming, so they have been employed mainly by large multinational firms and national governments. Some of the biggest Delphi surveys were conducted by the Japanese government: a survey on technological future trends in 1997 used over 4,200 experts (a much higher number compared with surveys in other countries). Such surveys can be of great use to managers. For example, a Japanese Delphi study in 1971 forecasted 'a widespread use of facsimile machine in Japanese households', and estimated that a large number of Japanese households would own a fax machine by about 1990. As it turned out, the future market for fax machines was estimated relatively well: in 1989 there were almost 5 million fax machines in Japan, and 90% of companies owned one. The success of the fax machine came as a surprise to many managers in Western firms, but not to Japanese managers, who had planned for it. Partly as a result of early technological forecasts, it was Japanese companies—not Siemens or IBM—who were prepared for the future and who pioneered the sale of fax machines in Japan and then in global markets (Cuhls 2001).

3.6.3 Scenario analysis

Herman Kahn and A. J. Weiner, who pioneered the use of scenario analysis, defined a scenario as 'a hypothetical sequence of events constructed for the purpose of focusing attention on causal processes and decision points'. Scenarios explore possible future events by looking at particular causes and seek to understand and explain why certain events might or might not occur. Scenario analysis is very different from other forecasting techniques, as it does not try to predict what will actually happen. Rather, scenario analysis tries to identify several possible futures (typically, two to four different scenarios), each of which is plausible but not assured. The value of scenarios lies in increasing awareness of possibilities and exploring 'what if' questions. By offering different forecasts and offering them in the form of a narrative/description, scenarios provide managers with a better understanding of the relationships between different factors and assumptions underlying different forecasts. Scenario analysis recognizes the shortcomings of most forecasts by considering a number of different and plausible assumptions about the future, rather than a single assumption which may prove wrong (Schnaars 1987).

The use of scenarios increased markedly after the oil crisis of 1973, when the world economy was disrupted by an Arab oil embargo. Using scenario planning from the late 1960s, managers at Royal Dutch/Shell were able to anticipate major disruptions in the global oil supplies in the 1970s, although scenario analysis did not specify in which year a crisis would happen. As a result of using scenarios, Shell was much better prepared to deal with the 1973 oil crisis than its international competitors, and the company improved its competitive position in the oil industry during the crisis (Wack 1985a; 1985b).

In comparison with trend extrapolation, scenario analysis and Delphi surveys are able to look into the long-term prospects of an industry. Trend extrapolation based on historical data typically looks five years ahead; more frequently, forecasts are made for much shorter periods, such as monthly or quarterly forecasts. Such studies fail to assist strategic decision-makers in industries where investments are made with much longer investment horizons, such as the oil industry, where investments may take longer than five years to pay off. Shell's scenarios in the late 1960s and early 1970s allowed managers to look fifteen years ahead and more. However, the main problem of forecasting is that the further you look into the future, the more unreliable the forecasts become. Therefore, different forecasts can fulfil different purposes: a three-year industry forecast based on trend extrapolation may help to adjust sales or product development in the short term; a fifteen-year scenario analysis may help managers to strategically plan the long-term future of the organization.

3.6.4 Forecasting and the challenge of internationalization

Internationalization of markets is a challenge for corporate forecasting, in that it is difficult to forecast distant markets from central company headquarters. This challenge is greatest when it comes to forecasting uncertain events such as the development of new technologies. Using internet sources or merely interviewing foreign managers may not always allow a firm to pick up 'weak signals' of important future trends. In technology forecasting, the most effective forecasting can be achieved when it is performed by the firm's research centres around the world, which collect information on the spot. Cheaper alternatives to establishing research centres include international 'listening posts' or 'technology scouts'. For example, the German pharmaceutical firm Bayer employs over a dozen technology scouts in addition to its research centres in Europe and elsewhere: two in Japan, six in the United States, and six in Europe; their task is to detect new research results, new technologies or partners worldwide (Reger 2001).

At the same time, it is important that central company headquarters have an overview of different forecasts, and that international forecasting activities are fed into strategic decision-making at the company's headquarters. It makes no sense for a company to have technology scouts around the world if top management is unable to act on their forecasts. In order to coordinate forecasting activities across its worldwide subsidiaries, Bayer formed a central forecasting group, which resides in the strategic analysis department.

3.7 Summary

This chapter has demonstrated that it is important to understand how changes in the external industry environment affect or do not affect a firm. The first step is to identify your precise market, because a focus on a broad industry may lead to an inaccurate understanding of the market and the nature of competition. In order to identify the precise market, firms can conduct a market segmentation analysis and a strategic group analysis.

A more comprehensive understanding of an industry can be gained through an analysis of its underlying economic and technical characteristics. Michael Porter suggested that managers should understand the rules of competition in their industry so that they become aware both of industry attractiveness and of their firm's own competitive position within the industry. In order to uncover these underlying rules, Porter suggested that managers should understand the five competitive forces in their industry: the entry of new competitors; the threat of substitutes; the bargaining power of buyers; the bargaining power of suppliers; and the rivalry amongst existing competitors.

The Five Forces and market conditions change over time as a result of industry evolution, so managers need to understand the causes underlying industry change. The concept of the Product Life Cycle can help to understand industry evolution. An extension of the concept, known as the International Product Life Cycle Model (IPLC), helps to explain why industry change may force firms to relocate parts of their business to other countries. The model suggests that advanced countries are the first to introduce new products; then the innovating country tends to lose its exports initially to other developed countries and subsequently to less-developed countries; eventually the innovating country may cease producing a specific product.

Ultimately, the strategic decision-maker would like to know what could happen to his/her industry in the future. Understanding industry evolution and forecasting future change is crucial, since the cost of changing strategy increases as the need for change becomes more obvious. So firms require 'strategic' forecasts—forecasts used to understand the future changes in the industry environment which may require major shifts in the firm's operations. A thorough understanding of the industry environment and its likely future should help the strategic decision-maker to develop more appropriate strategies.

KEY READINGS

- On strategic group analysis, see McGee and Thomas (1986).
- On the Five Forces Model and industry evolution, see Porter (1980).
- On the International Product Life Cycle, see Vernon (1966).
- On scenario planning, see Schnaars (1987).

DISCUSSION QUESTIONS

1 What is the difference between market segmentation analysis and strategic group analysis? How can strategic group analysis help managers in formulating a firm's strategy?

2 Take an industry of your choice. Conduct a Five Forces analysis of that industry. What are the key forces at work in that industry? What are the key drivers for change?

3 What problems do managers face in conducting a global Five Forces analysis?

4 To what extent does the IPLC model help or hinder our understanding of how an industry evolves?

5 Give five examples of situations when it would be suitable for a firm to use trend extrapolation to forecast its global industry environment, and five examples of when it would be suitable to use scenario planning.

Closing case study
The rise of Linux—the battle for the operating system market

The operating system (OS) is the master control program that runs your computer. It is usually the first program loaded when you switch on your computer. The OS usually controls only one computer, but it can also control groups of computers or even entire local area networks. The global OS market is dominated by Microsoft Windows, which was first introduced in 1983, and most computers today run on a Microsoft-produced OS such as Windows 2000 or Windows XP. By the early 1990s Microsoft was in an ideal global position:

- Microsoft suppliers had insignificant bargaining power (if you count, for instance, firms which supplied hardware on which Windows was developed and computer engineers who supplied their skills).

- There were very few competing or substitute products, such as Macintosh OS (which did not run on PCs) or Unix OS for networks.

- Entry barriers were very high: the development costs for a new widely available OS were enormous and Windows was protected through intellectual property rights. Due to early adoption of Windows in the entire market, the financial and psychological costs of switching to a different OS were enormous and a large number of companies in related sectors (from chip-maker Intel to software developers) developed products which worked in combination with Windows.

- Customers had little bargaining power, as most computers had Windows pre-installed on them. Average consumers had only the choice between Windows-operated computers or the much less common Macintosh.

But a new OS has challenged the dominant position of Windows in recent years: Linux. Linux was written by a Finnish graduate student called Linus Torvalds, who posted the first version of the OS on an internet discussion group in August 1991. Torvalds invited other amateur programmers to suggest improvements to his OS, and by December 1991 he had already released the tenth Linux version. By May 1992, Linux was in its ninety-sixth edition.

The main difference between Windows and Linux was that the source code of Windows was a closely guarded secret, while Linux was 'open-source' (i.e. all the basic information on the OS was publicly available). Indeed, a key driving force for Torvalds and his colleagues was to create an OS that did not cost anything, in contrast to the expensive Microsoft system. Since Linux was open-source, amateur programmers around the world were able to continue its development, frequently by using the internet and e-mail to exchange technical details.

For several years, Linux was mainly used by a small group of computer enthusiasts, and there were barriers to its widespread adoption. There were only a few software programmes which could run on Linux, and it was arduous to install it on a computer. But then small commercial companies such as Red Hat and Caledra began to sell application software for Linux; the companies distributed copies of Linux free, but charged for additional applications and customer support services. Until the arrival of Linux, OS producers such as Microsoft, Novell, and Sun were protected from new competitors through high development costs and the intellectual property rights on their products. Since the introduction of Linux, new firms can enter the market with a low capital investment, since Linux is not protected through patents, and production costs such as plant and machinery account for only a very small part of the cost structure of Linux distributors. With the quick growth of Linux distributors such as Red Hat, Linux began to be used for running entire clusters of computers.

By the late 1990s, large firms and government departments began to replace Windows with Linux to save costs. At the same time, multinational computer firms such as IBM and Oracle started to invest in Linux as an alternative to Windows. In 1998, Oracle started offering Linux versions for its software. In 2000, IBM declared that it would invest US$1 billion in Linux development, and assigned 250 engineers to work on Linux. In November 2003, Novell—a Microsoft rival and the maker of the NetWare OS—announced the takeover of the German firm SuSE, one of the companies distributing Linux, for US$210 million.

Despite the success of Linux, Windows still dominates the global OS market today, with a market share of more than 90%. But there are major differences between the desktop OS market (OS for individual computers) and the server OS market (OS for computer networks). According to the research analysts International Data Corp. (IDC), the market shares in 2002 were as follows:

Desktop operating systems	Server operating systems
93.8% Windows	55.1% Windows
2.9% Macintosh	23.1% Linux
2.8% Linux	11.1% Unix
	9.9% Novell Inc.'s NetWare

There are several reasons why Linux was less successful in the desktop OS market. Individual customers found it cumbersome to install Linux on their computers. Despite the introduction of new software applications such as StarOffice (which competes with Microsoft Office), there are still relatively few software applications and many popular applications do not run on Linux, which reduces its functionality. There are also high switching costs for individual customers; it takes time to familiarize yourself with a new OS and—if all your colleagues and friends use Windows applications—it makes sense to continue using the same software (e.g. when you want to swap text files written with Microsoft Office). But even if Linux were more user-friendly, Microsoft still has the advantage of a strong brand name, and it would require a gigantic marketing and sales effort to replace Windows with Linux. The perception that Windows is a superior product helps Microsoft to differentiate itself from Linux. Microsoft can spend hundreds of millions on marketing. As smaller firms such as Red Hat or SuSE cannot charge for distributing Linux, they have limited resources to fight Microsoft.

Large companies and government agencies found it easier to replace Windows with Linux for their computer networks. Because they had a large number of computers, the switching costs per computer unit were much lower than for an individual user. The low cost was a key attraction, while—at the same time—Linux proved to have some technical advantages over Windows. While Windows frequently 'crashed' for no apparent reason, Linux is said to allow more stable operations, which was of greater importance for computer networks than for individual users. Since Linux is open-source, it also allows technicians to amend certain parts of the programme or add new ones, so that upgrades can be easily completed without the involvement of Microsoft.

The low cost of Linux was also a key attraction for computer firms such as IBM. It has been estimated that the development cost for Windows 2000 was US$1 billion, so Microsoft needed to sell a vast number of copies to recover its investment. In contrast, the cost of developing Linux was very low, as many amateur programmers donated their time for free and many companies shared development costs. IBM's research and development costs for Linux-related systems were lower than for Windows-run systems, and the company was able to reduce its dependence on Microsoft. By early 2003 IBM had over 4,600 Linux customers, and was able to sell Linux servers worth hundreds of millions of dollars.

The domination of the OS market by Windows is likely to continue for some time. Indeed, Microsoft can look forward to growing Windows sales. According to a forecast by the research analysts IDC until 2007, sales for both Windows and Linux will grow, as the global market for client OS will expand at an average annual growth rate of 7.5%, while the server OS market will grow at a rate of 9.1% per year. But Microsoft is clearly worried about the threat from Linux. One major problem for Microsoft is that it does not simply face one rival (e.g. Novell, which in the 1990s was Microsoft's main rival in network OS), as there are many firms distributing and developing Linux. As James Allchin, the group vice-president of Microsoft's Windows business, admitted: 'We're used to competing with products and companies. It's different than anything else we've dealt with before.'

Sources: K. Subhadra and S. Dutta, 'Linux—gaining ground', case study at ICFAI Center for Management Research (ICMR), Hyderabad, India, 2003; R. Madapati and V. K. Thota, 'Linux vs Windows', case study at ICMR, Hyderabad, India, 2003; various articles and websites.

Discussion questions

1 Outline briefly how the five forces in the OS market affected Microsoft before and after the introduction of Linux.

2 What can Microsoft do to counteract the threat from Linux?

REFERENCES

Arthur, W. Brian (1996). 'Increasing returns and the new world of business', *Harvard Business Review* (July–Aug.): 100–9.

Baden-Fuller, Charles (ed.) (1990). *Strategic Management of Excess Capacity* (Oxford: Blackwell).

Bain, J. S. (1956). *Barriers to New Competition* (Cambridge, Mass.: Harvard University Press).

Caves, Richard, and Porter, Michael (1980). 'The dynamics of changing seller concentration', *Journal of Industrial Economics* 29(1): 1–15.

Cuhls, Kerstin (2001). 'Foresight with Delphi surveys in Japan', *Technology Analysis and Strategic Management* 13(4): 555–69.

D'Aveni, Richard (1994). *Hypercompetition: Managing the Dynamics of Strategic Maneuvering* (New York: Free Press).

Dean, T., and Brown, R. (1995). 'Pollution regulation as a barrier to new firm entry: initial evidence and implications for future research', *Academy of Management Journal* 38: 288–303.

Deephouse, D. L. (1999). 'To be different, or to be the same? It's a question (and theory) of strategic balance', *Strategic Management Journal* 20: 147–66.

Doyle, P. (1997). *Marketing Management and Strategy*, 2nd edn. (New York: Prentice Hall).

Flowers, Edward B. (1976). 'Oligopolistic reactions in European and Canadian direct investment in the United States', *Journal of International Business Studies* (fall/winter): 43–55.

Greve, Henrich R. (1998). 'Managerial cognition and the mimetic adoption of market positions: what you see is what you do', *Strategic Management Journal* 19(10): 976–88.

Grossman, G., and Helpman, E. (1991), 'Endogenous product cycles', *Economic Journal*, 1214–29.

Harvey, Michael, Novicevic, Milorad M., and Kiessling, Timothy (2001). 'Hypercompetition and the future of global management in the twenty-first century', *Thunderbird International Business Review* 43(5): 599–616.

Klein, Harold E., and Linneman, Robert E. (1984). 'Environmental assessment: an international study of corporate practice', *Journal of Business Strategy* 5(1): 66–75.

Knickerbocker, Frederick T. (1973). *Oligopolistic Reaction and Multinational Enterprise* (Boston, Mass.: Division of Research, Graduate School of Business Administration, Harvard University).

Levitt, Theodore (1965). 'Exploit the product life cycle', *Harvard Business Review* (Nov.–Dec.): 81–94.

Lieberman, Martin B. (1987). 'Excess capacity as a barrier to entry', *Journal of Industrial Economics* 35(June): 607–27.

Lustgarten, S. H. (1975). 'The impact of buyer concentration in manufacturing industries', *Review of Economics and Statistics* 57: 125–32.

MacMillan, Ian C., van Putten, Alexander B., and McGrath, R. G. (2003). 'Global gamesmanship', *Harvard Business Review* (May): 63–71.

Mann, H. Michael (1966). 'Seller concentration, entry barriers, and rates of return in thirty industries', *Review of Economics and Statistics* 48: 296–307.

Masson, R. T., and Shaanan, J. (1982). 'Stochastic dynamic limit pricing', *Review of Economics and Statistics* 64: 413–22.

————(1987). 'Optimal pricing and threat of entry', *International Journal of Industrial Organization* 5: 1–13.

Mauri, A. J., and Michaels, M. P. (1998). 'Firm and industry effects within strategic management: an empirical examination', *Strategic Management Journal* 19(3): 211–19.

McGee, John, and Segal-Horn, S. (1990). 'Strategic space and industry dynamics', *Journal of Marketing Management* (3): 173–93.

——and Thomas, Howard (1986). 'Strategic groups: theory, research, and taxonomy', *Strategic Management Journal* 7(2): 141–60.

Nair, Anil, and Kotha, Suresh (2001). 'Does group membership matter? Evidence from the Japanese steel industry', *Strategic Management Journal* 22(3): 221–35.

Oster, S. (1982). 'The strategic use of regulatory investment by industry sub-groups', *Economic Inquiry* 20: 604–18.

Peteraf, Margaret, and Shanley, Mark (1997). 'Getting to know you: a theory of strategic group identity', *Strategic Management Journal* 18 (summer special): 165–86.

Porter, Michael (1980). *Competitive Strategy: Techniques for Analysing Industries and Competitors* (New York: Free Press).

——(1985). *Competitive Advantage: Creating and Sustaining Superior Performance* (New York: Free Press).

Prahalad, C. K., and Lieberthal, K. (2003). 'The end of corporate imperialism', *Harvard Business Review* (Aug.): 109–17.

Reger, Guido (2001). 'Technology foresight in companies: from an indicator to a network and process perspective', *Technology Analysis and Strategic Management* 13(4): 533–53.

Rosenbaum, David I., and Lamort, Fabian (1992). 'Entry, barriers, exit, and sunk costs: an analysis', *Applied Economics* 24(3): 297–305.

Rumelt, Richard P. (1991). 'How much does industry matter?', *Strategic Management Journal* 12: 167–85.

Schmalensee, Richard (1988). 'Inter-industry studies of structure and performance', in Richard Schmalensee and Robert D. Willig (eds.), *Handbook of Industrial Organization*, 2nd edn. (Amsterdam: North-Holland).

Schnaars, Steven, P. (1987). 'How to develop and use scenarios', *Long Range Planning* 20(1): 105–14.

Vernon, Raymond (1966). 'International investment and international trade in the product cycle', *Quarterly Journal of Economics* 80 (May): 190–207.

Wack, Pierre (1985a). 'Scenarios: uncharted waters ahead', *Harvard Business Review* 63(5): 72–89.

___ (1985b). 'Scenarios: shooting the rapids', *Harvard Business Review* 63(6): 139–50.

Wells, Louis T. Jr. (1968). 'A product life cycle for international trade?', *Journal of Marketing* 32 (July): 1–6.

Yip, George (1982). 'Gateways to entry', *Harvard Business Review* 60 (Sept.–Oct.): 85–93.

4

Corporate social responsibility and stakeholder analysis

Learning outcomes

After reading this chapter you should be able to:

- understand the significance of new global actors in the external business environment, especially non-governmental pressure groups;

- understand the different views on corporate social responsibility and their business implications;

- explain the benefits of corporate social responsibility for multinational firm strategies;

- apply some techniques for conducting stakeholder analysis.

Royal Dutch/Shell is one of the largest multinational firms in the world. But two events in 1995 showed that the strategies of even the largest multinational firms might change as a result of globally operating non-governmental organizations.

On 30 April 1995, Shell managers were taken by surprise when activists from the environmental group Greenpeace boarded the Brent Spar, a floating oil storage facility in the North Sea. The Brent Spar was decommissioned and Shell planned to sink it in the Atlantic. The British government strongly supported Shell's disposal plans. But Greenpeace criticized the planned sinking of the Brent Spar, which they claimed contained some harmful substances, and advocated onshore disposal. For almost two months the Brent Spar issue dominated media reporting in the UK and many other countries. While Greenpeace occupied the Brent Spar, public protests took place elsewhere; they were strongest in Germany, where Shell faced a major decline in petrol sales. Finally, in June 1995, Shell announced a reversal of its decision to sink the Brent Spar. Greenpeace claimed victory and protests stopped.

Shell then faced criticism over its operations in the Ogoni area of Nigeria. For a number of years the Ogonis (an ethnic minority of some 500,000 people) had complained about major environmental damage caused by Shell, and demanded greater benefits from oil operations for the local people. They suffered from oil spills and other harmful side effects of oil production, while little oil money flowed back to the local communities. After local protests led by the Movement for the Survival of the Ogoni People (MOSOP), Shell withdrew from the Ogoni area in 1993. But in November 1995 the Nigerian government executed the prominent Ogoni leader and chief Shell critic Ken Saro-Wiwa and eight others. This galvanized non-governmental organizations into supporting the Ogoni cause and new anti-Shell protests erupted around the world.

As a result of these two crises, Shell underwent a major process of transformation. As Sir Mark Moody-Stuart, chairman of the Committee of Managing Directors, wrote: 'Shell is undergoing fundamental change. ... We have learned the hard way that we must listen, engage and respond to our stakeholder groups.' In 1996 the company initiated the 'Society's changing expectations' project, a sophisticated audit of the views of the company's stakeholders. The Shell group's 'Statement of general business principles' was revised to include statements in support of fundamental human rights and sustainable development. Shell engaged in a process of dialogue with a number of stakeholders including human rights organizations.

Shell's internal organization also changed, and a Social Responsibility Committee was established at the highest corporate levels of the two parent companies. Finally, the company's strategies for expansion changed. Shell has become an important global player in renewable energy; it now owns wind farms and is involved in solar energy and hydrogen development.

Sources: Jedrzej George Frynas, *Oil in Nigeria: Conflict and Litigation between Oil Companies and Village Communities* (Münster: LIT, 2000); Tony Rice and Paula Owen, *Decommissioning the Brent Spar* (New York: Spon, 1999); Richard Boele and Heike Fabig, 'Shell, Nigeria and the Ogoni', an MBA case study for the 3rd Annual Nestlé Canada MBA Case Competition in Business and Sustainability (Schulich School of Business, Toronto, York University, 28–9 Jan. 2000).

4.1 Introduction

The activist campaigns against Shell made managers of other companies re-evaluate the relationship between business and society. In both the Brent Spar and the Nigerian case, Shell relied on the British and the Nigerian governments respectively to 'sort things out'. In both cases it failed to scan the wider external business environment for opportunities and threats. Shell's actions were entirely legal; the company paid government taxes and believed that it had done nothing wrong. But new and important actors are emerging in the global business environment, and the public increasingly expects businesses to assume new roles.

Important new global actors are non-governmental organizations (NGOs) such as Greenpeace or Amnesty International. An NGO can be defined as a 'group whose stated purpose is the promotion of environmental and or social goals' (Bendell 2000: 16). An NGO does not pursue economic interests and does not stand in elections for political office. This definition excludes, for instance, the International Chamber of Commerce (ICC), which has an economic agenda. The ICC speaks on behalf of business in promoting the market economy; its member companies and associations are themselves engaged in international business, and the ICC provides services to firms, especially the ICC International Court of Arbitration (the world's most important venue for international commercial arbitration). So the ICC is not considered an NGO.

NGOs are often multinational. Like multinational firms, they operate in many different countries, they have complex structures, they use many modern management techniques, and their strategies are global in scope. For instance, the environmental group Greenpeace is present in forty countries across Europe, the Americas, Asia and the Pacific; its major activist campaigns are global in nature. However, NGOs have different aims and objectives from business. While business aims primarily at making profits, NGOs usually pursue social and environmental goals. One of their objectives is to scrutinize business activities and persuade companies to become more socially responsible. Why did these organizations emerge to challenge business?

> **KEY CONCEPT**
>
> A non-governmental organization (NGO) is a group whose stated purpose is the promotion of environmental and or social goals. An NGO does not pursue economic interests, and does not stand in elections for political office.

4.2 The emergence of NGO–business relations

Bendell (2000) identified three reasons for the growth in NGO–business relations:

- the emergence of a global economy;
- the disintegration of traditional views on the difference between political and economic institutions; and
- developments in global communications.

4.2.1 **The emergence of a global economy**

As Dicken (2003) observed, one of the most striking developments in international business in the last few decades has been an intensification in competitive bidding between states (or between communities within states) for internationally mobile investment. Multinational firms can exploit regulatory differences between states by relocating some of their manufacturing plants from one country to another, or by shifting to sourcing their supplies from a different country with a more advantageous regulatory regime, which is termed 'regulatory arbitrage' (Leyshon 1992). Large multinational firms may be able to play off one government against another as states compete against each other to attract foreign investment by offering the best incentive packages. For instance, when Toyota and Peugeot were searching for the location of a new car plant in eastern Europe, the governments of Poland, the Czech Republic, and Hungary raced against each other to put in bids. Many different towns in the three countries tried to outbid each other by offering incentives. When the representatives of a Polish town learned that a Czech town had offered Toyota-Peugeot an industrial estate at the rate of one euro per square metre, it offered an industrial estate for nothing. The Polish town further offered (among other inducements) to build a four-lane access road to the planned car plant, to finance the construction of houses for expatriate staff, and to give managers access to a local golf club (which was important to Japanese managers). Despite all these incentives, in late 2001 Toyota-Peugeot chose a location in the Czech Republic where the companies were offered government incentives worth over €200 million.

In addition to offering financial aid or favourable taxation rates for foreign investors, national governments may also be reluctant to impose environmental and social regulations on firms. There is, for example, some evidence that governments in Asia hampered the functioning of trade unions, preventing a rise in wages and improvements in working conditions, in order to keep operational costs to a minimum, as a means of attracting international clothing and footwear companies. In order to reduce costs further, clothing and footwear firms such as Nike have already relocated part of their production activities away from locations such as Hong Kong and Taiwan towards locations with cheaper labour, and where trade unions have less of an influence, such as Vietnam and mainland China (Frynas 2003).

Like national governments, inter-governmental organizations are also reluctant to impose regulations on firms. In 1973 the United Nations Centre for Transnational Corporations (UNCTC) was set up, and embarked on formulating an international code of conduct to regulate the activities of multinational firms. But the centre was closed in 1993 after twenty years of failed negotiations. In place of binding international commitments, inter-governmental organizations focused on voluntary agreements, self-monitoring by firms, and social audits performed by external consultants (Newell 2000). In 2002 the European Commission firmly rejected a regulatory approach to corporate social responsibility, making it clear that it does not at present intend to impose responsible behaviour on companies by regulation or directive. Even where international agreements for the protection of the environment or workers' rights exist, they are 'vaguely worded, slow to negotiate and difficult to enforce' (Newell 2000: 33).

There are clear international standards and even binding international law in a number of areas such as labour rights, such as the International Labour Organization conventions. But traditional political mechanisms for achieving social and environmental goals are often perceived by NGOs and the public as having failed to resolve many of the world's most pressing problems. The increased focus of NGOs on multinational firms may reflect frustration with the pace of inter-governmental environmental and social reforms (Korten 1995). In the new global business environment, NGOs perceive that firms are often more powerful than states. NGOs' targeting of multinational firms is indicative of their attempts to check the growth in the power of those firms associated with globalization. NGOs are actively working to develop global norms of corporate behaviour, which multinational firms find increasingly difficult to escape (Newell 2000). The recent growth of NGOs is a by-product of globalization.

4.2.2 Linkages between political and economic institutions

Previously, business has often been regarded as apolitical, with managers believing that they should stay out of politics if possible. Shell made it clear that the company 'had always been (and is) firmly apolitical. Even if oil companies dreamed of political control, they could not achieve it' (Howarth 1997: 236). Therefore, Shell could not use its influence in order (for instance) to ask the Nigerian government to improve the lot of the local people in oil-producing areas. But NGOs feel that such statements are dishonest, as multinational firms have used their power to influence governments when it was to their own advantage. After all, Shell and other international oil companies were members of the controversial Global Climate Coalition, which spent tens of millions of dollars trying to undermine the UN climate negotiations.

NGOs and a large segment of the public no longer accept the view that firms are apolitical and should stick to profit-making, while governments should stick to providing social welfare. With growing recognition of corporate power in shaping politics, the previous apolitical or asocial approach to corporate policy is changing (Bendell 2000). As multinational firms are interconnected with social and political issues, NGOs believe that firms should pursue certain social and environmental goals which were previously the sole responsibility of governments.

4.2.3 Developments in global communications

Global access to computers, fax machines, mobile phones, video cameras, and the internet has provided NGOs with greater knowledge and greater power (Bendell 2000). Through the availability of communications technology, NGOs can quickly gather information from some of the most obscure parts of the world. An activist in a remote part of the rain forest in Brazil can quickly contact his colleagues in London or New York and can instantly send images of polluted rivers or forests. Communications technology can help to distribute the message quickly across the world. NGOs use the internet for displaying information and images, which can be seen all over the world. E-mails sent to a few mailing lists can snowball into alerting individuals in many countries to a specific issue.

Communications technology can also be used as a campaign tool, for instance, for organizing petitions and for sharing information between groups of people in different countries. In the 1970s and 1980s, anti-apartheid activists operated complicated telephone networks to spread urgent messages. Today, the internet makes it much easier to share information and coordinate campaigns. The success of many global NGO campaigns depends on the ability to use internet tools (Bray 2000).

4.3 Arguments on Corporate Social Responsibility (CSR)

With the rise of NGOs, multinational firms are asked to take on new roles in promoting social and environmental objectives. But there are two major objections to firms assuming such new roles:

- The only purpose of businesses is to make a profit, and they should not pursue any other objectives.
- Ethical considerations differ between countries, and firms face a dilemma as to which national ethical system to follow.

4.3.1 Companies and profit maximization

Milton Friedman is probably the best-known advocate of the idea that private firms have no responsibilities beyond profit maximization. He stated (1963: 133) that there is 'only one social responsibility of business: to use its resources and energy in activities designed to increase its profits so long as it stays within the rules of the game ... [and] engages in open and free competition, without deception and fraud ...' According to this view, by pursuing social and environmental business objectives firms will ultimately hurt shareholders by generating lower profits. Indeed, according to Friedman (1963: 133), the idea that firms have any responsibilities beyond maximizing profits for their shareholders represents 'a fundamental misconception of the character and nature of a free economy'.

Furthermore, Friedman argued that firms do not have the expertise to engage in solving social problems. By implication, specialized institutions such as government agencies or charities are in a much better position to pursue social and environmental objectives.

Friedman's views are extreme, but they still find supporters today. When referring to oil companies, Marina Ottaway (2001) stated that companies 'are not the right organizations for furthering moral causes. Oil companies may be "organs of society", but they are highly specialized ones, and their strengths lie not in devotion to democracy and human rights but in finding, extracting, and distributing oil.' David Henderson (2001: 147–8) contended that CSR can damage the economic development of firms and nations, as 'welfare may be reduced, not only because businesses are compelled to operate less efficiently, but also because new forms of interventionism arising out of the adoption of CSR, including closer regulation, narrow the domain of competition and economic freedom'.

4.3.2 National differences and CSR

Even if firms decide to pursue social or environmental objectives, international business poses a difficulty, as different nations have different ethics. Indeed, managers in different countries have sometimes strikingly dissimilar views on the same business problems. A study of Hong Kong showed that managers there regarded taking credit for another person's work as being the most unethical activity, which is very different from Western managers, who would find bribery or acquiring competitor information as more unethical (McDonald and Zepp 1988). Business research demonstrates that, despite globalization, ethical concerns of managers continue to vary according to nationality (Jackson 2000).

One of the most hotly debated ethical issues in international business is corruption (Lane and Simpson 1984). Many studies have attempted to show that views on taking bribes vary widely between different countries. When confronted with exactly the same situation, managers from one country might consider a payment to a government official a bribe, while managers from another country might consider it a legitimate gift. Some countries are said to be more prone to corruption than others. For instance, one study suggested that corrupt practices in Russia are deeply ingrained because of historical and political factors (Taylor et al. 1997). Surveys amongst international managers consistently show that some countries are more corrupt than others. The annual reports on corruption by the German NGO Transparency International show that countries such as Nigeria and Indonesia are ranked as being amongst the most corrupt countries in the world year after year.

Many managers believe that business people should adapt to every country in which they operate. The view that morality is relative to a particular culture or community is called 'cultural relativism'. If paying bribes is prevalent in their host country, then managers should follow the rules of the land. Indeed, managers might say that not paying a bribe may damage business interests. Some US managers think that the Foreign Corrupt Practices Act of 1977, which prohibits US managers from giving bribes in foreign countries, puts them at a competitive disadvantage vis-à-vis non-US firms in many countries. If the only way to obtain a lucrative government contract is by paying a bribe, a US firm may lose important business opportunities by refusing to do so. This view is not necessarily supported by research (Graham 1983), but it is nonetheless an influential one.

Cultural relativism suggests that managers should not try to find morals in business but should simply follow the laws of the land wherever they operate. An activist group in Britain or the US cannot dictate what the company should do in South Africa or France, as managers have to follow South African or French laws and business traditions.

4.4 CSR and the stakeholder view

Few businesspeople and scholars share the view that the business community has no social responsibility to society. They have a very different view of CSR from that of Milton Friedman. The problem is that there are many definitions of CSR, and there is no universal consensus on which social objectives companies should pursue.

The World Business Council for Sustainable Development (WBCSD 2000) defined CSR as 'the commitment of business to contribute to sustainable economic development, working with employees, their families, the local community and society at large to improve their quality of life'. But any definition is problematic. When asked what CSR means to them,

Exhibit 4.1 Different views of Corporate Social Responsibility

The World Business Council for Sustainable Development (WBCSD) initially defined CSR as 'the continuing commitment by business to behave ethically and contribute to economic development while improving the quality of life of the workforce and their families as well as of the local community and society at large'. It asked businesspeople and non-businesspeople what they thought of this definition. This is what people in several countries had to say.

In Taiwan, it was suggested that the definition should address:

- benefits for future generations
- environmental concerns (damage prevention and remediation).

In the United States, people commented:

- include more emphasis on the role of the individual
- reflect the need for greater transparency
- the term 'economic development' does not adequately capture the breadth of the economic role of business in society.

In Ghana, it was suggested that the definition should include the notion of:

- a global perspective which respects local culture
- building local capacity leaving a positive legacy
- empowerment and ownership
- teaching employees skills and enabling communities to be self-sufficient
- filling-in when government falls short
- giving access to information
- partnerships, because CSR does not develop in a vacuum.

In Thailand, people stated it should try to capture:

- the concept that the bigger the company, the greater the obligation
- the importance of environmental mitigation and prevention
- the need for transparency
- the importance of consumer protection
- awareness of and change in people's attitudes towards the environment
- the relevance of youth and gender issues.

As a result of its dialogue with people in different countries, WBCSD modified its definition of CSR to mean 'the commitment of business to contribute to sustainable economic development, working with employees, their families, the local community and society at large to improve their quality of life'.

people from different countries emphasize different issues; for instance, environmental issues are stressed in Thailand, while Ghanaians stress the empowerment of local communities (see Exhibit 4.1). These differences suggest that managers must remain sensitive to cultural differences between countries.

The view that businesses should pursue certain social goals suggests that managers have broader responsibilities that extend beyond the company's owners and shareholders to include employees, customers, suppliers, and local communities. This view goes beyond corporate charitable donations, public relations exercises, or special employee benefits, all of which practices have long been pursued by companies. It stresses that companies have responsibilities to their stakeholders (Pegg 2003).

KEY CONCEPT

Corporate Social Responsibility (CSR) is the commitment of business to contribute to sustainable economic development, working with employees, their families, the local community, and society at large to improve their quality of life. But any definition is problematic, and people from different countries emphasize different issues in their understanding of CSR.

4.4.1 The stakeholder view of the firm

Many scholars and managers now accept the idea that a firm has stakeholders (Chang and Ha 2001; Handy 1994). A stakeholder is typically defined as 'any group or individual who can affect or is affected by the achievement of the organization's objectives' (Freeman 1984: 46). Stakeholders include employees, customers, suppliers, stockholders, banks, environmentalists, governments, and other groups who can either help or damage the firm (see Exhibit 4.2). Freeman (1984) simply summarized the stakeholder approach as 'the principle of who or what really counts'.

The stakeholder approach, which was originally devised as just another tool for understanding organizations and analysing the business environment, is now mainly associated with CSR. Since managers usually paid enough attention to suppliers or governments in the past, the literature on CSR usually emphasizes 'non-traditional' stakeholder groups such as NGOs and local communities. It is those groups which mostly advocate CSR and which have traditionally not been part of the firm's strategic analysis.

The stakeholder view of the firm undermines the notion that a firm should only maximize profits for shareholders. Rather, the goal of any firm should be to satisfy the aspirations of all of the main stakeholders.

KEY CONCEPT

A stakeholder is any group or individual who can affect or is affected by the achievement of the organization's objectives. Stakeholders include employees, customers, suppliers, stockholders, banks, environmentalists, governments, and other groups who can either help or damage the firm. Freeman summarized the stakeholder approach as 'the principle of who or what really counts'.

Exhibit 4.2 Generic stakeholder map of a multinational firm

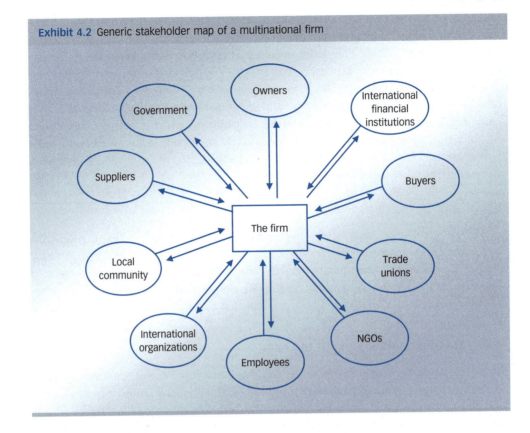

4.4.2 Stakeholder issues

Each stakeholder group has different agendas and concerns. So specific issues of concern vary between different groups.

Based on field studies, Clarkson (1995) identified some of the typical corporate and stakeholder issues for different stakeholder groups. These included issues concerning:

- employees (e.g. health promotion; women in management and on the board);
- shareholders (e.g. shareholder communications and complaints; shareholder advocacy);
- customers (e.g. product safety; customer complaints);
- suppliers (e.g. general policy; relative power); and
- public stakeholders (public health, safety, and protection; environmental assessment of capital projects).

One major problem with such a wide variety of stakeholder concerns is how to assess the firm's performance for addressing stakeholder issues. Traditionally, only the purely economic performance to the benefit of one stakeholder group—the shareholder—was taken into account. This gives rise to new ways of assessing the performance of the firm such as the triple bottom line concept.

4.4.3 Triple bottom line concept

Promoted by various NGOs, the triple bottom line (TBL) concept emerged from the recognition that firms are becoming accountable for social and environmental effects on society, in addition to generating profits. TBL is an expanded CSR concept, which suggests that social and environmental indicators should become as important as conventional profit indicators. On the most basic level, TBL states that companies should simultaneously be held accountable for their social, environmental, and financial performances (Elkington 1997).

TBL does not yet represent standard corporate wisdom, but it is being advocated, amongst other concepts, by various important socially responsible investment and mutual fund companies such as Calvert, Walder Asset Management, and Zurich (Pegg 2003). TBL is also increasingly taken into account by managers in large and small multinational firms. Information and indicators of financial, social, and environmental performance are now regularly reported by firms in very different sectors, ranging from IT companies such as the Finnish Novo Group to airport management companies such as the British BAA.

KEY CONCEPT

The triple bottom line concept is an expanded CSR concept, which suggests that social and environmental indicators should become as important as conventional profit indicators. TBL states that companies should simultaneously be held accountable for their social, environmental, and financial performances.

4.5 Business opportunities of CSR and stakeholder involvement

Non-traditional stakeholders such as NGOs do not only pose external threats to firms but they also present business opportunities. Local communities and NGOs can help to make government agencies more favourably disposed towards a firm; they can help to market a new product or build barriers to entry. Business opportunities are created as local communities and NGOs are becoming more prepared to work with business for common strategic goals.

4.5.1 Collaboration between business and NGOs

There is evidence that NGO–business relationships are now shifting from confrontation towards collaboration. A survey of NGOs and companies worldwide by Elkington and Fennel (2000) found a high convergence between companies and NGOs. Over 85% of the respondents believed that such partnerships would increase over the following five years. Neither firms nor NGOs expected an end to confrontation, but the opportunities for collaboration have grown.

Collaboration takes many forms. Sometimes firms may engage with an NGO for a specific project, for instance marketing an environmentally friendly product. At other times, several firms form a coalition with various NGOs on general issues of joint interest. A remarkable global strategic joint venture is the Global Reporting Initiative (GRI), which was established in 1997 by the Coalition for Environmentally Responsible Economies (CERES). The GRI, which brings together a number of NGOs and companies, has the mission of developing globally applicable guidelines for reporting on economic, environmental, and social performance, initially that of multinational firms and eventually for any business, government, or NGO (www.globalreporting.org/). In this way, a global NGO–business partnership aims to establish common global standards, which national governments are unable to provide.

There are various reasons for the growth of NGO–business partnerships, including the NGOs' need for more funding and technical expertise and the firms' desire to use NGOs to gain credibility with the public. However, the growth of such partnerships is inhibited by a number of factors, including firms' short-term financial concerns and NGOs' belief that firms are often merely seeking public relations benefits and not environmental or social improvements (see Exhibit 4.3). Above all, partnerships can be problematic because NGOs and firms have very different strategic objectives, different organizational cultures, and different ways of seeing the world.

4.5.2 Benefits of NGO–business partnerships

Stakeholder engagement can sometimes help firms to get ahead of the competition. For instance, the medium-sized refrigerator producer Foron from eastern Germany began a working relationship with Greenpeace in the early 1990s to promote a Foron-developed CFC-free refrigerator. Foron brought its technical expertise to the partnership, while Greenpeace could offer its media presence and high moral authority, which was more convincing to potential customers than any corporate advertising campaign. The Greenpeace–Foron partnership not only helped Foron to sell many refrigerators, it changed the entire marketplace. After strong initial resistance, all large refrigerator producers in Germany adapted the new technology and made the CFC-free refrigerator the market standard (Schneidewind and Petersen 2000).

According to Waddell (2000), the involvement of NGOs can help firms to achieve many corporate goals, including:

- risk management and reduction (e.g. providing stakeholder views as early warning of possible problems);
- cost reduction and productivity gains (e.g. leveraging non-tax status or educating the public);
- new product development (e.g. providing knowledge and lobbying for regulatory change);
- new market development (e.g. extending a trusting public image);
- human resource development (e.g. teaching and training about specific communities);
- building barriers to entry (e.g. building a distinctive image); and
- creativity and change (providing alternative viewpoints so as to reveal hitherto unrecognized assumptions and develop new integrative strategies).

Through stakeholder analysis, firms may be able to find business opportunities and resources which they ordinarily would not have been able to identify.

Exhibit 4.3 Drivers and constraints of NGO–business partnerships

Drivers for business engagement with NGOs

- markets
- NGO credibility with public on issues and priorities
- need for external challenge
- cross-fertilization of thinking
- greater efficiency in resource allocation
- desire to head off negative public confrontations
- desire to engage stakeholders

Drivers for NGO engagement with NGOs

- growing interest in markets
- disenchantment with government as provider of solutions
- need for more resources, e.g. funding, technical and management expertise
- credibility of business with government
- cross-fertilization of thinking
- access to supply chains
- greater leverage

Brakes on business-led initiatives

- concerns over confidentiality of information shared with NGOs
- difficulties of addressing broadening agenda of sustainability-focused groups
- inability to deal with schizophrenic tendencies of NGOs
- desire to protect 'weakest link in chain'
- short-term financial concerns
- concerns over splintering of NGO movement and corresponding reduction in business value of alliances

Brakes on NGO-led initiatives

- belief that company is only seeking public relations benefits, rather than real environmental improvement

→

→

- perceptions of inconsistency in company environmental behaviour (inability to deal with schizo-phrenic tendencies of companies)
- conflicts with membership and fundraising base
- decisions to devote energies to protecting environmental regulatory structure

Source: Elkington and Fennel (2000).

4.5.3 From stakeholder involvement to profit-making

We showed that the involvement of non-traditional stakeholders can bring very tangible benefits to companies. In general, there is evidence to suggest that becoming socially responsible can lead to higher profits. A study by the research firm Wiesenberger found that what it calls 'socially screened funds' had, on average, consistently done better than other mutual funds, although they tended to be more risky and marginally more expensive. On average, companies which include ethical commitments in their annual reports have also been found to outperform other companies financially (quoted in Pegg 2003).

It is important to remember, however, that social responsibility does not bring instant results. Good relationships with stakeholders take years to build, and so does a firm's reputation for being socially responsible. In essence, CSR is about creating value in the long term. A firm must assess strategic opportunities from socially responsible behaviour in the long term. For instance, Shell played down its ROACE (return on average capital employed) and earnings expectations in the new business areas of renewable energy such as wind and solar. At the same time, the company expects major market growth in these sectors in coming years and hopes to reap major profits in the longer term. One problem with this approach, however, is that some stakeholders—shareholders or financial institutions—may pressurize the firm to generate profits in the short term.

4.5.4 CSR without profits?

As the previous sections revealed, the involvement of non-traditional stakeholders such as environmental groups may help firms to reap major benefits and help to increase shareholder value in the long term. However, the point of CSR is that—unlike targeted corporate sponsorships or employee benefits—it does not always pay. The evidence on the profitability of socially responsible companies or investment funds is not entirely clear. Indeed, research suggests that social engagement by companies could, if not managed properly, lead to lower shareholder value (Hillman and Keim 2001). When managers start engaging with stakeholders, they do not necessarily know whether this will ever translate into higher profits or better corporate reputation.

Another major issue is that some stakeholders will not lend support to the company unless they are convinced that it is very sincere about CSR. An NGO such as Greenpeace will not publicly work with a company (as it did with Foron) unless it is convinced that top management demonstrates integrity and consistency in strategy and implementation of CSR. Companies which are perceived as insincere are shunned by NGOs. For instance, the biotechnology firm Monsanto started a series of advertisements in the UK in 1998 which even presented some opposing NGO viewpoints and invited the public to voice their views about the company. However, Monsanto was perceived as consulting stakeholders but then doing little or nothing to change its actual behaviour, so stakeholder analysis and management had very limited benefits for the firm (Elkington and Fennel 2000).

Somewhat paradoxically, in order to profit from CSR and stakeholder engagement, corporate leaders have to convert to the view that social issues are sometimes more important than profits. The success of many thriving socially responsible firms had much to do with CEOs such as Anita Roddick of the Body Shop or Rick George of Suncor, who became very credible supporters of CSR and turned their organizations around to follow CSR principles at all levels of organization and strategy formulation.

As Parkinson (1999) argued, socially responsible corporate behaviour can be a precondition for long-term profitability. But CSR concerns cannot be solely motivated by the hope of creating value for the firm. Parkinson (1999: 62) concluded that managers should accept that respect for social issues 'will sometimes require companies to make less than the maximum possible profits'.

But even if there are no profits to be made and a firm is unwilling to yield to stakeholder demands, managers may have to implement social and environmental improvements in order to retain acceptance of the firm in society. Firms may feel under pressure to imitate successful examples of socially and environmentally conscious firms in order to 'enhance their legitimacy' by society (Tsai and Child 1997). Some social and environmental initiatives may be necessary just to stay competitive in the new global business environment.

4.6 Stakeholder analysis in the global business environment

Stakeholder engagement is a complex process, ranging from identifying key stakeholders in the business environment to implementing CSR strategies and monitoring performance. In this chapter we deal only with the first steps of identifying who the stakeholders are and how businesses should decide which stakeholders are the most important ones to talk to.

4.6.1 Stakeholder mapping

Exhibit 4.2 showed a generic stakeholder map of a multinational firm. This can serve as a starting point for identifying the main stakeholders. 'Generic stakeholders' refers to categories of groups who can affect the firm or are affected by the firm, such as suppliers or government. While government is a category, it is the finance ministry, the environmental protection agency, or the country's parliament which can affect the achievement of strategic goals (Freeman 1984: 54).

However, the mapping of stakeholders is much more complicated than Exhibit 4.2 suggests, as a multinational firm faces different groups in different countries. Furthermore,

Exhibit 4.4 Stakeholders of Shell International

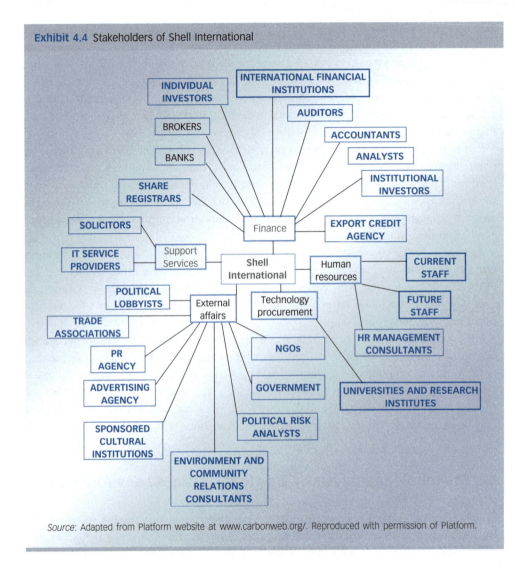

Source: Adapted from Platform website at www.carbonweb.org/. Reproduced with permission of Platform.

stakeholders can be very different for different organizations. For example, environmental NGOs may be crucial for a waste-treatment plant but may be of little importance to an on-line book retailer. Therefore, every firm must identify the specific stakeholders which are important to it globally and in every country in which it operates. Exhibit 4.4 shows a generic stakeholder map for the London-based Shell International. Under each of the headings such as government or non-governmental organizations, there may be very different groups with different interests. Furthermore, Shell's subsidiaries in different parts of the world will have many other stakeholders. For instance, the stakeholders of Shell's Nigerian subsidiary will include contracting firms such as Wilbros and Schlumberger, local host communities represented by village chiefs, youth leaders, and women's groups, and different government agencies such as the Nigerian environment ministry and the Nigerian state oil firm. A failure to identify an important stakeholder may be costly to the firm. For example, Shell in Nigeria failed to consider Ken Saro-Wiwa's MOSOP movement as a legitimate stakeholder and refused to talk to it in the early 1990s, which was one of the key reasons for the company's poor relations with local communities in Nigeria. This illustrates the importance of constructing precise stakeholder maps.

4.6.2 Problems in stakeholder mapping

It is not easy to construct a stakeholder map. Freeman (1984: 58) pointed out that two issues must be considered when stakeholders are identified. First, the same group can have different stakeholder roles for the company. For instance, for Shell in Nigeria, the Nigerian government is a stakeholder as government, but it is also an owner (as joint-venture partner) and a financial institution (the Nigerian Central Bank). Multiple roles for the same stakeholder group can give rise to conflicting demands on the company. Second, stakeholder groups are interconnected and may influence each other. For Shell in Nigeria, the local communities (especially MOSOP) had an impact on environmental NGOs; in turn, the media publicity generated by international NGOs led a financial institution (the International Finance Corporation—IFC—of the World Bank) to withdraw from its investment in a Shell gas project.

A further complication in constructing a stakeholder map is that such a map is only useful at a particular point in time for a specific purpose. Managers should never forget that the relative importance of stakeholders may be different for different issues and projects. Therefore, stakeholders require different degrees and types of attention depending on things such as their degree of power or the urgency of the issue, while levels of these attributes (and thereby the importance of a stakeholder) can vary from issue to issue and from time to time (Mitchell et al. 1997).

4.6.3 Who constructs stakeholder maps?

A stakeholder map is usually constructed by people from within the company. But there are problems in doing so. One study found that top managers ascribed more relative importance to stakeholders who played a part in the traditional activities of the firm (owners, customers, and employees) than to the government or non-traditional stakeholder groups (Agle et al. 1999). Jawahar and McLaughlin (2001) noted that 'functional managers, in order to increase their power, may exaggerate threats from their stakeholders, leading top managers to form an inaccurate picture of demands on the organization. Such acts of self-interest may cause the organization to be out of sync with the predictions of our stakeholder theory.' Finally, stakeholder attributes are socially constructed; they are not objective reality. Managers may have different perceptions of issues such as stakeholder legitimacy compared with a stakeholder's own perception (Mitchell et al. 1997). As Freeman (1984: 64) reminded us, when the managers' 'perceptions are out of line with the perceptions of the stakeholders, all the brilliant strategic thinking in the world will not work'.

For all of these reasons, it is sometimes better to let someone from outside the company conduct stakeholder analysis. Big consultancy firms such as Arthur D. Little have designed various management tools and structured workshops for that purpose. Large companies also use small specialized consultancy firms such as CoreRelation Consulting to collect information on stakeholder views or the social impact of the company's activities with regard to a particular project or country. However, stakeholder analysis cannot be left entirely to consultants. Since the managers' perceptions may be out of line with the perceptions of stakeholders, managers should use stakeholder analysis to reveal their own beliefs about the relevance of each stakeholder group (Freeman 1984: 95).

4.6.4 Stakeholders and the industry environment

Stakeholder mapping can be useful in surveying the industry environment. When we discussed the Five Forces Model in the last chapter, we highlighted the bargaining power of two stakeholder groups—buyers and suppliers. But other stakeholders can also constrain industries. For example, governments can raise or lower entry barriers through regulations, and NGOs can force firms to undertake costly investments. In order to reflect the power of all stakeholders in analysing the business environment, we are proposing a modified Four Forces Model (see Exhibit 4.5), which includes rivalry, the threat of new entrants, the threat of substitutes, and the power of stakeholders (which includes buyers, suppliers and others).

Exhibit 4.6 applies the Four Forces Model to the sports shoe industry. It shows that ordinarily the bargaining power of suppliers and buyers would be considered relatively low. However, by integrating other stakeholders, our model demonstrates that stakeholders could present a high threat. As low labour costs are very important in shoe manufacturing,

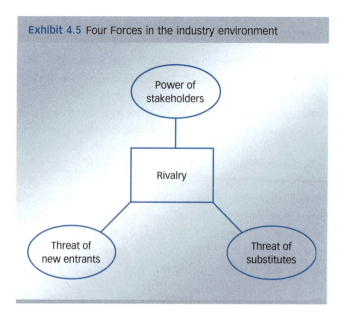

Exhibit 4.5 Four Forces in the industry environment

Power of stakeholders

Rivalry

Threat of new entrants

Threat of substitutes

Exhibit 4.6 Four Forces Model applied to the sports shoe industry

- Many suppliers in different Asian countries, little threat of forward integration; however, products are unique and the switching costs for firms such as Nike are high.
- Buyers' power is relatively low as there are many consumers and they are not concentrated; strong proprietary brand names mean low substitution threat.
- Well-organized NGOs which target sports shoe manufacturers; proprietary brand names are particularly vulnerable to media campaigns.

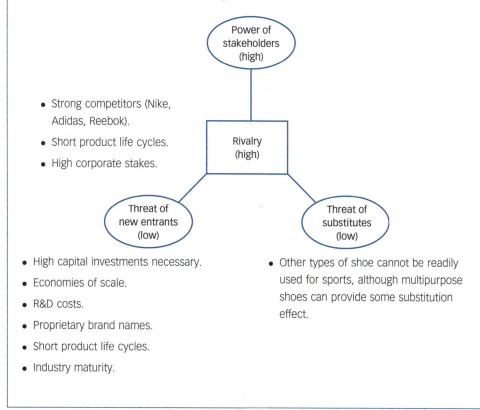

- Strong competitors (Nike, Adidas, Reebok).
- Short product life cycles.
- High corporate stakes.

- High capital investments necessary.
- Economies of scale.
- R&D costs.
- Proprietary brand names.
- Short product life cycles.
- Industry maturity.

- Other types of shoe cannot be readily used for sports, although multipurpose shoes can provide some substitution effect.

companies such as Nike and Adidas locate production in countries with low labour costs and poor labour rights records such as China, Vietnam, and Indonesia. Therefore, the shoe sector is more at risk than some other industries from NGOs which focus on labour rights. Proprietary brand names, which ordinarily have the advantage of raising entry barriers, are a disadvantage when dealing with NGOs: they make the firm more vulnerable to targeting by NGOs, as corporate reputation is at stake.

4.7 Identifying the key stakeholders of the multinational firm

Firms cannot accommodate the interests of every stakeholder. There are just too many of them. A multinational firm which operates in many different countries has thousands of stakeholders with very different agendas and demands. Furthermore, stakeholders may have contradictory interests. One environmental group may want the company to divest itself of a certain project, while another group may want the company to introduce anti-pollution measures but continue operating. But some stakeholders are just much more important than others, and it is important to identify who the main stakeholders are and how much power they have over the firm.

4.7.1 The primary stakeholders

According to Clarkson (1995), the most important stakeholders are those 'without whose continuing participation the firm cannot survive as a going concern'. These are called primary stakeholders; they are shareholders and investors, employees, customers, and suppliers. Furthermore, they include the so-called public stakeholder group: 'the governments and communities that provide infrastructures and markets, whose laws and regulations must be obeyed, and to whom taxes and other obligations may be due' (Clarkson 1995).

If a primary stakeholder group becomes discontented with the firm and withdraws its co-operation, the firm will suffer serious damage or may not be able to continue as a going concern. The fate of Dow Corning (a pioneer firm in the development of silicon-based materials and technology) is an example. Its inability in 1991 to keep its customer and public stakeholder groups satisfied with the safety of one of its products led to the breakdown of the stakeholder system for that product and Dow Corning's fall from its leading position in the breast implant market (Clarkson 1995).

4.7.2 The secondary stakeholders

Secondary stakeholder groups are defined as those who affect or are influenced by the firm, but are not engaged in transactions with the firm and are not essential for its survival. The media and a wide range of NGOs would be seen as secondary stakeholders under this definition (Clarkson 1995).

However, there are problems with this definition. In the global economy NGOs or local communities can also have a major impact on the survival of a firm, even if they are not engaged in transactions with the firm. For example, environmental interests such as communities are also thought to have at least loose quasi-contracts (and sometimes very specific ones) with firms (Donaldson and Preston 1995). Indeed, NGOs and local communities can threaten the survival of a company. For instance, when the UK-based building materials company RMC Group bought a former state-owned cement plant in the former East Germany in 1990, the local community wanted to see the plant closed because of its poor environmental record, despite the potential loss of local employment. In order to ensure the plant's survival, RMC had to engage with the community and the local government. After many environmental improvements had been introduced, including the EU Eco-Management and Audit Scheme (EMAS), not only was the plant able to survive but it received much endorsement from the local community. This example illustrates that some of the stakeholders previously defined as 'secondary' should perhaps be considered as 'primary' to the firm.

KEY CONCEPT

A firm has primary and secondary stakeholders. Primary stakeholders are those without whose continuing participation the firm cannot survive as a going concern. They include shareholders and investors, employees, customers, and suppliers, as well as the so-called public stakeholder group: the government and communities that provide infrastructures and markets. Secondary stakeholders are those who affect or are influenced by the firm, but are not engaged in transactions with the firm and are not essential for its survival. They include the media and a wide range of NGOs.

4.7.3 Which stakeholders should the firm focus on?

As we noted earlier, stakeholders can be very different for different organizations. Jawahar and McLaughlin (2001) observed that, since an organization is dependent on its environment for resources, 'the importance of a stakeholder will depend on the needs of the organization and the extent to which the organization is dependent on that stakeholder, relative to other stakeholders, for meeting its needs'.

The firm may need to focus on different stakeholder groups depending on several factors. One such factor is the firm's corporate nationality. Despite globalization, a firm's national origin can still account for many differences between multinational firms. Pauly and Reich (1997, mentioned in Chapter 2, section 2.9.3) found, for instance, that German and Japanese firms obtain most of their financing through banks, while US firms rely much more on capital markets. So banks would be more important stakeholders to a Japanese or a German firm. With regard to CSR, US and Western European firms were more frequently targeted by the mainly Western-based NGOs than were firms from other countries. So Greenpeace will be of greater importance to a German firm than to a Chinese firm.

As the needs of a firm change over time, the relative importance of stakeholders will change as it evolves. During the start-up stage, when the firm is most concerned about obtaining initial financing and entering the marketplace, the key stakeholders are likely to be shareholders, creditors, and customers. In contrast, during the maturity stage firms are likely to act proactively towards most of their stakeholders including communities and NGOs. On the one hand, firms are likely to be larger in the mature stage and will attract more scrutiny from stakeholders; on the other, firms will have more cash flow without particularly attractive investment opportunities (Jawahar and McLaughlin 2001).

The type of industry can also influence a firm's response to social demands by stakeholders. For instance, Greenpeace will be a key stakeholder for industries which cause major pollution, such as the oil industry; it will be of less relevance for textile manufacturers, which cause relatively little pollution. On the other hand, coffee roasters and retail chains such as Starbucks must pay attention to groups such as Oxfam or the US-based Global Exchange, which target coffee producers. A waste-disposal firm during the start-up stage will have to pay attention to the environmental concerns of local communities, in contrast to many other firms during the start-up stage.

4.7.4 Critique of stakeholder analysis

Stakeholder analysis has come under some criticism recently. Ulrich Steger (2003) suggested that in today's fast-moving global business environment managers often cannot be sure about either stakeholder groups or their demands. So the use of stakeholder maps may be of limited value because key stakeholders may change or their demands may change. According to Steger, a focus on stakeholder analysis can only work if you have all the information—who all your stakeholders are, what do they want at a given moment (which could change), and how to rank the urgency of dealing with the most important stakeholder groups. But firms rarely have all the relevant information in today's global business environment. Managers may not know whether Greenpeace or another stakeholder is planning a campaign against the organization, but they might be aware of a public debate about a specific issue—for instance about the proposed phasing out of a dangerous chemical or calls for better working conditions in a given industry or country.

Therefore, Steger (2003) suggested that managers should focus on issues which could become threats to the organization rather than on stakeholders. He believes that, rather than preparing stakeholder maps, firms should have an 'early warning system' (EAS), which will scan the business environment for early signs of problems. Companies may already have some form of EAS—for example, consumer research aimed at detecting new desires or shifts in social attitudes. But Steger believes that firms should also have an EAS for detecting and preventing trouble ahead. This can be done with the help of systematic information-gathering, dissemination of information within the organization, and simple management tools or checklists.

4.7.5 Issue analysis

One tool for issue analysis proposed by Steger (2003) is cross-impact analysis, which can be used by managers, for example, during brainstorming sessions (see Exhibit 4.7). By placing potential threats and opportunities in the business environment in relation to corporate objectives, managers can better understand how an issue could influence the organization. Steger recommends this tool for situations such as when ecological issues prompt customers to direct criticism at a company because of its products, and to begin switching to environmentally friendly products. It could also be used in situations when a firm is confronted with stricter regulations on product quality, which could make innovation more feasible. This type of analysis might indicate that the ability of customers to switch to another firm's products is high, or that the potential for innovation is higher than previously assumed.

Exhibit 4.7 Example of cross-impact analysis

Corporate issues	Potential environmental product-related developments			
	Potential for public criticism	Ability of consumers to switch to environmentally friendly substitutes	Stricter environmental regulations	Ability to innovate
Safeguarding of competitiveness	–	–	–	+
Profit	0	–	–	?
Qualified and motivated employees	–	–	?	+
Quality level of products—user-friendly image	0	0	?!	
Diversification	+	+	+	?
Globalization	0	0	–	+–
Distribution channels	?	?!	?	0

+ = positive influence; ? = ambiguous/uncertain influence; – = negative influence; ?! = unknown if it will have an influence or not and, if so, in which direction; 0 = neutral.

One assumption underlying issue analysis is that most issues do not come entirely out of the blue. In most cases managers could have detected them, as issues follow patterns or a set of criteria. In order to help managers decide how an issue might develop in future, Winter and Steger (1998) proposed a checklist which asks eight questions:

1. Are the arguments against the issue plausible?

2. Does the issue evoke emotion? Is it understandable—visual, touching—by the public?

3. Is the issue media-friendly?

4. Are there connections to other issues involving the company or other companies?

5. How strong is the key activist group?

6. How isolated is the company?

7. How far have the dynamics of the crisis already evolved?

8. How easy is the solution?

The checklist can help to understand some of the dynamics of social and ecological issues. For example, the pharmaceutical industry has been frequently criticized for unethical practices but it has rarely attracted major NGO campaigns in the same way as the oil or the mining industries. The checklist makes it clear that issues involving pharmaceuticals

Exhibit 4.8 A six-step process for 'FOSTERing' stakeholder relationships

Foundation	• clarify corporate values • develop social mission • communicate corporate commitment
Organizational alignment	• assess organizational readiness • adapt systems and structures to support • relationship-building
Strategy	• inventory and assess existing relationships • benchmark best practices • establish dialogue with key stakeholders • refine corporate goals and prepare strategy
Trust	• build collaborative relationships with key stakeholders • identify common goals • resolve conflict
Evaluate	• design conduct stakeholder audit • celebrate successes • learn from experiences
Repeat	• use results to refine corporate goals

Source: CoreRelation Consulting website at www.corerelation.com.

are usually very complex, difficult to understand, and not particularly media-friendly. The side-effects of a given medical drug may not be as easy to explain, not as easy to prove, and not as media-friendly compared with the direct effects of an oil spill on bird life. The activist groups which focus on pharmaceuticals are not as strong as activist groups focused on oil-related or mining-related issues. But major Western pharmaceutical firms have been targeted in campaigns related to AIDS drugs. Firms have been forced to cut prices for AIDS drugs sold in developing countries and to allow cheap imitations of drugs to be produced in those countries. The checklist could have helped pharmaceutical firms to forecast the rising importance of the AIDS issue. The issue evokes considerable emotion, the effects of high drug prices on poor HIV-infected Africans are easily understandable, and the issue is media-friendly.

As with stakeholder analysis, one problem with issue analysis is that some information may not be known to the firm. A lack of understanding by managers might call for a deeper investigation of the issue in order to detect any changes in the business environment. As Steger (2003) pointed out, a precondition for the use of cross-impact analysis is that no predominating opinion should be allowed to prevail and that advocates of minority opinions are brought into the brainstorming sessions as well as outsiders with a wide background. As with stakeholder analysis, issue analysis relies on managers being open-minded to new trends and developments.

4.7.6 From strategic analysis to strategy development

The idea of stakeholders and stakeholder analysis is useful in providing a tool for an understanding of the new business environment. But it is important to keep in mind that stakeholder analysis does not begin and does not end simply with identifying who the stakeholders are or what the key issues are. A firm needs to develop strategies to cope with the new pressures in the external business environment. In doing so, the firm's objective must be to foster friendly relationships with its stakeholders, avoid risks to its reputation, and benefit from working with stakeholders. It is not enough to know who your stakeholders are: you must have a strategy for dealing with them. Exhibit 4.8 shows a Six-Step Process developed by Ann Svendsen and CoreRelation Consulting for fostering stakeholder relationships. Without a proper process of stakeholder engagement, a firm's stakeholder analysis will not lead anywhere.

4.8 Summary

In a global business environment where national governments and inter-governmental organizations fail to address many of the world's most pressing problems, the public looks to business to perform social tasks previously accomplished by the state. In this global environment, NGOs have acquired a powerful influence on business activity. While managers may not necessarily like it, business is now expected to pursue social and environmental objectives. These new pressures have given rise to corporate social responsibility (CSR), which has been defined as 'the commitment of business to contribute to sustainable economic development, working with employees, their families, the local community and society at large to improve their quality of life'.

There are two major objections to multinational firms assuming new social and environmental roles. First, it has been argued that businesses serve the sole purpose of making a profit, and that they should not pursue any other objectives. Second, ethics differ between countries, and multinational firms face a dilemma as to which national ethics to follow. But views are changing, and many international businesspeople now accept that firms have a social responsibility to society. Indeed, CSR may provide various new business opportunities to multinational firms, such as through NGO–business partnerships.

Many international businesspeople have also come to accept the idea that a firm has stakeholders. A stakeholder is typically defined as 'any group or individual who can affect or is affected by the achievement of the organization's objectives'. In an increasingly complex globalizing world, firms need to engage with stakeholders, but stakeholder engagement is a complex process. The first step in this process is identifying the relevant stakeholder groups (for instance, through stakeholder mapping) and identifying the relevant stakeholder issues (for instance, through cross-impact analysis).

Our view is that firms will increasingly have to manage stakeholder issues in the same way as other strategic issues, as they are relevant to competing in a global market. Indeed, it is crucial that stakeholder concerns are not dealt with by a public relations or a stakeholder unit within the firm, but are incorporated into the formulation of strategic plans and financial budgets. To quote Michael Porter, 'Seeing strategy narrowly leads to missed opportunities and bad competitive choices.'

KEY READINGS

- On the social responsibility of multinational firms, see Jedrzej George Frynas and Scott Pegg (eds.), *Transnational Corporations and Human Rights* (London: Palgrave, 2003).
- On NGO–business relations, see Jem Bendell (ed.), *Terms for Endearment: Business, NGOs and Sustainable Development* (Sheffield: Greenleaf, 2000).
- A useful book on stakeholder theory is Freeman (1984).

DISCUSSION QUESTIONS

1 List and discuss the key arguments for multinational firms promoting social and environmental objectives.

2 What are the key arguments against multinational firms promoting social and environmental objectives?

3 What must a manager consider in engaging with an NGO?

4 Why might multinationals which are socially and environmentally conscious be more profitable in the long term than those multinationals which are not?

5 What problems do managers face in stakeholder mapping?

6 Take a multinational firm of your choice and list its primary stakeholders.

Closing case study
Stakeholders and Suncor Energy Inc. work together to create value (2002)

Suncor Energy Inc. is an integrated energy company headquartered in Calgary in the Canadian province of Alberta. Suncor's oil sands business, located near Fort McMurray, Alberta, extracts and upgrades oil sands and markets refinery feedstock and diesel fuel, while operations throughout western Canada produce natural gas. Suncor operates a refining and marketing business in Ontario with retail distribution under the Sunoco brand. US downstream assets include refining operations in Colorado and retail sales in the Denver area under the Phillips 66 brand. Suncor's common shares (SU) are listed on the Toronto and New York stock exchanges.

During the past decade Suncor has been transformed from an unprofitable, traditional integrated oil and gas company to a dynamic, highly profitable growth enterprise with a vision of becoming a successful, environmentally sustainable energy company that is dedicated to vigorous growth by meeting the changing expectations of current and future stakeholders.

This move towards becoming a sustainable energy company has meant enormous changes in attitude, management decision-making, business strategy, stakeholder relationships, and employee engagement. Suncor recognized that it takes more than a declaration to become a sustainable energy company; therefore, it began to take on a new approach to stakeholders in the early 1990s.

A new approach to stakeholder collaboration

One of the major objectives of Suncor's new framework was to increase communication, consultation, and collaboration with the company's stakeholders, so issues and concerns could be more clearly understood and resolved. This was a new approach for Suncor—the company had historically taken an approach of informing stakeholders, often after decisions had been made rather than at the planning stages of business opportunities. Under the new approach, however, it has sought to adopt a more comprehensive approach to address stakeholder relations. Underlying the need for stakeholder collaboration for building alliances and partnerships and developing inclusionary processes focused on solutions. This is built on a belief by senior management that supplying energy in a manner that meets the economic, environmental, and social expectations of stakeholders—customers, shareholders, communities, governments, employees, and interest groups—creates a solid foundation for increasing shareholder value over the long term.

To address the core of this initiative, Suncor began a process of canvassing the views of others and incorporating their ideas and concerns into business decisions. This led to stronger relationships with key stakeholders, sometimes even leading to specific memoranda of understanding that outlined mutual issues, obligations, and commitments.

Specifically, once identified, stakeholders are involved through:

- information-sharing (providing timely information to stakeholders through news releases, mailings, advertising, websites, community newsletters, and public meetings);
- consultation (meeting and working with stakeholders to resolve issues and concerns); and
- collaboration (providing opportunities for shared decision-making through partnerships, alliances, and multi-stakeholder forums).

There is no 'one size fits all' model for Suncor's approach to stakeholder relations. But some common steps are applied in every instance. To help identify stakeholders, Suncor considers:

- the environmental, economic, social (cultural, lifestyle) impacts of the business;
- a stakeholder's proximity to the company or project;
- the national/international interests and/or issues at stake; and
- critical landmarks of public interest (historical sites, environmentally sensitive areas).

Cumulative Environmental Management Association

An example of Suncor's multi-stakeholder collaboration is the Cumulative Environmental Management Association (CEMA), a voluntary process co-founded by Suncor that emerged as a result of rapid development of natural resources and the increasing concerns of the cumulative environmental impacts in the regional municipality of Wood Buffalo of Northern Alberta, Canada. While the process was inaugurated in June 2000, active participation and involvement of stakeholders preceded CEMA throughout the 1990s.

In 1997, after several oil sands companies publicly announced their intentions to expand current operations or construct new projects, a handful of these players gathered to discuss cooperative approaches to Cumulative Effects Assessment (CEA). As expansion of the oil sands developed, the societal demands for sustainable development increased. The public was demanding that cumulative environmental impacts be addressed and managed. It was evident from the beginning that regional stakeholders must play a meaningful role in CEA and ongoing environmental management. A series of consultation exercises and workshops with industry and stakeholders (regional First Nations and Metis Locals) were organized to gain a better understanding of the environmental issues.

During a period of intense project application reviews in late 1998, a smaller group of CEMA participants agreed a memorandum of understanding to advance the development of regional guidelines, objectives, and management systems for acidifying emissions and ground-level ozone. Early in 2000 CEMA was transformed into an official association, which is managed by an executive director and administrative staff. Currently, the association has forty-three members representing aboriginal groups, interest groups, all levels of government, and industry.

Results

Suncor found that strategic involvement of stakeholders often leads to better ideas, reduce risk, the resolution of outstanding issues, increased savings, and significant improvements in the decision-making process and the overall development of more sound solutions. Suncor has been able to ascribe many of its key successes to stakeholder engagement. Relationships have been built and trust has been improved between Suncor and the aboriginal communities and other environmental and social interest groups and individuals. This has allowed the company to benefit from a higher level of public acceptance for its commercial developments: amongst other developments, the company was able quickly to secure permission to expand significantly its oil sands development in the Athabasca oil sands region in northern Alberta.

Stakeholder relations have become an integral part of the way Suncor conducts business. Operating on a set of principles that guide and influence the company's relationships, Suncor has gained significant experience and respect among its stakeholders. Today, it is engaged with stakeholders and leads a number of regional, national, and international partnerships between local communities, environmental organizations, governments, and other industry partners to find solutions for global issues such as climate change and more regional issues such as smog, acid rain, water quality, and land reclamation. Suncor is an established leader on environmental issues in Canada and, as such, has a competitive advantage over other international energy companies in North America.

Suncor's approach to stakeholder engagement has been studied by the managers of many global companies. It provides an interesting example of how a company which has operations in only two countries (Canada and the US), serves as a role model for globally operating businesses.

Source: This case study was drawn from 'SUNCOR: success through stakeholder collaboration: valuing diversity', available from the World Business Council for Sustainable Development (WBCSD) website at www.wbcsd.ch. The case study is reproduced by permission of WBCSD and Suncor Energy Inc. For more information, contact Dianne Humphries, Suncor (DHumphries@Suncor.com).

Discussion questions

1 Discuss the main benefits of Suncor Energy's new approach to stakeholder collaboration.

2 What might be some of the problems of adopting this approach to stakeholder collaboration by a large global shoe-manufacturing firm with hundreds of suppliers in different countries?

REFERENCES

Agle, B. R., Mitchell, R. K., and Sonnenfeld, J. A. (1999). 'Who matters to CEOs? An investigation of stakeholder attributes and salience, corporate performance, and CEO values', *Academy of Management Journal* 42(5): 507–25.

Bendell, Jem (2000). 'Introduction: working with stakeholder pressure for sustainable development', in Jem Bendell (ed.), *Terms for Endearment: Business, NGOs and Sustainable Development* (Sheffield: Greenleaf).

Bray, John (2000). 'Web Wars: NGOs, companies and governments in an internet-connected world', in Jem Bendell (ed.), *Terms for Endearment: Business, NGOs and Sustainable Development* (Sheffield: Greenleaf).

Chang, S. J., and Ha, Daesung (2001). 'Corporate governance in the twenty-first century: new managerial concepts for supranational corporations', *American Business Review* 19: 32–44.

Clarkson, M. B. E. (1995). 'A stakeholder framework for analyzing and evaluating corporate social performance', *Academy of Management Review* 20(1): 92–117.

Dicken, Peter (2003). *Global Shift: Reshaping the Global Economic Map in the 21st Century*, 4th edn. (London: Sage).

Donaldson, Thomas, and Preston, Lee E. (1995). 'The stakeholder theory of the corporation: concepts, evidence, and implications', *Academy of Management Review* 20(1): 65–91.

Elkington, John (1997). *Cannibals with Forks: The Triple Bottom Line of 21st Century Business* (Oxford: Capstone).

——and Fennel, Shelly (2000). 'Partners for sustainability', in Jem Bendell (ed.), *Terms for Endearment: Business, NGOs and Sustainable Development* (Sheffield: Greenleaf).

Freeman, R. Edward (1984). *Strategic Management: A Stakeholder Approach* (Boston: Pitman).

Friedman, Milton (1963). *Capitalism and Freedom* (Chicago: University of Chicago Press).

Frynas, Jedrzej George (2003). 'The transnational garment industry in South and South-East Asia: a focus on labor rights', in Jedrzej George Frynas and Scott Pegg (eds.), *Transnational Corporations and Human Rights* (London: Palgrave).

Graham, J. L. (1983). 'Foreign corrupt practices: a manager's guide', *Columbia Journal of World Business* (fall): 89–94.

Handy, Charles (1994). *The Age of Paradox* (Cambridge, Mass.: Harvard Business School).

Henderson, David (2001). *Misguided Virtue: False Notions of Corporate Social Responsibility* (London: Institute of Economic Affairs).

Hillman, Amy J., and Keim, Gerald D. (2001). 'Shareholder value, stakeholder management, and social issues: what's the bottom line?', *Strategic Management Journal* 22: 125–39.

Howarth, S. (1997). *A Century in Oil: The 'Shell' Transport and Trading Company 1897–1997* (London: Weidenfeld & Nicolson).

Jackson, Terence (2000). 'Management ethics and corporate policy: a cross-cultural comparison', *Journal of Management Studies* 37(3): 349–69.

Jawahar, I., and McLaughlin, G. (2001). 'Toward a descriptive stakeholder theory: an organizational life cycle approach', *Academy of Management Review* 26(3): 397–414.

Korten, David C. (1995). *When Corporations Rule the World* (London: Earthscan).

Lane, H. W., and Simpson, D. G. (1984). 'Bribery in international business: whose problem is it?', *Journal of Business Ethics* 3: 118–37.

Leyshon, A. (1992). 'The transformation of regulatory order: regulating the global economy and environment', *Geoforum* 23: 249–67.

McDonald, Gael M., and Zepp, Raymond A. (1988). 'Ethical perceptions of Hong Kong Chinese business managers', *Journal of Business Ethics* 7: 835–45.

Mitchell, Ronald K., Agle, Bradley R., and Wood, D. J. (1997). 'Toward a theory of stakeholder identification and salience: defining the principle of who or what really counts', *Academy of Management Review* 22(4): 853–86.

Newell, Peter (2000). 'Globalization and the new politics of sustainable development', in Jem Bendell (ed.), *Terms for Endearment: Business, NGOs and Sustainable Development* (Sheffield: Greenleaf).

Ottaway, Marina (2001). 'Reluctant missionaries', *Foreign Policy* (July–Aug.): 44–54.

Parkinson, John (1999). 'The socially responsible company', in Michael K. Addo (ed.), *Human Rights Standards and the Responsibility of Transnational Corporations* (The Hague: Kluwer Law International).

Pauly, L. W., and Reich, S. (1997). 'National structures and multinational corporate behaviour: enduring differences in the age of globalization', *International Organization* 51(1): 1–30.

Pegg, Scott (2003). 'An emerging market for the new millennium: transnational corporations and human rights', in Jedrzej George Frynas and Scott Pegg (eds.), *Transnational Corporations and Human Rights* (London: Palgrave).

Porter, M. (1985). *Competitive Advantage: Creating and Sustaining Superior Performance* (New York: Free Press).

Schneidewind, Uwe, and Petersen, Holger (2000). 'Change the rules! Business–NGO relations and structuration theory', in Jem Bendell (ed.), *Terms for Endearment: Business, NGOs and Sustainable Development* (Sheffield: Greenleaf).

Steger, Ulrich (2003). *Corporate Diplomacy: The Strategy for a Volatile, Fragmented Business Environment* (Chichester: Wiley).

Taylor, T. C., Kazakov, A. Y., and Thompson, C. M. (1997). 'Business ethics and civil society in Russia', *International Studies of Management and Organisation* 27(1): 5–18.

Tsai, S. H. Terence, and Child, John (1997). 'Strategic responses of multinational corporations to environmental demands', *Journal of General Management* 23(1): 1–22.

Waddell, Steve (2000). 'Complementary resources: the win-win rationale for partnership with NGOs', in Jem Bendell (ed.), *Terms for Endearment: Business, NGOs and Sustainable Development* (Sheffield: Greenleaf).

Winter, M., and Steger, U. (1998). *Managing Outside Pressure: Strategies for Preventing Corporate Disasters* (Chichester: Wiley).

World Business Council for Sustainable Development (WBCSD) (2000). *Corporate Social Responsibility: Making Good Business Sense* (Geneva: WBCSD).

5

Analysis of the internal environment

Learning outcomes

After reading this chapter you should be able to:

- understand the significance of the internal environment and core competencies for the strategies of multinational firms;

- distinguish between the positioning perspective and the resource-based perspective;

- conduct a resource audit and apply the VRIO framework to a firm;

- conduct a value-chain and value-system analysis;

- understand the importance of comparative analysis.

The internet search engine Google has become one of the world's best-known brands since its launch in 1998. It was voted the top brand of 2003 in a survey of 4,000 branding professionals compiled by Interbrand. Not only is its own website the most popular search engine on the internet; Google also powers the search engines of major portals such as AOL. With a search index in ninety different languages and over twenty offices around the world, the company had over 70% of the global market in 2004, which means that seven out of ten people use Google's web page when they are looking for information on the internet. Annual revenues—through advertisements and technology licensing deals—are estimated to be as much as US$1 billion. How did Google overtake its rivals to become the world's most popular internet search engine?

When Google entered the market in 1998, the company was a latecomer to the search engine world and its success was by no means guaranteed. There were many established search engines, including AltaVista, HotBot, Lycos, Yahoo!, and WebCrawler and others. It was believed that first movers would triumph, as internet users would usually stick with the first search engine that they used. Google proved that this belief was wrong.

It all started when Sergey Brin and Larry Page, friends at Stanford University, began to collaborate on a new search engine in January 1996. Initially they did not want to start their own company, and they approached existing companies such as Yahoo! with the aim of selling their search engine technology. But no one was interested. One business executive told them: 'As long as we're 80% as good as our competitors, that's good enough. Our users don't really care about search.' Brin and Page then decided to go on their own.

From its launch in September 1998, the word quickly spread that Google was different from all the other search engines. The search results were more helpful to users and Google had the largest number of indexed pages—the search index grew to over one billion web pages by June 2000. Google introduced a number of innovations such as the Google Toolbar, which made it possible to use the search engine without visiting the Google homepage by using the Toolbar's search box or clicking on text within a web page; another improvement was the highlighting of keywords in search results. Finally, Google was faster than many competitors such as AltaVista, as search results were returned more quickly.

Another source of Google's success was simplicity. The Google team realized that the simple, stripped-down web page design and easy use were reassuring to both new and old users. The home page barely changed over the years, even though the direction of the company had progressively changed. While new functions were added to the website, Google kept away from adding new tools or features which would make it look less user-friendly or would require much new learning by the user.

Since its launch Google has changed, as the company has become more business-oriented and has concentrated more on generating revenue through advertisements. Google sought business partners and advertising clients to boost its revenues, announcing the first profits in late 2001—a major achievement for an internet firm at that time. However, the company founders Brin and Page refuse to compromise Google's search usefulness in pursuit of profits. In contrast to its chief rival, Yahoo!, Google refuses to charge for search inclusion. Google charges for paid searches, but those results are separate from its main search results and clearly differentiated for users, appearing in a distinct style under the heading 'Sponsored Links'. Yahoo! includes paid placements with other search results without telling the users. The refusal to accept money for manipulating search results helps Google foster its market leadership. 'We feel very strongly that user trust is key to our success', says Tim Armstrong, vice-president, advertising sales at Google.

It is not clear whether Google can remain No.1 search engine forever. One observer remarked that Google could lose its dominant position 'since it takes so little—only a bright idea by another set of geeks—to lose the lead'. Its chief rival, Yahoo!, has in recent years begun to buy up some of the other search engines—including AltaVista, Overture, and Inktomi—in order to increase its market share, and to acquire new technology. More worryingly for Google, perhaps, Microsoft has announced that the company is currently working on its own much superior search engine; the powerful Microsoft could become a major threat to Google if it decided to launch a direct onslaught on the search engine market.

However, Google managers do not seem particularly worried about competition. Even if Google has lost some of the technological ground to others in the past few years, it remains probably the web's largest and fastest and one of the most user-friendly search engines. Google is also likely to remain the undisputed market leader for some time thanks to its wide distribution network (including AOL), strong consumer brand, and product innovation. The Google executives believe that it is much more important to concentrate on how Google can leverage its resources, rather than on what the rivals are doing. Sergey Brin, the Google co-founder, commented: 'I've seen companies so obsessed with competition that they keep looking in their rear view mirror and crash into a tree.'

Sources: various newspaper articles and internet sources.

5.1 Introduction

The last three chapters have outlined the characteristics of the external business in which firms operate and stressed that the organization should adapt the strategy to the business environment. In contrast, the example of Google shows that international success can be achieved by focusing on the firm, rather than the external business environment. Many business writers—just like Google executives—believe that strategic decision-makers should focus on how a firm can leverage its resources, rather than on what the competitors and other stakeholders are doing.

Just as the external business environment is important, managers need to understand the unique strengths and weaknesses of their firm. They need to understand in what way the firm has unique resources and capabilities, what and who creates value within the firm, and how the firm resources compare with those of other firms. In short, they need to appreciate the 'internal' firm environment, which is the topic of this chapter.

The chapter starts by contrasting the view that the external business environment should be the starting point for formulating strategy with the view that the internal firm environment should guide strategy formulation.

5.2 Positioning perspective vs. resource-based perspective

In Chapter 3 we introduced the concept of strategic fit, which suggests that firms must adapt their resources and activities to take advantage of external business opportunities. But some writers have suggested that firms sometimes put too much emphasis on strategic fit. Hamel and Prahalad argued that the concept of fit is unbalanced, and should be supplemented by the idea of strategy development by 'stretch'.

While a firm must ultimately affect a fit between firm resources and the opportunities it pursues, the concept of 'strategic stretch' suggests that managers should try to identify and leverage the resources and competencies of the organization to yield new opportunities or to provide competitive advantage. Creating stretch relates to a misfit between resources and aspirations, and means going beyond what the business environment offers at a particular moment in time. The idea of stretch encourages managers to have high aspirations, and to exploit firm resources and capabilities in ways which rivals find difficult to match, or in genuinely new directions, or both.

The contrast between 'strategic fit' and 'strategic stretch' exemplifies different views on how firms should compete in global markets. Should strategies be developed by looking outward to the external business environment? Or should they be developed by looking inward, to the firm resources? The focus on the external business environment is associated with the 'positioning perspective' on strategy. The focus on firm resources is associated with the 'resource-based perspective' on strategy.

KEY CONCEPT

Strategic stretch is about identifying and leveraging the resources and competencies of the organization to yield new opportunities or to provide competitive advantage. Strategy development by stretch suggests that managers should exploit firm resources and capabilities in ways which rivals find difficult to match, or in genuinely new directions, or both.

5.2.1 The positioning perspective

The positioning perspective assumes that the external business environment determines a firm's freedom to manoeuvre. The successful firm must pay attention to the needs of customers and the actions of competitors, by adapting the company's strategy to its external environment. Firms must be market-driven and externally oriented (Day 1990; 1994). These assumptions underline the Five Forces Model presented in Chapter 3. Michael Porter (1985) argues that a thorough understanding of the five competitive forces will allow strategists to position the firm in a particular strategic group or market niche, which yields sustained profitability: 'Competitive strategy is the search for a favourable competitive position in an industry.'

The key to successful positioning is a thorough and continuous monitoring of the external business environment, which can be done, for instance, using the Five Forces Model. Understanding the business environment will allow the firm to anticipate future changes in market trends. Once a firm positions itself in an attractive market, it needs to respond to challenges by rival firms, it needs to react to shifts in customer needs, and it needs to deal with product and price changes by suppliers.

Advocates of the positioning perspective do not deny that firm resources matter; if the firm does not have the necessary resources to exploit a specific business opportunity, it will not be able to develop a strategy to take advantage of that opportunity. Nonetheless, the external business opportunity—not the internal resource—is considered the starting point for developing successful strategies.

5.2.2 The resource-based perspective

The resource-based perspective distinguishes between firms in terms of their strategic and resource endowments and stresses the uniqueness of every firm in contrast to previous emphasis on the opportunities and threats in the external business environment. This approach assumes that a firm can use superior resources and capabilities to modify the industry structure and/or change the rules of the competitive game (Wernerfelt 1984; Peteraf 1993). The Google founders in our opening case study were not worried about competitive forces in the external environment such as entry barriers and industry profitability, but instead focused on their unique strengths; they have changed the search engine market rather than trying to adapt to the market.

Indeed, many writers suggest that firms must focus on obtaining exclusive assets and developing unique resources and capabilities, which are difficult for rivals to imitate, in order to survive in the new global market. One of the main criticisms of the positioning perspective is that positioning can no longer lead to success in a world which is constantly changing (compare section 3.4.1).

Stalk et al. (1992) suggested that competition was a 'war of position' when the world was characterized by 'durable products, stable customer needs, well-defined national and regional markets, and clearly identified competitors'. It made sense to position a firm within a profitable market and to reap profits over time, if the market structures were relatively stable. But with the onset of globalization of markets, firms can no longer expect markets to remain stable. According to Stalk et al. (1992), the key to success is no longer *where* a company chooses to compete but *how*. So does the firm's external environment or its unique resources and capabilities dictate strategy and lead to success?

5.2.3 Industry profitability vs. firm profitability

Many academic studies have been conducted to determine whether corporate success (i.e. profits) depends on positioning a firm in a favourable market environment or on unique resources. The research findings are partly contradictory. A few studies have suggested that firm profitability depends primarily on the external business environment. Schmalensee (1985) found that the industry environment had by far the most important influence on firm profitability, although his statistical analysis has methodological shortcomings. But this view has now become far less popular: even Michael Porter now accepts that the effects of the industry environment are less important than the effects of firm skills. A study by McGahan and Porter (1997) found that 19% of the variance of return on assets was due to industry effects and 32% due to business unit effects (i.e. unique firm resources). Other studies are even more clear-cut. According to Rumelt's (1991) study, only 4% of the variance of return on assets was attributable to the influence of the industry, while 73% was due to business unit effects.

These results suggest that firms need to identify what they do best, and to see how they can leverage their unique resources to prevail against rivals. But it would be wrong to dismiss the importance of the industry environment—both the industry environment and the skills of the firm matter. Indeed, it would be highly unwise for a firm to focus on unique resources and to lose sight of its industry (see section 3.4.3). The debate between the positioning and the resource-based perspective is one of *relative* emphasis in formulating strategies.

> **KEY CONCEPT**
>
> The positioning perspective suggests that the business opportunity should be the starting point for developing successful strategies. The resource-based perspective suggests that unique firm resources should be the starting point for developing successful strategies.

5.3 Analysing firm resources and capabilities

Until now, we have loosely used the words 'resources', 'capabilities', 'assets', and 'skills'. But what exactly do they mean? Unfortunately for the student, there is no universal classification of these terms within strategic management. But we suggest that it is useful to distinguish between 'resources', 'capabilities', and 'core competencies' when analysing the internal firm environment.

5.3.1 Resources

There is no universal definition of a resource, and resources are usually defined very broadly. Jay Barney (1991) defined firm resources as 'all assets, capabilities, organizational processes, firm attributes, information, knowledge etc. controlled by a firm that enable the firm to conceive of and implement strategies that improve its efficiency and effectiveness'. The firm has so many different resources that it is difficult even to make a comprehensive list of all of them. They include both 'tangible' resources (e.g. machinery, equipment, and other physical resources; location of company premises; patents, trademarks, and other intellectual property) and 'intangible' resources (e.g. the knowledge of employees; managerial skills; a firm's reputation).

With a view to supporting the firm's strategies, it is useful to identify and classify the firm's resources as a first step towards exploiting them, through what is called a 'resource audit'. A resource audit can help the firm to leverage resources more effectively. For instance, the 'rediscovery' by the BBC and Walt Disney of their respective archives of old documentaries and films allowed them to leverage those resources by re-releasing old TV and radio material or selling licensed packages of films to other TV networks. Some of these resources—such as old BBC recordings of the Beatles or old Walt Disney movies—have proved highly profitable.

KEY CONCEPT

Resources are all assets, capabilities, organizational processes, firm attributes, information, knowledge, etc. controlled by a firm that enable the firm to conceive of and implement strategies that improve its efficiency and effectiveness. A resource audit identifies and classifies the resources controlled by the firm with a view to supporting the firm's strategies.

5.3.2 Capabilities

Resources are of limited use by themselves. The strategic decision-maker needs to know which specific resources provide the firm with a competitive advantage over other firms, and a firm must be able to integrate resources into effective strategies. Google's computer engineers, marketing experts, IT equipment, and brand name do not provide value by themselves; Google must have a capacity to combine resources in a meaningful way. A firm thus requires not only resources but also 'capabilities', which have been defined by Day (1994) as 'complex bundles of skills and collective learning, exercised through organizational processes, that ensure superior coordination of functional activities'. Capabilities are about the firm's ability to integrate different tangible and intangible resources in order to provide products or services to customers that are valued.

It would be very difficult to describe all possible capabilities because every firm develops its own set of capabilities that is rooted in the peculiar characteristics of its market, past activities, and anticipated requirements. Capabilities can be as diverse as the ability effectively to anticipate customer needs; the ability to monitor new technology; effective customer service delivery; skilful human resource management; or effective strategy development (Day 1994). For example, some of Wal-Mart's capabilities include effective use of logistics management techniques, its ability to provide lower prices, and its ability to work closely with suppliers through collaborative relationships.

Global competition requires further new capabilities such as effective currency hedging (see section 2.5.2) and global technology scanning (see section 2.7.1). Liesch and Knight (1999) found that tacit (i.e. unarticulated) knowledge on internationalization provided small and medium-sized multinational firms with a key competitive advantage in foreign markets. Unless firms develop new forms of capability, they may not be able to compete successfully in the emerging global markets.

Thinking in terms of capabilities can help managers to concentrate on what the firm can do to provide value for the customer. It provides a bridge between the firm's resources and the requirements of the market, by linking the different resources and business processes to serving customer needs.

> **KEY CONCEPT**
>
> Capabilities are complex bundles of skills and collective learning, exercised through organizational processes, that ensure superior coordination of functional activities. Capabilities are about the firm's ability to integrate different tangible and intangible resources in order to provide products or services to customers that are valued.

5.3.3 Core competencies

Not all of the firm's resources and capabilities have the potential to provide a competitive advantage for the firm. Many resources and capabilities are needed simply to survive in the global market. But some core assets critically underpin the firm's overall success—these are called 'core competencies', a term which refers to the combination of individual technologies and production skills that underlie a company's multiple production lines (Tampoe 1994; Campbell and Luchs 1997).

The concept of core competencies was originally devised by Prahalad and Hamel (1990), who argued that the success of the best international companies lay in core competencies underlying all their end products. For instance, Honda's core competence in engines and power trains gave them a competitive advantage in diverse businesses such as cars, motorcycles, lawn mowers, and generators. Canon's core competencies in optics, imaging, and microprocessor controls gave them a competitive edge in copiers, laser printers, cameras, and image scanners. 3M's competencies in substrates, coatings, and adhesives allowed them to develop post-it notes, magnetic tape, photographic film, and coated abrasives. In all these multinational firms, the secret of success lay in interlinkages between different business units based on a shared number of core assets. The core competencies gave rise to a number of core products, which in turn influenced the development of end products (see Exhibit 5.1). For instance, Honda's engines can be seen as the firm's core product: they help to deepen the firm's design and development skills and lead to the development of end products (Prahalad and Hamel 1990).

Prahalad and Hamel (1990) use the metaphor of a tree to describe the relationship between business units and competencies. The business units are like the branches of the tree, the end products are like the leaves, and the core competencies are like the roots of a tree. Prahalad and Hamel argue that if you analyse a company by looking only at end products, it is the same as if you assess the strength of a tree by looking only at its leaves.

Thinking in terms of core competencies can help multinational firms to concentrate on centrally pursuing innovation and centrally initiating the development of new end products. Otherwise, the firm may be in danger of concentrating too much on strategic groups (see section 3.2.2) rather than on spanning the boundaries of the different businesses using its core strengths. Focus on core competencies can help firms to think of markets in novel ways, to use existing resources in new ways, and to develop new businesses. According to Prahalad and Hamel (1990), core competencies are about 'communication, involvement and a deep commitment to working across organizational boundaries'.

Exhibit 5.1 Core competencies and competitiveness

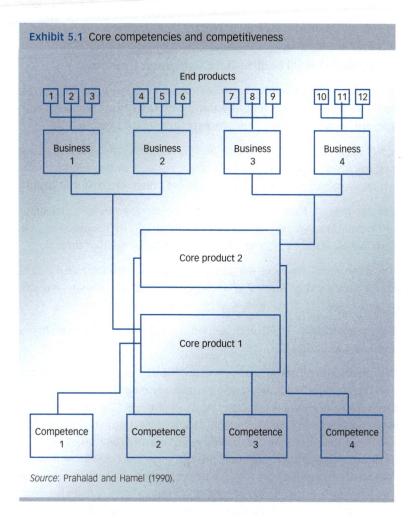

Source: Prahalad and Hamel (1990).

KEY CONCEPT

Core competencies refer to the combination of individual technologies and production skills that underlie a company's multiple production lines and critically underpin the firm's competitive advantage. Core competencies are about communication, involvement, and a deep commitment to working across organizational boundaries.

5.3.4 **The VRIO framework**

We have suggested that core competencies are important. But a practical question for managers is how to identify a firm's core competence. Prahalad and Hamel (1990) suggested that three tests can be applied to identify a core competence:

1. A core competence provides potential access to a wide variety of markets.

2. A core competence should make an important contribution to the customer's benefits of the end product.

3. A core competence should be difficult for competitors to imitate.

A more practical tool for identifying core competencies is the VRIO framework devised by Barney (1997: ch. 5), which asks four questions: whether a firm's resources and capabilities are valuable, rare, costly to imitate, and are exploited by the organization:

The question of value   Do a firm's resources and capabilities enable the firm to respond to environmental threats or opportunities? (A valuable resource or capability helps to neutralize environmental threats or to exploit opportunities to create value for the customer.)

The question of rareness   How may competing firms already possess particular valuable resources and capabilities? (A rare resource or capability is only possessed by few existing or potential competitors, and helps to distinguish the firm from other firms.)

The question of imitability   Do firms without a resource or capability face a cost disadvantage in obtaining it compared to firms that already possess it? (A costly-to-imitate resource or capability cannot easily/cheaply be developed by other firms.)

The question of organization   Is a firm organized to exploit the full competitive potential of its resources and capabilities?

Asking these questions will allow managers to analyse the potential of a broad range of firm resources and capabilities as sources of competitive advantage. For instance, rival firms may imitate new Sony end products through reverse engineering, but Sony's core competence in designing, manufacturing, and selling miniaturized electronic technology has been valuable, rare, difficult to imitate, and consistently exploited by the firm.

Sustainable competitive advantage only arises if firms have resources which combine *all* of these four attributes (see Exhibit 5.2). For instance, Xerox has possessed many knowledge resources which were valuable, rare, and difficult to imitate. Xerox had 'invented' the idea of a personal computer and made great innovations in copying machines over the years; however, the company was not able to exploit its advances in computing and failed to exploit the full potential of its innovations in copying machines.

The example of Xerox demonstrates that it is not sufficient for a firm to spend vast sums on research and development or to have unique resources and capabilities. A firm must be market-oriented and must be able effectively to coordinate all its activities to deliver value to the customer. In other words, a firm cannot afford to ignore the business environment, just as it cannot ignore the development of unique resources and capabilities.

KEY CONCEPT

The VRIO framework asks a set of four questions: whether a firm's resources and capabilities are valuable, rare, costly to imitate, and exploited by the organization. Using the VRIO framework can help managers to identify their firm's core competencies, and ultimately their firms' competitive advantage.

Exhibit 5.2 VRIO framework

Is a resource or capability...				Competitive implications	Economic performance
Valuable?	**Rare?**	**Costly to imitate?**	**Exploited by the organization?**		
No	–	–	No	Competitive disadvantage	Below normal
Yes	No	–		Competitive parity	Normal
Yes	Yes	No		Temporary competitive advantage	Above normal
Yes	Yes	Yes	Yes	Sustained competitive advantage	Above normal

Source: Barney (1997).

5.3.5 Resources and capabilities in multinational firms

Multinational firms have complex structures, with affiliates scattered around the world. A specific resource or capability may exist in some parts of the firm but not in others. Not all valuable assets are located at the company's headquarters (i.e. in the home country). So a key challenge for a multinational firm is not simply how to acquire and develop resources and capabilities, but how to recognize valuable resources and capabilities in its subsidiaries in different countries, and how to diffuse these resources and capabilities to other parts of the company.

As a result of the globalization of markets, resources and capabilities of subsidiaries of multinational firms have gained in importance (Birkinshaw et al. 1998; Birkinshaw and Hood 1998; Gupta and Govindarajan 2000). Global—as opposed to international—strategies demand a high level of subsidiary specialization, as each subsidiary may concentrate on a specific task or activity on behalf of the entire firm. For instance, we suggested in Chapter 2 that firms may conduct global technology scanning by locating the company's research centres in countries where relevant cutting-edge research is pursued (see section 2.7.1). As a consequence, the flow of resources and capabilities from the foreign subsidiary back to the firm's headquarters becomes as crucial as the flow of knowledge from the headquarters to its subsidiaries. Managers are therefore advised to monitor closely the development of resources and capabilities in the firm's international subsidiaries.

Some resources and capabilities in subsidiaries are 'location-bound', i.e. their value is limited to a specific country or area of operations. But other resources and capabilities are not location-bound and may be transferred to the company's headquarters or the firm's subsidiaries in other countries. These resources and capabilities have the potential to contribute to the multinational firm's overall competitive advantage (Birkinshaw et al. 1998). According

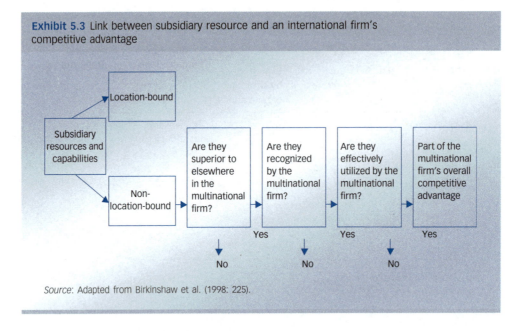

Exhibit 5.3 Link between subsidiary resource and an international firm's competitive advantage

Source: Adapted from Birkinshaw et al. (1998: 225).

to Birkinshaw and his colleagues, this potential can translate into international competitive advantage, if three conditions are fulfilled (see Exhibit 5.3):

1. An affiliate has a resource or capability, which is superior to those resources and capabilities found elsewhere in the firm (otherwise there is no point in transferring that resource or capability to other countries).

2. Corporate managers in other parts of the firm recognize and accept the affiliate's superior resource or capability (otherwise managers in other countries will not be willing to adopt that new resource or capability).

3. The affiliate's superior resource or capability is effectively transferred and is utilized in other parts of the multinational firm (otherwise the resource or capability will not contribute to the multinational firm's overall competitive advantage).

5.4 Global value chains and value systems

Thinking about firm resources and capabilities has become much more critical with the onset of globalization, as firms have come under immense pressure to obtain many value-creating activities from outside the company. In many global industries there is a strong pressure towards achieving more with fewer resources at a faster rate. Multinational firms are expected to restructure, downsize, and re-engineer. The result has been a proliferation of international strategic alliances (see Chapter 7) or simply the outsourcing of certain business functions by buying goods and services from other firms in the market (Insinga and Werle 2000). Many multinational firms have outsourced various functions that were previously considered core to their industries. For instance, car manufacturers hire contractors to do much of their manufacturing for them (Takeishi 2001), while international banks outsource some of their critical information system functions (Insinga and Werle 2000).

Therefore, a key question is *which* resources and capabilities the organization should retain inside the company and which assets it should obtain from outside the company (this point will be fully explained in Chapter 9). In global strategic management, another crucial question is *where* the resources and capabilities should be located. In Chapter 2 we suggested that multinational firms can scan the entire world for the cheapest production location (see section 2.5.1). Therefore, many multinational firms do not simply obtain resources and capabilities from other firms in the market; they must integrate the resources and capabilities of many different firms located in many different countries. For instance, international clothing retailers no longer buy their clothes directly from a large manufacturer, but instead buy from a large number of smaller manufacturers in developing countries such as Vietnam and China, who in turn may subcontract the work to even smaller manufacturers; the buyers often outsource many of the essential processes including the placing of product orders and quality control (see Exhibit 5.4). But how should the firm decide when to obtain resources and capabilities from outside and when it should obtain such external resources and capabilities from foreign locations?

One simple economic rule is that a firm should obtain resources from outside when the costs of obtaining an activity from the market are lower than the costs of doing it yourself. Similarly, a firm should obtain resources from a foreign source when the cost is lower compared with a domestic source. Therefore, managers must understand the economic value of the different activities that a firm performs. The concepts of value added, value chain analysis, and value system analysis can help them in this task.

5.4.1 Value added

Resources and capabilities add value by turning inputs (e.g. raw materials) into outputs (e.g. finished goods). Value added is the difference between the cost of inputs and the market value of outputs; it is the value that a firm adds to bought-in materials and services through its own production and marketing efforts within the firm. A typical passenger car, for example, is made of more than 30,000 parts produced by a myriad of firms in many different countries. Different parts of the car have a different value added, so it is useful to know which parts provide most value added, or—put differently—which activities are most profitable for the firm.

An analysis of value added is equally useful for relatively simple products such as South African canned peaches (see Exhibit 5.5). This analysis shows that South African agriprocessing firms only earn a small share of the value added from the production of canned peaches, with the biggest share going to foreign supermarkets. Indeed, the value added of South African firms may be further eroded due to the growing rivalry between producers and growing concentration among international supermarket chains. As a result of the changing value added in the global market, two of South Africa's largest fruit manufacturers have moved into the more profitable global sourcing and distribution and have opened

Exhibit 5.4 Global sourcing in the clothing industry

In some cases in the clothing industry, resources and capabilities have stayed within the boundaries of the firm. For example, Marks & Spencer buys a large proportion of its clothes from several international manufacturers such as Courtauld, who may import clothes directly from a Courtauld-owned factory in Thailand or elsewhere (see Fig. A).

But such a simple trade relationship has become rare today, and the clothing trade typically involves middlemen, local producers, and subcontractors. Some clothing retailers have their buying offices in Asia, which buy directly from local producers (see Fig. B). For example, C&A France purchases clothes through Mondial, a 100% C&A-owned venture with offices in a number of countries such as Hong Kong, which in turn buys clothes from the local manufacturers in a country or in an entire geographical region.

In the majority of cases, the trading patterns are more complex than the two examples mentioned above. In many cases a retailer employs an intermediary, which can range from a single local agent to an international trading company with wholly owned or controlled clothing factories (see Fig. C). The intermediary can, at one extreme, merely facilitate a business deal between a buyer and a manufacturer or, at the other extreme, can offer a range of services, including placing orders with the local producer as well as managing the quality control process. The services of an intermediary may reduce the profit margins for the retailer or the manufacturer, but they offer a number of advantages, especially in terms of providing the retailer with local knowledge and contacts. The intermediary may buy or facilitate a purchase from a manufacturer. In some cases, the manufacturer may subcontract part or all of the output. In the Philippines, for example, manufacturers reportedly subcontract as much as 75% of their clothing production.

The trading patterns can be even more complex than those described above. An international retailer may procure clothes through a buying office from an intermediary. The intermediary may buy from a local producer, who buys from a subcontractor, who in turn subcontracts the work. Indeed, the international buyer may never learn the names of the subcontractors involved. In addition, a retailer may hire an independent firm to manage the quality control process such as SGS, a Swiss firm specializing in quality control. The search by retailers for cheaper clothes has forced a shift in the global chain for manufacturing clothes.

Source: J. G. Frynas and S. Pegg, *Transnational Corporations and Human Rights* (Basingstoke: Palgrave, 2003), 164–6.

Fig. A   Direct trade between TNCs

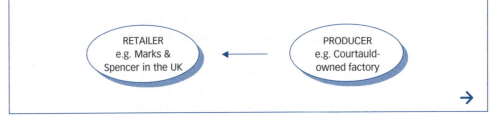

→

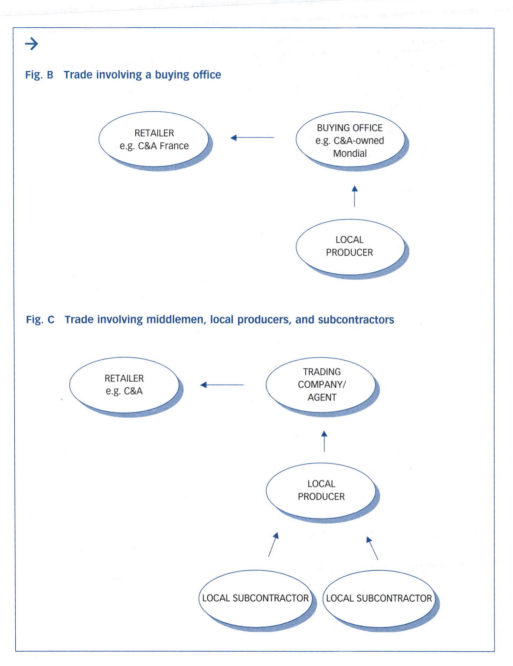

Fig. B   Trade involving a buying office

Fig. C   Trade involving middlemen, local producers, and subcontractors

offices in Jersey and the UK respectively, just as they have sought to reduce their processing operations in South Africa (Kaplan and Kaplinsky 1999).

Unfortunately, detailed information on the value added of different business processes is often unavailable in practice, as managers may not have all of the information on the different business activities (e.g. it may prove impossible to put a value on some types of

Exhibit 5.5 The product value of South African peaches

The firm activity	Contribution to final product value (%)
Within South Africa	
Peaches	12.4
Cans	11.6
Sugar	4.2
Canning, of which:	14.7
7.4% Labour	
7.3% Other (depreciation, utilities, internal transport, etc.)	
Total inside South Africa	42.9
Outside South Africa	
Shipping, duties, insurance, landing charges	24.2
Importer's margin	6.3
Supermarket margin	26.7
Total outside South Africa	57.1

knowledge) or it may be difficult to calculate the value added (e.g. if the firm uses the same overheads to create many different products). But it is important for the strategic decision-maker to have at least a rough idea of the value added of the different activities performed by the firm. For instance, does the firm generate most value added when designing the car, manufacturing the engine, or assembling the final vehicle? Value chain analysis helps to understand where value is created within the firm.

KEY CONCEPT

Value added is the difference between the cost of inputs and the market value of outputs; it is the value that a firm adds to its bought-in materials and services through its own production and marketing efforts within the firm.

5.4.2 Value chain analysis

Most goods and services are produced by a series of vertical business activities, which can include product development, manufacturing, marketing, distribution, and after-sales service. The total economic value created is split amongst them, with some parts of the chain creating more value added than others. Value chain analysis depicts the main activities inside the firm, and aims to reveal the relative value added amongst the different parts of the firm's operations. Undertaking a value chain analysis helps the firm to understand its cost position and to identify its competitive strengths.

Porter (1985) divided the value chain into primary and support activities (see Exhibit 5.6).

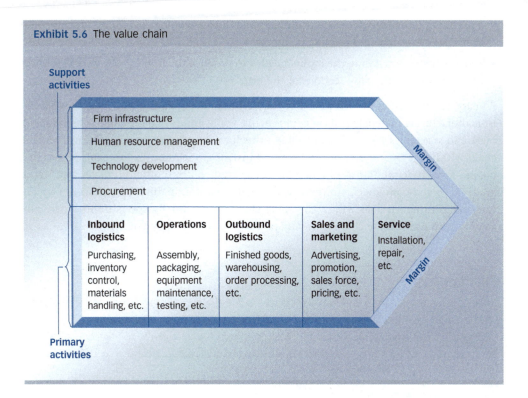

Exhibit 5.6 The value chain

Primary activities deal with those activities needed to create or deliver a product or service, while support activities are designed to improve the effectiveness of primary activities. 'Margin' refers to the value added.

Primary activities include:

- 'inbound logistics': receiving goods from suppliers, storing them and transporting them;
- 'operations': activities needed to convert the inputs into final products and services;
- 'outbound logistics': distributing the final product or service to the customer;
- 'marketing and sales': activities which help to make customers aware of the products or services;
- 'service': activities which maintain or enhance the value of the product or service.

Support activities include:

- 'firm infrastructure': planning and control systems which are important to the firm's performance in its primary activities, and which encompass finance, legal support, government relations, corporate strategy, etc.;
- 'human resource management': recruiting, training, developing, and rewarding people within the organization;
- 'technology development': knowledge activities needed to improve a firm's products and

services or processes used to create products and services, which encompass process equipment, basic research, and product design;

- 'procurement': purchasing the inputs needed to produce the firm's products and services, which may occur in many sections of the firm.

Primary activities differ in each industry. For a car manufacturer, inputs will include specialist manufacturing materials and car components, while inputs of a restaurant chain include meat and vegetables. Vertically integrated firms have more primary activities in the value chain within the boundaries of the firm. For instance, Shell and Exxon explore for crude oil, produce crude oil, transport crude oil, refine crude oil into other products, and sell oil products to end-consumers. However, even the largest multinational firms do not usually carry out all the activities within the value chain. Firms usually specialize in a particular activity, so a firm's value chain is usually part of a larger 'value system'.

KEY CONCEPT

Value chain analysis depicts the main activities inside the firm and aims to reveal the relative value added amongst the different parts of the firm's operations. Undertaking a value chain analysis helps the firm to understand its cost position and to identify its competitive strengths.

5.4.3 Value system analysis

Since firms usually do not carry out all the primary activities in an industry, it is useful to undertake an analysis of all the different activities inside the firm as well as the value chain activities not performed by the firm. A firm is part of a wider system of creating value which involves the value chains of its suppliers, distributors, and customers, which is known as a value system. Value system analysis depicts the main activities inside and outside the firm and aims to reveal the firm's linkages with its suppliers' value chains, its distributors' value chains, and its customers' value chains (see Exhibit 5.7). The value system concept is essentially an extension of the value chain concept to inter-firm relationships. While the value chain is specific to each company, different companies may sometimes use similar value systems; two competing firms may use the same suppliers and the same distribution channels. Somewhat confusingly for the student, writers sometimes use other terms, such as 'value chains', 'supply chains', or 'production networks', when referring to value systems.

Globalization of markets has led to the development of global value systems—sometimes referred to as 'global commodity chains' or 'global value chains'—involving many firms from many different countries linked through contracts and partnerships (Gereffi and Korzeniewicz 1994). Indeed, globalization has led to a shift in value systems in many industries. Global value systems have moved away from vertically integrated firms and value systems based around a lead firm (which gave detailed instructions to its suppliers) towards value systems based around loose connections between firms (Gereffi et al., forthcoming). For instance, in the clothing industry discussed earlier (Exhibit 5.4), traditional value

Exhibit 5.7 The value system

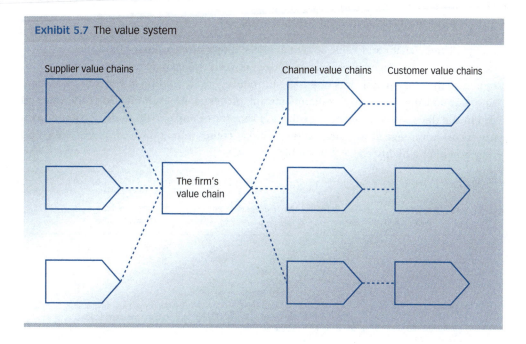

systems involving large retailers such as Marks & Spencer and large manufacturers such as Courtauld have given way to new value systems; globalization has enabled new players such as Chinese and Korean trading firms to become an important element of new global value systems by providing a vital link between US and European retailers and local Asian clothing manufacturers. Exhibit 5.8 shows how the distribution of the value added is changing within global value systems of four industries.

Nonetheless, there is no best way of organizing global value systems. Some multinational firms such as Sony and Samsung benefit from retaining a vertically integrated value chain, as integral product architecture makes it difficult to break the value chain. Similarly, in the clothing industry Zara's success in achieving extremely fast product cycles—bi-weekly in some cases—has been supported by the firm's in-house textile manufacturing subsidiary and close relationships with sewing workshops which are highly dependent on Zara (Gereffi et al., forthcoming). These examples illustrate the point that a firm's value chain and its value system must, above all, match its business strategy.

KEY CONCEPT

A value system is a wider system of creating value which involves the value chains of the firm's suppliers, distributors, and customers. Value system analysis depicts the main activities inside and outside the firm, and aims to reveal the firm's linkages with its suppliers' value chains, its distributors' value chains, and its customers' value chains.

5.4.4 Value analysis and cost advantages

Applying value chain and value system analysis allows firms to understand their organization's cost structure, which provides a bridge between strategic management and accounting. Indeed, value analysis was originally introduced as accounting analysis to understand the value added within complex manufacturing processes. An examination of the value added in the different parts of the organization can, for example, help to demonstrate that a firm's cost advantage in the international market comes from a low-cost physical distribution system or a highly efficient assembly process.

Exhibit 5.8 The changing distribution of value added in four industries

Sector	Links in value chain	Prime source of economic rent			Implications for production activities
		Past	**Present**	**Future**	
Fresh fruit and vegetables	Seed design ↓	Growing	Seed design and new product development	Seed design, new product development	Growing capabilities (climatic specific) are generalized and competition high
	Growing ↓				
	Post-harvest processing ↓		Coordination of value chain efficiency		Economic rents in intangibles (seed design, growing practices, phyto-sanitary practices, etc).
	Exporting ↓				
	Retailing	Wholesale	Retail chains		Battle between retail chains and brand names for shelf dominance
Canned deciduous fruit	Seed design ↓	Growers in South Africa and Australia	European and US growers and fruit canners	Buyers	Growing capabilities (climatic-specific) are generalized and competition high; intense competition leads to falling terms of trade. Low barriers to entry mean *that rents are low throughout the chain*
	Growing ↓				
	Post-harvest processing ↓		Buyers and export agents	Retail chain own brands	*Within individual links*, economic rents are increasingly in intangibles (seed design, growing practices, phyto-sanitary practices, brand names and marketing).
	Exporting ↓				
	Buyers ↓				
	Retailing	Wholesale	Brand names		Battle between retail chains and brand names for shelf dominance
Footwear	Leather ↓	Leather			
	Design ↓		Design	Design	Design is critical as increasing competition in production forces declining terms of trade
	Assembly ↓	Assembly			
	Exporting ↓				
	Buyers ↓		Buying	Buying	Buyers play dominant role in global sourcing
	Retailing		Retailing	Retailing	Brand names of growing importance

→

→

Sector	Links in value chain	Prime source of economic rent			Implications for production activities
		Past	Present	Future	
Automotive components	Raw material processing ↓		Coordination of value chain	Coordination of value chain	Manufacturing competencies become widespread; growth of global sourcing, but intense competition leads to falling terms of trade. Rent achieved *by moving to different links* in the chain
	Design ↓	Design	Design	Design	
	Forming ↓	Forming	Some in forming and assembly		
	Assembly ↓	Assembly			
	Exporting ↓		OEM brand name	OEM brand name	*Within individual links*, economic rents are increasingly in intangibles (design, knowledge inputs into production, brand names and marketing)
	OEM user ↓				
	Spares ◀				

Source: R. M. Kaplinsky, 'Globalisation and unequalisation: what can be learned from value chain analysis?', *Journal of Development Studies* 37(2) (2000), 133.

OEM = original equipment manufacturer.

Knowledge about where value is created in the firm can further help managers to take important investment decisions. It can help the firm to detect where further investment is needed to lower the cost of inputs (e.g. through new machinery) or increase the value of outputs (e.g. through further marketing). Furthermore, value analysis can facilitate outsourcing decisions, which was the starting point of this section. Activities which generate no value added or below-average value added within the firm may simply be outsourced to lower-cost firms. Alternatively, the firm may decide to move into new activities which promise a higher value added, as the two South African agri-processing firms have done in our earlier example (see section 5.4.1).

5.4.5 Value analysis and strategic linkages

The strictly economic value of business functions cannot be the only criteria for deciding which activities the firm should focus on. Some activities may be obtained more cheaply in the market, but they may be of strategic importance to the company and it may be essential for the firm's survival to retain a capability in strategically important areas. Following a strictly economic analysis may indeed have disastrous consequences if the firm relinquishes an activity which is of critical strategic importance to its survival. For example, the US computer hardware company Apricot subcontracted all of its manufacturing to the Japanese firm Mitsubishi in 1988; Mitsubishi later purchased the entire hardware business from Apricot, leaving the latter to operate independently only in software. Outsourcing was an unfortunate strategic choice in this case, as Apricot's corporate reputation critically depended on hardware production which the company no longer controlled (Child and Faulkner 1998: 92).

The story of Apricot illustrates that managers must understand the strategic import-ance of carrying out various business functions, which goes back to our discussion of core competencies. Procurement of high-quality materials or superior product design may provide no cost advantages, but they may help to differentiate the firm from its competitors in the eyes of customers.

Porter (1985) pointed out that value analysis cannot be sufficient to guide strategic decision-making; the linkages between the different activities are also vital. Competitors can perhaps imitate your firm's low-cost physical distribution system, but they may not be able to imitate the unique linkages between resources and capabilities within your firm. Value analysis should therefore be used to identify the firm's unique linkages between activ-ities and, in combination with the VRIO framework (section 5.3.4), can help to identify the firm's core competencies. A firm must excel in *at least* one value-creating activity (a valu-able, rare, difficult-to-imitate resource or capability), and be no worse than its competitors in any other, to sustain its competitive advantage.

As previously mentioned (section 5.4.1), the detailed information on the value added of the firm's different activities is often unavailable in practice. So value analysis is typically carried out without detailed quantification of the value added, and concentrates on rel-atively broad activities (e.g. production, procurement etc.) to identify the strategic contri-bution that each activity makes. Just like the strictly economic analysis, this can help to make vital investment and outsourcing decisions. The main rule for the strategist is that value-adding activities, which are of crucial strategic importance to the firm, should never be outsourced. If Apricot had followed that rule, it could have avoided its mistakes.

5.4.6 Value analysis and global location decisions

An understanding of cost advantages as well as strategic linkages can help firms to decide *which* activities should be carried out inside or outside the organization. As stated at the start, value analysis can also help multinational firms to identify *where* activities should be located in the global value system.

The general rule is that a firm should locate a value activity in those countries that possess a comparative advantage in terms of a specific factor of production. Kogut (1985) suggested that managers should make a location decision based on the distinction between labour-intensive and capital-intensive activities in the value chain. Labour-intensive activities such as clothing manufacturing or food processing depend heavily on the availability of cheap unskilled labour, so they should be located in countries where the cost of production is low (see Chapter 2, section 2.5.1). Capital-intensive activities such as research and develop-ment and manufacturing of new products depends heavily on a highly trained workforce and sophisticated process technologies, so they should be located in countries where the cost of capital is low (see Chapter 2, section 2.5.3). Exhibit 5.9 compares a range of value chain activities in terms of their capital-intensity and labour-intensity (Kogut 1985). The distinction between labour-intensive and capital-intensive activities explains the basis of the International Product Life Cycle we discussed in Chapter 3 (section 3.5.1); the location of

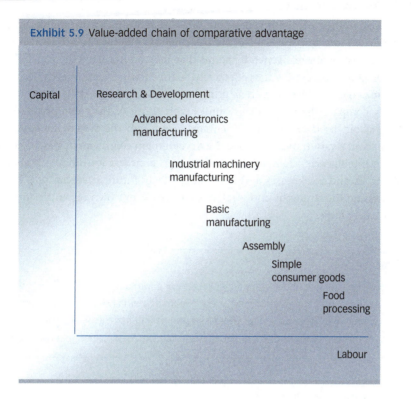

Exhibit 5.9 Value-added chain of comparative advantage

Capital

Research & Development

Advanced electronics
manufacturing

Industrial machinery
manufacturing

Basic
manufacturing

Assembly

Simple
consumer goods

Food
processing

Labour

manufacturing moves from developed countries towards developing countries, as the basis of competitive advantage moves from capital-intensity towards labour-intensity.

Multinational firms also need to keep in mind the importance of strategic linkages when selecting a specific foreign location. This is particularly important when a firm's competitive advantage depends on continuous innovations; in that case, it may be important for the firm to locate in a technology cluster (see section 2.7.1). The Diamond Model discussed in Chapter 2 (section 2.8) may help in choosing a location where innovation is more likely.

5.5 Comparative analysis

The previous discussion suggested that firms should assess their resources and capabilities and their strengths and weaknesses in the different stages of the value chain. But how do managers know whether something is valuable or rare? You can only be judged to have a specific above-average resource or capability if you compare yourself with your peers. If you do not know how many other firms have the same capability, how can you claim that it is rare? Therefore, an integral part of an internal firm analysis must be a comparison with your competitors.

Unfortunately, managers frequently neglect the gathering of information about competitors. An Australian survey of top managers found that 67% of managers see their firms as above average in their competitiveness; but 60–70% rely largely on rumours, personal contacts, sales staff, and newspapers for the information they use to arrive at their strategic decisions. Indeed, managers generally admit that they do not have the capability to gather information about competitiveness effectively relative to their firms' needs (Hall 2001: 4–5). How can managers believe that their firms have above-average skills if they are not able to properly compare their firm's capabilities with those of their competitors? The firm's knowledge about itself can be greatly enhanced through the systematic collection of information about rivals in order to assist the development of firm strategies, which is termed 'competitor intelligence'. Competitor intelligence is aimed at learning both about competitors' strengths and weaknesses and about their likely future strategies and initiatives, as well as assessing the strengths and weaknesses of the firm's own resources and capabilities relative to other firms.

> **KEY CONCEPT**
>
> Competitor intelligence is the systematic collection of information about rivals in order to assist the development of firm strategies. It is aimed at learning both about the competitors' strengths and weaknesses and about their likely future strategies and initiatives, as well as assessing the strengths and weaknesses of the firm's own resources and capabilities relative to other firms.

5.5.1 Competitor intelligence

Competitor intelligence is aimed at collecting information about every company against whom the firm directly competes. But even before you start collecting competitor information, it is important to have an intelligence plan by asking yourself what business decisions you require the information for, and what specific question you need to ask in order to reach a decision (O'Guin and Ogilvie 2001). Competitor intelligence must be an integral part of a firm's strategic development process from the start. Otherwise, you will simply accumulate a lot of data without much effective use.

A practical problem is how to find information. While some key information may be kept secret by the competitor, many sources of information are available to the analyst. The search can start with publicly available newspapers or stock exchange filings by competing firms. It can end with personal conversations with suppliers, customers, and former insiders. It is important to start with publicly available data and then moving progressively closer to the target of your information search, just like gradually peeling an onion (see the 'intelligence onion' in Exhibit 5.10). Publicly available sources may contain much useful data, and the analyst needs to accumulate a minimum amount of knowledge before talking to insiders. The more knowledge you acquire, the more useful questions you can pose to suppliers or former insiders (O'Guin and Ogilvie 2001). Crucially, a firm must be able to analyse the data effectively and integrate the findings into its own strategic development. Indeed, above-average ability to gather competitor intelligence can become a key capability, and could become a source of competitive advantage (Fahey 1998).

A general rule is that competitor intelligence is most crucial in concentrated industries

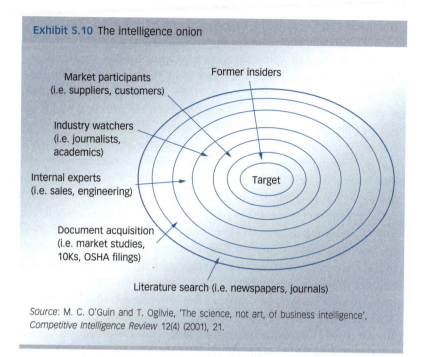

Exhibit 5.10 The intelligence onion

Market participants (i.e. suppliers, customers)

Former insiders

Industry watchers (i.e. journalists, academics)

Internal experts (i.e. sales, engineering)

Target

Document acquisition (i.e. market studies, 10Ks, OSHA filings)

Literature search (i.e. newspapers, journals)

Source: M. C. O'Guin and T. Ogilvie, 'The science, not art, of business intelligence', Competitive Intelligence Review 12(4) (2001), 21.

where the business environment is dominated by a few competitors, whose strategic behaviour is highly interdependent. Chen (1996) suggested that firms should compare themselves with competitors along two dimensions in order to anticipate their strategic behaviour: 'resource similarity' and 'market commonality'. Market commonality refers to the degree of presence that a competitor manifests in the markets where it overlaps with your firm. Resource similarity refers to the extent to which a given competitor possesses strategic endowments comparable in type and quantity to those of your firm. If your competitor shares the same markets with your firm (so the market is important to them) and has similar resources and capabilities to those of your firm (so the competitor's strategies have similarities to yours), then there is a high likelihood that the competitor will retaliate against your firm's strategic moves. To put it differently, if your firm has a lot in common with a competitor, your competitor will watch you carefully and may initiate similar strategies; if you start a price war, for instance, the competitor may respond with the same weapon. This helps to explain why competition is sometimes most intense in concentrated global industries with only two main rivals, such as soft drinks (Pepsi vs. Coca-Cola), photographic films (Kodak vs. Fuji), and civilian aircraft (Boeing vs. Airbus). So competitive intelligence may not only help you to assess the strengths of your own resources and capabilities, but may also help you to understand your competitors' likely strategies.

5.5.2 Benchmarking

When managers lack information about their competitors, they may develop strategies based on wrong assumptions. When low-cost Japanese copiers produced by Canon came to pose a competitive threat to Xerox in the US market in the 1980s, Xerox managers were convinced that Canon sold copiers below production cost to gain high market share at the expense of profits. In order to gain competitor intelligence, Xerox managers travelled from the United States to Japan, where Xerox had a joint venture with Fuji for manufacturing photocopying machines. During their stay in Japan, Xerox managers dismantled a Canon copier and found that it was not only cheaper to make but also of a higher quality than Xerox products. Subsequently, Xerox imitated Canon's materials and methods in order to improve the quality and lower the cost of its own products. This experience led Xerox managers to develop the benchmarking approach, which has since been adopted by many other multinational firms (Cox and Thompson 1998; Camp 1989; Watson 1993). Benchmarking has been defined by Camp (1989: 12) as 'the search for industry best practices that will lead to the superior performance of a company'. The aim of benchmarking is to find better practice processes which show higher levels of performance, and which can be copied or adapted internally by the organization (Cox and Thompson 1998).

The Xerox–Canon case is an example of 'competitive benchmarking', i.e. benchmarking your competitors. Competitive benchmarking can be very successful, for instance, through reverse engineering of a competitor's product. But beyond such simple methods, competitive benchmarking is difficult in practice, as competitors are reluctant to reveal their secrets. An alternative method is 'functional benchmarking' (also called 'generic benchmarking'), which involves benchmarking organizations with regards to specific business activities or processes. This allows firms to benchmark organizations outside the industry or strategic group which may not even share the same value systems, and can help to avoid problems of confidentiality of information (Cox and Thompson 1998). For instance, Xerox benchmarked the direct-mail clothing manufacturer LL. Bean in terms of stock control and warehousing systems and benchmarked Disney's equipment maintenance approaches. British Airways improved aircraft maintenance by studying the processes surrounding Grand Prix racing pit stops, while the English Law Society learned how to improve its phone system from telephone call centres. Indeed, by focusing on the best practice in a specific shared activity (e.g. warehousing or employee training), the organization may learn how 'it is best to do things' in that specific field globally, rather than just learning how 'it is best to do things' in its industry.

> **KEY CONCEPT**
>
> Benchmarking is the search for industry best practices that will lead to the superior performance of a company. The aim of benchmarking is to find better practice processes which show higher levels of performance, and which can be copied or adapted internally by the organization.

5.5.3 Internal comparative analysis

We have so far concentrated on comparing the firm's resources and capabilities with those of competitors and other external organizations. But it is equally important for the multinational firm to compare different parts of the company. We suggested earlier that globalization has increased the importance of resources and capabilities of subsidiaries of multinational firms (section 5.3.5). So a key challenge for an organization is not simply how to learn from others but also how to diffuse its resources and capabilities within its own boundaries.

Internal comparative analysis can be performed in different ways, such as informal discussions involving subsidiary managers from different countries, a comparison of profitability measures between subsidiaries, or internal benchmarking. It is essentially a top-down process. The headquarters of the multinational firm identifies best practices in specific subsidiaries and then diffuses them to other parts of the company. An alternative to such internal comparative analysis is a bottom-up process, by which the firm's headquarters gives subsidiary managers some freedom to demonstrate their expertise and their willingness to take on additional responsibilities (Birkinshaw et al. 1998). But internal comparative analysis such as internal benchmarking has the advantage of providing the headquarters with an overview of performance by all subsidiaries of the company, and helps it to take strategic decisions on how to develop specific resources and capabilities across the entire firm.

Internal benchmarking can lead to major improvements in a multinational firm. For instance, Rank Xerox—the European subsidiary of Xerox—had been less profitable than the US subsidiary for many years. In turn, there were also considerable performance differences between Rank Xerox affiliates in different European countries. While affiliates in countries such as the Netherlands and Portugal could boast a return on assets (ROA) of more than 20% (comparable with Xerox's US affiliate), other affiliates had an ROA of well below 20%. Rank Xerox then identified, documented, and transferred best practices from its best-performing affiliates to other affiliates, which led to revenue improvements of some US$100 million in the first year alone. This example demonstrates that comparative analysis needs to take place at various levels. The challenge for organizations is as much to diffuse best practices as it is to learn from others.

Nonetheless, whether a firm engages in external or internal benchmarking, there will be times when benchmarking may be inappropriate. Even Rank Xerox found that certain practices—such as instituting optimal sales behaviours for salespeople within the company—were difficult to implement in practice. For instance, managers may over-rely on quantitative data rather than trying to understand the reasons for performance measures; it may be very difficult to implement someone else's best practice in a different context; or it may simply not be possible to obtain the relevant data. So a firm should start by carefully asking questions such as 'What is to be benchmarked?' and 'Who is to be benchmarked?' (Cox and Thompson 1998). Exhibit 5.11 sets out the Xerox 'Ten-step benchmarking process'.

5.5.4 Comparative analysis in global markets

Some observers believe that competitor analysis and benchmarking are no longer sufficient to be successful in a global market. Competitor analysis may fail to recognize important trends, which may affect the company; for instance, the firm may fail to prepare for the entry of a new competitor because the new competitor comes from outside the recognized strategic group (see section 3.2.2). Imitation of other firms through benchmarking also has

Exhibit 5.11 Xerox ten-step benchmarking process

Planning	1. Identify what is to be benchmarked. 2. Identify comparative companies. 3. Determine method of data collection and do it.
Analysis	4. Determine current performance gap. 5. Project future performance levels.
Integration	6. Communicate findings and gain acceptance. 7. Establish functional goals.
Action	8. Develop Action Plans. 9. Implement specific actions and monitor progress. 10. Recalibrate benchmarks.

pitfalls, since an imitation-based strategy may only lead to reproducing the cost and quality advantages that your competitors already possess in specific activities; it does not lead to a 'competitive revitalization' (Babbar and Rai 1993).

But comparative analysis still has a major role to play in global markets. As the earlier Xerox–Canon example illustrated, a comparative analysis can help to discover best practice, respond to increasing competition, gain a tactical advantage, or to reduce complacency. Since firms can benchmark the best performers from other industries, adopting a new practice from outside the industry can give a specific firm a competitive advantage over the established competitors inside the industry. Furthermore, since multinational firms have resources and capabilities scattered around the world, internal comparative analysis is important to ensure the diffusion of best practices within the organization on a global scale.

Globalization does not mean an end to comparative analysis; it means that firms must constantly develop and transplant their internal resources and capabilities in order to stay ahead of competitors. At the same time as multinational firms need to devote attention to resources and capabilities, globalization means that firms need to look far beyond their established strategic group and must scan the entire world for opportunities and threats.

5.6 **Summary**

Some writers have suggested that managers sometimes put too much emphasis on strategic fit, i.e. matching a firm's resources and activities to the external environment in which it operates. Hamel and Prahalad argued that the concept of fit is unbalanced and should be supplemented by the idea of strategy development by 'stretch', i.e. identifying and leveraging the resources and competencies of an organization to yield new opportunities or to provide competitive advantage. The contrast between 'strategic fit' and 'strategic stretch' exemplifies different views on how firms should compete in global markets: the positioning perspective and the resource-based perspective.

It is important for strategic decision-makers to understand thoroughly their firm's 'resources', 'capabilities', and, above all, 'core competencies'. 'Core competencies' refers to the combination of individual technologies and production skills that underlie a company's multiple production lines. They can be identified, amongst other methods, using the VRIO framework, which asks four questions regarding value, rareness, imitability, and organization. Prahalad and Hamel argued that the success of the best multinational firms lay in core competencies underlying all their end products.

Not all resources and capabilities have to be located within the firm's boundaries. In many global industries there is a strong pressure towards obtaining many value-creating activities from outside the company, either through outsourcing or through strategic alliances. The concepts of value added, value chain analysis, and value system analysis can help strategic decision-makers in identifying where value is created in the firm. This knowledge can aid economic decisions related to the firm's cost structure and strategic decisions related to the selection of activities the firm should focus on.

Resources and capabilities can only be judged to be valuable or rare if a firm compares itself with the competitors. Competitor intelligence and benchmarking can help the firm to compare itself with others, so that managers avoid overestimating their own abilities. However, even if competitor analysis is used properly, one needs to be cautious about over-relying on resources and capabilities. The firm's resources and capabilities may become less rare than they used to be, or they may lose the strategic fit with the external environment. Furthermore, if there is a radical change in the external business environment (e.g. as a result of a major technological shift), the firm's existing assets could become a liability by hindering the firm from adapting to the new external environment. Therefore, managers must pay equal attention to the internal firm environment and the external business environment. Neither the resource-based perspective nor the positioning perspective can guide strategy development by itself.

KEY READINGS

- On the resource-based perspective, see Peteraf (1993).
- On core competencies, see Prahalad and Hamel (1990).
- On value chains, see Porter (1985).
- On benchmarking, see Cox and Thompson (1998).

DISCUSSION QUESTIONS

1 What is the difference between the resource-based perspective and the positioning perspective?

2 Take an organization of your choice. Identify the key resources, capabilities, and core competencies of that organization. How easy is it for competitors to imitate your organization's resources, capabilities, and core competencies? What changes in the external business environment can make those resources, capabilities, and core competencies less valuable to the organization?

3 Take the same organization. Identify its value chain and value system. Would you advise the managers to improve or change the organization's current value activities?

4 To what extent can competitive intelligence and benchmarking help a firm's global strategy?

Closing case study
Outsourcing at F&C Management

As with most other fund managers, Robert Jenkins, head of F&C Management, a subsidiary of Eureko, a pan-European financial services group, thought long and hard about outsourcing the administration of a €60 billion pension fund business. There were pros and cons.

On the one hand, fund administration was not one of F&C's specialisms—it was something that had to be done. On the other, it was an important service that, if wrong, could upset clients.

In the end, Mr Jenkins elected to outsource for three main reasons. 'One was to convert a fixed cost to a variable cost', he explains. F&C had considerable fixed costs—mainly staff. So, in down times, he had no easy way of shifting the costs to reflect worsening financial conditions. Outsourcing the fund administration operation, handled by more than 90 people at F&C's headquarters near Liverpool Street station in London, was an easy way of doing this. Also, it meant that when market conditions improved, he did not have to go on a hiring spree, competing with others and pushing up employee costs.

'A second reason was to ensure a higher level of service at an acceptable cost for us and for our clients', he says. By outsourcing, fund managers, in effect, pay for the custody bank to update the technology needed to carry out fund administration. If several firms use the custody bank's services, then their pooled resources can be used to invest in the technology, thereby cutting the overall amount they have to pay.

'Above all', says Mr Jenkins, 'outsourcing would allow us to focus on our core competency, which is managing money.' Few fund managers regard fund administration as a differentiator. So, by handing it over to specialists who do, F&C's management was able to devote valuable extra time to the business of portfolio investment.

Having established the rationale, Mr Jenkins then embarked on the tricky business of selecting an appropriate custody bank. He drew up a list of eight to start with. 'We had the full list of suspects', he recalls. Then, he whittled this down to two: the Bank of New York and Mellon Financial. 'They were equally competitive in terms of price and the quality of the bid', he says. 'We wouldn't have gone wrong with either one. It was a close call.'

After some debate, F&C plumped for Mellon, even though it was smaller than the Bank of New York. Mr Jenkins says that Mellon, which already had a tie-up with ABN Amro, the Dutch bank, appeared to be very committed to the European market. For a London-based company with a pan-European outlook and strong Dutch connections, this was important. Also, Mellon had an existing mandate to provide fund accounting services for F&C, something that had been in place since 1989.

F&C entered exclusive talks in July 2003. For Mellon, it was a major business win. Richard Godfrey, managing director of Mellon's European investment administration division, says it felt like going through a classic merger and acquisition process—with all the elation that follows.

But the deal had not yet been finalized. A further four months of talks took place, with Mellon briefing

F&C's fund administration staff who were going to transfer under the terms of a so-called 'lift out' arrangement. 'We wanted the staff to go through a full consultation process in order to make sure that we had a "hearts and minds" transfer', says Mr Godfrey.

By November 2003 a formal deal had been reached, and 93 F&C staff transferred to Mellon. In April 2004 the staff moved into Mellon's new London headquarters near Blackfriars Bridge.

So far, so good. 'Both parties are satisfied', says Mr Jenkins.

But it is not over yet. Later in 2004, F&C's fund administration operation was planning to undergo what specialists call a 'systems migration', and the business will switch to Mellon's technological platform.

Even after this it won't be over as such. 'This is not a typical M&A deal', says Mr Godfrey. 'There, you generally shake hands and separate. Here, you have to live with the deal and your partner.'

F&C and Mellon have an agreement that will see the fund management house paying out according to a variable rate card, as Mr Jenkins terms it. The payment will vary according to four factors: the amount of assets under management, the number of client accounts, the number of securities held in clients' portfolios, and volume of share trading.

'Under the old system', says Mr Jenkins, 'we would have had to have paid our people, whether we were making more or less money.' According to F&C's calculations, its variable costs as a percentage of personnel costs will rise from 27% in 2002 to 40% in 2004. As a percentage of overall costs, variable costs will rise from 19% in 2002 to 33% this year.

It is too early to say if there has been any impact yet. But, if these calculations are right, F&C will be among the most efficient fund management businesses in Europe.

Discussion questions

1　Why did F&C Management decide to outsource an important service such as fund administration?

2　What does this case teach us about the practical challenges of obtaining resources and capabilities from outside the firm?

Source: Simon Targett, 'Why outsourcing made good sense CASE STUDY F&C MANAGEMENT', *Financial Times* (FT Report), 30 June 2004. Reprinted with permission of the FT.

REFERENCES

Babbar, Sunil, and Arun, Rai (1993). 'Competitive intelligence for international business', *Long Range Planning* 26(3): 103–13.

Barney, Jay B. (1991). 'Firm resources and sustained competitive advantage', *Journal of Management* 17(1): 99–120.

___(1997). *Gaining and Sustaining Competitive Advantage* (Reading, Mass.: Addison-Wesley).

Birkinshaw, Julian, and Hood, Neil (1998). 'Multinational subsidiary evolution: capability and charter change in foreign-owned subsidiary companies', *Academy of Management Review* 23(4): 773–95.

_____and Jonsson, Stefan (1998). 'Building firm-specific advantages in multinational corporations: the role of subsidiary initiative', *Strategic Management Journal* 19(3): 221–41.

Camp, R. C. (1989). *Benchmarking: The Search for Industry Best Practices that Lead to Superior Performance* (Milwaukee: ASQC Quality Press).

Campbell, A., and Luchs, S. K. (1997). *Core Competency Based Strategy* (London: International Thomson Business Press).

Chen, M. J. (1996). 'Competitor analysis and interfirm rivalry: toward a theoretical integration', *Academy of Management Review* 21(1): 100–34.

Child, John, and Faulkner, David (1998). *Strategies of Cooperation: Managing Alliances, Networks, and Joint Ventures* (Oxford: Oxford University Press).

Cox, Andrew, and Thompson, Ian (1998). 'On the appropriateness of benchmarking', *Journal of General Management* 23(3): 1–19.

Day, G. S. (1990). *Market Driven Strategy: Processes for Creating Value* (New York: Free Press).

——(1994). 'The capabilities of market-driven organizations', *Journal of Marketing* 58 (Oct.): 37–52.

Fahey, Liam (1998). *Competitors: Outwitting, Outmaneuvering, and Outperforming* (New York: Wiley).

Gereffi, G., and Korzeniewicz, M. (eds.) (1994). *Commodity Chains and Global Capitalism* (Westport, Conn.: Praeger).

——Humphrey, John, and Sturgeon, Timothy (forthcoming). 'The governance of global value chains', *Review of International Political Economy*.

Gupta, A., and Govindarajan, V. (2000). 'Knowledge flows within multinational corporations', *Strategic Management Journal* 21(4): 473–96.

Hall, Chris (2001). 'The intelligent puzzle', *Competitive Intelligence Review* 12(4): 3–14.

Insinga, Richard C., and Werle, Michael J. (2000). 'Linking outsourcing to business strategy', *Academy of Management Executive* 14(4): 58–70.

Kaplan, David, and Kaplinsky, Raphael (1999). 'Trade and industrial Policy on an uneven playing field: the case of the deciduous fruit canning industry in South Africa', *World Development* 27(10): 1787–1801.

Kogut, Bruce (1985). 'Designing global strategies: comparative and competitive value-added chains', *Sloan Management Review* (summer): 15–28.

Liesch, P., and Knight, G. (1999). 'Information internationalization and hurdle rates in small and medium enterprise internationalization', *Journal of International Business Studies* 30(2): 383–94.

McGahan, Anita M., and Porter, Michael (1997). 'How much does industry matter, really?', *Strategic Management Journal* 18 (special issue): 15–30.

O'Guin, C. M., and Ogilvie, T. (2001). 'The science, *not art*, of business intelligence', *Competitive Intelligence Review* 12(4): 15–24.

Peteraf, Margaret A. (1993). 'The cornerstones of competitive advantage: a resource-based view', *Strategic Management Journal* 14(3): 179–91.

Prahalad, C. K., and Hamel, G. (1990). 'The core competence of the corporation', *Harvard Business Review* 68(3): 79–93.

Porter, Michael (1985). *Competitive Advantage: Creating and Sustaining Superior Performance* (New York: Free Press).

Rumelt, Richard P. (1991). 'How much does industry matter?', *Strategic Management Journal* 12(3): 167–85.

Schmalensee, Richard (1985). 'Do markets differ much?', *American Economic Review* 75: 341–51.

Stalk, G., Evans, F., and Shulman, L. (1992). 'Competing on capabilities', *Harvard Business Review* (Mar.–Apr.): 57–70.

Takeishi, Akira (2001). 'Bridging inter- and intra-firm boundaries: management of supplier involvement in automobile product development', *Strategic Management Journal* 22(5): 403–33.

Tampoe, M. (1994). 'Exploiting the core competences of your organization', *Long Range Planning* 27(4): 66–77.

Watson, G. H. (1993). 'How process benchmarking supports corporate strategy', *Planning Review* (Jan.–Feb.): 12–15.

Wernerfelt, B. (1984). 'A resource-based view of the firm', *Strategic Management Journal* 5(2): 171–80.

'Given this reality, we are moving fast—as digital markets demand—to transform our business portfolio, with an emphasis on digital commercial markets. The digital world is full of opportunity for Kodak, and we intend to lead it, as we have led innovation in the imaging industry for more than a century.'

Chairman and chief executive Daniel Carp

Kodak, the company that 'made photography available to all', acquired PracticeWorks, Inc. on 7 October, 2003, to cement its position in the dental practice management software (DPMS) and digital radiographic imaging market (Exhibit: I & II). With them, Kodak would be able to provide a full spectrum of dental imaging products and services, ranging from film, photography and digital radiography.

In the 1990s, the traditional photography industry came under tremendous pressure from the digital alternative. Therefore, Kodak started changing from the traditional film business into a more contemporary digital business. It concentrated on the medical imaging business to reduce its dependence on the waning film business. And this deal might be a hatchet to cling to in its stormy, core business of photography.

Why dental imaging?

Along with the deal, the company was also moving into commercial printing, by hiring a Hewlett-Packard (HP)[1] veteran to head its new commercial printing unit. Though Kodak has been there in the commercial printing business, with its NexPress[2] digital printing system joint venture and Kodak Polychrome Graphics, the business was now given the status of a business unit, with its own head. The commercial printing division is one among the company's five divisions, the others being: display and components, health imaging, digital and film imaging systems and commercial imaging. Furthering the push into commercial printing, Kodak said that it would also get into digital asset management (tracking and storing of digital files), since the market is growing because of the increasing need of companies to store information digitally. It would continue to work with its existing joint venture partners like Heidelberger Druckmaschinen AG[3]. While Kodak was getting into new businesses, it was also broadening its product portfolio (Exhibit: III). It acquired television post-production company Laser-Pacific Media Corp[4] and even the PracticeWorks, Inc. acquisition served the same purpose. Medical imaging was considered an area of profitable growth and Kodak was a strong player in the market. In 2003, Kodak was the world leader in dental x-ray film, and PracticeWorks was a US leader in the fast growing DPMS market. Alexis

---

[1]HP is a technology solutions provider to consumers, businesses and institutions globally. The company's offerings span IT infrastructure, personal computing and access devices, global services and imaging and printing for consumers, enterprises and small and medium businesses. HP is a worldwide leader in ink-jet printing.

[2]NexPress offers world-class color production printing solutions and services to help build your business.

[3]A German printing machinery manufacturer.

[4]Laser-Pacific Media Corp., is one of the world's most technically advanced, digital, high definition post production facilities, offering the full range of services needed by creators of filmed and digitally captured content to prepare their creative asset for distribution.

Exhibit I Eastman Kodak Company

It was July 1888, when George Eastman, the founder of Kodak, first released his camera to the public. But it was the film inside the camera that really allowed for its mass marketing. Eastman developed the first rolled film, which was contained in his Kodak camera.

Eastman Kodak Company is primarily engaged in developing, manufacturing and marketing traditional and digital imaging products, services and solutions for consumers, professionals, healthcare providers, the entertainment industry and other commercial customers. The company operates in four segments: Photography, Health Imaging, Commercial Imaging and Components Group. The company sells traditional film products in its consumer imaging, professional and entertainment imaging businesses within the Photography segment. Products and services of the Health Imaging segment enable healthcare customers to capture, process, integrate, keep in archive and display images and information in a variety of forms. The Commercial Imaging segment encompasses Kodak's operations in imaging solutions, providing image-capture, analysis, printing and keeping in archives. The Kodak components group is comprised of the Kodak display business, the imaging sensor solutions business and an optics business.

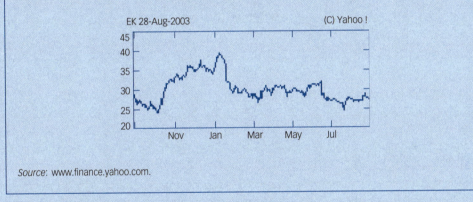

Source: www.finance.yahoo.com.

Gerard, President, Future Image Inc.[5], the leading provider of digital imaging information and analysis, said 'Kodak's focus on Infoimaging—which includes the proposed purchase of PracticeWorks, Inc.—points the company in the right direction. Medical imaging is both a lucrative market in and of itself, and one where Kodak can develop visual information management systems that will later apply to broader markets.[6]'

In 2003, the dental digital radiography sales worldwide were estimated to be $100–120 million annually, but the penetration rates remained abysmally low in the US and other big markets. Recognizing such a potential, the company had long made inroads into this market. Its medical imaging thrust started with the acquisition of Imation Inc.[7] in 1998, followed by a joint venture with Hewlett-Packard for developing photofinishing equipment, which again, was followed by the acquisition of Lumisys[8].

[5] Digital Imaging Group (DIG), an open non-profit industry consortium founded by Adobe, Canon, Eastman Kodak, Fuji, Hewlett-Packard, IBM, Intel, Live Picture and Microsoft to promote the growth of digital imaging. Source: www.futureimage.com.
[6] In an e-mail interview given to ICFAI Press in August, 2003.
[7] Imation Inc., maker of data storage and information management products.
[8] A producer of digital imaging systems for the medical industry.

Exhibit II **PracticeWorks, Inc.**

PracticeWorks, Inc. provides information management technology products and services for dentists, orthodontists and oral and maxillofacial surgeons. The company offers software-based systems, which handle the financial and practice management needs of its customers. The company's practice management software applications help customers in the administration of their practices and in the financial management of their businesses, and include treatment planning, charting and other clinical applications. Cosmetic digital imaging software capability is a recent addition to the company's offerings. The company has recently begun offering digital radiography systems as well as distributor for Trophy Dental, a developer and manufacturer of digital X-ray equipment and software.

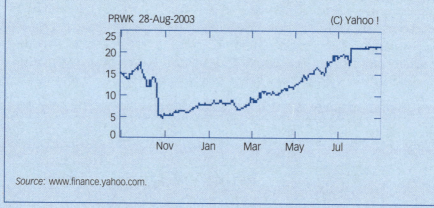

PRWK 28-Aug-2003   (C) Yahoo !

Source: www.finance.yahoo.com.

Product development under Kodak

Kodak's first cameras were simple dry-plate cameras. Later, the company developed a 'detective camera', so called because of its tiny size. George Eastman reasoned that the average person would be more attracted to a small camera than a big one. In 1888, Eastman introduced an improved version of his compact camera, that was small and easy to use.

In 1900, Kodak launched its user-friendly Brownie camera. Unlike other cameras, the Brownie camera was made specifically for children. The important feature that made the Brownie camera a success, besides its simple and effective design, was its price. Each Brownie was priced at $1. As the demand increased, the company set up subsidiaries: Kodak SAF in Paris and Kodak GmbH in Berlin.

By 1935, Kodak was producing Kodachrome, a colour film first used for motion pictures and then for slides and home movie cameras. In 1950, Kodak built a plant in Texas to produce chemicals, plastics, and fibres used in film production. It also designed products for the corporate sector. The company's Carousel slide projectors[9] became very popular in corporate offices in the 1960s.

In 1963, Kodak launched the Instamatic line of 'foolproof' cameras. The Instamatic became Kodak's biggest success. The camera, with the film in a foolproof cartridge, eliminated the need for loading in the

---

[9]The company introduced the first in its very successful line of KODAK CAROUSEL Projectors, which featured a round tray holding 80 slides.

Exhibit III Kodak's Product Portfolio

Products

- Aerial & Industrial Products
- Display Products (OLED)
- Document Imaging
- Scanners
- Micrographics
- Microfilm
- Reference Archive
- Graphics & Printing
- Wide Format Inkjet
- Digital Production Presses
- Graphics Arts Materials
- Imaging & Data Analysis Software
- Image Sensors—CCD & CMOS
- Optical Products
- Precision Optics
- Image Collection Solutions
- Commercial Remote Sensing
- Optical Systems/Space Science
- Scientific Imaging

Product Service & Support

- Document Imaging Products
- Encad Products
- OEM Document Imaging & Storage Products

Other Services

- Document Imaging Services
- Enhancement Services
- Global Manufacturing Services
- Imaging Services
- Imaging Services & Support
- Professional Services

Government

- Federal Government Contracts
- Government Applications

dark. Kodak also became one of the first companies to develop a Camcorder, but the company management was against its launch, thinking that it would be very costly and might detract from sales of amateur movie products.

In 1975, Kodak introduced the Ektaprint Copier-Duplicator[10], pitching itself into direct competition with two firmly entrenched rivals, Xerox[11] and IBM[12]. Having committed itself to a line of high-volume machines, Kodak found itself in the wrong segment, as more users turned to low volume photocopiers.

Kay R. Whitmore[13] continued Chandler's[14] effort to focus the company's effort on its four basic business segments: imaging, information, chemicals and health. Whitmore began to favour development of new electronic products to record, store, transmit, and deliver image outputs.

In 1992, Kodak introduced the Photo CD, a compact disk capable of storing photographs. Here a photographer's roll of film was developed by a photo-finisher, and images were transmitted to the disk, rather than being printed as paper pictures. Storing images on a CD gave users the ability to preserve a large number of pictures on a single disk. Besides, the images could be viewed on a television screen with a special CD Photo CD player, or on a computer screen with a CD-ROM. It was also suitable for emerging telephone transmission and multimedia applications.

In February 1995, Kodak announced its next generation Photo CD imaging workstation, which allowed commercial laboratories and photo-finishers the ability to offer their customers copyright infringement protection for their digital images. Kodak also announced an alliance with Space Imaging Inc. to develop and market imaging products and services for commercial remote sensing markets, such as civil engineering and construction, land management, agriculture, mining, environmental monitoring, tax assessment, and infrastructure planning and management. In March 1995, Kodak introduced a full-featured digital camera. The Kodak Digital camera 40 was targeted at business people who wanted to add digital pictures to their reports, presentations, and other documents published on desktop computers. Kodak also announced agreements with four other companies, to make their digital imaging products more accessible to customers.

- Kodak signed an agreement with Kinko[15] for installed document imaging software and workstations, which would help customers add pictures to their documents for the PHOTO CD Disc[16].

- Microsoft collaborated with Kodak on walk-up imaging kiosks for producing photographs and PHOTO CD Discs. The two companies also agreed to co-brand software to make it more obvious, which Microsoft consumer applications supported digital images.

- IBM joined Kodak in announcing agreements in digital imaging, including one on an internet-based network image exchange.

- Kodak tied up with Hewlett Packard to use HP printers in its complete imaging solution.

---

[10]Kodak introduced the KODAK EKTAPRINT 100 Copier-Duplicator, which received immediate industry acclaim for its high quality copies and the user-friendliness made possible by an on-board microcomputer.

[11]Xerox Corporation offers an innovative array of colour and black-and-white digital printers, digital presses, multifunction devices, and digital copiers, as well as a broad range of services, solutions, and software.

[12]IBM is the manufacturer of the industry's most advanced information technologies, including computer systems, printing systems, software, storage systems and microelectronics.

[13]Kay R. Whitmore was appointed as CEO in 1990.

[14]Colby Chandler was appointed as CEO in 1983.

[15]Kinko Optical Co., Ltd is a Taiwan-based company, which produces high precision items including camera zoom lenses, digital camera lenses, scanner lenses, LCD projector lenses.

[16]The Photo CD system builds a bridge from professional photography to the desktop computer. It combines the quality, convenience and low cost of conventional picture-taking with the benefits of digital technology—the ability to display, enhance, store and transmit images electronically.

In the consumer photography market, the most important development for Kodak was the introduction of its Advantix family of cameras and films[17]. In January 1997, Kodak introduced four new GOLD Films that employ COLORSHARP Technology.

- KODAK GOLD 400, 200, and 100 Films provide the best combination of colour accuracy, colour saturation, and sharpness, across the entire colour spectrum, of any 35 mm colour-negative consumer film.

- KODAK GOLD Max Film is an 800-speed film that delivers excellent picture quality in virtually any picture-taking conditions—indoors or outdoors, stills or fast action.

These new films reflect the consumers' demand for photographic products that are more intuitive and convenient, freeing them to decide simply how they want to use their film, not which film to use.

In 1998, Kodak announced its lowest priced yet digital camera, the KODAK DIGITAL SCIENCE™ DC200 Camera with 'megapixel' (million pixels per image) image quality. The camera operated like a conventional point-and-shoot camera and fitted into a coat pocket. It has built-in automatic flash and a 1.8-inch colour liquid crystal display, that serves both as a viewfinder and as a viewer for reviewing, organizing, and deleting pictures. In the same year, America Online Ltd. (AOL)[18] and Kodak announced an alliance to offer AOL members an exclusive online service. Members will be able to have their processed pictures delivered to their 'You've Got Pictures!' box on AOL. They will also be able to order reprints, enlargements, and other personalized merchandise from photo retailers and to let friends and relatives have access to the images, for viewing and ordering.

In March 1999, Kodak announced that it was expanding Cinesite Inc.,[19] to help drive the rapid convergence of film, digital, and hybrid motion imaging technologies in the motion picture industry. Cinesite will have three separate divisions with the following emphases:

- Digital Mastering—offering its powerful tool for the release of motion pictures in all formats for cinema and television to help ensure that today's films will be long-term assets compatible with future distribution formats.

- Film Scanning and Recording—making high-quality digital film conversion services accessible and affordable, wherever motion pictures are produced, forming alliances with film labs and post-production facilities around the world, and installing and supporting Kodak digital film scanners and recorders at these sites.

- Cinesite Visual Effects—operating visual effects facilities with large creative and technical staff in Los Angeles and London for the creation of motion pictures and TV commercials.

In 2001, Kodak introduced 'Kodak Polychrome Graphics CTP1 Processor'. Kodak Polychrome Graphics provides one of the broadest product and solutions portfolios available in the graphic arts industry today, including a wide range of conventional lithographic plates and thermal plates for computer to plate solutions, Kodak branded graphic arts films, and digital proofing products.

---

[17]The Advantix cameras were based on a hybrid digital-and-conventional technology called APS, or Advanced Photography System. It combines the drop-in convenience of the Instamatic with near 35 mm quality, while adding a host of new features. Advantix also lets a person switch among three different size photographs on the same roll.

[18]America Online, Inc. is a wholly owned subsidiary of Time Warner Inc. the top Internet access-provider in the world. For years, America Online has been the undisputed worldwide heavyweight of the dial-up ISP industry. AOL blows away the rest of the competition when it comes to customers, serving more than 31 million worldwide users.

[19]Cinesite is a Kodak subsidiary and part of the company's Entertainment Imaging division. Cinesite's Hollywood facilities offer digital intermediate and mastering, digital restoration, and scanning and recording services for the motion picture industry.

Kodak Under M. C. Fisher

M. C. Fisher[20], who began his tenure as Eastman Kodak's chairman, president, and CEO in 1993, re-focused the company on its roots—making pictures by selling Eastman Kodak's pharmaceutical and over-the-counter drug businesses. This drastic decision was essential, he said. 'If you don't have the resources to implement a strategy, then you don't have a strategy—and we didn't[21].'

Refocusing the company on making pictures, rather than film and chemical processing, allowed Eastman Kodak to build itself into the digital future, rather than be eliminated by it. Fisher focused on emerging markets where the growth opportunity was higher; the earlier company executives had not focused on developing countries, because they convinced themselves that profit margins would be lower because the price was half. As digital image making became popular, many at Eastman Kodak felt threatened, but he took a different view. 'Digital technology is the biggest enabler of growth and the internet is becoming the primary vehicle for services.' He identified these strategic areas to focus on:

- Marketing—the internet has revolutionized marketing by allowing companies direct contact with customers;

- Watch out for Wal-Mart—old-economy giants will be formidable when they get fully trained on internet opportunities;

- New Value Propositions—new-economy businesses often give away what old-economy companies produce, so traditional companies must create their own new value propositions;

- New Market Values—Dot.com values are not based on traditional earnings/share ratios but on the capacity to create future customers, and they may be priced right.

Even at the internet speed of today's economy, he noted, some traditional business concepts such as valuing customers and employees still count.

Kodak under Daniel A. Carp

Daniel A. Carp[22], who succeeded M. C. Fisher, carried the digital transformation from traditional film into digital imaging, ending a 123-year reliance on film due to drop in sales. He told the investors at a meeting in New York that the company would stop making major investments in its consumer-film business, after a three-year drop in sales[23]. Instead, Kodak would devote the cash to expand into areas such as ink-jet printers and digital imaging for hospitals, pitting itself against companies like Hewlett-Packard Co. and Canon Inc.[24]

Carp also said that he spent as much as $3 billion on acquisitions over the next three years. Carp also emphasized a strategic approach towards new growth opportunity in infoimaging, a $385 billion in-

[20]M. C. Fisher did advanced degrees in engineering and mathematics from MIT. Before joining Eastman Kodak, Fisher served as CEO and chairman of Motorola, Inc., a current member company of CTPID's Internet and Telecom Convergence Consortium. Fisher is a member of the Business Council and a member and past chairman of the U.S.–China Business Council and the Council on Competitiveness. He is an elected member of the American Academy of Arts and Sciences and the National Academy of Engineering. Source: Nancy Duvergne Smith, 'Eastman Kodak's corporate refocus pays off', George M. C. Fisher's Leaders in Technology and Management Lecture, www.web.mit.edu.

[21]'Eastman Kodak's corporate refocus pays off', George M. C. Fisher's Leaders in Technology and Management Lecture, www.web.mit.edu.

[22]Daniel A. Carp took over as Chief executive on 1 Jan in 2000.

[23]Source: Carol Wolf, 'Kodak stocks hit 18-year low', www.insidevc.com, 26 September, 2003.

[24]Originally a maker of 35 mm cameras, Canon Inc. has become one of the world's leading manufacturers in other fields, such as copying machines and computer peripherals, mainly laser beam and bubble jet printers. The company's products also include business systems such as faxes, computers, micrographics and calculators. Canon's camera business consists mainly of SLR cameras, compact cameras, digital cameras and video camcorders.

dustry, created by the convergence of image science and information technology like Health Imaging, The Common Picture Exchange Environment (CPXe)[25] and Kodak's Easy Share Digital Camera System[26]. Carp stressed that although these examples involve the convergence of complex technologies, companies in the infoimaging industry[27] would not be successful, if they focused on the consumer benefits of technology and not on technology alone.

Carp outlined Kodak's four key strategies for driving growth: driving image output in all its forms, making digital imaging easier, maximizing the value of film and developing new businesses in the market.

Driving image output in all its forms was a major opportunity for growth. It was one where pictures could be taken with either a film camera, a digital camera or a mobile phone-camera. People would be able to view, organize, share and print those pictures from any device to any device.

Making digital imaging easier for professional photographers was the second strategic thrust. It was well-known that the Japanese professional photographer demands and accepts only the highest level of imaging quality. Kodak is working hard to make digital as simple as possible for snap shooters.

Maximizing the value of film was going to be a central imaging technology for a long time to come. So, Kodak planned to continue to improve upon film's unrivaled ability to capture high level of image information. It would be designed to meet the exciting, high quality standards of the Japanese professional market. And in the US markets, the new Kodak Plus digital one-time-use camera provides picture-takers with an easy and inexpensive way to get digital pictures without a more expensive digital camera.

Developing new business in new markets was the fourth strategy, which was critical to success. Carp noted that alliances with other companies—including competitors—were essential for infoimaging companies to thrive. Kodak teamed up with a number of players. An example of such an alliance is NexPress, a joint venture by Kodak with Heidelberg[28]. Kodak is currently working with IBM and JVC[29] on a Digital Camera Operating system that would play an important role[30]. Another alliance driving growth was Phogenix imaging, a joint venture that blends Kodak's image science and photofinishing expertise with Hewlett-Packard's thermal inkjet technology.

The digital demon

Two days after the announcement of the deal, on 23 July, 2003, Eastman Kodak posted a 60% fall in the second-quarter profits, largely due to feeble camera and film sales, especially in China (See Exhibit: IV). On the same day, it said that it would slash up to 9% of its global work force, amounting to about 6,000 jobs. The three-year slump in film sales, because of film-less digital cameras, created a dent in Kodak's sales.

Kodak made more money by selling film rolls than cameras, much like in the printing business, where the printer cartridges generate more revenue than the printers. With digital cameras, that source of revenue was eliminated. Therefore, the company was restructuring its photography division into the digital

[25]Through CPXe consumers will be able to capture photos with any digital camera, upload them to any participating photofinisher, and order prints for home delivery or in-store pick up.

[26]It enables images to be digitally captured, easily transferred to a PC, edited, sent by e-mail, and printed.

[27]Infoimaging is the evolution of communications through pictures, enabling people and businesses to communicate, conduct commerce and work together. Kodak is a leader in the $385 billion infoimaging industry, being one of the only companies that compete in all three sectors of infoimaging: devices, infrastructure and services & media. Source: www.ameinfo.com.

[28]One of the world's foremost providers of printing and graphic arts equipment.

[29](JVC) Founded in 1927, Victor Company of Japan (JVC) manufactures VCRs, TVs (high definition, plasma display panel), and home and car stereos. The consumer electronics maker's other products include DVD players, camcorders, media (CDs, DVDs, videotapes), and information and security systems. JVC has been affiliated to Matsushita Electric, since that company bought a majority stake in 1954 (it now owns 52%). Source: www.biz.yahoo.com.

[30]Source: www.kodak.com.

Exhibit IV Eastman Kodak Company and Subsidiary Companies CONSOLIDATED STATEMENT OF EARNINGS—UNAUDITED (in millions, except per share data)

	Three Months Ended June 30		Six Months Ended June 30	
	2003	2002	2003	2002
Net sales	$3,352	$3,336	$6,092	$6,042
Cost of goods sold	2,236	2,082	4,152	3,928
Gross profit	1,116	1,254	1,940	2,114
Selling, general and administrative expenses	716	656	1,282	1,196
Research and development costs	179	192	373	379
Restructuring costs and others	44	—	76	—
Earnings from continuing operations before interest, other charges, and income taxes	177	406	209	539
Interest expenses	34	44	71	88
Other charges	9	22	30	53
Earnings from continuing operations before income taxes	134	340	108	398
Provision (benefit) for Income taxes	22	54	(1)	71
Earnings from continuing operations	112	286	109	32
Earnings (losses) from discontinued operations, net of income tax benefits for the three and six months ended June 30, 2002 of $1 and $2, respectively	—	(2)	15	(4)
NET EARNINGS	$112	$284	$124	$323
Basic and diluted net earnings (losses) per share:				
Continuing operations	$0.39	$0.98	$0.38	$1.12
Discontinued operations	0.00	(0.01)	0.05	(0.01)
Total	$0.39	$0.97	$0.43	$1.11
Number of common shares used in basic earnings (losses) per share	286.5	291.7	286.4	291.5
Incremental shares from assumed conversion of options	0.1	0.1	0.2	0.1
Number of common shares used in diluted earnings (losses) per share	286.6	291.8	286.6	291.6
Cash dividends per share	$0.90	$0.90	$0.90	$0.90

Source: www.kodak.com.

and film division, that would oversee the emerging operations like Ofoto.com, a web site that allows the uploading, sharing and printing of digital images.

In 2003, the company operated in three segments—photography, health imaging and commercial imaging, of which the photography segment comprising the film business, was the least profitable one, while the health imaging segment was the most profitable and the commercial imaging's contribution was marginal. Consumer and professional film, photo paper, cameras, photo processing and digitization services, including online service were the offerings from the portfolio of the photography segment.

Digital products like imagers, radiography, medical products and services as well as speciality products in oncology and dental fields were the offerings in the health-imaging segment. Whereas, the commercial Imaging segments constituted microfilm equipment, printers, scanners and other business equipment.

S'i'mile of change

The photography industry was changing rapidly as consumers prefer to take, store and exchange pictures electronically (See Exhibit: V). It was a fundamental shift in the mindset of consumers. Said Alexis Gerard[31], of Future Image: 'The combination of digital imaging and the Internet—particularly, the wireless Internet—is driving a fundamental shift in communication patterns, by enabling people both in their personal and business lives to communicate what they see through taking and sending pictures, rather than having to "convert" that visual information into language (i.e. to describe what they see verbally or in writing which is what all of us have done most of our lives).' So he was of the view that, accordingly, image taking and viewing will change from an occasional activity, as is now the case, to an everyday activity, and the opportunity for imaging companies will be orders of magnitude greater than anything they have experienced historically. And, he adds, 'Many people at Kodak understand this clearly. However, monetizing this opportunity requires transitioning from a value proposition based on materials, regardless of whether they involve chemical or digital technology, to a value proposition based on information.' Eventually, he says, 'It's no longer about the value of a roll of film or a memory card, or a silver halide print or an inkjet print. It's about the value of the content of the image.' Such potent changes had resulted in a spurt in all kinds of devices having access to the Internet and with inbuilt cameras like the camera mobile phones. So, on the one hand, there was competition from Sony, Canon and on the other side from Nokia and other phone companies. In that view, specialized business areas where Kodak is already strong, like medical imaging, are a safe bet.

The film still rolls on

It was not that Kodak hadn't recognized the shift (Daniel A. Carp and former CEO M. C. Fisher made efforts to tap the potential of digital technology); it was only that the shift had been too rapid for the company to respond. In fact, Kodak confessed that consumers were going digital, much faster than it had originally anticipated. Kodak had digital photo development capabilities, but hadn't come up with digital cameras and its rivals like Canon and other smaller players were flourishing with the increase in sales of their digital cameras.

In 2003, consumer and professional photography businesses accounted for nearly 60% of Kodak's annual sales and it was under tremendous pressure to reduce the dependence on consumer film, as its global sales declined by 6% in the second quarter. At a time when analysts believed that for the first time in the US, by 2003 year-end, digital cameras would outsell traditional ones. Then, IDC estimated that the sales of digital cameras in the US would grow to 13 million units in 2003 and 20 million in 2007, as against 10 million in the year 2002. To mitigate the threat or rather to grab the opportunity, Kodak was launching several digital cameras of its own that year. Also, there were chances of the film business reviving and Kodak's prospects brightening. 'There are preliminary indications that the film market is improving, and visibility on the magnitude of the restructuring plan of Kodak emphasizing its digital focus', said Shannon Cross of Cross Research. She went on to say that risks remained with regard to pricing pressure, increasing digital penetration and the need to acquire in order to grow to the top line.

[31] Alexis Gerard is President of Future Image Inc, the leading publisher of business-to-business information and analysis for the digital imaging industry, which he founded. He is a past President of the Digital Imaging Group (DIG), an open non-profit industry consortium founded by Adobe, Canon, Eastman Kodak, Fuji, Hewlett-Packard, IBM, Intel, Live Picture and Microsoft to promote the growth of digital imaging. Source: www.futureimage.com.

Then again, even with digital eating into film, Kodak continued to find strong demand for its film in areas like China, India and Latin America, not to forget professional areas such as health care (even in dental) and movies. Digital's growth was tied to the penetration of the PC and that of the Internet and other means of Internet access devices like mobile phones.

Kodak's future outlook

Kodak's plan to enter the printer market will put it in competition with entrenched consumer electronics firms including Hewlett-Packard, Canon, Seiko's Epson[32], Lexmark[33], and Computer vendor Dell[34], which has recently started selling relabeled printers manufactured by others.

Kodak planned not to make any more significant investment in traditional consumer film, though it would continue to make private-label film to sell under non-Kodak brand names. Designed to shift investment into digital markets, the company official said its strategy would centre on three broad categories: commercial, consumer, and health[35]. Its commercial initiatives included developing imaging services, such as on-demand digital colour printing, for business customers. The consumer initiatives included accelerating growth of Kodak's Easy Share digital camera business and increasing the printing of pictures at home or at retail location. Kodak's health initiatives involved gaining more market share in digital capture of medical images and building an information services business.

Kodak's move to build its professional digital printing business in areas such as health care, in competition with Xerox Corp., could cost as much as $2 billion for a moderate size acquisition over the next three years and more investment in new growth areas[36]. Additionally, Kodak is likely to sell or close about $1 billion worth of an array of businesses, including the slide-carousel group, which would lead to more job losses[37].

Kodak's management also recommended the dividend rate cut, because the company needed to maintain financial flexibility, while taking advantage of the cash-generation capability of its traditional businesses to achieve the revenue goals[38].

Kodak sets revenue goals based upon its planned expansion into the new range of businesses. According to Kodak officials, a more diversified business portfolio had the potential to generate $16 billion in sales by 2006 and $20 billion by 2010[39]. Kodak expected the strategy to increase revenue by 5 or 6 percent a year, though it would not achieve 6 percent growth this year. The company said that it would also strive to reduce its net debt to below the $2.0 billion level it held at the end of 2002 (Exhibit: VI). It expects an annual earning per share of $3.00 by 2006[40].

[32]Seiko Epson is a global firm based in Japan. Seiko Epson Corporation is in development, manufacturing, sales, marketing and servicing of information-related equipment (computers and peripherals, including PCs, printers, scanners and projectors), electronic devices (semiconductors, displays, and quartz devices), precision products (watches, plastic corrective lenses, and factory automation equipment) and other products. Source: www.epson.co.jp.

[33]Lexmark International, Inc., based in the United Kingdom, is a leading developer, manufacturer and supplier of printing solutions—including laser and inkjet printers, multifunction products, associated supplies and services—for offices and homes in more than 150 countries. Source: www.Lexmark.co.uk.

[34]Headquartered in Round Rock, Texas-based PC maker Dell would enter the market by linking up with an original equipment manufacturer (OEM) or a branded printer maker such as Lexmark, which would then make hardware that gets sold under the Dell brand name. Dell currently sells Hewlett-Packard, Lexmark and Epson branded printers. Source: www.news.zdnet.co.uk.

[35]'Kodak develops a new strategy', www.multexinvestor.com, 26 September, 2003.

[36]'Kodak redevelops itself', www.money.cnn.com, 25 September, 2003.

[37]'Kodak redevelops itself', www.money.cnn.com, 25 September, 2003.

[38]'Kodak unveils digitally oriented strategy to accelerate Growth', www.money.cnn.com.

[39]'Kodak develops a new strategy', www.multexinvestor.com, 26 September, 2003.

[40]'Kodak redevelops itself', www.money.cnn.com, 25 September, 2003.

Kodak's revenue goal would feature short, medium and long-term objectives. Over the next 2 years, it would cut cost and manage its traditional film business for cash and manufacturing share. Two to five years from 2003, Kodak would use cash generation to strengthen its strategic growth forays. After five years, it would expand its reach to build new business in commercial workflow management, mobile imaging, and both flat-panel and flexible film display[41].

Kodak announced a new mobile service on 11 December, 2003, as a move to boost revenue[42]. It launched 'kmobile.com website', through which camera phone users would beam their pictures directly to the Internet to be stored, accessed and viewed from anywhere via camera phone or personal computer (PC). And the user could also log on to order Kodak prints. The company also said that, starting in the first quarter of 2004, cell phone users would be able to beam the photos they want printed to the 24,000 printing kiosks the company has in US retail stores such as Wal-Mart Stores[43] and CVS[44]. Currently, only camera phone users whose handsets have removable memory cards can use these kiosks[45]. Kodak also cut a special deal with Nokia[46], which would put a direct wireless link to Kodak's kiosks on its phone screens. Besides these, Kodak has a deal with Cingular Wireless[47], as a part of which, it will be the

---

Exhibit V Digital camera vs. film camera

The fundamental difference between digital and 35 mm cameras[48] is that 35 mm cameras use traditional 35 mm film, which can be purchased at gas stations, discount stores, grocery stores or anywhere. But digital cameras don't use any type of film at all. Digital cameras record the photographed image onto a built-in-chip, a memory card or a disk. Digital cameras excel in the area of image developing. Because there is no film in a digital camera, there is no cost or time involved in developing the image, unlike 35 mm camera. If the digital camera has an LCD screen, image would turn out immediately after taking the picture. The camera can be directly attached to the printer or printer that has a slot for the camera's memory card, and then photos can be directly printed from the camera. Otherwise, uploading them onto computer would print that. But in the case of 35 mm camera, it is easy to have 35 mm film developed. After shooting off a roll of film, the developing part will be done by the photo developer.

In the under $400 price range, many film cameras offer special focusing features like fixed focus[49] and auto-focus[50] but a few digital cameras priced under US$400 have both fixed and auto-focus abilities. Under this price range, there are 35 mm camera zoom lenses of up to 200 mm but digital cameras provide shorter zoom range[51].

Source: www.cameras.about.com.

---

[41] 'Kodak develops a new strategy', www.multexinvestor.com, 26 September, 2003.
[42] 'Kodak polishes its (mobile) image', www.forbes.com, 11 December, 2003.
[43] Wal Mart is a major retailer and has stores in most of the US states.
[44] Consumer Value Corporation (CVS), headquartered in Woonsocket, R.I., is America's largest drug store chain with more than 4,000 stores in 24 states and the District of Columbia. Source: www.verifone.com.
[45] Penelope Patsuris, 'Kodak polishes its (mobile) image', 11 December, 2003.
[46] Nokia, based in Finland, is the world leader in mobile communications. Source: www.nokia.com.
[47] The No. 2 wireless carrier that is a joint venture between SBC and BellSouth.
[48] 35 mm camera is known as film camera because it uses 35 mm film.
[49] Fixed focus keeps the entire scene crisp and in focus.
[50] Auto-focus keeps the subject in focus, but leaves the rest of the scene blurred, which gives a dramatic look.
[51] Source: www.cameras.about.com.

exclusive photo site for Cingular. With so many initiatives, Kodak seems to be cementing its position in the digital era. However, many analysts feel that it will be very difficult for Kodak to return to its golden days when photography and camera were synonymous with the company name 'Kodak'.

Exhibit VI Eastman Kodak Company and Subsidiary Companies Consolidated Statement of Earnings

(in millions, except per share data)	For the Year Ended December 31		
	2000	2001	2002
Net sales	$ 13,994	$ 13,229	$ 12,835
Cost of goods sold	8,375	8,661	8,225
Gross profit	5,619	4,568	4,610
Selling, general and administrative expenses	2,514	2,625	2,530
Research and development costs	784	779	762
Goodwill amortization	151	153	—
Restructuring costs (credits) and others	(44)	659	98
Earnings from continuing operations before interest, other (charges) income, and income taxes	2,214	352	1,220
Interest expenses	178	219	173
Other (charges) income	96	(18)	(101)
Earnings from continuing operations before income taxes	2,132	115	946
Provision for income taxes	725	34	153
Earnings from continuing operations	$ 1,407	$ 81	$ 793

→

→

(in millions, except per share data)	For the Year Ended December 31		
	2000	2001	2002
Loss from discontinued operations, net of income tax benefits of $15, $2 and $0 for the years ending December 31, 2002, 2001 and 2000, respectively	—	$ (5)	$ (23)
Net earnings	$ 1,407	$ 76	$ 770
Basic net earnings (loss) per share			
Continuing Operations	$ 4.62	$ 0.28	$ 2.72
Discontinued Operations	—	(0.02)	(0.08)
Total	$ 4.62	$ 0.26	$ 2.64
Diluted net earnings (loss) per share			
Continuing Operations	$ 4.59	$ 0.28	$ 2.72
Discontinued Operations	—	(0.02)	(0.08)
Total	$ 4.59	$ 0.26	$ 2.64
Number of common shares used in basic earnings per share	304.9	290.6	291.5
Incremental shares from assumed conversion of options	1.7	0.4	0.2
Number of common shares used in diluted earnings per share	306.6	291.0	291.7
Cash dividends per share	$ 1.76	$ 2.21	$ 1.80

Source: www.kodak.com.

REFERENCES

1. 'Kodak develops a new strategy', www.marketmavens.com, 26 September, 2003.
2. 'Kodak redevelops itself', www.money.cnn.com, 25 September, 2003.
3. 'Kodak unveils digitally oriented strategy to accelerate growth', www.money.cnn.com, 25 September, 2003.
4. 'Kodak directions for the 21st century', www.kodak.com, 12 June, 2003.
5. 'The Kodak case', www.aurorawdc.com.
6. 'Digital cameras vs. film cameras', www.cameras.about.com.
7. Bruce Upbin 'Kodak's digital moment', www.forbes.com 8 August, 2000.
8. Carol Wolf, 'Kodak stocks hit 18-year low', www.insdevc.com, 26 September, 2003.
9. 'Kodak CEO outlines emerging platform for economic expansion: Infoimaging', www.businesswire.com.
10. Art Jahnke, 'Kodak stays in digital picture', www.cnn.com, 6 August, 1999.
11. Chana R. Schoenberger, 'Can Kodak make up for lost moments?' www.forbes.com, 10 June, 2003.
12. Nancy Duvergne smith, 'Eastman Kodak's corporate refocus pays off', George M. C Fisher's Leaders in Technology and Management Lecture, www.web.mit.edu.
13. 'Kodak launches digital film service', www.dpreview.com, 3 February, 2000.
14. Chana R. Schoenberger, 'Can Kodak make up for lost moments?' www.forbes.com, 10 October, 2003.
15. 'Eastman Kodak disappoints', www.fool.com, 16 September, 2003.
16. 'Film vs. digital: can Kodak build a bridge', www.businessweek.com, 2 August, 1999.
17. Art Jahnke, 'Kodak stays in the digital picture', www.cnn.com.
18. www.kodak.com.

PART III

Global strategic development

6

Managing the internationalization process

Learning outcomes

After reading this chapter you should be able to:

- understand the motives for internationalization;

- explain the theories underpinning the internationalization process;

- explain the Born Global concept;

- understand the different modes of entry strategies employed by multinational firms;

- understand the de-internationalization process.

Opening case study
The internationalization of Carrefour—life the way we want it!

In 1959 the Fournier and Defforey families established the Carrefour company. A few months later, in the summer of 1960, the company opened its first supermarket in Annecy, Haute Savoie, in France. In 1963 Carrefour invented a new store concept—the hypermarket. The hypermarket concept was novel, and revolutionized the way French people did their shopping. It moved daily shopping from small stores to enormous stores where customers find everything they want under one roof, in addition to self-service, discount price, and free parking space. The first Carrefour hypermarket store was established at the intersection of five roads—hence the name Carrefour, which means 'crossroads'. The first Carrefour hypermarket opened in Sainte Geneviève des Bois, with a floor area of 2,500 m², twelve checkouts, and free parking space for 450 cars. By 2003 Carrefour had become the leading retailer in Europe and the second largest worldwide. It is now the market leader in nine countries and has more than 9,200 stores in thirty countries. In 2003 more than 50% of its revenues came from its international stores.

In 1969 Carrefour opened its first hypermarket store outside France, in Belgium. Although French consumers welcomed the hypermarket concept, smaller stores lobbied against the spread of hypermarket stores in the late 1960s and early 1970s, and in 1973 the French legislature introduced the Royer Law, which restricted the introduction of more hypermarkets. Carrefour had no choice but to expand internationally. It first moved to neighbouring European countries: Switzerland in 1970, Britain and Italy in 1972, and Spain in 1973. However, Carrefour soon withdrew from the Belgian and British markets, focusing mainly on southern European and Latin American countries where the distribution system was not yet modernized. In 1975 it expanded its format outside Europe, to Brazil. Carrefour's internationalization strategy further accelerated in the 1980s and 1990s (see Exhibit A).

Carrefour's international strategy is based on the hypermarket format with local adaptability. For example, while the store format is the same anywhere around the world, the company sells hot meals to French customers in France and pasta in Argentina and Italy, and has sushi bars in most Asian countries. The success of Carrefour's export of its hypermarket concept is due, at least in part, to its careful choice of countries and to its ability to adapt its format to local business environments. As shown in Exhibit A, most countries are emerging economies with a growing urban middle-class population that find the hypermarket concept appealing.

The international concept of Carrefour is based on:

- A simple and clear idea: People in major cities prefer to do all their shopping under one roof. Carrefour's logic is based on the belief that choice, self-service, free parking, and low prices have universal appeal. Although these principles might seem simple, the introduction of free parking in South Korea and Singapore was considered revolutionary given the high cost of land in these countries;

- Evolving ideas: Each hypermarket around the world is expected to keep reinventing itself to meet the demands of local customers. For instance, the company has recently introduced organic food in France, optical shops and tyre fitting in Taiwan, and petrol stations in Argentina.

As shown in Exhibit A, different formats are present in different countries. While the hypermarket model is the only format in emerging economies in South America (with the exception of Brazil and Argentina) and Asia, different formats exist in European countries. This is mainly due to (1) planning restrictions on building hypermarkets in Western European countries and (2) historical growth through acquisition of small outlets. In addition, in contrast to its standard entry mode by ownership, Carrefour entered several countries—the United Arab Emirates, Madagascar, Qatar, Romania, the Dominican Republic, Tunisia—through a franchise partnership.

Exhibit A International development of Carrefour

Year	Country and mode of entry	No. of stores (1999)	Formats
1969	Belgium—Carrefour's first hypermarket outside France	483	60(HM), 423(SM)
1973	Spain: under the store Pryca banner. In 1979 it introduced the hard discount store in Spain.	3,098	117(HM), 180(SM), 2239(HD), 532(CS), 30(CC)
1975	Brazil	193	69(HM), 124(SM)
1982	Argentina	300	22(HM), 133(HD), 145(SM)
1989	Taiwan—the first in Asia	32	HM
1993	Italy	912	38(HM), 288(SM), 532(CS), 9(C&C), 47(FF)
1993	Turkey	32	7(HM), 25(HD)
1994	Mexico	17	HM
1994	Malaysia	6	HM
1995	China	23	HM
1996	Thailand	10	HM
1996	Korea	15	HM
1996	Hong Kong	2 (in 1988)	HM
1997	Poland	16	7(HM), 27 Global (SM)
1997	Singapore	1	HM
1998	Chile	2	HM
1998	Colombia	2	HM
1998	Indonesia	7	HM
1999	Czech Republic	5	HM
2000	Greece	313	14(HM), 133(SM), 166(HD)

Note: HM = hypermarkets, SM = supermarkets, HD = hard discount, CS = convenience store, C&C = cash and carry.

Sources: P. Kamath and C. Codin, 'French Carrefour in South-East Asia', *British Food Journal* 103(7) (2001): 479–94; E. Colla and M. Dupuis, 'Research and managerial issues on global retail competition: Carrefour/Wal-Mart', *International Journal of Retail and Distribution Management* 30(2) (2002): 103–11; and Carrefour's website: **www.carrefour.com**.

6.1 Introduction

Understanding the motives behind a firm's decision to internationalize its business activities helps to explain why and how firms should engage in international business activities. For example, Carrefour was compelled to make its first international move in the 1970s because of the introduction of the Royer Law, which restricted its growth in France. Later on, it was attracted by opportunities in Asian and Middle Eastern markets. In this chapter we discuss factors that push and pull firms to internationalize their business activities.

In addition to the motives for internationalization, we need to understand the different modes of entering a foreign country or a region. There is no best way to enter a foreign market. For example, Carrefour's mode of entry differed from one country or region to another. The company started its first international experience cautiously, expanding to countries it knew quite well and in moves which involved small risks. As it gained more experience in foreign markets and confidence in its ability to operate effectively outside its home market, its attitudes towards operating and risk in foreign markets changed. This resulted in further expansions into more challenging and unknown markets, such as the Middle Eastern and Asian markets.

6.2 Motives and decision to internationalize

In addressing the question of why certain firms are engaged in international business activities while others are not, researchers have focused on the elements stimulating a firm's decision to initiate foreign market entry (Albaum 1983). Internationalization stimuli can be defined as those internal and external factors that influence a firm's decision to initiate, develop, and sustain international business activities.

Two factors lead firms to consider the possibility of operating outside their home market: organizational factors arising from within the firm, and environmental factors which are outside the firm's control (Aharoni 1966).

6.2.1 Organizational factors

Organizational factors can be split into two forces: decision-maker characteristics and firm-specific factors (see Exhibit 6.1).

Decision-maker characteristics

Recognition by the top manager, or the top management team, of the importance of international activities is an essential part of the process of internationalization. The top manager's (or top management team's) exposure to foreign markets is a critical component in the decision to internationalize (Karafakioglu 1986). Management characteristics such as perceptions of risk in foreign operations have a strong influence on management

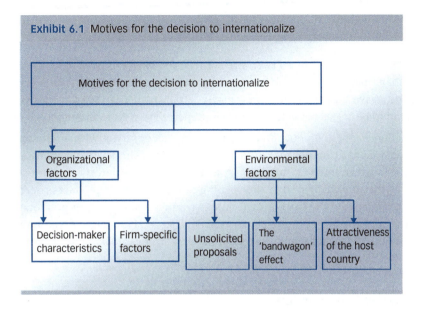

Exhibit 6.1 Motives for the decision to internationalize

perceptions of international business activities. Reid (1981) found the following character-istics positively influenced the internationalization decision:

- Foreign travel and experience abroad: Managers who travel abroad extensively are more open-minded and interested in foreign affairs, thus being more able and willing to meet foreign managers and form business partnerships. They also have more opportunities to observe first-hand the advantages that foreign partnerships and foreign countries may offer, have a foreign business network in place, and are able to attract and negotiate with managers from different cultures.

- Foreign language proficiency: The number of languages spoken by the top manager is a good indication of his or her interest in international activities. Managers who speak several languages tend to travel more to foreign countries and thus are more able to establish social and business contacts, understand foreign business practices better, are better placed to negotiate a good deal for the company, and communicate not only with top managers of foreign affiliates who could speak the home country's language but with line managers and employees as well.

- The decision-maker background: Having been born abroad, lived abroad, or worked abroad could influence one's view of risks and opportunities in foreign markets. For example, international work experience exposes managers to foreign opportunities, and therefore makes it easier for them to take the first step into foreign markets.

- Personal characteristics: Natural risk-takers are more likely to engage in an international activity than risk-averse managers. Similarly, managers with high ambitions tend to internationalize more than managers with low personal ambitions.

Firm-specific factors

There are two firm-specific factors:

- Firm size: As will be discussed later, size matters, and bigger firms tend to internationalize more than smaller ones. This is because large firms possess more managerial and financial resources, have greater production capacity, attain higher levels of economies of scale, and tend to be associated with lower levels of perceived risks in international operations.

- International appeal: Production of a unique product or service with an international appeal could act as a stimulus for international expansion. This is often demonstrated by the speed with which international sales are first obtained after start-up. The source of appeal could be the concept as seen in the opening case study, or the product or service offered by the company on the basis of their unique features and quality, or promotion through heavy advertising, sales promotion, and public relations. Products like Nike trainers, Levi's jeans, Pepsi, McDonald's, and Coca-Cola have all crossed global borders because of their international appeal.

6.2.2 Environmental factors

The external business environment has a major impact on the strategic direction of a firm. Many external driving forces stimulate a firm to internationalize. Among the most important of these are:

Unsolicited proposals

Some unsolicited proposals from foreign governments, distributors, or clients are hard to resist and may stimulate a firm to go international (Wiedersheim-Paul et al. 1978). For example Volkswagen decided to enter the Chinese auto market after a Chinese delegation visited Volkswagen's headquarters in Germany in 1978 and proposed a joint venture that had the blessing of the Chinese government.

Thanks to the internet, firms are now receiving unsolicited inquiries through the firm's website. For example, the first international contract of the Indian software development firm Ekomate came from a British firm, which came across Ekomate's website on the internet by accident. After its first international encounter, Ekomate expanded into the US market. Ekomate's clients and partners in the early 2000s include multinational firms such as IBM, Ford, and Citibank.

The 'bandwagon' effect

Competing firms tend to observe, benchmark, evaluate, and imitate each other's strategic moves, especially in industries with only a few big players (Knickerbocker 1973). If one firm internationalizes, it is likely that others will mimic its strategic move and create a bandwagon effect.

Attractiveness of the host country

Attractiveness describes the degree to which the country's host market is desirable for business operations by foreign firms. Multinational firms may be attracted because of the host country's market size. Market size is attractive to foreign firms because it offers greater potential for growth, profit, and stability of operations. In addition to market size, per capita income is a good measure of a country's attractiveness for market seeking multinationals. Customers in countries with high per capita income have high purchasing power, and high demand for industrial and consumer goods. Another factor that attracts foreign firms is favourable foreign investment regulations (Bilkey and Tesar 1977).

KEY CONCEPT

Internationalization stimuli are those internal and external factors that influence a firm's decision to initiate, develop, and sustain international business activities. Two sets of factors lead firms to consider the possibility of operating outside their home market: organizational factors arising from within the organization and environmental factors which are outside the organization's control.

6.3 The internationalization process

The previous section explained *why* firms internationalize (the motives for internationalization). Another crucial question is *how* they internationalize (the internationalization process). An influential explanation of the internationalization process was offered by Swedish researchers (Johanson and Wiedersheim-Paul 1975; Johanson and Vahlne 1977).

Johanson and Wiedersheim-Paul (1975) made two observations about the way in which firms internationalize. First, firms start exporting to neighbouring countries or countries that are comparatively well known or have relatively small 'psychic distance'. Psychic distance is the sum of the factors preventing the flow of information from and to the market (e.g. cultural differences or differences in government regulations). In other words, a firm's international expansion depends on its experiential knowledge of foreign markets. Experiential knowledge is knowledge obtained from experience. By implication, there is a direct link between market knowledge and market commitment. The better the knowledge of a market, the stronger the commitment to that market.

Second, firms expand their international operations step by step. In other words, a firm's international expansion occurs as a result of incremental decisions. Johanson and Wiedersheim-Paul (1975) studied the internationalization process of four large Swedish multinationals, and found that the internationalization patterns of these firms were marked by a number of small incremental changes. They identified four successive stages in the firm's international expansion:

1. no regular export activities;

2. export activities via independent representatives or agents;

3. the establishment of an overseas subsidiary;

4. overseas production and manufacturing units.

These two observations form the basis of the Uppsala Model, which suggests that a firm's international expansion is a gradual process dependent on experiential knowledge and incremental steps. Johanson and Wiedersheim-Paul's (1975) work was further developed and refined by Johanson and Vahlne (1977), who formulated a 'dynamic' Uppsala Model—a model in which the outcome of one cycle of events constitutes the input to the next (see Exhibit 6.2).

6.3.1 The Uppsala Model

The Uppsala Model posits that firms proceed along the internationalization path in the form of logical steps, based on their gradual acquisition and use of information gathered from foreign markets and operations, which determine successively greater levels of market commitment to more international business activities. The concept of market commitment suggests that resources located in a particular market present a firm's commitment to that market, so foreign direct investment means higher market commitment than exporting or licensing. Market commitment is composed of two factors: the amount of resources committed and the degree of commitment. The amount of resources refers to the size of investment in a given market. The degree of commitment refers to the difficulty of finding an alternative use for the resources and transferring them to the alternative use.

The Uppsala Model assumes that the more the firm knows about the foreign market, the lower the perceived market risk will be, and the higher the level of investment in that market. The perceived risk is primarily a function of the level of market knowledge acquired through one's own operations (Forsgren 2002). So over time, and as firms gain

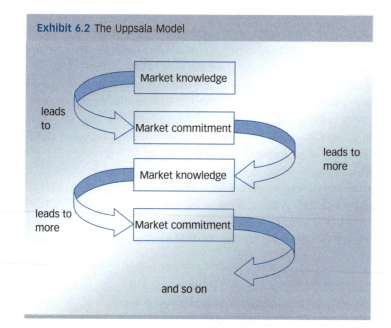

Exhibit 6.2 The Uppsala Model

Market knowledge

leads to

Market commitment

leads to more

Market knowledge

leads to more

Market commitment

and so on

foreign commercial experience and improve their knowledge of foreign markets, they tend to increase their foreign market commitment, and venture into countries that are increasingly dissimilar to their own. This in turn enhances market knowledge, leading to further commitment in more distant markets.

The model helps to understand a firm's initial choice of international location and its mode of entry into foreign markets. For example, German firms would initially export to Austria and Switzerland before making direct investments in France, the United States, or Africa. At the same time, firms would initially export to other countries or would engage in strategic alliances with foreign firms, before committing capital towards foreign investments. It should be pointed out that there are three exceptions to the Uppsala Model. First, firms that have large resources and experience can take larger internationalization steps. This helps to explain why small- and medium-sized enterprises follow the Uppsala Model more closely than very large multinational firms. Second, when market conditions are stable and homogeneous, relevant market knowledge can be gained from sources other than experience. Third, when the firm has considerable experience of markets with similar conditions, it may be able to generalize this experience to any specific market.

KEY CONCEPT

The Uppsala Model suggests that a firm's international expansion is a gradual process dependent on *experiential knowledge* and *incremental steps*. It assumes that firms proceed along the internationalization path in the form of logical steps, based on the gradual acquisition and use of information gathered from foreign markets and operations, which determine successively greater levels of market commitment to more international business activities.

6.3.2 Limitations of the Uppsala Model

Despite the intuitive appeal of the Uppsala Model, there is much concern about its current usefulness. First, the model does not explain what triggers the first internationalization step. Second, it does not explain the mechanism by which experiential knowledge of a foreign market affects commitment of resources to that market (Anderson and Gatignon 1986). Third, there is ample evidence to suggest that attitudes of managers to the risks and incentives in relation to internationalization do not differ according to the number of foreign markets in which their firms have operated (Sullivan and Bauerschmidt 1990).

Fourth, the basic assumption of the Uppsala Model is that lack of knowledge about foreign markets is a major obstacle to international operations—but what if the firm acquired knowledge through external recruitment rather than firm experiential knowledge? By heavily relying on 'learning by doing' as the basic logic for internationalization, the Uppsala Model fails to pay attention to other forms of learning such as learning through imitation, learning through international strategic alliances, or learning through incorporating people.

Fifth, the argument that multinational firms enter countries that are culturally and geographically close to theirs before entering culturally and geographically distant countries does not always hold. For example, after Starbucks achieved phenomenal success in the US market, it made its first international venture in 1995 in the Japanese market through a joint venture with Sazaby Inc. Further, in 1996, the company extended its international presence to Hawaii and Singapore. It did not enter the French market until January 2004, when it opened its first store in Paris. Sometimes a firm's international expansion is not the outcome of a learning process (as the Uppsala Model suggests) but the outcome of a rational strategic choice (i.e. a conscious choice to enter a specific foreign market). For example, if a European firm makes a deliberate decision to relocate its manufacturing production to a low-cost country, it may be more likely to invest in distant China than in a neighbouring European country. This helps to explain why many Norwegian firms did not make initial foreign investments close to the home country and would not necessarily internationalize in incremental steps (Benito and Gripsrud 1992).

Finally, there are firms which do not follow the traditional internationalization process, but which are multinational firms from the very start. These firms are called Born Global firms.

6.3.3 The Born Global firm

In 1993 the consultants McKinsey published the findings of a survey for the Australian Manufacturing Council on the internationalization of small and medium firms in Australia (McKinsey 1993). The report put forward evidence that a large number of the surveyed firms in Australia viewed 'the world as their marketplace from the outset and see the domestic market as a support for their international business' (p. 9). The McKinsey report referred to these firms as Born Global firms.

Several researchers observed the Born Global phenomenon, even in the 1980s, but used different terms to describe it. Hedlund and Kverneland (1985) used the term 'leapfrogging' to describe firms that jumped over stages in the traditional models such as the Uppsala Model. Similarly, McDougall et al. (1994) coined the term 'International New Ventures' (INV) to describe firms that right from their birth seek competitive advantage by using resources from different countries and by selling their products in multiple countries. They defined an INV as:

> a business organization that, from inception, seeks to derive significant competitive advantage from the use of resources and the sale of outputs in multiple countries. The distinguishing feature of these start-ups is that their origins are international, as demonstrated by observable and significant commitments of resources (e.g. material, people, financing, time) in more than one nation. (McDougall et al. 1994: 49)

Characteristics of Born Global firms

Born Global firms are generally small and medium high-tech firms using well-known technology. These firms are able to standardize production, distribution, and marketing processes and position themselves in global niche markets. Knight and Çavusgil (1996) argue that the increasing importance of the global niche markets facilitated the emergence of Born Global firms. Global niche markets are a product of increasing specialization or 'stick to the knitting' strategy adopted by firms in the 1990s and beyond. Because of the small size of niche markets, firms have to sell internationally to be competitive. The fact that they are high-tech enables Born Global firms to sell their product or service to global customers with minimum adjustments.

Another characteristic of Born Global firms is their country of origin. Firms originating from small countries such as Nordic countries are more likely to adopt a Born Global strategy than firms from large countries such as the US. For example, Lindmark et al. (1994) reported that nearly 50% of high-tech start-ups in the Nordic countries began exporting within two years of their establishment. The small size of the home market makes it important for firms to sell their products globally to be competitive.

One of the major characteristics of Born Global firms is the commitment of the manager or founder to internationalization. Generally, Born Global firms are managed or founded by people who have greater international exposure than managers of gradually internationalizing firms. Further, they generally have higher risk tolerance than managers of gradually internationalizing firms (Kotha et al. 2001).

KEY CONCEPT

A Born Global firm has virtually no domestic market, internationalizes within a short period from inception, and generates most of its sales in foreign markets.

6.4 Entry mode strategies

We have previously referred to modes of entry into foreign markets. When firms decide to enter a foreign market, they are faced with a large array of choices of entry mode, which could be grouped into five main categories: export, licensing, franchising, international joint venture, and wholly owned operations. This section will focus only on four modes of entry, leaving aside international joint ventures. Because of the importance and complex nature of international joint ventures and strategic alliances, we have allocated a whole chapter to this issue (see Chapter 7).

6.4.1 Export

A simple definition of exporting is the action by the firm to send produced goods and services from the home country to other countries. This can be ascribed to the fact that exporting does not need the commitment of large resources and is thus less costly than alternatives such as joint ventures (Morgan and Katsikeas 1998). It is also easier for the multinational firm to withdraw its operations with minimum damage (see Exhibit 6.3). Because of the physical distance, the export strategy, however, does not enable the multinational firm to control its operations abroad.

Export is a frequently employed mode of internationalization and one of the most simple and common approaches adopted mainly by small and medium-sized firms in their endeavour to enter foreign markets.

Exhibit 6.3 Advantages and disadvantages of the different modes of entry

Mode of entry	Advantages	Disadvantages
Export	• Does not require a high resource commitment in the targeted country • Inexpensive way to gain experiential knowledge in foreign markets • Low-cost strategy to expand sales in order to achieve economies of scale	• Hard to control operations abroad • Provides very small experiential knowledge in foreign markets
Licensing	• Speedy entry to foreign market • Does not require a high resource commitment in the targeted country • Can be used as a step towards a more committed mode of entry • Low-cost strategy to expand sales in order to achieve economies of scale	• Hard to monitor partners in foreign markets • High potential for opportunism • Hard to enforce agreements • Provides a small experiential knowledge in foreign markets
International franchising	• Speedy entry to foreign market • Requires a moderate resource commitment in the targeted country • Moderate-cost strategy to expand sales in order to achieve economies of scale	• High monitoring costs • High potential for opportunism • Could damage the firm's reputations and image • Does not provide experiential knowledge in foreign markets
Wholly owned ventures Greenfield strategy	• Low risks of technology appropriation • Able to control operations abroad • Provides high experiential knowledge in foreign markets • Low level of conflict between the subsidiary and the parent firm • Does not have the problem of integrating different cultures, structures, procedures and technologies • Managers of foreign subsidiaries have a strong attachment to the parent firm	• Could not rely on pre-existing relationships with customers, suppliers, and government officials • Potential difficulty in accessing existing managers and employees familiar with local market conditions • Adds extra capacity to the existing market • The firm is seen as a foreign firm by local stakeholders
Mergers and acquisitions	• Low risks of technology appropriation • Able to control operations abroad • Provides high experiential knowledge in foreign markets	• Problem of integrating foreign subsidiaries into the parent's system • Managers of acquired foreign subsidiaries may have a weak attachment to the parent firm

→

→

Mode of entry	Advantages	Disadvantages
	• Could rely on pre-existing relationships with customers, suppliers, and government officials	
	• Access to existing managers and employees familiar with local market conditions	
	• Does not add extra capacity to the market	

There are three different exporter categories according to firms' level of export involvement: *experimental involvement*, where the firm initiates restricted export marketing activity; *active involvement*, where the firm systematically explores a range of export market opportunities; and *committed involvement*, where the firm allocates its resources on the basis of international marketing opportunities (Çavusgil 1984).

As shown in Exhibit 6.3, generally firms export for two reasons. First, firms need experiential knowledge, and exporting has the potential to provide firms with international experience without their taking high risk or strong commitment. Second, firms use exporting to expand their sales in order to achieve economies of scale.

Risks of exporting

Export strategy, compared with the other modes of entry, is a low-risk strategy. The major risks of exporting are:

• When countries experience major political instability, export could be disrupted, with consequential delays and other defaults on payments, exchange transfer blockages, or confiscation of property.

• The multinational firm has no control over some costs, such as costs of land transport to the port, transfers, shipping costs, insurance, and foreign exchange risk.

6.4.2 Licensing

International licensing is 'the transfer of patented information and trademarks, information and know-how, including specifications, written documents, computer programmes, and so forth, as well as information needed to sell a product or service, with respect to a physical territory' (Mottner and Johnson 2000: 171).

Licensing does not mean duplicating the product in several countries. Most products going into foreign countries require some form of adaptation: labels and instructions must be translated; goods may require modification to conform with local laws and regulations; and marketing may have to be adjusted.

Benefits of licensing include speed to market, especially when a firm lacks sufficient skills, capital, or personnel to enter a foreign market quickly (see Exhibit 6.3). For example, 7-Eleven, a US company founded in Dallas, Texas, in 1927, uses international licensing to enter foreign markets. In January 2003 the company claimed that it owned approximately 18,600 7-Eleven stores and operated by area licensing in sixteen countries.

In addition to being used as an entry mode to foreign markets, licensing may also be used as a step towards a more committed mode of entry such as a joint venture or a wholly owned form. For example, when in 1997 Phoenix AG, a German manufacturing concern, agreed to license the production of its automotive and railway components in India to Sigma Corp. of Delhi, the licence agreement was no more than a step towards establishing a joint venture, which would integrate Sigma's manufacturing capability into Phoenix's global strategy (Mottner and Johnson 2000).

Risks of licensing

Several risks are associated with international licensing. Mottner and Johnson (2000) identified the following risks:

- Sub-optimal choice: This risk is associated with the possibility of licensing being not the best possible choice and or selecting the wrong partner—hence not realizing the full potential of the partnership.

- Risk of opportunism: The possibility that the licensee takes the opportunity to appropriate the technology or process that has been licensed to it and internalizes it.

- Quality risks: These risks are associated with the possibility that some licensees might not be able or willing to maintain the quality of the product or service and hence compromise the reputation of the licensor.

- Production risks: These risks are related to the possibility that licensees will not 'produce in a timely manner, or will not produce the volume needed, or will overproduce'.

- Payment risks: There are risks associated with licensees not being able to or decide not to pay for royalties.

- Contract enforcement risk: This risk is associated with licensors not being able to enforce the agreed contract. This usually occurs in emerging economies where there is weak infrastructure for commercial law enforcement.

- Marketing control risk: This risk is related to the possibility that some licensees may not market the licensed product or process properly—under-spending on marketing activities, using inappropriate channels of distribution, and so forth.

6.4.3 International franchising

Franchising has been increasingly utilized as a method of business expansion over the last thirty years (Eroglu 1992). Several multinational firms, such as the Body Shop, Benetton Group, and McDonald's, have developed a successful international franchising network.

International franchising is 'a contract-based organizational structure for entering new markets' (Teegen 2000: 498). It involves 'a franchisor firm that undertakes to transfer a business concept that it has developed, with corresponding operational guidelines, to non-domestic parties for a fee'. Teegen notes that:

> once the potential franchisor has established a reputation for its business concept, this develops demand as a 'leasable' commodity. The franchisor packages the business concept, operational guidelines and access to its trade and brand marks, and offers this business format to firms, who purchase the rights to exploit commercially the concept and trade names for a given period of time (typically between five and fifteen years) in a given geographical territory. Typical franchise contracts require an up-front payment to the franchisor as well as royalty payments based upon sales in the stipulated territory.

Franchisers are responsible for improving the product/service mix, policing outlet quality, and promoting the brand in the host country.

The franchise network system implies mutual cooperation and commitment between often distinct and, at least to some degree, autonomous firms. This cooperation is based not only upon mutual advantages but also on reciprocity. Thus, successful cooperation between franchisers and franchisees requires a high level of trust to alleviate the fear of opportunistic behaviour and to enhance the performance of the franchise.

Multinational firms are increasingly relying on master franchisers to manage their franchise network in a particular country. Generally, master franchisers are from the host country. They are given the rights to develop and manage the franchise network in a particular country or region. Their duties include selecting suitable local franchisees, providing them with the necessary assistance, and collecting the franchise fee.

Risks of international franchising

While using a master franchiser with knowledge of local markets and cultural awareness has several advantages, it involves several risks (see Exhibit 6.3). These are:

- The master franchiser may not follow the directives of the franchisor.
- Franchisers may not understand the fundamental concept of the franchisor and as a result may communicate the wrong concept to the franchisees.
- The fact that franchisers are responsible for improving the quality of the product, policing outlet quality, and promoting the brand may increase the potential for franchisees to free-ride, in the belief that the franchiser's efforts are sufficient for the franchise to succeed. This can result in franchisees attempting to increase profits by reducing the quality of inputs (e.g. by under-staffing).
- A franchise may damage the franchiser's image and reputation in the host country, because customers often cannot distinguish between franchised and company-owned outlets: a poor experience in one franchise outlet may hurt the reputation of the entire chain.

Because of these risks, several multinational firms do not use a franchise system. For example, Starbucks Coffee Company uses only three business structures in international markets: joint ventures, licences, and company-owned operations. It states on its website that the company does not:

sell individual franchises or sub-franchise. Starbucks Coffee Company will either operate our coffeehouses directly (or through a local subsidiary) or will enter into a business agreement with a company or group of individuals. This company or group is granted the right to develop and operate coffeehouses throughout a defined region. (www.starbucks.com)

6.4.4 Wholly owned ventures

In contrast to exporting, licensing, and franchising, wholly owned subsidiaries involve a higher degree of risk. Multinational firms have two options: greenfield investment in a completely new facility, or acquisition of or merger with an already established local firm.

The greenfield strategy

A greenfield strategy entails building an entirely new subsidiary in a foreign country from scratch to enable foreign sales and/or production.

Typically, a greenfield investment signifies that the parent firm has decided to clone its strategy and structure in the foreign plant by transferring its technology, supply chain, organizational structure, and corporate culture (Hennart and Park 1993). For instance, during the 1980s and 1990s Japanese firms adopting a global strategy structure preferred to clone their home country structure and strategy in foreign markets through greenfield strategies (Harzing 2002).

Generally, greenfield investments are preferred when specific technical and organizational skills define a firm's ability to compete. For example, Japanese multinationals with weak competitive advantage tend to use mergers and acquisitions (M&As), while those with strong advantages prefer greenfield investments to transfer their advantages to foreign markets (Hennart and Park 1993).

Risks of the greenfield strategy   The greenfield strategy is a high-risk strategy. In addition to the above risks associated with other modes of entry, such as political instability in the host country, other risks specific to the greenfield strategy (see Exhibit 6.3) include:

• the risk of not being able to build relationships with customers, suppliers and government officials in the new country;
• the risk of not being able to recruit managers and employees familiar with local market conditions;
• the risk of being seen as a foreign firm by local stakeholders.

The mergers and acquisitions (M&As) strategy

An international merger is a transaction that combines two companies from different countries to establish a new legal entity. International acquisition refers to the acquisition of a local firm's assets by a foreign company. In an acquisition, both local and foreign firms may continue to exist. Barkema and Vermeulen (1998: 405) noted that 'for companies to prefer acquisition to greenfield entry, the cost of constructing new facilities, installing equipment, and hiring and training new labour force must exceed the costs of purchasing and recasting existing properties'.

There is ample evidence to suggest that, in the short-term, cross-border M&As have positive benefits for the shareholders of the acquired firm. In the longer term, however, profitability gains through increased efficiency, or increased market share, are often nonexistent or limited (Rene 1994). Grinblatt and Titman (1998: 702) state that, on the basis of the available evidence,

> we cannot say whether mergers, on average, create value. Certainly, some mergers have created value while others were either mistakes or bad decisions. Of course, many mistakes were due to unforeseen circumstances and were unavoidable. These unforeseen circumstances often occur at the implementations stage. They include problems and challenges such as: the degree of compatibility, or lack thereof, of management practices between the two national values and practices and organizational structures and cultures; the extent to which parties want to retain and value their organizational integrity; and the nature of the relationship between the two organizations.

There are three types of M&A: horizontal, vertical, and conglomerate:

- Horizontal M&As involve two competing firms in the same industry. This type of M&As is more common in industries where consolidation is required, such as automobile, petroleum, and pharmaceutical industries.

- Vertical M&As involve a merger between firms in the supply chain. This involves, for example, a distributor or a supplier merging with a manufacturer.

- Conglomerate M&As involve a merger of two companies from two unrelated industries. Conglomerate M&As were very popular in the late 1980s, but have been declining ever since as firms retreated to their core business during the 1990s and early 2000s. As a result, the share of conglomerate M&As fell from 42% in 1991 to around 27% in 1999 (UNICTAD 2000).

The motives for M&As can be classified into three distinct motives: strategic, economic, and personal (Hopkins 1999: 212)

Strategic motives   Strategic motives aim to improve the overall strategic position of the multinational firm. This includes intention to create synergy, to strengthen market power, and to gain speedy access to foreign markets (Hopkins 1999: 212). Synergy is the potential ability of two firms to be more successful as a result of a merger or an acquisition. If synergy is achieved, the combined firm's value after the merger or acquisition should be higher than the combined value of the two firms operating independently. Because synergy seems straightforward and intuitively appealing, it often tops the list of motives in survey and academic studies. It is, however, much harder to achieve in practice. An example of synergy gone wrong is the acquisition of WordPerfect by Novell for $1.4 billion. Novell failed to achieve the intended synergy, and had to sell WordPerfect to Corel for only $200 million.

A firm may also be motivated to merge with or acquire another firm in order to leverage its core competencies. A company that develops a core competence in negotiating with foreign governments, such as Shell, or in acquiring political resources, such as Volkswagen, may try to acquire another firm in order to capitalize on its core competencies and use it in different industries to strengthen its market.

Further, international M&As provide multinational firms with speedy access to foreign markets. By acquiring an already established firm in a foreign market, the firm gains a strong foothold in the acquired firm's home market.

As opposed to entry through a greenfield strategy, M&As provide access to foreign markets without adding access capacity. This is very important in mature industries where the market is already saturated, such as the auto industry. In addition, acquiring an established brand name in a foreign market gives rapid entry and access to existing proprietary assets (technology, skills, organization, information, supplier networks, brands, contacts, etc.). For example, when Wal-Mart acquired Asda, Wal-Mart capitalized on Asda's customer loyalty and trusted brand name, which gave Wal-Mart a strong avenue by which to access the UK market and slowly introduce its brand name to UK customers.

Economic motives   There are four economic motives for international M&As:

- the desire to achieve economy of scale by joining productive forces;
- cost reduction by eliminating redundant resources after the M&As; this is often the case in horizontal M&As;
- differences in the growth of national economies motivate firms from slow-growing economies to acquire firms in high-growth economies;
- if firms are perceived to be undervalued in particular countries, they will be a target for cross-border M&As (Gonzalez et al. 1998).

Personal motives   A top management team may venture into an international M&A for personal reasons. This is likely to happen when managers are stronger that stakeholders. This could be simply to satisfying their hubris and ego through 'empire-building', or for motives of self-interest such as increasing their reward package and job security.

Risks of the M&A strategy   The major risks associated with the M&A strategy (see Exhibit 6.3) include:

- The different corporate and national cultures, structures, technology and procedures may cause great problems for integrating the acquired subsidiary into the parent company's system. This may result in inferior performance and in some cases the subsequent failure of the acquired subsidiaries.
- Managers of the acquired foreign subsidiary may not accept the parent company, which results in a weaker degree of attachment between the managers of the acquired foreign subsidiary and the parent firm.

6.4.5 Entry modes and risk vs. control

Each of the five entry modes has its advantages and drawbacks. Therefore, multinational firms have to make trade-offs when they decide on the most suitable entry mode strategy. *Control*—the desire to influence decisions, systems, and operations in the foreign affiliate— and *risk* are the two most important factors in the decision formula when deciding on the type of entry mode (see Exhibit 6.4). The two factors often go hand in hand. To obtain

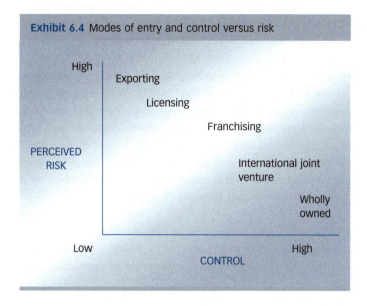

Exhibit 6.4 Modes of entry and control versus risk

control, the multinational firm must commit resources to, and take responsibility for, the management of its foreign plants. In other words, more control requires high risk and vice versa (Anderson and Gatignon 1986).

When selecting the appropriate entry mode, multinational firms have to answer two questions: What level of resource commitment are they willing to make? And what level of control over the operation do they desire? The firm has to look at the risks in the general environment, risks in industry, and firm-specific risks. For markets where total perceived risk is low, firms use entry strategies that involve a high level of resource commitment, such as wholly owned and joint-venture strategies (Brouthers 1995). In markets where the perception of risk is too high, however, the management might no longer believe that it has control over the risk. In this case the management must abandon its desire to control and adopt a low resource commitment strategy by sharing risk with other firms through a joint venture or franchise, or pass the risk management to another firm—to a licensing or a franchise partner—which might be better qualified to manage the risks (see Exhibit 6.4).

KEY CONCEPT

Multinational firms have to make trade-offs when they decide on the most suitable entry mode strategy. More control involves high risk and vice versa. When perceived risk is low, the multinational firm should use entry strategies that involve a high level of resource commitment, such as wholly owned and joint-venture strategies. In contrast, when the perceived risk is high, the multinational firm should adopt a low resource commitment strategy by sharing risk with other firms through a joint venture or franchise, or pass the risk management to a local firm through a licensing or a franchising agreement.

6.5 De-internationalization

Internationalization is a two-way street. Multinational firms do not only enter new markets. They may have to reduce their international activities by pulling out—partially or totally—of a country or a region, or by putting an end to their international aspirations when necessary. We refer to the endgame as 'de-internationalization strategy'. 'De-internationalization' refers to 'any voluntary or forced actions that reduce a company's engagement in or exposure to current cross-border activities' (Benito and Welch 1997: 8). It includes total withdrawal of a firm from an operational presence in a foreign market. Exit may result from failure, closure, or a successful sale of the firm. Exit may be accomplished through sale of assets, international store swaps, bankruptcy, or related events (Burt et al. 2002).

The de-internationalization process is more complicated than the internationalization entry process. While countries tend to welcome multinational firms, governments and interest groups do not feel the same way when foreign companies decide to leave, as the closing case study shows.

Multinationals must develop an endgame strategy and execute it very carefully. Choosing the wrong de-internationalization strategy, or implementing the correct strategy poorly, can increase the cost of exit (Burt et al. 2002). For example, the closing case study illustrates how a bad handling of the de-internationalization process could be very costly.

6.6 Summary

Two main motives lead a firm to a decision to internationalize its business activities: organizational factors arising from within the firm, and environmental factors that are outside the organization's control. These two motives combined lead firms to consider the possibility of operating outside their home market.

In addition to the motives to internationalize, one needs to understand the different modes of entry into a foreign country or a region. When firms decide to enter a foreign market, they are faced with a large array of choices of entry mode, ranging from export to wholly-owned operations. There is no best way to enter a foreign market and the mode of entry may differ from one country or region to another, as the opening case on Carrefour demonstrates. Multinational firms have to make trade-offs when they decide on the most suitable entry mode strategy. *Control*—the desire to influence decisions, systems and operations in the foreign affiliate—and *risk* are the two most important factors in the decision formula when deciding on the type of entry mode.

The Uppsala Model seeks to explain the process or the internationalization steps. Its main argument is that firms generally proceed along the internationalization path in the form of logical steps, based on their gradual acquisition and use of information gathered from foreign markets and operations, which determine successively greater levels of commitment to more international business activities. They start with no regular export activities, then move to export activities via independent representatives or agents; after that they tend to establish an overseas subsidiary; and finally, they commit themselves to overseas production and manufacturing units.

There are five entry modes available to international firms: export, licensing, franchising, international joint venture and wholly-owned operations. Managers need to take risk and control into consideration when deciding the appropriate entry mode. This chapter has focused only on four modes of entry. The next chapter will focus on international joint ventures and strategic alliances.

KEY READINGS

- J. P. Buckley and P. N. Ghauri, *The Internationalization of the firm: A Reader* (London: Thompson Business Press, 1999) is a collection of some of the key articles on internationalization.

- Y. Aharoni, *The Foreign Investment Decision Process* (Boston: Graduate School of Business Administration, Harvard University, 1966), although an old book, provides an excellent analysis of the foreign decision-making process.

- Useful papers on entry modes and risk and control are K. Brouthers, 'The influence of international risk on entry mode strategy', *Management International Review* 35(1) (1995): 7–28, and K. Brouthers, 'The influence of international risk on entry mode strategy in the computer software industry', *Management International Review* 35(1) (1993): 7–28.

DISCUSSION QUESTIONS

1 Select a multinational firm and identify and discuss the internal and external motives for internationalization. Was it pushed or was it pulled? You may use the opening case study to discuss this question.

2 Do all multinational firms follow the Uppsala Model? Justify your answer with examples.

3 Identify a Born Global firm and discuss its internationalization process.

4 'There is no one best way to enter foreign markets. It is a case of horses for courses.' Discuss this statement.

5 Why is the de-internationalization process more complex than the internationalization process? Refer to the closing case study.

Closing case study
Marks & Spencer's exit from France

In 1998 Marks & Spencer, the legendary British retailer, faced a crisis that threatened its very survival. Prior to the crisis, M&S had been one of the most successful British retailing companies. By 1998 the business had retail sales of almost £8 billion, traded from almost 500 stores around the world, and owned Brooks Brothers and Kings Supermarkets in the United States.

Although growth has never been rapid or smooth in Europe, and although in 1999 two stores in France and four in Germany were closed, M&S had a high-profile European presence, particularly in France. The stores themselves were smaller than the standard UK stores and sold a more restricted range of goods, but included the classic St Michael clothes and food ranges (41% of sales).

In an attempt to turn around the company, in February 2000, Luc Vandevelde (a Belgian national) was appointed as chairman. He joined M&S from Promodes, a French multinational retailer (6,000 stores in sixteen countries), where he was president and chief operating officer for four years.

In October 2000, M&S started a strategic review of its business activities. On 29 March 2001, the company announced a fundamental overhaul of its business, described by the chief executive and chairman, Luc Vandevelde, as an 'urgent' plan for recovery, totally focused on the UK business. The measures announced included the closure (by 31 December 2001) of all its company-owned stores in continental Europe except for those in Ireland, the franchising of the company-owned stores in Hong Kong, and the sale of American chains Brooks Brothers and Kings Supermarkets. There were also changes to UK operations and approach and a reconstruction of the balance sheet through property value release. £2 billion was to be returned to shareholders. The company reported that it was losing £34 million a year in continental Europe. M&S budgeted £250–300 million as the cost of withdrawing from continental Europe.

On 29 March 2001, M&S sent a message by e-mail to its management in European branches informing them of the plan to close its operations in Europe and to place 'total focus on the recovery of the UK business'. Shortly after receiving the information, the company's closure plan was presented to the central works council of the French subsidiary at an extraordinary meeting. These communications took place a few minutes before the London Stock Exchange opened, and the formal announcement was made through the Stock Exchange. M&S share prices rose by 7% on the day of the announcement. Following the announcement, workers organized demonstrations outside M&S stores in France, against the closure plan and the way it was announced. Some stores closed for the day. The demonstrations marked the start of a series of unanticipated and undesirable consequences for M&S.

M&S management misjudged the extent to which France's unions, media, and political class would unite in condemning both the closure and the way the company handled the closure announcement.

Three days after the announcement, French trade unions launched a legal action against M&S to forestall the planned closure. Under French and European law, local and multinational firms must hold annual meetings with employee-elected works councils. Further, the works councils must be informed and consulted about business relocation or closure proposals as they arise. The unions believed that M&S had not consulted at all, and had simply announced a closure plan. This impression was reinforced in the M&S media conference in London where the plan was described as 'final'. M&S argued that the announcement in its press release made it clear that the plan was subject to consultation ('intends to divest or close non-core businesses and assets, subject to consultation with its employees'). The issue was thus one of timing and sincerity of consultation.

The closure dominated national news for several weeks. The closure was seen as controversial. Furthermore, the political class had immediately united against M&S. The French prime minister, Lionel Jospin, commented:

> The case of' M&S is particularly unacceptable. It appears that employees and even, seemingly, the managers of outlets in France were advised by the British management at the same time as the press and the Stock Exchange, by e-mail ... The employees who enriched M&S shareholders should be treated better. Such behaviour [by the company] should be punished. (Agence France Presse, 31 March 2001)

The French finance minister, Laurent Fabius, argued, 'We are in the twenty-first century and you can't really treat staff in that way, without any consideration.' The French labour minister, Elisabeth Guigou, called upon the state prosecutor to launch an investigation under penal law that could impose a prison sentence of up to one year on M&S's senior French management, as well as a FF25,000 fine. At the European level, the European commissioner for social affairs branded the act of the announcement 'shameful'. A French judge quickly (9 April 2001) found that, in failing to consult its workforce about the proposed closures, M&S had breached French and EU law. The judge fined the company for 'manifestly illegal trouble-making', ordering M&S to suspend its closure plans, undertake a proper consultation process, and develop a new 'social plan' (i.e. a redundancy and/or re-employment package). Elsewhere in Europe, and particularly in Belgium and Germany, similar concerns over M&S were raised. However, outside France there was no basis for legal intervention.

In addition to the arguably crass errors of process, the unfortunate timing of the announcement exacerbated the reaction. The closure was announced during a heated political debate over workers, rights and work conditions in France (*Economist*, 16 June 2001). A 'social modernization' bill was passed by the French parliament on 11 January 2001. The core of the legislation aimed to strengthen the right to work, improve redundancy prevention, and tackle 'precarious' (i.e. casual and temporary) employment.

On 2 May 2001, M&S France appointed a new president, Alain Juillet, to lead the closure operation in France. He had extensive experience in restructuring companies in France, and added new perspectives to the M&S closure strategy. Though the objective remained the same—to manage market exit by the end of 2001—Juillet's aim was to carry out the process in a 'socially responsible' manner. From the outset, Juillet changed the tone. For example, he stated: 'Un salarié ne se jette pas comme un Kleenex' (employees should not be disposed off like a Kleenex) (*Nouvelle Observateur*, 17 May 2001). He repeatedly stressed that M&S would apply the legal requirements and particularly the *code du travail*. He noted that M&S had never wanted to break the French law. A new 'social' scheme was proposed. There would be no dismissals. All employees would be offered another job. The transfer of any stores would be accompanied by the best possible protection of the employees, by offering current employees the chance to continue in their job (*Nouvelle Observateur*, 2001). This represented a fundamental rethinking of the approach. This does not mean that the relationships eased. Negotiations about the closure and the 'social plan' stuttered onwards. Employees occupied the company's French headquarters in June and went on strike over pay rates. They felt they had nothing to lose.

In July 2001, however, M&S decided to 'sell' rather than 'close' its French stores and began the process of looking for a purchaser. Galeries Lafayette, a leading French retailer, made an offer to buy the French M&S stores. On 30 November 2001 the workers' council at the French division announced that it would not contest the M&S plans to sell its stores to Galeries Lafayette.

Sources: 'Europe: don't sack your workers', *Economist* 359 (16 June 2001), 52; 'Marks & Spencer: il n'y aura pas de licenciements', *Nouvelle Observateur* 1908 (17 May, 2001).

Discussion questions

1 Critically examine the way M&S handled the closure of its shops in France.

2 What do you think M&S should have done differently?

REFERENCES

Aharoni, Y. (1966). *The Foreign Investment Decision Process* (Boston, Mass.: Graduate School of Business Administration, Harvard University).

Albaum, G. (1983). 'Effectiveness of government export assistance for smaller-sized manufacturers: some empirical evidence', *International Marketing Review* 1(1): 68–75.

Anderson, E., and Gatignon, H. (1986). 'Modes of foreign entry: a transaction cost analysis and propositions', *Journal of International Business Studies* (fall): 1–26.

Barkema, H., and Vermeulen, F. (1998). 'International expansion through start-up or through acquisition: a learning perspective', *Academy of Management Journal* 41: 7–26.

Benito, G. R. G., and Gripsrud, G. (1992). 'The expansion of foreign direct investments: discrete rational location choices or a cultural learning process?', *Journal of International Business Studies* (third quarter): 461–76.

——and Welch, L. S. (1997). 'De-internationalization', *Management International Review* 37(2): 7–25.

Bilkey, Warren J., and Tesar, George (1977). 'The export behaviour of smaller Wisconsin manufacturing firms', *Journal of International Business Studies* 8: 93–8.

Brouthers, K. (1995). 'The influence of international risk on entry mode strategy', *Management International Review* 35(1): 7–28.

Burt, S. L., Mellahi, K., Jackson, P., and Sparks, L. (2002). 'Retail internationalisation and retail failure: issues from the case of Marks and Spencer', *International Review of Retail, Distribution and Consumer Research* 12(2): 191–219.

Çavusgil, S. T. (1984). 'Differences among exporting firms based on their degree of internationalisation', *Journal of Business Research* (12): 195–208.

Eroglu, S. (1992). 'The internationalisation process of franchise systems: a conceptual model', *International Marketing Review* 9(5): 19–30.

Forsgren, M. (2002). 'The concept of learning in the Uppsala internationalisation process model: a critical review', *International Business Review* 11(3): 257–77.

Gonzalez, P., Vasconcellos, G. M., and Kish, R. J. (1998). 'Cross-border mergers and acquisitions: the undervaluation hypothesis', *Quarterly Review of Economic Finance* 38(1): 25–45.

Grinblatt, M., and Titman, S. (1998). *Financial Market and Corporate Strategy* (Boston, Mass.: Irwin/McGraw-Hill).

Harzing, Ann-Wil (2002). 'Acquisition versus greenfield investments: international strategy and management of entry mode', *Strategic Management Journal* 23(3): 211–27.

Hedlund, G., and Kverneland, A. (1985). 'Are strategies for foreign markets changing?', *International Studies of Management and Organization* 15(2): 41–59.

Hennart, J. F., and Park, Y. R. (1993). 'Greenfield vs. acquisition: the strategy of Japanese investors in the United States', *Management Science* 39(9): 1054–70.

Hopkins, H. D. (1999). 'Cross-border mergers and acquisitions: global regional perspectives', *Journal of International Management* 5: 207–39.

Johanson, Jan, and Vahlne, Jan-Erik (1977). 'The internationalization process of the firm: a model of knowledge development and increasing foreign commitments', *Journal of International Business Studies* 8(1): 23–32.

——and Wiedersheim-Paul, Finn (1975). 'The internationalization of the firm: four Swedish cases', *Journal of Management Studies* 12: 305–22.

Karafakioglu, Mehmet (1986). 'Export activities of Turkish manufacturers', *International Marketing Review* 3(4): 34–43.

Knickerbocker, F. T. (1973). *Oligopolistic Reaction and Multinational Enterprise* (Boston, Mass.: Division of Research, Graduate School of Business Administration, Harvard University).

Knight, G. A., and Çavusgil, S. T. (1996). 'The born global firm: a challenge to traditional internationalisation theory', *Advances in International Marketing* 8: 11–26.

Kotha, S., Rindova, P. V., and Rothaermel, F. T. (2001). 'Assets and actions: firm-specific factors in the internationalization of U.S. internet firms', *Journal of International Business Studies* 32(4): 769–91.

Christensen, P. R., Lindmark, L., Vatne, E., Eskelinen, H., Forsström, B., and Sørensen, O. J. (1994). *Småföretagens Internationalisering: en Jämförende Studie*, (Copenhagen: NordREFO).

McDougall, P., Shane, S., and Oviatt, B. M. (1994). 'Explaining the formation of international new ventures: the limits of theories from international business research', *Journal of Business Venturing* 9(6): 469–87.

McKinsey and Co. (1993). *Emerging Exporters* (Melbourne: Australian Manufacturing Council).

Mellahi, K. (2003). 'The de-internationalization process', in *Internationalization: Firm Strategies and Management*, C. Wheeler, F. McDonald, and I. Greaves (eds.), (London: Palgrave).

Morgan, R. E., and Katsikeas, C. S. (1998). 'Exporting problems of industrial manufacturers', *Industrial Marketing Management* 29(2): 161–76.

Mottner, S., and Johnson, P. J. (2000). 'Motivations and risks in international licensing: a review and implications for licensing to transitional and emerging economies', *Journal of World Business* 35(2): 171–88.

Reid, R. S. (1981). 'The decision-maker and export entry and expansion', *Journal of International Business Studies* 12(2): 101–12.

Rene, Olie (1994). 'Shades of culture and institutions in international mergers', *Organization Studies* 15(3): 381–405.

Sirower, Mark L. (1997). *The Synergy Trap: How Companies Lose the Acquisition Game* (New York: Free Press).

Sullivan, D., and Bauerschmidt, A. (1990). 'Incremental internationalization: a test of Johanson and Vahlne's thesis', *Management International Review* 30(1): 19–30.

Teegen, H. (2000). 'Examining strategic and economic development implications of globalising through franchising', *International Business Review* 9(4): 497–521.

UNICTAD (2000). *World Investment Report: Cross-Border Mergers and Acquisitions and Development* (New York: United Nations).

Weidersheim-Paul, F., Olson, H. C., and Welch, L. A. (1978). 'Pre-export activity: the first steps in internationalization', *Journal of International Business Studies* 9(1): 47–58.

7

International strategic alliances: partnership and cooperation

---

Learning outcomes

After reading this chapter you should be able to:

- understand the importance of international strategic alliances;

- understand the difference between different types of international strategic alliance;

- explain the drivers for international strategic alliances;

- list and discuss the motives for international strategic alliances;

- select an international strategic alliance partner;

- outline some common dilemmas concerning terminating an international strategic alliance.

In a growing hunt to lure customers with seamless service and one-stop shopping, companies around the world—from publishers to manufacturers—are acquiring international partners through mergers and joint ventures. The tag-line for this year's Hollywood remake of the movie *Godzilla* applies to the global marketplace as well: 'Size does matter.'

The trend toward strategic alliances has spread to the professional services arena. Normally, a large US law firm like Minneapolis-based Faegre & Benson (**www.faegre.com**) would spend its time facilitating mergers and joint ventures for its corporate clients. But in August 1997 Faegre & Benson launched its own international strategic alliance, teaming up with the London firm of Hobson Audley Hopkins & Wood to create a multinational partnership, Faegre Benson Hobson Audley. Their innovative bid to create an efficient service arrangement across two separate firms in two different countries has attracted considerable attention in London, generating profiles in publications such as the *Financial Times* and *The Lawyer*. Many members of the US legal community have been watching to see whether the joint-venture approach is, in fact, a promising new trend for firms trying to navigate the tricky waters of international law. 'Very few American firms have the size and experience to handle the complexities of English law on their own', explains Scott James, who has been part of Faegre & Benson's presence in London for more than twelve years. 'As a result, many clients end up hiring big firms on both sides of the Atlantic. But the American and English firms are often strangers to one another, with no history of working together. That's inefficient and expensive for the client.'

Historically, American firms have tried to overcome these obstacles by opening up London offices of their own. Since the early 1990s, when a change in English practice rules allowed American and English lawyers to join forces, a number of American firms have built up sizeable offices of English solicitors. But success in London's crowded, sophisticated legal market has proved elusive. 'American firms sometimes expect legal practice in London to be little more than American law with a British accent', said James. 'It's not. There are cultural, practical, and professional differences. When you try to integrate English lawyers into an "American" practice, it's not uncommon to have problems.'

Faegre & Benson adopted another solution to the problems that have tripped up other firms. Rather than hiring English lawyers one by one into a larger international office, they concluded they could better serve US businesses by establishing a relationship with a separate firm with roots in London. 'We wanted a partner whose practice would complement ours and meet the needs of our corporate clients in the United States', said James. 'Hobson Audley's lawyers had the breadth of expertise in English business law we were looking for. Plus, I've known Gerald Hobson and Max Audley for many years. That personal relationship goes a long way.'

Despite their familiarity, neither firm was ready to jump into a formal merger. 'The last thing we wanted to do was barge in and try to make them do things our way', said James. Instead, they created a partnership involving selected lawyers from both firms. Then they began building working relationships to leverage their separate strengths. The two firms had plenty of experience helping their clients face the challenges of similar joint ventures. But now they had to face those challenges themselves. Could they make it work?

As lawyers, the firms had an advantage in nailing down the legal requirements of a partnership. But not all the hurdles were on paper. James acknowledges that different technology and accounting systems don't always make good bedfellows. The back-office process is more labour-intensive at the moment than he would like. But James sees those concerns being resolved over time.

'The administrative issues of working together are still falling into place', he said. 'But we wanted to start doing business together, so we focused on client service first. If we had tried to build a large office from scratch, we'd still be figuring out our culture and our infrastructure. Instead, we've already proven we can deliver results.'

Indeed, even in their short time together, the American and English lawyers have a couple of significant successes to boast about. In March 1998, Faegre Benson Hobson Audley represented shareholders of 4-Sight, an English software company that was sold to an American company, WAM!NET, in a complex transaction involving a mixture of cash and stock. Faegre & Benson's corporate lawyers in Minneapolis handled the due diligence, while lawyers for Faegre Benson Hobson Audley negotiated, drafted, and closed the deal in London.

In April 1998, Faegre Benson Hobson Audley petitioned the English High Court on behalf of a Faegre & Benson client in Iowa. The lawyers won a groundbreaking injunction under the UK Arbitration Act by establishing for the first time that the High Court could intervene to secure English assets of an American defendant in advance of judgment in American arbitration proceedings. 'Those are examples of the advantages we can achieve by working together', James believes. 'Through Faegre Benson Hobson Audley, we can offer our clients a depth of knowledge—and efficient delivery—that isn't easy to find in the international legal market.'

He may be right. Faegre Benson Hobson Audley has top-notch lawyers on both sides of the ocean, but what's more important is these two firms truly seem to get along. Lawyers regularly shuttle back and forth for seminars and client consultations, and the two firms have launched an exchange programme, sending associates to each other's offices for extended stays. They're also sharing new ideas for technology and marketing. 'You have to have the raw legal talent to make this work', said James. 'But that's not enough. You can find good lawyers at many firms in the United States and England. The real extra value for clients comes out of the relationship. The more we share resources—the more we know about each other's strengths—the better the results will be for clients. I think this is the beginning of a beautiful friendship.'

Source: R. Zelade, 'Hands across the sea', *International Business* 11(4) (1998): 12–13.

7.1 Introduction

Over the past few years, international strategic alliances have grown exponentially in number, and are now a very popular instrument in global market competition. While the majority of international alliances still involve large multinational firms with global value chains, since the late 1990s there has been a surge of alliance activities involving firms from traditionally non-international sectors such as business services and small and medium firms. Many financial and business services companies, like Faegre Benson Hobson Audley, are joining together to cope with a fast-changing global business environment. Further, international strategic alliances are being formed across a broad range of sectors, including airlines, manufacturing, pharmaceuticals, computers and electronic equipment, and—as the opening cases study shows—legal services.

The current surge in international strategic alliances is prompted by a range of motives. In a global business environment characterized by fierce competition, rapidly changing technologies, shorter product life cycles, and high R&D cost, one of the sources of sustainable competitive advantage for multinational firms is their ability to economize on production and research costs, and access intangible assets such as managerial skills and knowledge of different markets more cheaply and faster than competitors.

The above trends are forcing multinational firms to re-examine the feasibility and wisdom of traditional 'go it alone' market development methods, marketing, distribution, and market entry strategies. Inevitably, multinational firms have come to realize that no matter how strong and resourceful a company, there is no way it can have competitive advantage in each and every step of the value-added process in all national markets, nor can it maintain a cutting edge in all the different critical technologies required for the development, production, and marketing of today's sophisticated products and services.

Consequently, multinational firms now assume that they should forge international strategic alliances unless they can find a good reason not to. If managed properly, international strategic alliances can help multinational firms to transform their operations and gain access to new technologies, accelerate time-to-market, and gain insights that would be extremely difficult for the multinational firm to learn and act on its own.

Many multinational firms that had previously shunned alliances are becoming heavily involved in partnerships. For example, in 1966 General Motors's (GM) policy statement stated that 'unified ownership for coordinated policy control of all operations throughout the world is essential for effective performance as a worldwide firm'. In recent years, however, GM has gone on to forge scores of alliances with competitors and others throughout the world. For example, in September 2001 GM and the Suzuki Motor Corporation of Japan strengthened their strategic alliance which started in September 2000. GM increased its equity ownership in its Japanese partner from 10% to 20%. In addition, GM and Suzuki agreed to produce the jointly developed Chevrolet YGM-1 concept car (a small passenger car designed primarily for the Asian market). The two companies also agreed to exchange personnel in key functional areas, and to include GM representation on the Suzuki board of directors. GM and Suzuki also developed plans to expand their cooperation in areas such as R&D, purchasing, finance, and information systems to further leverage resources.

7.2 The concept of international strategic alliances

What is an international strategic alliance? According to Webster's Dictionary an alliance is an 'association of interests'. In a broad context, the term 'alliance' refers to 'relationships that provide *opportunities for mutual benefit* and results beyond what any single organization or sector could realise alone' Austin (2000: 47). In a specific business and management context, Gulati and Singh (1998) define an alliance as 'any *voluntarily* initiated cooperative agreement between firms that *involves exchange, sharing, or co-development,* and it can include contributions by partners of capital, technology, or firm-specific assets'.

Parkhe (1991: 580) defines international strategic alliances as:

> the relatively enduring interfirm cooperative arrangements, involving cross-border flows and linkages that utilize resources and/or governance structures from autonomous organizations headquartered in two or more countries, for the joint accomplishment of individual goals linked to the corporate mission of each sponsoring firm.

That is, an international strategic alliance is a strategic cooperative agreement, or agreements, between two or more firms, from at least two different countries, which involves exchange, sharing, or co-development for achieving strategically significant objectives that are mutually beneficial and beyond what a single firm could achieve alone.

The above broad definitions comprise a vast array of corporate linkage arrangements, ranging from almost an arm's length vendor–customer relationship to an affiliation just short of a complete merger. These include joint ventures, cross-licensing, reciprocal distribution and promotion arrangements, technology swaps, information exchange agreements, collaborative research programmes, sharing of complementary assets, and cooperative product development and servicing contracts (Hung 1992).

Understanding strategic alliances also requires understanding what they are not (Mockler 1999: 5). Mockler argues that mergers and acquisitions do not constitute strategic alliances because they 'do not involve two or more independent firms sharing benefits and control over a continuing time period'. It is important to note that international joint ventures (IJVs) 'may or may not be true strategic alliances, depending on the circumstances'. It depends on the importance of the contribution and nature of the relationship. If the contribution of one or all parties is minimal, then they only 'nominally can be considered a strategic alliance'.

KEY CONCEPT

An international strategic alliance is a strategic cooperative agreement, or agreements, between two or more firms, from at least two different countries, which involves exchange, sharing, or co-development for achieving strategically significant objectives that are mutually beneficial and beyond what a single firm could achieve alone.

7.3 International strategic alliances: drivers, needs, motives, and pitfalls

7.3.1 Drivers of international strategic alliance formation

Underlying the increasing popularity of international strategic alliances are two broad drivers: globalization and technological factors (see Exhibit 7.1).

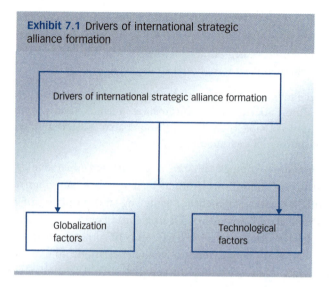

Exhibit 7.1 Drivers of international strategic alliance formation

Globalization

In the current global world economy there is a growing acceptance that, no matter how strong the multinational firm, a strategy based on competition by itself does not necessarily ensure sustainable competitive advantage. In effect, simultaneous competition and cooperation between individual multinational firms are needed to ensure the survival of multinational firms in a dynamic, highly competitive, and increasingly uncertain global business environment.

Although political obstacles to ownership and market entry are diminishing, there are still national and cultural differences that make international strategic alliances attractive vehicles for entering new markets. For instance, Mooij and Hofstede (2002) found that converging technologies, and even the disappearance of income differences across countries, will not lead to homogenization of consumer behaviour across countries. They argue that consumer behaviour will become more heterogeneous because of cultural differences across cultures. As a result, it is very important for multinational firms to work with local companies that understand consumer behaviour better than large multinational firms.

Technological factors

The proliferation of international strategic alliances in recent years has definitely been enhanced by improved communication technology such as the internet, which links geographically dispersed companies easily and cheaply and which enables multinational firms to share know-how and information and to forge integrated distribution networks in different countries simultaneously.

Further, the world market of today is characterized by shortened product life cycles, faster rates of product obsolescence, soaring cost of capital, including the cost of research and development, and ever-growing demand for new technologies which prompt the need to share resources and risks. The cost of developing a new product is also very high. Therefore, multinational firms must minimize the cost of new product development and reduce the chance of product failure. This has led multinationals to forge cross-border strategic alliances to share the cost of new product development, and to develop global product and industry standards.

7.3.2 Motives for international strategic alliances

Multinational firms entering international strategic alliances may be prompted by several motives, including enhancement of their technology development capabilities in order to access or develop new technology, sharing R&D cost and knowledge in order to defray the cost of R&D and improve research capability, and increasing market power through, for example, cartels (Buckley and Glaister 1996). Further, in the current global business environment characterized by short product life cycle, speed-to-market is of the essence, and strategic partnerships greatly increase this speed.

It is necessary to identify when strategic alliances should be considered and when other decisions, such as M&As, are a better option. International strategic alliances are relevant only when there is an advantage in combining the capabilities of two or more international firms, and when the combinations of the capabilities must yield a total value that is greater than if the capabilities were used separately. A case in point here is the alliance formed by the three US auto makers (Ford, General Motors, and Chrysler) to develop an efficient battery for an electric car to meet a regulation in the state of California which requires that a certain percentage of cars on the road should not use gasoline.

International strategic alliances are relevant when a full merger between the firms would be costlier than a series of alliances. An example here is the alliance between the chemical giant Dupont and the pharmaceutical giant Merck. The former brought its productive discovery capabilities along with imaging agent's business experience, while the latter contributed its development expertise, capital, market rights to several brands, and established skills in bringing products to commercial fruition. Merck wanted to speed the costly process of bringing products to market. Dupont wanted to establish itself as a force in the pharmaceutical market. The main motivating force behind this inter-industry alliance is the pooling of expertise to create synergy (Huston, 1991).

The above benefits notwithstanding, international strategic alliances have their pitfalls, of which the major examples are listed in Exhibit 7.2.

7.4 Types of alliance

Most international strategic alliances can be categorized as vertical, i.e. alliances between buyers and suppliers, or horizontal, i.e. alliances between competitors (Nooteboom 1999).

7.4.1 Vertical relationship

Vertical relationships are formed between international suppliers and buyers that agree to use and share their skills and capabilities in the supply chain (see Exhibit 7.3). An example

---

Exhibit 7.2 Pitfalls of international strategic alliances

- The potential for a multinational firm entering a strategic alliance to become too dependent on the partner(s). Rather than carrying out its own consistent strategy, it bases its moves on its partners' moves. As a result, it does not move in a planned direction towards its goal since so much depends on what the partners agree to do.

- Excessive use of strategic alliances to build competitive advantage, without considering the dangers of long-term dependence on partners, could lead to the deterioration of the firm's ability to learn.

- If the alliance is not managed properly, the firm could 'give away too much' or even lose control over its core competencies. For instance, most Japanese are better at managing international strategic alliances, and often learn more from alliances, than their Western counterparts. This is partly because of their ability to imitate while Western firms are driven by the desire to innovate. In addition, Japanese firms tend to keep the same technicians and managers in the alliance for longer periods than their Western counterparts, and often have a clearer idea about what is to be learnt from the alliance than Western partners.

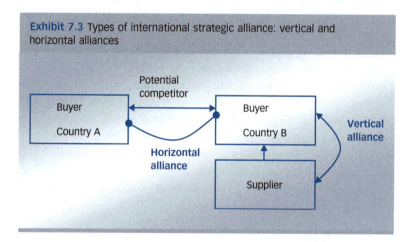

Exhibit 7.3 Types of international strategic alliance: vertical and horizontal alliances

here is Microsoft's several vertical strategic alliances with governments: governments and Microsoft work together to develop e-government strategies, IT-related security issues, and so on.

7.4.2 Horizontal relationship

Horizontal relationships are formed between rival firms selling the same or similar goods and services. They are often called *collaborative* alliances. Though cooperating with one another, the partner firms in such alliances retain their strategic autonomy. They are formed by existing or potential rival companies in order to enhance their respective capabilities and competitive positions in non-competing lines of operations or markets. Yet, at the same time, these firms may face each other as competitors in different lines of operations or markets. Notable examples are the alliances formed by General Motors and Toyota, Siemens and Philips, Canon and Kodak, Thomson and JVC, Apple and Canon, Honeywell and NEC, Texas Instruments and Hitachi, IBM and Apple, and Northern Telecom and Motorola (Hung 1992).

7.5 Selecting and managing partners

In order for international strategic alliances to achieve their goals and objectives, multinational firms must 'select the right partners, develop a suitable alliance design, adapt the relationship as needed and manage the end game appropriately' (Reuer 1999: 13). In this section we discuss the criteria for partner selection, the importance of fit in the international strategic alliance relationship, the balance between trust and risk, and management of the endgame or alliance dissolution.

7.5.1 Partner selection criteria

Arguably one of the most important factors for the success of an international strategic alliance is the selection of the most appropriate partner. The selected partner must bring valuable mix of skills, resources, and competencies to the collaboration. Managers should consider two types of criterion when selecting a partner: *partner-related criteria* such as partner characteristics, compatibility, motivation, commitment, and reliability; and *task-related criteria* which include financial resources, marketing resources, customer service, R&D technical resources, organizational resources, and production resources. The complementarity of both the characteristics and the task-related suitability of the chosen partner provides the basis for success or failure, and dictates the level of benefit achievable from the partnership (Geringer 1990). Medcof (1997) suggests that managers should pay attention to the 4Cs—capability, compatibility, commitment, and control—when selecting a partner (see Exhibit 7.4).

> **KEY CONCEPT**
>
> Two types of criterion should be considered when selecting a partner: *partner-related criteria*, such as partner characteristics, compatibility, motivation, commitment, and reliability; and *task-related criteria*, which include financial resources, marketing resources, customer service, R&D technical resources, organizational resources, and production resources.

7.5.2 International strategic alliances and fit

Successful international strategic alliances should achieve three types of fit: strategic fit, operational fit, and culture fit.

> **Exhibit 7.4 The four Cs when selecting a strategic alliance partner**
>
> Is the prospective partner *capable* of carrying out its role in the alliance?
> Is the prospective partner *compatible* operationally?
> Is the prospective partner *committed* to the alliance and its strategic aims?
> Are the *control* arrangements for the coordination of the alliance appropriate?
>
> *Source*: Based on Medcof (1997).

Strategic fit

Strategic fit is the degree to which a potential alliance partner augments or complements a partner's strategy (Jemison and Sitkin 1986). Strategic fit includes non-conflicting corporate strategies, absence of hidden competitive agendas, and combined opportunity which is greater than that offered by going it alone. For instance, in scale alliances or horizontal alliances, where partners contribute more or less similar capabilities and resources in an attempt to maximize the utilization of similar assets, strategic fit requires all partners to have similar resources and capabilities and to contribute the same amount of resources and capabilities. In vertical alliances, where partners contribute different capabilities in an effort to learn from each other, strategic fit requires partners to contribute equally valuable but different resources and capabilities.

Operational fit

Operational fit includes compatibility of processes, of information systems, of location of facilities, and of profitability and cash flow. That is, deriving value from strategic alliances requires multinational firms and their partners to have compatible systems, procedures, and technologies that can fit or work together.

Cultural fit

There are two types of cultural fit: corporate cultural fit and national culture fit. 'Corporate cultural fit' refers to 'the way we do things around here'. Firms in the same country do things differently. Corporate cultural fit is the compatibility between partner firms as reflected in the similarity of their organizational management style, which include the levels of employee participation or authoritarian management, delegation of responsibility, and decision-making process—centralized or decentralized (Parkhe 1991). When managers consider corporate cultural fit, they should also take into consideration soft issues such as ethics, responsiveness to change, and corporate governance. Cartwright and Cooper (1993: 57–60) state that many alliances fail to meet expectations because the cultures of the partners are incompatible, and the degree of culture fit that exists between combining organizations is likely to be directly related to the success of the alliance.

'National culture' refers to patterns of beliefs and values that are manifested in practices, behaviours, and various artefacts shared by members of the same nation. Because organizations are, in many ways, embedded in the larger society in which they exist, managers should examine both corporate and national cultures.

International strategic alliances work better when the management practices are compatible with the national culture. International strategic alliances could suffer from problems in communication, cooperation, commitment, and conflict resolution caused by partners' values and behavioural differences, which in turn could cause interaction problems and adversely influence the alliance performance. Generally, alliances between culturally similar partners are more likely to be successful than alliances between culturally dissimilar partners. For example, while both US and Japanese partners relate their commitment to perceived benefits from the alliance, they differ in their perception of satisfaction. While the US partners are often concerned with immediate results and use these latter as an important factor for commitment, the Japanese are more concerned with long-term organizational performance. This makes US managers impatient when entering international strategic alliances with Japanese firms.

7.5.3 Strategic alliances in emerging economies

Most Western multinationals are motivated to forge joint ventures with partners from emerging economies because their home markets are saturated and they need to establish a 'bridgehead' in potential foreign markets, and/or to gain access to cheap labour and raw material (Hoon-Halbauer 1999). These motives, however, are not that important for local partners. In most emerging economies, local firms have a customer base and knowledge of local markets, but their technology, management skills, and know-how are outdated. Partners in emerging economies forge alliances with Western multinationals to access financial assets, technical capabilities, and modern technology. Such conflict of objectives may lead to problems in managing the alliance (Hitt et al. 2000).

It is important to note here that the motives for forging strategic alliances differ from one emerging economy to another. Hitt et al. (2004: 183) suggest that multinationals

> should understand that local firms in various emerging-market countries are likely to have different needs and seek different types of partners for strategic alliances. Thus, multinational firms should expect that the motives for forging partnerships with western multinationals to be different from one emerging economy to another.

For example, Kotabe et al.'s (2000) study of the motivations for seeking partners from the perspective of local Latin American enterprises noted that foreign firms seeking entry into Latin America via a partnership with local firms need to address the question of why local firms are motivated to collaborate. The study suggests that access to technical expertise, marketing expertise, financial resources, foreign markets, risk and cost reduction, and competitive markets are the most important factors.

In Mexico, however, Gillespie and Teegen (1995) reported that Mexican firms tend to see foreign partners as little more than sources of financial resources to invest in new technology as well as bringing technological know-how. Understanding the motives behind the alliance helps parties involved to select the appropriate partner and manage the partnership more effectively in emerging economies.

7.6 International strategic alliances: balancing trust and risks

Multinational firms engaged in international strategic alliances face many different kinds of risk. Because of the nature of international strategic alliances, they are inherently more likely than strategic alliances within the same country to be associated with high opportunity to cheat, high behavioural uncertainty, high instability, and poor performance. Shenkar and Yan's (2002) study of the failure of the Ramada–Guilin hotel strategic alliance in China found that the lack of a clear legal framework in China, problems dealing with Chinese institutions, partners' politics, and cross-cultural clashes led to the failure of the alliance.

Das and Teng (1999) organize risks in strategic alliances into two broad categories: relational risk and performance risk. Relational risks are unique to strategic alliances, as single firms' strategic moves are not subject to such risk. Relational risk in strategic alliance refers to 'the probability and consequences of not having satisfactory cooperation'. Opportunistic behaviours include 'shirking, appropriating the partner's resources, distorting information, harbouring hidden agendas, and delivering unsatisfactory products and services'. Das and Teng (1999; 2001) argue that relational risks are an unavoidable—and quite problematic—element of strategic alliances.

Performance risk is the likelihood that 'an alliance may fail even when partner firms commit themselves fully to the alliance' (Das and Teng 1999). This could be due to external factors such as unprecedented fierce competition, political change, government policy change, *force majeure* such as wars, or internal factors such as 'lack of competence in critical areas'.

Gomes-Casseres (2001) notes that because alliances are often based on 'incomplete and evolving contracts', alliances agreements are typically open-ended and contain 'gaps' to deal with unforeseen circumstances. Accordingly, each partner runs some risks that the other partner could 'opportunistically' takes advantage of. Gomes-Casseres (2001) argues that partners in strategic alliances practise 'mutual forbearance' by forgoing short-run opportunistic actions in the interests of maintaining the relationship, which partners expect will yield long-run benefits.

It is clear from the above discussion that trust between partners *is* the most important factors for successful alliances (Parkhe 1998a; 1998b). One key challenge for firms in strategic alliances is to protect themselves effectively from losing their core resources and competencies to their competitors. Exhibit 7.5 provides some basic guidelines in dealing with risks in international strategic alliances.

KEY CONCEPT

Many of the risks associated with strategic alliances, such as poor compatibility with partners, unintended knowledge leaks, loss of skills, and loss of technology often results when managers choose the wrong partner and/or manage the alliance poorly.

Exhibit 7.5 Managing strategic alliance risks

1. Emphasize protection of your own primary resource. Remember that:
   - Risks are relatively low in protecting physical and financial resources, including patents, contracts, logos, and trademarks (ownership protected by law).
   - Risks are high in protecting technological, managerial, and organizational resources. Be careful about unintended transfer of knowledge and imitation; you have little legal protection here.

2. Exercise control through contracts, equity, and management. Employ, as appropriate:
   - Contractual control (specify usage of properties).
   - Equity control (majority or shared ownership).
   - Managerial control (have one's own staff in key positions, regular meetings, frequent interactions and communications).

3. Retain flexibility through short-term recurrent contracts, limiting commitment, and effective exit provisions. You need the ability to adapt, to be free from rigid contracts, and to be able to recover invested resources. Hence:
   - Have contracts specifying an incremental process of alliance-making.
   - Avoid joint ventures and minority equity alliances in favour of less engaging forms such as licensing, shared distribution, and product bundling.
   - Insist on specific costing and pricing formulas and clear property rights, as alliance activities tend to blur ownership contours.

4. Safeguard continued security by limiting exposure to knowhow:
   - Maintain the knowledge barrier by forming alliances in which partners work separately, such as funded R&D and outsourcing agreements, unless you are willing to work closely with partners, as in joint ventures.
   - Make clear to partners and your own staff that unauthorized learning will need to be prevented.

5. Ensure increased productivity by emphasizing superior alliance performance:
   - Focus on knowledge productivity, particularly by seeking compatibility of organizational routines and culture of partners.
   - Identify and eliminate internal stickiness and learning barriers that prevent integration with partner's superior knowledge.

Source: T. K. Das and Bing-Sheng Teng, 'Managing risks in strategic alliances', *Academy of Management Executive* 13(4) (1999), 50–62.

7.7 Endgame: alliance dissolution

Alliance failure leads to wasted resources, diverted management attention, organizational conflicts, and, most seriously, a failure to serve the strategic interests of the partners. Research shows that international strategic alliance failure rate is around 50%. The answer to the question when an alliance should be terminated is not clear. Interestingly, managers are often inclined to escalate their commitment to a failing strategic alliance rather than terminate it. Inkpen and Ross (2001) observed the following:

- Alliances are often difficult to form, making managers reluctant to walk away quickly after protracted and expensive negotiations.

- If alliances are viewed as critical for corporate advantage, persistence becomes like peer pressure: 'If my competitors are forming alliances, we must do the same, and we had better stick with them because termination will be viewed negatively.'

- For many firms, especially those with limited alliance experience, alliance performance is difficult to measure. Thus, whereas an experienced firm may understand when failure is imminent, an inexperienced firm may opt for the benefit of the doubt.

- Alliances often entail high levels of visible senior management involvement and, consequently, both executive ego and political exposure resist feedback.

- Alliances are by definition a combination of resources from multiple firms. Difficulties with assessment of partner competencies may lead to a willingness to persist in the belief that the partner can 'fix things'.

- Alliance endgames can be as protracted as the formation negotiations, leaving firms stuck in an almost endless loop of poor performance and conflict over how to end the alliance.

Because of the above, managers tend to rationalize a failing alliance by, for instance, viewing the losses as the price of future returns. Termination of a strategic alliance is even harder in international strategic alliances. In addition to the above, multinational firms invest more time negotiating the deal with international partners, commit more resources, and put their international reputation at stake. As a result, when an alliance fails they tend to throw good money after bad in the hope that more resources will save the alliance. They may attribute problems with international strategic alliance to the difficulties of doing business in a particular country instead of the poor management of the strategic alliance.

Managers must know when to give the strategic alliance another chance and when to terminate it. Alliances may be terminated for any number of reasons. The collaborative relationship may break down in partner disputes that cannot be resolved; the alliance may accomplish its mission and therefore outlive its purpose; partner strategies may change, eliminating the need for the alliance; or adverse action by regulatory authorities force the alliance to break up.

When and how alliances terminate should be negotiated in advance if possible, allowing for a more or less graceful exit by the alliance partners. There is a great deal of value in knowing that there is a clear way out of the alliance if need be, and in knowing how shared assets will be distributed or disposed of if a partner exits.

KEY CONCEPT

Strategic alliances do end. Endings are not necessarily failures. The only thing that counts is whether an alliance has fulfilled its strategic purpose before termination. Most alliances represent a temporary co-alignment of interests between different parties. When the objective of the alliance is achieved, there is little rationale for the alliance to continue.

7.8 Summary

The current surge in international strategic alliances is prompted by a range of motives, including fierce global competition, rapidly changing technologies, shorter product life cycles, and high R&D costs. One of the sources of sustainable competitive advantage for multinational firms is their ability to forge and successfully manage strategic alliances to reduce R&D cost and to access intangible assets such as managerial skills and tacit knowledge of different markets more cheaply and faster than competitors. With these pressures has come the realization that competitiveness can be enhanced by combining complementary capabilities and competencies of different organizations in close long-, medium-, or short- term relationships rather than opt for the 'go it alone' strategy.

Strategic alliances have several pitfalls. Multinational firms may become too dependent on external partners rather than carrying out their own strategies. This may also lead to the deterioration of the multinational firm's ability to learn. Further, if the alliance is not managed properly, the firm may not be able to protect its core competencies and may 'give away too much' to external partners, some of whom may be direct competitors. Therefore, it is of extreme importance that the firm chooses the right partner—a partner that is trustworthy and meets both related criteria, such as partner characteristics, compatibility, motivation, commitment, reliability, and task-related criteria, such as financial resources, marketing resources, customer service, R&D technical resources, organizational resources, and production resources. In addition to selecting the right partner, for strategic alliances to be successful they should achieve three types of fit: strategic fit, operational fit, and cultural fit. Choosing the wrong partner, or lack of fit between partners, may lead to unintended knowledge leaks and to loss of skills and technology. Furthermore, choosing the right partner is only the first step towards a successful alliance. As an allianice develops, partners need to carefully manage the alliance relationship.

Like all temporary relationships, strategic alliances do and must end. One should not confuse termination with failure. Not all endings are necessarily failures. If the alliance fulfils its strategic purpose it is a success, even if it ends earlier than expected or planned.

KEY READINGS

- Mockler (1999) is useful in providing insights into practical strategies in international strategic alliances.
- A useful book on international strategic alliances is Farok J. Contractor and Peter Lorange (eds.), *Cooperative Strategies in International Business* (Lexington, Mass.: D. C. Heath, 1998).

- Inkpen and Ross (2001) provides a comprehensive analysis to why managers tend to escalate their commitment to a failing strategic alliance.
- Useful papers on partner selecting in emerging economies are Hitt et al. (2000), and Tina M. Dacin, Michael A. Hitt, and Edward Levitas, 'Selecting partners for successful international alliances: examination of US and Korean firms', *Journal of World Business* 32(1) (1997): 3–16.

DISCUSSION QUESTIONS

1 Identify the motives for the strategic alliance between Feagre & Benson and Hobson Audley. (Refer to the opening case study.)

2 Write a short executive brief to the CEO of a multinational firm explaining how international strategic alliances could be used to develop a new high-tech product. Be sure you present your critique of both the advantages and pitfalls of international strategic alliances.

3 By using specific examples, explain how multinational firms balance (or not as the case may be) trust and risks in international strategic alliances.

4 Explain why Japanese multinational firms tend to learn more from international strategic alliances than their Western counterparts.

5 Explain why most international strategic alliances persist beyond their useful life.

Closing case study
Proteome Systems—dancing with the big pharmas

Sydney-based Proteome Systems is an example of a company whose success can be attributed to international strategic alliances. Established in 1999 by a small number of academics who left Macquarie University to establish the company, Proteome Systems has quickly become one of the world's major forces in proteomics (the study of entire protein systems). Proteome Systems is headquartered in Sydney, Australia, and has premises in the Boston area in the United States. The company is dedicated to the development of proteomics technology, the discovery of biomarkers and drug targets, and to proteomic bioinformatics. The company's business strategy aims to generate near-term revenues 'from collaborating with companies in the Pharmaceutical and AgBiotechnology industries in return for research and development payments and a combination of milestone payments and royalties based on achievement of commercial outcomes'.

Because of the company's small size and shortage of necessary managerial and financial resources, its management quickly realized that it could not achieve its objectives without forging global strategic alliances (Ashiya 2000). Keith Williams, chief executive and founder, noted that 'you have got to dance with the big pharmas but you don't necessary have to sell to them' (quoted in Ashiya 2000: 6).

Proteome Systems' first strategic alliance was with Dow AgroSciences in 1999. The two companies signed a multi-year joint research agreement to collaborate on several projects in the area of proteomics. This included research to characterize more completely an entirely new class of proteins being developed by Dow AgroSciences, and to identify new enzymes and novel pathways in the biosynthesis of plant products. Other successful alliances have been established with: Shimadzu Corporation, Japan, to develop a new instrumentation for proteomics based on Proteome Systems' patented technologies and gain access to the Japanese market; and GeneBio Geneva, Switzerland, to be the exclusive distributor of Proteome Systems' GlycoInformatic databases and tools (see Exhibit B). In March 2001, Proteome Systems signed an agreement with the Millipore Corporation, USA, to develop and market novel kits in the rapidly emerging field of proteomics. Two months later, it entered another global proteomics alliance with the Sigma Chemical Company and the new biotech division of the Shimadzu Corporation, Shimadzu-Biotech.

In November 2001 it finalized another global strategic alliance with IBM, aimed at conducting advanced scientific studies into proteins' role in preventing, causing, and treating diseases. According to the alliance agreement, IBM will provide the IT backbone for Proteome Systems' commercial offerings, including its platform for proteome analysis, called ProteomIQ. The latter offers a comprehensive suite of software, instruments, and technologies for integrating, analysing, and managing a full range of protein data, including images and biological samples. Furthermore, the two companies will collaborate on research initiatives, as well as marketing programmes designed to drive sales and to deploy solutions to research institutions, biotechnology, and pharmaceutical companies. Further, IBM will supply hardware and software, and services, as needed, for Proteome Systems' in-house research programs and databases that address and

---

Exhibit B International strategic alliance partners

- **IBM:** Global strategic alliance with IBM Life Sciences. Collaboration in which IBM will supply information technology infrastructure for ProteomIQ. This includes hardware and software, and services as required.

- **The Proteomics Alliance (see www.theproteomicsalliance.com):** Includes *Sigma-Aldrich*, and undertakes such projects as the development of ProteomIQ, the totally integrated proteomics platform.

- **Shimadzu Corporation and Kratos Instruments:** Development and distribution of Xcise, automated instrumentation for the processing of gels for mass spectrometry analysis. Development of the 'chemical printer', an automated solution for high-throughput mass spectrometric analysis of proteins. Partnering on software development for automated high-throughput proteomics analysis on Kratos' Axima mass spectrometer.

- **Sigma-Aldrich:** Manufacturing and distribution of proteomics products developed by proteome Systems.

- **Millipore Corporation:** Development and distribution of consumables and kits for proteomics.

- **ThermoFinnigan:** Collaboration in liquid chromatography, ion-trap mass spectrometry for integration into ProteomIQ. This includes development of sample LC-MS preparation kits and integration of informatics into Proteome Systems, BioinformatIQ, an informatics package.

- **CSIRO (Commonwealth Scientific and Industrial Research Organization):** Collaboration in statistics, data management, software architecture, and industrial image analysis.

- **GeneBio (Geneva, Switzerland):** GeneBio is the exclusive distributor of Proteome Systems' GlycoInformatic databases and tools.

examine proteins involved in cancer, infectious diseases, and age-related illnesses. Proteome Systems can also tap into a wide range of sales, education, training, and technical support programs available through IBM's PartnerWorld for Developers Program—a worldwide program designed to help software developers reach broader markets faster and lower their costs of doing business.

Since 1999 Proteome Systems has quickly grown to become one of the world's major forces in proteomics. With over eighty staff, half of whom hold PhDs or MScs, it has developed a suite of novel technologies to make the world's first integrated, high-throughput platform for proteome analysis. This platform, currently deployed on a large scale in the Sydney laboratories and soon to be deployed in many sites around the world, is massively accelerating Proteome Systems' discovery research. Significant commercial opportunity exists in the commercialization of proteomics technology, and in the application of this technology to the discovery of biomarkers and drug targets.

Sources: M. Ashiya, 'Proteome Systems Limited', case study no. 9-602-039, Harvard Business School, 2000; Proteome Systems Limited's website: www.proteomesystems.com.

Discussion questions

1 Discuss the main drivers for global strategic alliances at Proteome Systems.

2 Discuss the advantages and disadvantages of Proteome Systems' global strategic alliance strategy.

REFERENCES

Austin, J. E. (2000). *The Collaboration Challenge: How Nonprofits and Businesses Succeed through Strategic Alliances* (San Francisco, Calif.: Jossey-Bass).

Buckley, P. J., and Casson, M. (1988). 'A theory of cooperation in international business', in Farok J. Contractor and Peter Lorange (eds.), *Cooperative Strategies in International Business* (Lexington, Mass.: D. C. Heath).

____and Glaister, W. K. (1996). 'Strategic motives for UK international alliance formation', *Journal of Management Studies* 33(3): 301–32.

Cartwright, S., and Cooper, L. C. (1993). 'The role of culture compatibility in successful organizational marriage', *Academy of Management Executive* 7(2): 57–70.

Das, T. K., and Teng, S. B. (1999). 'Managing risks in strategic alliances', *Academy of Management Executive* 13(4): 50–62.

_____ (2001). 'Trust, control, and risk in strategic alliances: an integrated framework', *Organization Studies* 22(2): 251–83.

Geringer, Michael J. (1990). 'Strategic determinants of partner selection criteria in international joint ventures', *Journal of International Business Studies* (first quarter): 41–62.

Gillespie, K., and Teegen, H. (1995). 'Market liberalization and international alliance formation: the Mexican paradigm', *Columbia Journal of World Business* 30 (winter): 58–69.

Gomes-Casseres, Benjamin (2001). 'Inter firm alliances'. In: *Routledge Encyclopedia of International Political Economy* (London: Routledge).

Gulati, R., and Singh, H. (1998). 'The architecture of cooperation: managing coordination costs and appropriation concerns in strategic alliances', *Administrative Science Quarterly* 43(4): 781–814.

Hitt, A. M., Ahlstrom, D., Dacin, T. M., Levitas, E., and Svobodina, L. (2004). 'The institutional effects on strategic alliance partner selection in transition economies: China vs. Russia', *Organization Science* 15(2): 173–85.

Hitt, M. A., Dacin, M. T., Levitas, E., Arregle, J. L., and Borza, A. (2000). 'Partner selection in emerging and developed market contexts: resource-based and organizational learning perspectives', *Academy of Management Journal* 43: 449–67.

Hoon-Halbauer, S. K. (1999). 'Managing relationships within Sino–foreign joint ventures', *Journal of World Business* 34(4): 344–69.

Hung, C. L. (1992). 'Strategic business alliances between Canada and the newly industrialised countries of Pacific Asia', *Management International Review* 32(4): 345.

Huston, P. (1991). 'When two companies capitalise on each other's strengths', *Medical Marketing and Media* (Feb.): 16–25.

Inkpen, A. C., and Ross, J. (2001). 'Why do some strategic alliances persist beyond their useful life?', *California Management Review* 44(1): 132.

Jemison, D. B., and Sitkin, S. B. (1986). 'Corporate acquisitions: a process perspective', *Academy of Management Review* 11(1): 145–63.

Kotabe, H. M., Teegen, P. S., Aulakh, M. C. C., de Arruda, R. J., Salgado, S. R., and Greene, W. (2000). 'Strategic alliances in emerging Latin America: a view from Brazilian, Chilean and Mexican companies', *Journal of World Business* 5(2): 114–32.

Medcof, J. W. (1997). 'Why too many alliances end in divorce', *Long Range Planning* 30(5): 718–32.

Mockler, J. R. (1999). *Multinational Strategic Alliances* (New York: Wiley).

Mooij, M. D., and Hofstede, G. (2002). 'Convergence and divergence in consumer behavior: implications for international retailing', *Journal of Retailing* 78: 61–9.

Nooteboom, B. (1999). 'Voice- and exit-based forms of corporate control: Anglo-American, European and Japanese', *Journal of Economic Issues* 13(4): 845–60.

Parkhe, A. (1991). 'Interfirm diversity, organizational learning, and longevity in global strategic alliances', *Journal of International Business Studies* 22(4): 579–601.

——(1998a). 'Understanding trust in international alliances', *Journal of World Business* 33(3): 219–41.

——(1998b). 'Developing trust in international alliances', *Journal of World Business* 33(4): 417–38.

Reuer, J. J. (1999). 'Collaborative strategy: the logic of alliances', *Mastering Strategy* (4 Oct.): 12–13.

Shenkar, O., and Yan, A. (2002). 'Failure as a consequence of partner politics: learning from the life and death of an international cooperative venture', *Human Relations* 55(5): 565–601.

8

The subsidiary-level strategy

Learning outcomes

After reading this chapter you should be able to:

- identify and describe levels of global strategy;

- identify and describe subsidiaries strategic roles;

- discuss the advantages and disadvantages of the different subsidiary roles;

- identify and discuss the generic strategies;

The old axiom may encourage companies to 'think globally and act locally', but experts say too much local action is hindering the deployment of global e-business processes and content management technology.

As the smoke clears from the internet technology revolution, many multinational companies are struggling with disparate, uncoordinated websites and initiatives. Hewlett-Packard, for instance, estimates that 1,500 sites cropped up among its regional and business units over the past few years.

'One of the hardest parts of our globalization effort is standing up and telling those people that all of this has to look like a single site', said Stephanie Acker-Moy, general manager of HP.com.

Like many multinationals in a range of industries, HP now has a program to standardize its Web technologies and centralize its global content management. But centralizing Web technology often means integrating or replacing 'renegade' sites, and local units often resist central guidance in order to gain more control over e-business initiatives.

The proposed solution—globalization technology—comprises translation, currency conversion, customs documentation, and other tools that facilitate the exchange of Web data among customers and suppliers in different countries. These software and services are often linked to central content management applications, such as those from Vignette and BroadVision.

But multinationals are not racing to buy these. The 20 leading providers of globalization services, for instance, will generate just over $1 billion in revenue this year [2001] and will grow at around 28% a year through 2004, according to an IDC report issued this month. Previous projections by other research firms, however, pegged annual growth rates at as high as 50%.

The problem, experts say, is that local units are so anxious to deliver e-business services to their constituents that they do not wait for corporate headquarters to develop content and technology standards. Such units often contract with local vendors to build and maintain their websites, noted AMR research analyst Louis Columbus.

But these autonomous efforts can lead to millions of dollars in redundant spending and create a mishmash of websites that behave very differently from country to country. For instance, a site in Scandinavia might present completely different information about a product than a site in Asia, leading to confusion among buyers and suppliers.

By building a common web content repository shared across regions, companies can unify their e-business efforts, IT managers said.

'What we used to call worldwide marketing was just an umbrella term for all the different regional efforts', said Kenn Perry, senior director of e-business solutions at computer chip maker Xilinx Inc., which has implemented a global web commerce scheme based on tools from Idiom Technologies Inc. 'But by bringing those efforts together on a common platform, we now can truly do worldwide marketing.'

Centralized globalization planning can also speed time-to-market. Castrol Inc. is using web services from ClearCross to monitor international regulations on its petroleum products so that it can develop a single product that complies with guidelines in every country, rather than regional products that must be rolled out separately. 'It's helped us to avoid costly product launch delays', said Cliff Betton, environmental health and safety manager at Castrol.

In the past, many US companies rolled out products region by region, first in the most lucrative areas. But with e-business, companies are being forced to roll out products simultaneously, experts explained. A centralized content management strategy, which lets companies create a single repository of new product information and then translates it simultaneously for use in multiple regions, is an important step in doing global e-business, they said.

A centralized approach can also reduce web development expenses. HP expects to save 25% on its content development by centralizing the creation of web content, such as product and catalogue data, Acker-Moy said. Castrol expects its multi-million-dollar web globalization initiative, launched in the second quarter, to pay for itself within four months.

Yet despite all the promised benefits, many local and regional offices resist centralized web globalization efforts, observers said. 'There's a mentality that is focused only on the local budget', said Fred Lizza, CEO of Idiom Technologies. 'For a centralized globalization effort to work, it has to be sold at the top so that those local interests will comply.'

HP has ordered some of its local units to rip out the products and tools they had purchased previously and replace them with technology that follows the corporate standard, Acker-Moy said.

But as companies consolidate their international e-business initiatives, they must be careful not to over-centralize their web content, which would make it difficult for local offices to adapt corporate messages to their customers and culture, experts said.

HP, for example, sets stringent standards for product information but gives units flexibility on product positioning 'because some cultures have very different needs and ways of buying', Acker-Moy said.

Corporate headquarters and local offices must strike a peace agreement, said Xilinx's Perry. 'It's sort of like our government, where there is a federal authority that dictates the common platform and state governments that handle local issues', he said. 'You will always have some people pushing for more federal power and others pushing for states' rights. The trick is to strike a balance.'

Source: Tim Wilson, 'Global e-biz mishmash: multinationals push to standardize efforts, but units often resist', *Internet Week* 875 (27 Aug. 2001).

8.1 Introduction

The internet is a powerful medium for reaching and servicing customers around the world. The Boo.com case study (Chapter 3) and the opening case study here, however, demonstrate that cross-national differences in infrastructure, national regulation, local consumer preferences and habits, payment methods, currencies, languages, and attitudes towards pricing and quality all militate against global internet strategies that approach all national markets as if they were the same (Frynas 2003). For instance, payment methods through the internet vary widely across countries. Further, while English may have become the global language, and around 80% of websites in the world are in English, only around 50% of internet users have English as their first language, and the number is decreasing as the internet spreads to more developing countries where English is not the language of business or communication. Goods and services sold over the internet also differ systematically in the extent they may force the firm to be locally responsive or globally integrated. For example, products such as CDs and DVDs are sold around the world without significant adaptation to local markets. In contrast, products such as clothes and accessories require major adaptation to local peculiarities. For these reasons, several companies like Yahoo! and eBay have adapted their websites to specific markets. In early 2000s Yahoo!, for instance, operated twenty-two country-specific portals in thirteen different languages.

However, as the opening case shows, allowing each subsidiary to develop its own website creates serious challenges as well. The multinational firm has to strike a balance between having a single global strategy, such as a single website for the whole company, or having mini-replicas around the world, each developing its subsidiary strategy.

8.2 Global strategy levels

In multinational firms, strategies are initiated at two distinct levels. There is a strategy for the multinational firm and all its subsidiaries which is called headquarter or corporate-level strategy. And there is a strategy for each subsidiary which we refer to as subsidiary-level strategy (see Exhibit 8.1). We will use the terms 'headquarter' and 'corporate-level strategy' interchangeably. At both corporate level and subsidiary level there are several sub-strategies dealing with specific management functions such as finance, human resources, marketing, and operations. This chapter focuses on the subsidiary-level strategy.

Corporate-level strategy deals with the question of *what* business or businesses to compete in, and the overall game plan of the multinational firm. In other words, the corporate-level strategy revolves around the definition of businesses in which the multinational firm wishes to compete, and the acquisition and allocation of resources to its different subsidiaries. The headquarter-level strategy will be discussed in the next chapter.

Exhibit 8.1 Level of global strategy

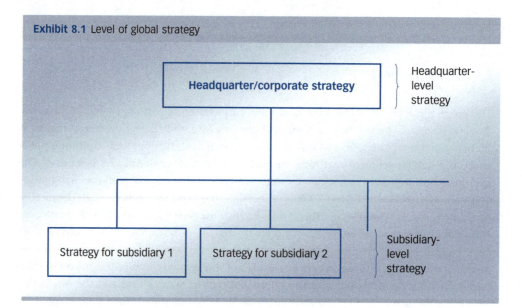

In contrast, subsidiary-level strategy refers to the game plan of each subsidiary. It is concerned with the question of *how* a subsidiary positions itself among local and international rivals to achieve its strategic goals (Dess et al. 1995: 374). It also deals with the integration of subsidiary-level strategy with the corporate-level strategy. Toward this end, the subsidiary level strategy is concerned principally with crafting a strategy that is congruent with the overall corporate-level strategy, and at the same time addressing specific strategic issues facing the subsidiary in its particular industry and or geographical location.

> **KEY CONCEPT**
>
> In multinational firms, strategies are initiated at the corporate/headquarter level and the subsidiary level. Each of the two levels of strategy has an important and distinct role to play in achieving and sustaining competitive advantage. Although key elements of the multinational firm strategy are formulated at the corporate level, strategies dealing with the implementation of the strategy are typically done at the subsidiary level.

8.3 Strategic role of subsidiaries

We broadly define the strategic role of subsidiaries as the significance of the subsidiaries' contribution to the overall global success of the multinational firm. The strategic role of subsidiaries in multinational firms varies from simply meeting the challenges of implementing the global headquarter-level strategy to taking the lead in developing a specific strategy for the subsidiary. Some subsidiaries may be given the authority to make strategic and operating decisions autonomously, whereas others may be passive implementers of headquarters-developed strategy (O'Donnell and Blumentritt 1999: 194; O'Donnell 2000).

The degree to which subsidiaries are actively involved in the formulation and implementation of corporate strategy, and the degree to which they are creators or passive users of knowledge within the multinational firms, varies from one multinational firm to another, and sometimes from one subsidiary to another within the same multinational firm.

Three key factors determine the level of a subsidiary's strategic role. First, corporate-level managers should give the authority to subsidiaries to make strategic decisions when the subsidiary faces conditions of high environmental uncertainty. For instance, when subsidiaries face local uncertainties in their business environment which require quick intervention, headquarter-level managers should give subsidiaries the authority and power to make strategic and operational decisions to deal with these uncertainties.

Second, corporate-level managers should give authority to subsidiaries when the subsidiary production technologies are non-routine and require complex and specific knowledge located at the subsidiary level. Corporate-level managers should keep interference in the strategy of the subsidiary to the minimum because they are not well equipped to respond adequately to local exigencies facing these subsidiaries.

A third major factor determining the degree to which subsidiaries set their own strategy is how much the multinational firm needs to adapt its overall strategy to local conditions.

At one extreme are multinational firms which use a standardized strategy worldwide with little or no modification. At the other extreme are multinational firms that give absolute power to subsidiaries to tailor their strategy to their local business environment. However, in practice it is not a case of all or nothing, but a matter of degree.

8.4 Types of subsidiary-level strategy

Generally, there are three broad types of subsidiary-level strategy. It must be pointed out that it is not a case of either/or, but rather of to what extent the multinational firm is pursuing type 1, type 2, or type 3 strategy. Below we discuss the three types of subsidiary-level strategy.

8.4.1 Support and implementation

Under this approach, multinational firms have a dominant corporate-level strategy, and the job of the subsidiary is to implement the corporate-level strategy. The centre in this case controls most of the multinational firm's activities and makes most strategic decisions. In brief, a dominant corporate-level strategy occurs when a subsidiary produces a component or a product under assignment from the parent for the multinational firm as a whole. Since the subsidiary is simply making an 'assigned' product, very little strategizing is required at the subsidiary level (Crookell 1986).

This is an appropriate strategy in industries where consumers worldwide have roughly the same preference. In these industries, firms should avoid the pressure and temptation to produce completely different products for different geographical markets. As discussed in Chapter 1, extreme customization is a very expensive strategy, and often the returns do not justify the high cost. Instead, firms are advised to produce variations on the basic products. This will obviously increase design, production, and marketing cost, but will have the advantage of greater acceptability by customers in different geographical locations and therefore higher returns.

The support and implementation role is also appropriate when little strategizing is needed at the subsidiary level in cases where, for example, subsidiaries in different countries face similar competitive environments and use standard processes. The role of subsidiary managers in this case is devoted primarily to improving the efficiency of their existing operations. The success of the subsidiary, therefore, requires an internal focus, specifically on achieving operating efficiencies.

Another minor but critical role of subsidiaries is localization of products. Note that under the support and implementation role, the subsidiary is involved more in localization than in adaptation. 'Localization' refers to 'the changes required for a product or service to function in a new country'. Adaptation, however, refers to changes that 'are made to customer tastes or preferences' (Johansson 2004: 392). A subsidiary *localizes* its products by, for example, making adjustments to its electrical equipment to make it compatible with local technical requirements such as electrical voltage. It *adapts* its products to local preferences when, for example, it produces shapes and colours that are popular in that country. Subsidiaries pursuing a support and implementation role are involved more in localization than in adaptation.

One must point out that a support and implementation role should not be taken to mean *total* centralized authority at the parent or corporate level, where the parent acts as the sole command and control. Some strategic elements of global corporate strategy are—and, according to many, should be—dispersed across multiple subsidiaries.

Multinational firms adjust the level of delegation to the subsidiary level by weighing the trade-off between the virtues and the vices of decentralization.

Advantages of support and implementation role strategy

A support and implementation strategy, like most strategic business alternatives, involves trade-offs. The benefits of pursuing a support and implementation strategy must be weighed against possible drawbacks.

Most multinational firms would prefer to have a single standard corporate strategy if their products and services are accepted around the world. Subsidiary managers in this case would not need to redesign their products to suit different customer needs and expectations, or develop a new strategy to compete in their local markets.

Further, from the corporate-level perspective, a sense of unity among its subsidiaries, a willingness to act as part of a single global strategy, is a strategic resource of enormous value, often more valuable than giving subsidiaries the flexibility to design their own strategy with little reference to the global corporate strategy. Having a global corporate strategy means that strategic disagreements and rivalries between subsidiaries are resolved within the context of the global strategy, and once a decision on the direction of a firm has been reached, it will be honoured by all subsidiaries.

Key advantages of the support and implementation role of the subsidiary level strategy include the following:

- Evidence suggests that multinational firms perform better when subsidiary strategies are integrated with corporate-level strategy. This is partly because consensus between corporate-level managers and subsidiary managers allows for strategic decisions to be easily coordinated and implemented, which may lead to better performance.

- A standard global design strategy with a common standard design for the entire market eliminates the sources of additional costs through economies of scale. As explained in Chapter 1, the cost of production tends to decline as the firm gains experience with a particular production process.

- A standard global design strategy with a common standard design for the entire market creates a cost advantage through faster organizational learning. This is because a global design strategy eliminates complexity by focusing on a smaller set of homogeneous tasks, and leads the firm to a faster path of learning through familiarity and repetition.

- A standard global design strategy can enhance efficiency for the multinational firm by producing fewer product varieties in longer production runs in different national plants.

- When subsidiaries focus on implementing and supporting the corporate-level strategy, they are likely to gain strengths in pursuing operational efficiencies.

The support and implementation strategy has several disadvantages. The strategy is not suitable in industries or regions where customers are increasingly more demanding and less willing to accept standard global products and compromise their specific needs and wants. Also, the strategy is not adequate when subsidiaries face conditions of high environmental uncertainty, or when they use non-routine production technologies that require complex and specific knowledge located at the subsidiary.

8.4.2 Mini-replica role

In a truly mini-replica role, the subsidiaries are able not only to select their own strategies in the matters allocated to them but to define their own goals with little interference from the corporate headquarters.

In this approach, while subsidiaries have the authority to design their own subsidiary-level strategy unconstrained by corporate dictates, they must do so within recognized boundaries set by the corporate parent. The key challenge here is how to decentralize the strategy-making process to the subsidiary level without breaking the umbilical cord between the corporate parent and the subsidiaries.

Generally, the mini-replica role is appropriate when subsidiaries operate in highly uncertain business environments, use non-routine processes, and/or require complex and specific knowledge located at the subsidiary. The mini-replica strategy is sometimes also motivated by a basic lack of corporate unity, primarily in a highly diversified company, and by the unwillingness of some subsidiary managers to submit to centralized corporate parent control. This happens when subsidiary managers feel: that they will be discriminated against in the larger unit; that resources within the geographical region or particular industry they inhabit will not be used for the benefit of their subsidiary; that policies will be imposed on them that they find intolerable or damaging; or simply that they want to retain their own identity.

Advantages and disadvantages of the mini-replica strategy

When implemented properly, the mini-replica strategy has several important advantages.

- The first and most obvious advantage is that the more power subsidiaries have, the more opportunity they have to develop a strategy that fits their unique business environment.
- Another advantage of the mini-replica approach is that it frequently leads to better decisions at the subsidiary level, since managers at subsidiary levels are likely to have a clearer view of the business environment in which they operate.
- In a highly dynamic business environment, when the strategy has to be constantly reviewed, the mini-replica approach speeds up decision-making. Often valuable time is lost when subsidiary managers must wait for decisions to arrive from the centre.
- The mini-replica approach also causes subsidiaries to accept responsibility and be accountable for their strategy and action. This may help subordinate managers take initiatives to capitalize on local opportunities that otherwise would be lost.

Drawbacks of the mini-replica strategy include:

- There are costs associated with moving key activities away from the corporate centre. A mini-replica strategy increases manufacturing costs by reducing capacity utilization. Because subsidiaries produce products tailored to their specific markets, cooperation between subsidiaries is minimal.

- Multinationals following a mini-replica strategy may produce too many product varieties in sub-optimally small production runs.

- The mini-replica strategy raises the cost of operations because it is more expensive to hold an inventory of multiple items with each item requiring a minimum level of safety stock. If the local designs are substantially different from each other, such a strategy requires entirely different production processes for different designs, which leads to a higher investment and subsequent higher cost of operation.

- The mini-replica strategy involves promoting multiple products for different segments of the market. It involves a higher level of investment in advertising and marketing management.

- It requires increased effort in market planning and coordination for marketing multiple products for multiple segments of the market, as compared to a global product for all segments of the market.

- In several industries, continued global convergence of customer preferences means that multinational firms can no longer maintain their high cost mini-replica structure.

8.4.3 Global product mandate

Global or world product mandates are defined as the full development, production, and marketing of a product line in a subsidiary of a multinational firm (Rugman 1986). A global or world product mandate gives the subsidiary global responsibility for a single product line, including development, manufacturing, marketing, and exporting (Crookell 1986).

The global product mandate grants subsidiaries the power and authority to undertake high value-added activities in the subsidiary, as well as providing subsidiary management with the opportunity to develop and grow the mandate over time (Birkinshaw 1995). In other words, under the global product mandate, the subsidiary acts more like an equal partner of the corporate parent than a subordinate entity. It can also expect a much higher level of operational autonomy under the world mandate arrangement than under dominant corporate-level strategy.

Multinational firms grant subsidiaries a global product mandate when tariffs to operate in certain countries are prohibitively high, or when firms wanting to sell products in particular markets have to make them locally. Because the global product mandate gives the subsidiary the power and responsibility to act beyond its market, the subsidiary has to have an externally oriented strategy in that it must continually search for untapped or emerging market opportunities for its product. The subsidiary should have relatively great freedom to enter and leave markets in a timely fashion.

The global product mandate has several implications for the multinational firm. First, under the global product mandate functions such as R&D, production, marketing, and strategic management will be located at subsidiary level (Rugman 1986). Second, because subsidiaries with a global product mandate may have unique control within the multinational corporation (MNC) of certain products, they are both integrated within the MNC, because they export finished goods to other MNC subsidiaries, and autonomous, because they have a high degree of independence over strategic product-related decisions.

Advantages and disadvantages of the global product mandate

The global product mandate is similar to the mini-replica strategy. In fact it is a mini-replica strategy but with a mandate to develop, produce, and market a specific product or family of products. The mini-replica strategy, however, grants subsidiaries a broader mandate, which may include different products and/or different markets.

Given the similarities between the mini-replica strategy and the global product mandate strategy, the advantages and disadvantages of the global product mandate are the same as those of the mini-replica strategy.

8.5 Global generic strategies

No matter which type of subsidiary-level strategy is used, the key question for the headquarters is how a subsidiary creates value for the organization as a whole (see Chapter 5 for a discussion of value analysis). Understanding how value is created can help executives in developing a strategy for achieving competitive advantage. According to Michael Porter (1985: 3):

> Competitive advantage grows out of value a firm is able to create for its buyers that exceeds the firm's cost of creating it. Value is what buyers are willing to pay, and superior value stems from offering lower prices than competitors for equivalent benefits or providing unique benefits that more than offset a higher price. There are two basic types of competitive advantage: cost leadership and differentiation.

The two basic types of competitive strategy mentioned by Porter are known as 'generic' strategies, because they can be employed in any type of business in any industry. They can be employed either at corporate level or subsidiary level, or at both in a coordinated fashion. In a multinational firm which has many subsidiaries with diverse strategies, they are of the greatest importance at the subsidiary level.

The subsidiary of the multinational firm, or the corporate level when the multinational has a single standardized strategy, first has to decide what it wants to accomplish with the particular product it offers. The multinational firm and its subsidiaries must decide whether to offer their product to a broad segment of the market or to target a niche market. Ford, for example, produces cars that appeal to, and can be afforded by, a large segment of the population. In contrast, Ferrari produces cars with unique features for mainly young customers with high disposable income. The competitive scope of Ford's products is much larger than the competitive scope of Ferrari's products.

Therefore, a firm's relative position within an industry is given by its choice of *competitive*

Exhibit 8.2 Generic strategies and examples

Generic strategies	Characteristics	Examples
Cost leadership	Competitive scope: broad target Competitive advantage: lower cost	easyJet
Differentiation	Competitive scope: broad target Competitive advantage: differentiation	Mercedes cars
Focus cost	Competitive scope: narrow target Competitive advantage: lower cost	Poundstretcher
Focus differentiation	Competitive scope: narrow target Competitive advantage: differentiation	Ferrari

advantage, i.e. cost leadership or differentiation, and its choice of *competitive scope*, i.e. broad target or narrow target. Based on these two distinctions, Michael Porter has distinguished four generic strategies that firms can pursue: cost leadership, differentiation, focused low cost, and focused differentiation (see Exhibit 8.2). These are discussed in the following sections.

Both internal and external factors determine the choice of competitive strategies at the subsidiary level. Externally, the choice of the competitive strategy is determined by conditions in the subsidiary's competitive market, such as rivalry intensity, and by host country resources and infrastructure. For example, the low level of disposable income and lack of skills and of modern industrial infrastructure forced Western car manufacturers operating in China during the 1980s and early 1990s to follow a low-cost strategy. Because of a shortage of skilled workers, and a lack of firms able to supply high-quality parts, they were not able to produce high-quality cars. Even if they had been able to import high-quality cars, Chinese customers would not have been able to afford them.

Internally, the choice of the subsidiary's competitive strategy is shaped by the role of the subsidiary as set at the corporate level, and by the distinctive resources and capabilities of the subsidiaries that can be deployed overseas (Gupta and Govindarajan 2004) (see Chapter 5 for internal firm analysis).

KEY CONCEPT

A firm's relative position within an industry is given by its choice of *competitive advantage*, i.e. cost leadership or differentiation, and of *competitive scope*, i.e. broad target or narrow target. Based on these two distinctions, Michael Porter has distinguished four generic strategies that firms can pursue: cost leadership, differentiation, focused low cost, and focused differentiation.

8.5.1 Cost leadership strategy

Subsidiaries pursuing a cost leadership strategy appeal to price-sensitive customers. The strategy involves setting out to become the lowest-cost producer relative to local or other foreign rivals in the same market.

The subsidiary's goal in pursuing a cost leadership strategy is to outperform competitors in its market by producing goods and services at a lower cost. As a result, when all competitors in the market charge the same price for their products, the cost leader makes higher profits because its costs are lower. Furthermore, if price wars develop and competition increases, then it is most likely that high-cost companies will be driven out of the industry before the cost leader.

This strategy requires the subsidiary to be fully and continually devoted to cutting costs throughout the value chain. Thus, the subsidiary must vigorously pursue cost minimization activities by tightly controlling overhead costs, and by minimizing costs in activities such as R&D, marketing and advertising, and process innovation. The cost leadership strategy also requires achieving cost advantages in ways that are hard for competitors to copy or match.

Multinational firms and subsidiaries must be careful when pursuing a cost leadership strategy. The subsidiary must reduce cost without compromising product features and services that buyers consider essential. Compromising essential product features in the quest to minimize cost may lead to poor-quality products rather than value-for-money products. Skoda is a case in point here. In its quest to produce cheaper cars in the 1980s and early 1990s, it produced poor-quality cars that became the butt of car-users' jokes (see Exhibit 8.3).

Cost leadership is appropriate when the industry's product is perceived by buyers to be much the same from one producer to another; when the marketplace is dominated by

---

Exhibit 8.3 Skoda: from customers' joke to respected low-cost car

In its quest to produce cheaper cars in the 1980s and early 1990s, the Czechoslovakian car manufacturer Skoda produced cars that became the butt of car-users' jokes ridiculing its quality. Customers did not see a Skoda as a low-cost car; rather, it was perceived as a poor-quality car. This view was reflected in jokes such as:

What do you call a Skoda with a sun-roof? Answer: A skip.

Why does a Skoda have a heated rear windscreen? Answer: To keep your hands warm when you push it.

What do you call a Skoda with twin exhaust pipes? Answer: A wheelbarrow.

In 1991, Volkswagen took a 30% stake in Skoda and, while it continued with the cost leadership strategy, the new venture aimed to produce cars to Western quality standards. Volkswagen invested over £2 billion in the plant, research, development and new models. As a result, in 1994 Skoda launched the successful Felicia model. Although it was built on an old-style Skoda platform, it enjoyed the benefit of Volkswagen features. The second successful model, the Octavia, launched in 1998, was fully built on the Volkswagen group platform. As a result, Skoda has become one of the fastest-growing low-cost car brands in Europe. Although the costs of improving Skoda's quality pushed Skoda's prices up, demand for its products increased. In the UK alone, Skoda's sales rose by 24% in 2001 as opposed to the average market growth of 10.7%. In 2001 Volkswagen took total control of the business.

cut-throat price competition, with highly price-sensitive buyers; when there are few ways to achieve product differentiation that have much value to buyers; and when switching costs for buyers are low.

The cost leadership strategy and the subsidiary–headquarters relationship

Subsidiaries pursuing a cost leadership strategy produce a large volume of fairly standard-ized products that appeal to large price-sensitive segments of the market. They are often internally focused, and their main concern is cost reduction.

The parent and other subsidiaries assist the subsidiary to achieve its cost leadership stra-tegy by supporting activities that lead to cost reduction, such as scale economy in sourcing and cost-effective management skills (see Exhibit 8.4 below). For example, by sourcing glob-ally the parent is able to obtain scale economy in purchasing. The high volume of raw materials or parts purchased by the parent allows the subsidiary to take advantage of volume discounts. Further, the parent is better positioned to scan the international market for the least expensive raw materials or parts. The parent can also shift labour-intensive operations from subsidiaries in countries where labour cost is high to countries where it is low. The subsidiary can also benefit from sharing knowledge and value chain functions with other subsidiaries. For example, a subsidiary located in a country where certain skills for carrying out a specific process are abundant and inexpensive, performs the process for all subsidi-aries. Further, when a single global brand name is used worldwide, the subsidiary makes savings in advertising costs and sales efforts. This support enables the subsidiary to produce and market its product at a lower cost, and thereby gain a competitive advantage.

> **KEY CONCEPT**
>
> A cost leadership strategy involves setting out to become the lowest-cost producer relative to the firm's rivals.

8.5.2 Differentiation strategy

A subsidiary employing a differentiation strategy seeks to be unique in its industry along some dimensions that are perceived widely as unique and valued by customers. While differ-entiation typically involves higher costs, the uniqueness associated with its products allows the subsidiary to compensate by appealing to a broad cross-section of the market willing to pay premium prices. While a subsidiary pursuing a low-cost strategy such as Volkswagen's Skoda may produce a car that is safe, reliable, and durable, Volkswagen's Audi subsidiary follows a differentiation strategy and produces cars with extra-quality features such as ex-pensive leather seats, expensive wood in the dashboard, and so on.

In contrast to the cost leadership strategy, subsidiaries pursuing a differentiation strategy must focus on continuously investing in and developing features that differentiate their products in ways that customers perceive as unique and valuable.

When a subsidiary pursues differentiation, it seeks to distinguish itself along as many dimensions as possible. These dimensions can include brand image, innovation, physical characteristics of the product such as quality or reliability, customer service, or distribution network. For example, in addition to providing high quality and reliability in its products, Rolex, the Swiss-based watch manufacturer, has created a global network of specialists who alone are qualified to guarantee to Rolex owners the authenticity of their watch and the dependability of the features that ensure its longevity in order to safeguard its reputation.

Uniqueness may also relate to the psychological need of customers, such as status or prestige. For example, high-quality cars such as Audi and quality watches such as Rolex are not just reliable and technologically sophisticated products, they also appeal to customers' prestige needs. The development of a distinctive competence, such as Federal Express with its fast reliable service, is also a base for uniqueness.

Differentiation strategy and the subsidiary–headquarters relationship

Subsidiaries pursuing a differentiation strategy require strong support from the parent and other subsidiaries in terms of sharing technology, process innovation, and product development and marketing (see Exhibit 8.4 below). The quality of the product produced by the subsidiary is likely to be thoroughly tested by the parent.

Because differentiation requires constant innovation in order to produce unique products suited to local customers' demand preferences, subsidiaries must share knowledge, processes, and technologies with one another. That is, subsidiaries following a differentiation strategy are likely to depend more on support from the parent and continued resource sharing within the corporate group than subsidiaries following a cost leadership strategy. Note that while in both cost leadership and differentiation strategies the subsidiary requires the support of the parent and other subsidiaries, the type of support the subsidiary needs is different. Subsidiaries following a cost leadership strategy require support that helps them lower cost. In contrast, subsidiaries pursuing a differentiation strategy need support that helps them acquire capabilities necessary for producing differentiated products.

> **KEY CONCEPT**
>
> A subsidiary employing a differentiation strategy seeks to be unique in its industry along some dimensions that are perceived widely as unique and valued by customers.

8.5.3 Focused low-cost strategy

A subsidiary following a focus strategy puts emphasis on a niche market segmented by geographical region, income level, and/or product specialization. A focused low-cost strategy is a market niche strategy, concentrating on a narrow, specific, and recognizable customer segment and competing with lowest prices, a strategy which requires the subsidiary to be the cost leader in its niche. This strategy works well when the firm is able significantly to lower cost to a well-defined customer segment.

Examples of firms employing a focused cost strategy include youth and backpacker hostels, which provide cheap accommodation for students and backpackers looking for a place to stay, or low-cost retailers such as Poundstretcher (www.poundstretcher.co.uk), a UK-based retailer established in 1981 that offers products at a discount to price-sensitive shoppers.

Exhibit 8.4 Generic strategies and headquarter–subsidiary support

Generic strategies	Support from headquarters
Cost leadership	Strong support from headquarters to reduce cost Strong cooperation between subsidiaries to share best practice to reduce cost
Differentiation	Very strong support from headquarters to maintain quality and innovation Very strong cooperation between subsidiaries to maintain quality and innovation
Focus cost	Low support from headquarters Very low support from and cooperation between subsidiaries
Focus differentiation	Very strong support to maintain quality of products and services Very strong support from and cooperation between subsidiaries to maintain quality of products and services

KEY CONCEPT

A subsidiary following a focused low-cost strategy selects a narrow, specific, and recognizable segment whose requirement is less costly to satisfy compared to the rest of the market, and tailors its strategy to serve customers in this segment.

Focused low-cost strategy and the subsidiary–headquarters relationship

Because subsidiaries following a focused low-cost strategy concentrate on a small segment of the market and offer specific products, using well-defined technology and processes, they need only a small degree of support from the corporate parent (see Exhibit 8.4). Further, the link with other subsidiaries may also be weak because subsidiaries following a focused low-cost strategy tend to focus on their local market, which may be served differently from one country to another.

8.5.4 Focus differentiation strategy

A second market niche strategy is focused differentiation strategy. The subsidiary here concentrates on a narrow customer segment and competes through differentiating features.

To be successful, the subsidiary must be able to offer its target market something they value highly and which is better suited than other firms' products to their specific and unique requirements. Further, the strategy must have a strong brand and the subsidiary must have a thorough understanding of its targeted market's unique tastes and preferences, and the ability to offer products with world-class attributes.

Examples of focus differentiation include high-fashion clothing boutiques in Paris and Milan, and sports car manufacturers such as Ferrari, or makers of prestigious cars such as Rolls-Royce. Customers buying from such companies are willing to pay a high premium for the finest products and services.

Focused differentiation strategy and the subsidiary–headquarters relationship

In contrast to focused low-cost strategy, subsidiaries following a focused differentiation strategy need strong support from the parent and peer subsidiaries (see Exhibit 8.4). Producing products with world-class features requires specific resources and competencies that develop from cooperating and sharing information with the parent and other subsidiaries. Also, it is imperative that the parent assist subsidiaries to acquire the necessary resources and competencies in order for them to produce and/or offer products that consistently conform to the highest standards. Although the costs associated with the extensive sharing of information and coordination between the parent and subsidiaries and within subsidiaries is quite high, customers are willing to pay a high premium for the product.

KEY CONCEPT

A subsidiary following a focused differentiation strategy concentrates on a narrow customer segment and competing through differentiating features.

8.5.5 Integrated strategy or 'stuck in the middle'

Multinational firms sometimes adopt a hybrid strategy—also known as integrated strategy—balancing the emphasis on cost reduction against an emphasis on differentiation. The hybrid or integration strategy seeks to provide customers with the best cost/value combination. This strategy has a dual strategic emphasis, appealing to value-conscious customers who are sensitive to both price and value.

Several writers have criticized such a hybrid strategy. Michael Porter and several other writers, while accepting that each generic strategy has pitfalls and that there are different risks inherent in each strategy, argue that a hybrid strategy leads to mediocrity. Porter argues that the two basic generic strategies—cost leadership and differentiation—are incompatible and fundamentally contradictory, requiring different sets of resources and competencies and appealing to different customers; that any firm attempting to combine them would eventually end up 'stuck in the middle'; and that, as a result, such a firm will be outperformed by competitors who choose to excel in one of the basic strategies. Michael Porter (1985:12) noted:

> if a firm is to attain a competitive advantage, it must make a choice about the type of competitive advantage it seeks to attain and the scope within which it will attain it. Being 'all things to all people' is a recipe for strategic mediocrity and below-average performance, because it often means that a firm has no competitive advantage at all.

8.5.6 Criticisms of generic strategies

Several writers have challenged Porter's typology and questioned his claims about the exclusivity of the generic strategies. They argued that, contrary to what Porter advocates, sustainable competitive advantage rests on the successful combination of cost leadership and differentiation strategies (Deephouse 1999). One of the key reasons for adopting an integrated strategy is the turbulent global business environment, which requires multinational firms to adopt flexible combinations of strategies. For instance, Shanghai Volkswagen initially concentrated on a cost leadership strategy and produced cars to be used as taxis in the Shanghai area. Through its operations in China, Shanghai Volkswagen gained a strong market position in its market as well as valuable knowledge on the Chinese car market. Although Shanghai Volkswagen captured leadership in its particular segment, management realized that concentration on a single strategy involved higher than normal risks. New competitors started invading Shanghai Volkswagen's segment by imitating its strategy. There were signs that customers were starting to switch to competitors. As a result, Shanghai Volkswagen expanded its segment, and now follows a multi-segment strategy by pursuing low cost and differentiation strategies simultaneously.

To multinational firms such as Volkswagen, a hybrid strategy combining elements of cost leadership and differentiation is not only possible but is the most successful strategy for them to pursue. The hybrid strategy deals with the many inherent disadvantages of cost leadership and differentiation strategies. When properly employed in the right target market, it is likely to have higher performance than a pure cost leadership or differentiation strategy.

Nonetheless, Porter's generic strategies make a valuable contribution by emphasizing that firms need to make strategic choices between pursuing a certain type of strategy. For instance, when Volkswagen decided to increasingly differentiate its products in China, its costs invariably increased due to extra features offered in its cars. Therefore, firms need to weigh up the benefits of spending more money on more differentiated products as opposed to cutting costs in order to offer customers a low-cost product.

8.6 Summary

In multinational firms, strategies are initiated at two distinct levels. Strategies for the whole multinational firm are formulated at the headquarters *level* and called 'headquarter-level' or 'corporate-level' strategies. Strategies for each subsidiary are formulated at the subsidiary level, and are termed 'subsidiary-level strategies'. Corporate-level strategy deals with the question of *what* business or businesses to compete in, and the overall game plan of the multinational firm. Subsidiary-level strategy is concerned with the question of *how* a subsidiary positions itself among local and international rivals to achieve its strategic goals, and deals with the integration of subsidiary-level strategy with the corporate-level strategy.

As far as the relationship between headquarters and subsidiaries is concerned, we identified three types of subsidiary-level strategy: support and implementation, mini-replica, and global product mandate. Each strategy has advantages and pitfalls. The role of managers is to weigh the advantages against the disadvantages of each strategy before selecting the most appropriate strategy for their organization.

Multinationals cannot, and should not, target all customers in a particular market or country. They need to target a specific segment, large or small, using three specific strategies called generic strategies—cost leadership, differentiation, and focus. The subsidiary can also combine, or integrate, cost leadership strategy and differentiation generic strategies. The integrated strategy is a challenging strategy and has several risks. However, if implemented properly and successful, such integrated strategy enables the subsidiary to enjoy superior performance and enhance its competitive position.

KEY READINGS

- On the relationship between the headquarter and subsidiaries, read O'Donnell (2000).
- On the structures of subsidiaries, see Birkinshaw and Morrison (1995).
- On generic strategies, see Porter (1985).

DISCUSSION QUESTIONS

1 Briefly describe the two levels of global strategy.
2 Identify and briefly describe the roles of subsidiary-level managers.
3 Explain the three different types of subsidiary-level strategy, and discuss some of the pitfalls associated with each type.
4 Briefly describe the three generic strategies—cost leadership, differentiation, and focus—and discuss the pitfalls associated with each of the three generic strategies.
5 Explain the relationship between the three generic strategies and the headquarters–subsidiary relationship.
6 Can subsidiaries—and multinationals as a whole—combine generic strategies of cost leadership and differentiation? Put forward arguments for and against.

Closing case study
Vive la différence

Design harmonization of products is clearly high on the agenda of companies operating in international markets. A few multinationals began the process at the end of the 1980s. Perhaps inevitably, they were US companies. Castigated when they first entered Europe in the 1950s for arrogantly treating the region as one bloc, by the 1990s they were subsequently more admired than despised for emphasizing cross-border similarities instead of being daunted by cultural differences.

One of the most high-profile cases, and perhaps a landmark on the road to design harmonization, was the brand realignment which Mars carried out in the early 1990s. It simply and ruthlessly dropped well-established brand names in local markets and replaced them with what it decreed would be the American versions. In Europe, the chocolate bar, Marathon, became the horrendously named Snickers. Howls of protest followed from the public and press at this monstrous example of US imperialism. But ultimately protesters buckled under because they knew a good chocolate bar when they tasted one, whatever it was called.

There are a number of reasons for the trend towards design harmonization. First, and probably fore-most, companies continue to look for ways to drive out excess costs. Organizational structures, which once included a manufacturing unit in every main market to produce localized versions of the same brand, have been severely rationalized, as have the operational systems which supported them. Likewise, mul-tinationals of every hue are consolidating their promotional strategies into fewer advertising agencies, so it was inevitable that companies would begin to appreciate the benefits of rationalizing design inconsist-encies around the world. As Richard Williams, founder of UK packaging design specialists Design Bridge and now an independent consultant, puts it, 'If you can mastermind the brand centrally, you can reduce manpower and cut production costs.'

This clarion call for centralization has its dangers, of course. The challenge is knowing just how far to go, since the more we are the same, the more we love our differences. The Dutch love to smother their fries with mayonnaise (and a special type at that)—perhaps a tricky poser for the boffins in the Mayo Packaging faculty at McDonald's Hamburger University? The Spanish, for their idiosyncratic part, refuse to buy foam bath or shower gel in the same-size bottles as the rest of Europe. The packaging for a frozen fish meal in Germany has to have the fish topping lined up perfectly with the edge of the fish, whereas in the UK it needs to drip over the edge. The list goes on and on.

A multinational ignores these cultural differences at its peril. And there is another danger in adhering too unswervingly to the cause of consistency: global blandness. Sam Blass, planning director at design consultancy FLB, which has worked with companies such as Heinz and Spillers, argues, 'If the lowest common denominator is used for packaging across countries, it can become quite passive—it has to rely on advertising to give it character. This can leave the door open for an interesting domestic product to nip at its heels.' And if you don't watch out, today's awkward Scottish terriers can turn into tomorrow's corporate Rottweilers.

Finally, before you even so much as think about harmonizing design, make sure you understand how you want your corporate name (as well as your product) to fit into the international 'big picture'. Compan-ies need to be perceived in the 'right way' internationally—and not just for the benefit of the customer. It's also necessary for the workforce, wherever they are and whatever they do, so that they know 'who they are, what they do, where they are going and how they are going to get there', as John Sorrell, chair-man both of the consultancy Newell and Sorrell and of the Design Council, rather neatly puts it. This (of course) is all just common sense—after all, it is the corporate name, as well as goods and services, that is crossing borders. But not thinking clearly about the basics is perhaps the biggest mistake companies can (and still do) make when it comes to harmonizing design.

Source: Laura Mazur, *Management Today* (Oct. 1996): 101–2.

Discussion questions

1 Discuss the advantages of a centralized strategy. Illustrate your answer with examples from the case study.

2 Discuss the potential downside risks associated with a global 'harmonization' design. Illustrate your answer with examples from the case study.

REFERENCES

Birkinshaw, J., and Morrison, A. J. (1995). 'Configurations of strategy and structure in multinational subsidiaries', *Journal of International Business Studies* 26(4): 729–53.

Crookell, Harold H. (1986). 'Specialization and international competitiveness', in H. Etemad and L. S. Dulude (eds.), *Managing the Multinational Subsidiary* (London: Croom Helm).

Deephouse, David (1999). 'To be different, or to be the same? It's a question (and theory) of strategic balance', *Strategic Management Journal* 20: 147–66.

Dess, G., Gupta, A., Hennart, J.-F., and Hill, C. (1995). 'Conducting and integrating strategy research at the international, corporate, and business levels', *Journal of Management* 21(3): 357–93.

Frynas J. G. (2003). 'The limits of globalization: legal and political issues in e-commerce', *Management Decision* 40(9): 871–80.

Gupta, K. A., and Govindarajan, V. (2004). *Global Strategy and Organization* (New York: Wiley).

Johansson, K. J. (2004). *Global Marketing*, 3rd edn. (New York: McGraw-Hill).

O'Donnell, S. W. (2000). 'Managing foreign subsidiaries: agents of headquarters or an interdependent network?', *Strategic Management Journal* 21(5): 525–48.

___ and Blumentritt, T. (1999). 'The contribution of foreign subsidiaries to host country national competitiveness', *Journal of International Management* 5(3): 187–206.

Porter, Michael E. (1985). *Competitive Advantage* (New York: Free Press).

Rugman, Alan M. (1986). 'New theories of the multinational enterprise: an assessment of internalization theory', *Bulletin of Economic Research* 38: 101–18.

9

Headquarter-level strategy

Learning outcomes

After reading this chapter you should be able to:

- understand major headquarter-level strategic management responsibilities;

- understand global sourcing strategies;

- discuss the advantages and disadvantages of vertical integration strategy;

- discuss the advantages and disadvantages of outsourcing;

- list and discuss the different diversification strategies;

- discuss the advantages and disadvantages of the different diversification strategies;

- develop a global market portfolio matrix.

Tata began its activities in 1847 in India as a single business company operating as a textile mill. It is now India's largest and most admired conglomerate. When India won its independence in 1947 the Indian government introduced legislation against monopoly industries and high tax dividends. As a result, over the years Tata had to diversify into unrelated businesses to invest its revenues in different sectors rather than pay high taxes. Tata's activities span most key sectors of the Indian economy including steel, auto manufacturing, hotels, telecommunication, financial services, chemicals, and electricity, IT consultancy, tea, and watches. Nearly 40% of the group's companies are publicly traded, and they account for around 10% of the total capitalization of India's publicly traded companies. All the subsidiaries are linked together by the Tata brand name (with a few exceptions which include Voltas, Indian Hotels Company (Taj Group), Rallis India, and Titan Industries) and are managed by a core of corporate managers dealing with interlocking investments between and within the different subsidiaries.

After India began liberalizing its economy in 1991, Tata intensified its diversification strategy. This was a result of four key factors. First, Tata had been successful in leveraging its well-recognized and admired brand name across a variety of unrelated businesses, and the liberalization of the Indian economy created new business sectors and opportunities which led Tata to diversify even further. Second, Tata is well known in India as a 'good employer', and downsizing or exiting existing businesses was going to damage its image as a trusted employer. Third, Tata needed to update its portfolio of businesses and expand into fast-growing business in India such as IT, as explained by Kishore Chaukar, MD, Tata Industries, '[Tata is] looking at businesses that show promise . . . The logic behind the diversification is to expand the group's presence in the service sector, which is growing faster than manufacturing.' Fourth, several Western companies wanted to enter into partnership with reputable Indian companies. Tata's reputation for integrity, honesty, and good connections with the political and administrative elite in India made it the preferred partner. This led to joint ventures with several Western firms, such as AT&T and Daimler Benz.

Tata's corporate strategy is to manage by a central group of corporate managers. On the one hand their task is to act as a buffer between the different subsidiaries, so that each subsidiary is accountable for its activities. On the other hand, their task is to act as a bridge across the different subsidiaries, so as to enable expansion into new businesses and regions and assistance to businesses that need capital help from the centre. As a result, every time Tata has needed to expand into new business it has acted as a venture capitalist, using capital generated from the different industries to finance the new venture. Because of its aggressive expansion in the mid-1990s, the company's portfolios were not able to generate the necessary capital to finance the new ventures. As a result, it had to sell some of its stakes in several industries. In 1995, for example, it sold its stake in Tata industries to Jardine Matheson.

Similarly, when in 2000 Tata made a landmark deal by acquiring the Tetley brand—a well-known UK-based tea company with a global brand name—for £271 million, it generated the capital for the takeover from different industries. This was and still is the largest cross-border acquisition in India's corporate history. The deal made Tata the second largest tea company in the world after Unilever, which owns Brooke Bond and Lipton. Tetley's price of £270 million was more than four times the net worth of Tata Tea. The purchase of Tetley was funded by a combination of equity, subscribed by Tata Tea, junior loan stock, subscribed by institutional investors, and senior debt facilities, arranged and underwritten by Rabobank International.

In addition to using existing portfolios to raise the necessary capital, new ventures benefit from being able to recruit or borrow skilled managers and employees from existing businesses, or recruit directly from TAS (Tata Administrative Services), Tata's prestigious in-house training programmes. Tata encourages its different business to let its talented employees and managers move from one industry to another to discourage them from moving outside the group. For instance, it has a 'Tata group mobility plan' to assist skilled employees and talented managers to move from one industry to another without losing benefits.

Tata borrowed several Western style tools to manage its diverse portfolio. For example, it introduced the TBEM (Tata Business Excellence Model), which is based on the Malcolm Baldrige Award—an award given for quality for US-based companies that have achieved excellence in quality management—to identify and reward high achievers in the portfolio and assist and support under-performing groups or industries. The award is applied across Tata's different industries. The TBEM approach includes systems for reviewing talents and offering careers opportunities across functions within the same industries within the group.

Tata ranks its different industries according to points scored on the TBEM scale. For instance in 2002, Tata Steel topped the list by scoring 666 points, followed by Titan Watches with 524 points. The aim of the scheme is to help every industry or group in the Tata group to achieve business excellence and develop and sustain a competitive advantage in their respective industries.

In addition to standardized approaches such as TBEM, each group or industry develops its specific approach to managing its respective sector. In 2000, for example, to demonstrate its commitment to its employees the Taj Group—a group of around sixty hotels located in India and abroad run by Indian Hotels Company Limited (IHCL) as part of the Tata group—introduced the Taj People Philosophy (TPP). TPP deals with employees' career plans, training and development, appraisal, and several other aspects of their employment. It was based on the TBEM model. In 2001 the Taj Group started a programme to develop and reward employee loyalty called the 'special thanks and recognition system' (STARS). The STARS programme was used across Taj's group chain of hotels in India and abroad. These practices won the Taj Group the prestigious international Hermes Award in 2002 for 'best innovations in human resources' in the hospitality industry.

Sources: M. P. Chandran, *Implementing Tata Business Excellence Model in Tata Steel* (Centre for Management Research, Hyderabad, 2003); M. P. Chandran, *The TAJ's People Philosophy and STAR System* (Centre for Management Research, Hyderabad, 2003); C. Venkatakirishnan, *Tata Tea's Leveraged Buyout of Tetley* (Centre for Management Research, Hyderabad, India, 2001); U. Wieher, *Tata Tea Limited* (INSEAD, Fontainebleau, 2004); 'Tata group eyes logistics, biotech sectors for diversification', *Economic Times* (19 May 2003); www.tata.com.

9.1 Introduction

To be able to manage a large portfolio of unrelated businesses, multinational firms must have appropriate corporate-level strategy as well as the processes and integrating mechanisms to ensure that the corporate parent adds value. The multinational firm's performance will suffer if its corporate managers do not carefully consider their role in managing relationships with and between subsidiaries. The corporate centre needs simultaneously to act as a buffer between and a bridge across the different subsidiaries. To be able to do the latter, it must act as an arbitrator between the different subsidiaries which themselves have varied and sometimes conflicting interests.

In the last chapter, we examined strategy at the subsidiary level. In this chapter, we examine strategy at the corporate level. Most successful multinational firms expand into different businesses and regions. The role of the corporate strategy is to develop a well-defined and coherent strategy that guides decisions on the scope and types of business to engage in competencies to acquire, countries the firm should operate in, as well as allocation of resources into new business opportunities and re-allocation of resources away from undesirable business. For instance, Tata's management team at the corporate centre acts as a 'command and control' body, setting the direction for the entire organization and managing the corporate portfolio of businesses by selecting sectors in which to compete and by exiting unprofitable or unattractive businesses.

9.2 The role of the corporate parent

The role of the corporate parent is a complex one. 'Corporate parent' refers here to headquarters level. The corporate parent looks for common opportunities to minimize costs and maximize benefits between and within the different subsidiaries. Managers at the centre should possess the expertise and discipline necessary to derive additional value from a portfolio of disparate businesses. For these additional values to be created, however, requires deliberate intervention from the centre. The corporate parent has three key roles (see Exhibit 9.1).

- First, the corporate parent must determine the overall strategic direction and structure of the multinational firm. Managers at the corporate centre do this by providing the basis for identifying new businesses, including major acquisition and divestment, and prioritizing the allocation of resources. The management team at the centre must also articulate clearly and communicate effectively the firm's vision, mission, core values, and objectives.

- Second, the corporate parent must determine the scope of operations by defining the extent of the firm's involvement across different operations and countries. The corporate centre must examine whether the firm is better off with more or with less involvement. The centre must also decide on the extent to which the firm produces its own inputs or owns its distribution channel.

- Third, the management team at the corporate level needs to develop a basis for maintaining an overview of performance across all subsidiaries. The corporate centre does this by continuously reviewing the overall performance of subsidiaries, both to demonstrate how well each subsidiary is performing in relation to its corporate objectives and priorities and to indicate where action is needed to achieve improvement in performance.

9.3 Global sourcing strategies

As shown in Exhibit 9.1, one of the key roles of the corporate parent is developing and managing a global sourcing strategy. The global sourcing strategy must enable the multinational firm to exploit both its own and its suppliers' competitive advantages and the

Exhibit 9.1 Roles of corporate parent

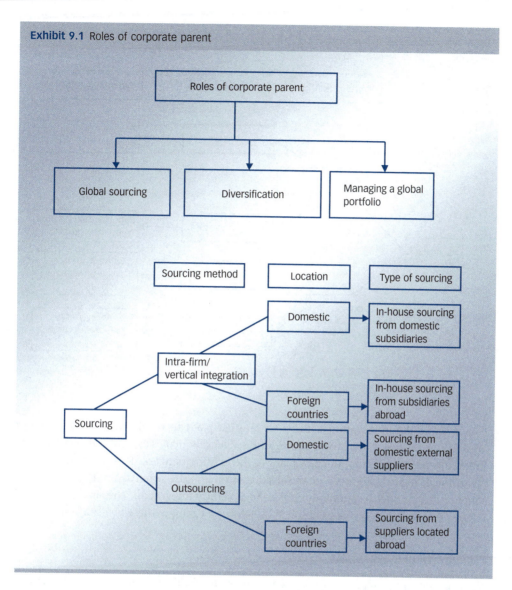

comparative locational advantages of various countries in global competition (Kotabe and Murray 2004). Multinational firms take advantage of locational advantages by sourcing components from foreign markets to take advantage of low production costs in certain countries or regions, or to take advantage of specific skills and technologies located abroad.

Kotabe and Murray (2004) define global sourcing strategy as the management of 'logistics identifying which production units will serve which particular markets and how components will be supplied for production'. Sourcing refers to the process by which multinational firms manage the flow of components and finished goods to serve domestic and international markets. A multinational firm's global sourcing strategy may include vertical integration, outsourcing, or both.

Exhibit 9.2 Outsourcing strategies

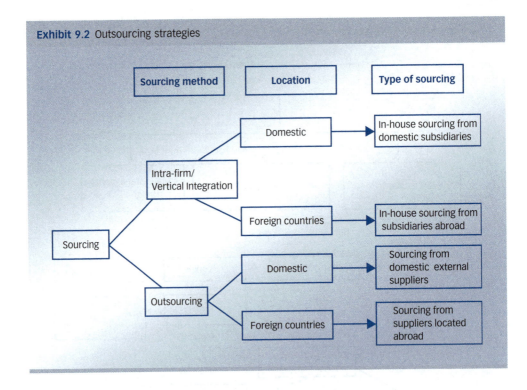

Every time the multinational firm adds another plant to its global network of subsidiaries, it must develop a sourcing strategy to deliver raw materials, and finished and semi-finished goods to and from the new plant to the existing network. This can be done internally through the existing network of subsidiaries on an intra-firm basis or through external suppliers. The former is commonly referred to as vertical integration. The latter is commonly referred to as outsourcing (see Exhibit 9.2). Below we examine these two strategies.

9.3.1 Vertical integration

Vertical integration represents the expansion of the firm's activities to include activities carried out by suppliers or customers. A vertically integrated firm oversees the flow and processing of raw and finished materials, information, and finances as they move in a process from suppliers to manufacturers to wholesalers to retailers to consumers.

Vertical or intra-firm sourcing can be domestic or international. Firms source components in-house domestically when the costs of producing them abroad outweigh the benefits. This is the case when the cost of producing and distributing the components domestically is lower than the cost of producing them in foreign markets, and/or where the quality of the components cannot be guaranteed abroad.

When the firm's sourcing strategy cuts across national boundaries, it is referred to as 'global intra-house sourcing strategy'. It involves coordinating and integrating the flow of inputs both within and among subsidiaries in different countries. To be able to source intra-firm from abroad, the firm needs a network of globally integrated facilities which are able to procure raw materials, transform them into intermediate goods and then final products, and deliver the final products to customers, often in different countries, through an integrated distribution system.

During the 1960s and 1970s, the ability to carry out everything internally at major multinational firms such as IBM, General Motors, and AT&T was considered a powerful competitive advantage. Since the 1980s, however, ample evidence has emerged to suggest that vertical integration may slow multinational firms down, and that in most cases it is better for multinational firms to outsource non-essential activities than do everything in-house. As a result, successful multinational firms such as Dell and Cisco, which outsource many of their operations to partners, are held up as exemplars of good practice. Several successful multinational firms and industries, however, remain vertically integrated. The European package tour business is an example of a vertically integrated sector. Most major European tour operators run their own travel agencies, airlines, hotels, resorts, etc. TUI, the world's largest tourism firm, manages nearly 100 brands, owns over 3,000 travel agencies and nearly 300 resorts, and owns 81 tour operators; it operates around 100 aeroplanes, and has incoming agencies in 17 countries.

KEY CONCEPT

Vertical integration represents the expansion of the firm's activities to include activities carried out by suppliers or customers.

Motives for vertical integration

There are several motives for vertical integration.

- Just after entering a new country, multinationals tend to be vertically integrated because of the lack of suppliers able to produce high-quality inputs. For example, when European and US car manufacturers entered the Chinese market in the 1980s there were no Chinese suppliers capable of producing high-quality auto parts to meet the standards required by multinational firms. As a result, Western car manufacturers had to take control of the supply chain, and often imported complete kits from their home country. As the auto industry grew in China, a network of suppliers capable of producing high-quality parts developed. Consequently, in the early 2000s most car manufacturers in China were using Chinese suppliers rather than producing the parts in-house.

- When competencies needed at the different stages of the value chain are similar, vertical integration provides the multinational firm with the opportunity to transfer best practices, and helps it secure access to critical knowledge and resources at different stages of the value chain.

- Vertical integration enables multinational firms to cross-subsidize one stage of the value chain by another in order to squeeze out competitors. For example, TUI is able to subsidize one of its businesses, such as its airline business, to squeeze out more focused competitors.

- Vertical integration provides multinational firms with the opportunity to retain control over proprietary knowledge, thus preventing leakage of proprietary knowledge to competitors and preventing suppliers from becoming competitors. Vertically integrated multinationals can keep proprietary technology and knowledge within the confines of their corporate system without passing it on to competitors or suppliers. In contrast, multinational firms that are not vertically integrated have to disclose and dissipate knowledge that could compromise their competitive position. For instance, many Asian firms have entered Western markets by first entering as a supplier for Western multinationals and subsequently marketing their own brand independently (Gilley and Rasheed 2000).

- Vertical integration enables firms to foreclose—or at least raise the cost of—input and output markets to competitors (Osegowitsch and Madhok 2003). For example, focused competitors are not able to use—or must use at a higher cost—hotels and tour operators owned by TUI.

- Vertical integration reduces uncertainties in demand and price (Osegowitsch and Madhok 2003). TUI, like other firms in the tourism industry, often faces fluctuation in demand due to external factors such as wars, epidemics, and change in weather. By being able to access data on all phases of the value chain, vertically integrated multinationals are aware of potential problems and are able to plan accordingly.

- Vertical integration enables multinational firms to reduce quality uncertainty by having control over the quality of inputs at all stages of the value chain.

- Vertical integration enables multinational firms to add value at different stages of the value chain. This is very important in sectors where value has immigrated from one stage of the value chain to another. In some industries value added has migrated downstream in the value chain. For example, the number of cars in use is much higher than the number of cars produced. This has led to a considerable shift of value added away from manufacturing to servicing existing products. Thus it makes sense for the manufacturing firm to expand its operations into downstream activities such as after-sales services. Manufacturing firms like IBM, Cisco, GE, and Compaq have moved into computer services and consultancy.

Disadvantages of vertical integration

Studies have identified a number of disadvantages of vertical integration. Below we list three key disadvantages.

- By engaging in several activities, the multinational cannot concentrate on certain core tasks it does best, and as a result more focused competitors may outperform a vertically integrated one.

- Vertically integrated multinationals often have higher costs relative to multinationals which pursue an outsourcing strategy. This is because vertical integration requires higher investment in plants and equipment than outsourcing firms.

- In fast-changing global business environments, and particularly in industries where barriers to exit are high, vertical integration increases inflexibility. For example, when technology or customers' preferences change, vertically integrated multinationals cannot change their technology or product quickly and cheaply. In contrast, outsourcing multinationals can switch their suppliers quickly and at much lower cost than vertically integrated ones.

9.3.2 Outsourcing

Outsourcing has become a significant corporate strategy since the 1990s. Organizations large and small, local and global, are turning to outsourcing in an attempt to improve their performance. Kotabe (1992: 103) defines outsourcing by multinational firms as inputs 'supplied to the multinational firm by independent suppliers from around the world'.

In the 1970s and 1980s multinational firms from Western countries outsourced primarily low-value work and labour-intensive activities to plants in developing countries. Typical of industries that led the way in outsourcing to developing countries were clothing and shoe industries, followed by electronics. For example, Nike outsourced its shoe-making activities to plants located in the Asia Pacific region. In the late 1980s and early 1990s, several firms in the software development sector in Western developed countries started outsourcing their activities to plants in India, Ireland, Taiwan, and South Korea. By the mid-1990s, largely because of the influence of the internet, firms around the world were able to transmit, quickly and cheaply, messages containing graphs, images, and audio and video files. This enabled multinational firms to outsource activities that were technically difficult or prohibitively expensive before the advent of the internet. As a result, firms are now outsourcing activities ranging from basic research to financial analysis. Further, the cost-saving justification for international outsourcing in the 1970s and 1980s has been gradually supplanted by concerns for quality and reliability in the 1990s and 2000s. Large multinational firms such as IBM and Hewlett-Packard all have outsourced their activities to plants in countries such as India and China, because of the low cost of operations as well as the quality and reliability of products produced in these countries. For instance, it is expected that around 3.3 million office jobs and $136 billion in wages will be moved from the US to low-cost countries by 2015. Half of these jobs will be for office support, 14% for computer and computer-related jobs, and only 10% for operations—actual processing and production of goods and services.

KEY CONCEPT

Outsourcing by multinational firms comprises the inputs supplied to the multinational firm by independent suppliers from around the world.

Conditions of outsourcing

Not all activities can be outsourced. To be successful at outsourcing a task in the value chain to a supplier, a firm must meet three conditions (Christensen 2001).

- First, it must be able to specify what attributes it needs from the supplier. If the attributes are not specified, the supplier may add, delete, or modify attributes that are key to the final product.

- Second, the technology and processes to measure those attributes must be reliably and conveniently accessible, so that both the company and the supplier can verify that what is being provided is what is needed.

- Third, if and when there is a variation in what the supplier delivers, the company needs to know what else in the system must be adjusted. That is, the company needs to understand how the supplier's contribution interacts with other elements of the system so that the company can take what it procures and plug it into the value chain with predictable effect.

Types of outsourcing

As shown in Exhibit 9.2, a multinational firm can outsource its activities domestically or abroad. Firms prefer domestic outsourcing when the disadvantages of producing goods abroad far outweigh the advantages. This is the case when the cost of producing and distributing the components by a domestic supplier is lower than the cost of producing them by foreign suppliers, and where foreign suppliers do not posses the necessary skills and technologies needed to produce the components.

In order to reduce production costs under competitive pressure, most multinational firms are increasingly turning to outsourcing of components and finished products from abroad, particularly from newly industrialized countries such as India, China, South Korea, Taiwan, Brazil, and Mexico.

The type of relationship with suppliers can be categorized as arm's-length or strategic outsourcing. A firm's decision to pursue arm's-length or strategic outsourcing is often based on the type of component needed and the firm's country of origin. For example, car manufacturers would acquire necessary but not strategic input from independent suppliers on an arm's-length basis to obtain lower cost of these inputs (Kotabe and Murray 2004: 8). Examples here include belts, tyres, batteries, and entertainment equipments. However, inputs of critical components or processes which are customized and which differentiate the firm's product from its competitors are sourced from suppliers based on strategic partnerships that enable the firm to gain access to suppliers' capabilities and to control the quality of products produced by the suppliers (Kotabe and Murray 2004: 8).

National differences also have an impact on the outsourcing strategy. US firms, for instance, tend to manage their suppliers in an arm's-length fashion. In contrast, Japanese firms divide their suppliers according to the type of input. Suppliers of core products that are crucial to differentiate the product are managed through exclusive, long-term relationships called *keiretsu*. Suppliers of standardized, non-core products, however, are managed on an arm's-length basis.

KEY CONCEPT

Firms prefer domestic outsourcing when the disadvantages of producing them abroad far outweigh the advantages. This is the case when the cost of producing and distributing the components by a domestic supplier is lower than the cost of producing them by foreign suppliers, and where foreign suppliers do not possess the necessary skills and technologies needed to produce the components.

Advantages of outsourcing

Outsourcing has several advantages:

- Cost saving: On average, outsourcing multinationals achieve cost advantages relative to vertically integrated multinationals (Gilley and Rasheed 2000: 765). Cost saving typically occurs because the cost of accessing suppliers in low-cost countries is lower than investing in manufacturing facilities in these countries.

- Access to proprietary knowledge: Outsourcing enables multinational firms to make use of proprietary knowledge to which the company would not otherwise have access. For instance, when US and European retailing firms entered into partnership with Japanese distribution networks by outsourcing their marketing and distribution activities to them, Japanese distribution networks provided them with valuable knowledge on marketing and distribution in Japan such as Japanese shopping behaviours and distribution networks. Further, by accessing proprietary knowledge, the multinational may start producing and marketing the product directly.

- Focus on core competence: Outsourcing frees up internal resources to concentrate on tasks in which the multinational has distinctive capabilities and does them better than competitors. For example, Nike's core competence is in designing and marketing shoes rather than manufacturing them. Nike has outsourced virtually all its manufacturing tasks to outside manufacturers in the Far East and South America, allowing the company to focus on the design and marketing aspects of the shoe industry.

- Flexibility: Outsourcing makes multinational firms 'footloose', enabling them to switch suppliers and countries as new practices, technology, or processes become available through a new supplier or in a different country.

- Competition: Outsourcing promotes competition between suppliers, thereby reducing cost and increasing quality of inputs.

Disadvantages of outsourcing

Like all strategies, outsourcing has several disadvantages.

- Outsourcing may lead to 'hollow firms' offering innovative concepts and designs without investing in physical capital such as manufacturing plants. As a result, as *Business Week* (1986) puts it, by outsourcing, multinationals 'risk putting their brand names on foreign made products'.

- Outsourcing in general and global outsourcing in particular have high failure rates. Research by Dun and Bradstreet (2000) found that around a quarter of all outsourcing agreements fail within the first two years and around half fail within five years. Results from a survey of Fortune 1000 companies reported several problems with global outsourcing including unanticipated increases in cost, culture clashes, and service-level failure. In fact, several firms could not cope with outsourcing related problems, and decided to reverse their outsourcing strategy and perform previously outsourced tasks in-house.

- Unforeseen operational and cultural problems may arise, primarily when Western firms outsource tasks that require repeated interface with customers in the home market. A case in point is Dell technical support in India. Dell received a large volume of complaints from its customers in the US, who complained that operators in India were very rigid in their response because of the standard scripted answers given to employees in India and the difficulty in understanding Indian accents. As a result, Dell considered reversing its move to base its technical support in India.

● Outsourcing may damage the multinational firm's ethical image. When multinational firms outsource, parts of their value chain are outside their physical boundaries and difficult to monitor. For example, Marks & Spencer (M&S) was accused in January 1996 by a British TV channel, Granada, in its *World in Action* programme, of deliberately misleading its customers through labelling its St Michael own-brand products with incorrect country-of-origin stickers. Moreover, it was alleged that M&S had used under-age workers in the production process. M&S implemented a £1 million action plan by creating a 'hit squad' to audit its suppliers through randomly visiting foreign factories to ensure that they did not employ under-age workers. The company also wrote to all its suppliers reminding them of the strict code of conduct and service obligations of being a part of the M&S supply chain.

9.4 Diversification strategies

Some organizations stick to the business they know well, following what is called a 'concentration strategy'. The overwhelming majority of multinational firms, however, operate in more than one business and diversify their operations either across multiple businesses ('industrial diversification') or across different national markets ('global diversification'), or both (see Exhibit 9.3 p. 259).

Most well-known firms, such as Eastman Kodak and Virgin, began their existence serving a single market in a single country, with a single product or service or a small group of products and services. Several large and successful multinational companies, such as Domino's Pizza and McDonald's, are still pursuing a single-market strategy. This is the concentration strategy. Concentration on a single business entails important advantages as well as dangerous disadvantages. On the one hand, by focusing on a single market the firm is better positioned to obtain in-depth knowledge of the business in which it operates than are firms operating in several markets. Further, by concentrating all its resources and capabilities in a single business, the firm should be in a better position to develop a competitive advantage over firms operating in several businesses. On the other hand, pursuing a concentration strategy is dangerous, especially when risk is substantial; when the product or service the company provides becomes obsolete; or when the industry reaches maturity and starts declining (Amit and Livnat 1988).

The rule of thumb is that the firm should stick to its core business unless: the risk of operating in that particular business is high; the firm's existing business stagnates or starts to shrink; or the firm acquires or develops unique competencies that are key success factors and valuable competitive assets in other industries.

As noted above, multinational firms diversify their operations either across multiple businesses (industrial diversification) or across different national markets (global diversification), or both (see Exhibit 9.3)

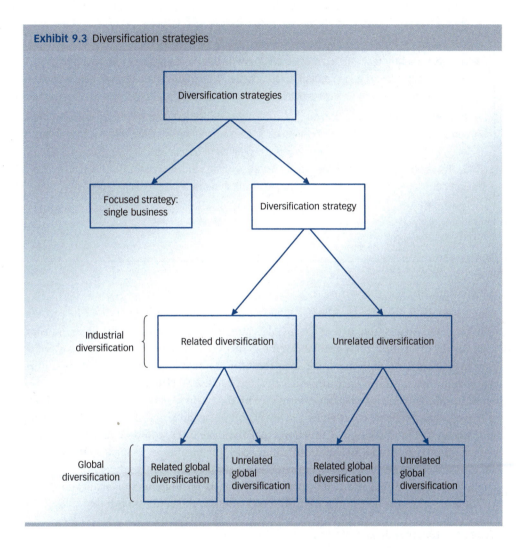

Exhibit 9.3 Diversification strategies

9.4.1 **Industrial diversification**

In the 1960s most commentators and corporate strategists extolled the virtues of diversification in Western economies, and as a result a large number of US and European firms adopted industrial diversification strategies. Accumulated evidence, however, suggests that diversification is not always the best strategy (Datta et al. 1991). As noted earlier, most well-known global companies such as Microsoft, Nokia, Amazon, McDonald's, Coca-Cola, Gillette, and Xerox all obtained their initial success through a single business. Attempts by

---

Exhibit 9.4 Three tests for judging a diversification move

- **The industry attractiveness test.** The new businesses must be attractive enough to yield consistently high returns on investment. The key issue here is sustainability of the forces generating good returns on investment. Temporary factors such as being the fashion of the day should not be relied on as measures of the long-term attractiveness of the new businesses.

- **The cost-of-entry test.** The cost of entering the new businesses should be low enough to allow the potential for good profitability and high enough to prohibit a flood of new entrants and erode the potential for high profitability.

- **The better-off test.** Diversification must offer potential for generating synergy between the current business and the new businesses and/or among the new businesses. This occurs when the whole business becomes greater than different businesses on their own, i.e. $1+1 = 3$. This is possible when the combined businesses lead to lower costs of operations, create a better image, leverage existing resources, and create new or stronger competencies and capabilities.

Source: Based on Thompson and Strickland (2003).

---

some of these companies to diversify failed miserably, and they quickly returned to their core business. An example here is Coca-Cola's attempt to diversify into the wine industry.

Industrial diversification is justifiable if it enhances shareholder value. It does so when the new businesses perform better under the parent firm's umbrella than they would perform as stand-alone businesses (Thompson and Strickland 2003: 294). The parent can only justify itself if its influence leads to better performance by the businesses than they would otherwise achieve as independent, stand-alone entities (Thompson and Strickland 2003: 308). The parent can do this by carrying out functions that the businesses would be unable to perform as cost-effectively for themselves, or by influencing the businesses to make better decisions than they would have done on their own (Goold et al. 1998: 308).

Thompson and Strickland (2003) propose three tests for judging a diversification move: the industry attractiveness test; the cost-of-entry test; and the better-off test (see Exhibit 9.4).

Types of industrial diversification

Several industrial diversification options are available to the firm. The firm has to choose whether to diversify into closely related business ('related diversification') or into completely unrelated business ('unrelated diversification'). Related diversification measures dispersal of activities across business segments within industries. Unrelated diversification measures the extent to which a firm's activities are dispersed across different industries.

Related diversification

A firm diversifies into related business when it enters new businesses that have valuable relationships among the activities constituting their respective value chains (Thompson and

Strickland 2003: 295). A related diversification involves adding new businesses that are stra-tegically similar to the existing business (Davis et al. 1992). For example, Johnson & John-son diversified into products such as baby products, first-aid products, women's sanitary and personal care products, skin care, prescription and non-prescription drugs, surgical and hospital products, and contact lenses. Similarly, the Gillette portfolio includes blades and razors, toiletries, toothbrushes (Oral-B), shavers (Braun), batteries (Duracell), and writing instruments (Parker pens, Mate pens). These portfolios provide these companies with op-portunities to share technological and managerial know-how, to lower costs, to capitalize on common brand names usage, and to benefit from cross-collaborations between the dif-ferent businesses (Ghoshal et al. 1994).

Related diversification presents firms with three key opportunities:

- Economies of scope. Because related business often use similar production operations, marketing, and administrative activities, related diversification provides firms with the opportunity to reduce manufacturing costs, share distribution activities, rationalize sales and marketing activities, and rationalize managerial and administrative support activit-ies (Davis et al. 1992). For instance, firms with closely related manufacturing activities can save costs by sharing knowledge on cost-efficient production methods between one business and another. Further, because of the closely related distribution activities the dif-ferent businesses can perform better together than apart. By managing all the businesses under one corporate umbrella, the firm saves costs by centralizing overlapping managerial and administrative activities such as finance, accounting, R&D, customer support centres, and some of the marketing activities. For example, 3M leverages its capabilities and com-petencies in adhesive technologies to several businesses such as automotive, construction, education, and telecommunication.

- Market power. Related diversification means using common suppliers across the businesses. This gives the firm greater power over its suppliers, and as a result it may secure volume discounts because of the large volume ordered from the same supplier.

- R&D competencies. Related diversification provides firms with the opportunity to transfer valuable know-how from one business to another, and to combine knowledge generated in separate businesses into a single R&D centre. By so doing the firm saves R&D costs, reduces 'new product-to-market' lead time, and is better positioned to develop new products.

KEY CONCEPT

Two industrial diversification options are available to the firm. The firm may diversify into closely related business or into completely unrelated business. The former is known as related diver-sification and the latter as unrelated diversification. Related diversification measures dispersal of activities across business segments within industries. Unrelated diversification measures the extent to which a firm's activities are dispersed across different industries.

Related diversification and synergy   Diversification must offer potential for generating synergy between the current business and the new businesses and/or among the new businesses. The transfer of best practices, however, is often hampered by 'stickiness' (Szulanski 1996; Zander and Kogut 1995; Cohen and Levinthal 1990). General Motors had great difficulty in transferring manufacturing practices between divisions (Gupta and Govindarajan 1986; 1991). Barriers to transfer of best practices include inter-divisional jealousy, lack of incentives, inclination to 'reinvent the wheel' by subsidiaries, lack of commitment, and lack of capacity from the recipient to absorb new knowledge.

The corporate centre can enhance the transfer between subsidiaries by developing the learning capacities of subsidiaries, systematically analysing and communicating best practice, and fostering closer relationships between subsidiaries. Further, parent companies should reward their subsidiaries' managers for working together, to make it worthwhile for these managers to cooperate. For instance, companies such as Enerson and RTZ had problems in the past achieving synergy because they did not reward their subsidiary managers for working together. In contrast, Unilever, ABB, and Canon place a strong emphasis on synergies, and reward managers for working together with other units. Goold and Campbell (2000) listed eight synergy killers (see Exhibit 9.5).

Unrelated diversification

A firm diversifies into unrelated business when it enters businesses whose value chains are so dissimilar that no real potential exists to transfer technology or management know-how from one business to another, to transfer competencies to reduce costs, to achieve competitively valuable benefits from operating under the same corporate umbrella, or to combine similar activities (Thompson and Strickland 2003: 295). For example, Virgin diversified into the airline industry (Virgin Atlantic), railway transport (Virgin Trains), soft drinks (Virgin Cola), and music (Virgin Superstores). Similarly, Giorgio Armani has been leveraging its well-known brand and association with fashion and haute couture into everyday clothes, cosmetics, spectacles, watches, and accessories, as well as furniture (Casa Armani), chocolate and food (Armani *dolce*), flowers (Armani *fiore*), nightclubs (in Milan), and hotels (in Dubai). Although under a common corporate umbrella, these businesses are too dissimilar to present Virgin and Giorgio Armani with any opportunity to share technological and managerial know-how, lower costs, and cross-collaborations between the different businesses.

Further, unrelated diversification, if not managed properly, may lead to what is known as 'contamination'. Contamination occurs when two businesses with different critical success factors are encouraged to work closely together in the name of synergy, and pollute each other's thinking and strategies. For example, when Benetton merged with Benetton Sportsystem in 1998, the 'new' Benetton faced a new form of competition. For instance, while in the casualwear market, Benetton competes through a special network of relationship with its retailers; in the sports business, however, the company has to deal with a host of different distributors, from big distribution chains to small specialized shops and retail agents.

If the corporate parent cannot benefit from leveraging its core competencies, or sharing its activities across businesses, what motivates a firm to diversify into unrelated businesses? The reason in most cases is the quest for a good profit opportunity. For example, a firm may acquire a firm whose assets are undervalued, or a firm that is financially distressed, for less than full market value and make quick capital gains by restructuring it and reselling it as one company or separate parts, whichever is more profitable.

Exhibit 9.5 The eight synergy killers

- **Inhibiting corporate strategy**. Unclear corporate strategy results in confusion about corporate priorities and murky lines of responsibility. As a result, unit managers may be excessively cautious about who to collaborate with and when and how to collaborate. Mixed signals from the corporate parent towards collaboration between units may paralyse unit managers.

- **Infighting between the barons**. This could be due to personality clashes, jealousy, competition for promotion, or infighting between units. Whatever the reason, infighting between unit managers hinders collaboration between units.

- **A culture of secrecy**. Lack of openness reduces people's willingness to share information and trust one another.

- **Misaligned incentives**. If the company does not give credit for working with and contributing to other units' performance and the corporate enterprise as a whole, unit managers will focus on their business units and become lukewarm about working with and helping other units (Ghoshal and Bartlett 1988).

- **Excessive performance pressure**. High performance targets push unit managers to be inward-looking and concentrate exclusively on their own unit's performance.

- **Insulation from performance pressure**. Insulation from performance pressure through e.g. cross-unit subsidies may weaken the motivation to seek out mutually rewarding synergies.

- **Domineering corporate staff**. When unit managers perceive corporate staff to be domineering, inflexible, and arrogant, they resist and often reject decisions made at the centre. As a result, genuine calls for collaboration between units may be opposed by unit managers.

- **Mistrust**. If unit managers mistrust each other, it will be very hard if not impossible for the corporate centre to convince them to work together.

Source: Based on Goold and Campbell (2000).

Unlike in related diversification, where the corporate parent adds value by exploring synergies *across* the different businesses, with unrelated diversification the corporate parent adds value by exploring synergies *within* the different businesses. The corporate parent does this by using its 'parental advantage' (Campbell et al. 1995). The 'parental advantage' stems from expertise in, and support from, the centre. The corporate parent, in this case, makes positive contributions to the different businesses by providing them with skills and competencies hard to obtain without the help from the parent, such as expert help (otherwise not available to them or available only at very high cost) on strategic moves, use of brand names, legal processes, divestment and downsizing strategies, and human resource policies.

Thompson and Strickland (2003: 3003) argue that 'the basic promise of unrelated diversification is that any company that can be acquired on good financial terms and that has satisfactory profit prospects presents a good business to diversify into'. They propose six criteria that firms should use to select an industry into which to diversify (see Exhibit 9.6).

> **Exhibit 9.6 Six criteria that firms should use to select an industry into which to diversify**
>
> - Whether the business can meet corporate targets for profitability and return on investment
> - Whether the new business will require substantial infusion of capital to replace out-of-date plants and equipment, fund expansion, and provide working capital
> - Whether the business is an industry with significant growth potential
> - Whether the business is big enough to contribute significantly to the parent firm's bottom line
> - Whether there is a potential for union difficulties or adverse government regulations concerning product safety or the environment
> - Whether there is industry vulnerability to recession, inflation, high interest rates, or shift in government policy
>
> *Source*: Thompson and Strickland (2003: 3003).

Risks and pitfalls of diversification

Since corporate managers must divide their time and energy between a number of businesses in the portfolio, they will always be less close to the affairs of each business than its own management team. Inevitably, there is a danger that their influence will be less soundly based than the views of the managers running the business.

Further, central cost has a tendency to creep upwards, as unproductive central interference goes unchecked (Oijen and Douma 2000: 309). Goold and Campbell (2002: 219) argue that parents inevitably destroy some value by incurring overhead costs, slowing down decisions, and making some ill-judged interventions, and that many corporate parents do not add enough value to compensate. In these cases the net effect of corporate parent's activities is negative, and it would be better to break up the group.

Diversification may also lead to the use of cross-subsidies which allow poorly performing subsidiaries to drain resources from better-performing ones (Berger and Ofek 1995). That is, diversification enables poorly performing subsidiaries to access free resources as part of a diversified firm, rather than being on their own. This may demotivate highly performing subsidiaries. For example, Michael Walsh reported that when he joined Tenneco as CEO he found that some of Tenneco's profitable businesses such as auto parts and chemical divisions were not striving as they could have done because their surplus was dumped into the company's money-losing businesses such as farm equipment.

Another major risk of diversification is corporate parents' interference in the running of subsidiaries. Interference from parents may inhibit the initiative of subsidiary managers and impel them to take on tasks for which they are ill-suited. For example, Coca-Cola, under Dough Ivester, CEO from 1997 to 1999, was criticized by subsidiary managers for becoming too centralized. The head of Coke Europe, Charlie Frenette, commented, 'if I wanted to launch a new product in Poland, I would have to put in a product approval request to Atlanta. People who had never ever been to Poland would tell me whether I could do it or not' (*Economist* 2001).

This is not to suggest that parents should play a hands-off role. On the contrary, the role of the parent is to develop and communicate clear responsibilities to subsidiaries without excessive detail. Absence of the latter will result in confusion about the specific roles and responsibilities of different subsidiaries, and a danger of destructive conflict between subsidiaries.

Diversification in emerging economies

While managers in Western developed economies are advised to stick to their core business unless they have good reasons to diversify, managers of large firms in emerging economies are advised to diversify into different lines of businesses unless they have good reasons to follow a focused strategy. This has led to the development of highly diversified companies in emerging economies.

Highly diversified businesses in emerging economies include *chaebols* in Korea, *grupos* in Latin America, and business houses in India. This is because, in emerging markets, institutions that support key business activities are not yet developed. According to Khanna and Palepu (1997: 3), companies in emerging economies operate in a market without effective securities regulation and venture capital firms, and as a result focused companies may not be able to raise adequate financing to start or support a new business opportunity. In most cases they are forced to generate the money from within the firm. To be able to do this, firms in emerging economies have to diversify to generate the financial capital to expand the business internally.

Further, without strong educational institutions, firms in emerging economies struggle to hire skilled employees. For example, Tata, like many large groups in emerging economies, has its own management training schools to develop the necessary skills needed to manage the company.

Also, unpredictable government behaviour can stymie any operation in emerging economies (Khanna and Palepu 1997: 4). To guard against this risk, firms have to pursue a diversification strategy to spread the risk of government behaviour. Khanna and Palepu (1997: 6) found that the larger the size of the group, the easier it is to carry out the cost of maintaining government relationships. For instance, Tata and other large groups in India have 'industrial embassies' in New Delhi, the capital of India, to facilitate interaction with bureaucrats and government officials.

Furthermore, in emerging economies, because of lack of information and weak law enforcement, it is very hard for customers to verify claims by firms regarding the quality and performance of products. While the cost of building a trusted brand is very high, once the brand becomes credible, the firms can leverage the power of a trusted and well-known quality image to new products and markets across different businesses. For example, a company like Tata, with a reputation for delivering on its promises, can use its trusted brand name to help it enter new businesses quickly at low cost.

Thus, diversification of a large company in emerging economies provides competitive strength in each market it enters, and helps the company deal with market imperfections in these countries (Lins and Servaes 2002). In contrast, as a result of these imperfections, focused firms would find it very hard to survive in emerging markets. For these reasons, Khanna and Palepu (1997: 3) noted that 'although a focused strategy may enable a company to perform a few activities well, companies in emerging markets must take responsibility for a wide range of functions in order to do business effectively'.

> **KEY CONCEPT**
>
> Companies in emerging economies are advised to pursue a diversification strategy for the following reasons: institutions that support key business activities are not yet developed; lack of strong educational institutions; unpredictable government behaviour; lack of information and weak law enforcement to verify claims by firms regarding the quality and performance of products.

9.4.2 Global diversification

Recent commentators have often extolled the virtues of global diversification. The main motivations for global diversification include the search for new foreign markets in an effort to exploit unique assets in foreign markets; to gain access to lower-cost, higher-quality input, or both; to build scale economies and other efficiencies; and to pre-empt competitors who may seek similar advantages in strategic markets (Kim et al. 1989).

On the one hand, increased integration of the global economies and opening of new markets has increased the feasibility of global diversification. On the other, heightened global competition has forced more firms to focus on their core line of business. That is, while global diversification has increased over time, industrial diversification has declined over the same period. It must be noted here that global diversification is not replacing industrial diversification. The causes of the recent increase in global diversification are different, and not related to the causes of the decline in industrial diversification. Indeed, research shows that, on average, firms with high global diversification have a higher level of industrial diversification than firms operating in a single country or a very small number of countries (Denis et al. 2002: 1953).

Related and unrelated global diversification

There are two types of global diversification: related global diversification and unrelated global diversification. Related global diversification is the dispersion of a global firm's activities across countries within relatively homogeneous cluster of countries (Vachani 1991: 307–8). Unrelated global diversification is the dispersal of the global firm's activities across heterogeneous geographic regions (Vachani 1991: 308). Let us assume that Western European countries can be regarded as a homogeneous cluster. A British firm that sells its products in five countries all of which are Western European would be regarded as having relatively highly related global diversification. However, a British firm that sells its products in five countries with one each in Africa, the Middle East, South America, Asia Pacific, and

Western Europe would be regarded as having highly unrelated global diversification. To distinguish between related global diversification and unrelated global diversification, one needs to consider three factors:

Physical proximity Buckely and Casson (1976) argue that communication cost in multinationals depends on the physical distance between the countries in which the firm operates. This is because of the costs associated with coordinating and controlling a widely dispersed network of subsidiaries. Accordingly, multinationals that operate in countries clustered physically close to each other should have lower costs of managerial coordination, and their managers may benefit from intimate personal contact. It must be pointed out here that, as noted in Chapters 1–3, the impact of recent technological advances such as the internet are reducing the importance of physical proximity.

Cultural proximity Generally, multinationals that operate in a cluster of countries with similar cultures and a common language may enjoy efficiencies because of reduced complexities in management operations. These complexities may arise because of dissimilarities in the language, culture, and socio-economic environment (Buckley and Casson 1976). Generally, the larger the cultural distance between the centre and the subsidiary the harder the task of transferring technical and managerial knowledge.

Level of economic development Intangible assets are generally hard to transfer to certain types of countries. For instance, if a multinational's success is associated to a large extent with intangible assets, which are highly valued in Western countries, it may find it easier to operate in similar Western countries than in developing countries, where customers value tangible assets more than intangible assets.

Benefits of global diversification

Global diversification can help the multinational firm achieve numerous benefits:

- Global diversification enhances shareholder value by exploiting firm-specific assets, by increasing operating flexibility, and by satisfying investor preferences for holding globally diversified portfolios (Hitt et al. 1997; Kim et al. 1989; Tallman and Li 1996).

- Global diversification may also enhance value by creating flexibility within the firm to respond to changes in relative prices, differences in tax systems, and other institutional differences (Hitt et al. 1997).

- Global diversification gives multinational firms the flexibility to shift production to the country in which production costs are low, or shift distribution to the country in which market demand is highest.

- Global diversification gives the multinational firm the ability to lower the firm's overall tax liability by exploiting differences in tax systems across countries, and to raise capital in countries in which the costs of doing so are lowest. The benefits of global diversification can raise investors' diversification preferences. This is the case when multinational firms are able to diversify globally at a lower cost than individuals.

- Global diversification may also benefit corporate managers through increased power and prestige, through compensation arrangements, or through personal risk reduction (Denis et al. 1997).

- Risk-spreading is one general reason for global diversification. Global diversification enables multinationals to spread risks across markets.

Costs of global diversification

Costs associated with global diversification include:

- A globally diversified firm is more complex than a purely domestic firm. This complexity could lead to high costs of coordinating a globally dispersed network of subsidiaries.

- Global diversification can lead to the inefficient cross-subsidization of less profitable business units. This often happens when subsidiary managers exert influence to increase the assets under their control. This leads, in some cases, to less profitable divisions being subsidized by more profitable subsidiaries.

- Managers may have the personal incentive to adopt and maintain value-reducing diversification strategies, even if doing so reduces shareholder wealth. Managers can benefit from global diversification in at least three ways. First, managing a large company, with subsidiaries all around the world, confers greater power and prestige on the manager (Jensen 1986). Second, levels of managerial compensation tend, on average, to be positively correlated with firm size (Jensen and Murphy 1990). Third, global diversification reduces the risk to the managers' relatively undiversified personal portfolio (Amihud and Lev 1981). Hence, if these private benefits exceed the manager's private costs, the firm may pursue value-reducing global diversification.

- It is possible that the costs of coordinating corporate policies in diversified firms, and the difficulties in monitoring managerial decision-making in globally diversified firms, increase the likelihood that the costs of global diversification outweigh the benefits (Denis et al. 2002: 1976).

9.5 Managing global portfolios

9.5.1 The roles of corporate parent

The corporate parent must provide a basis for a continuous review of performance at the different subsidiaries to be able to judge their performance. Further, the continuous review will allow subsidiaries to compare themselves with others and identify aspects for further improvement. It must be pointed out that the quest from the corporate centre to achieve consistency of performance measurement, and to ensure a sufficient degree of rigour and objectivity in measuring and reviewing performance, may create tension between the corporate centre and subsidiaries which want to retain control over their operations, and which seek to 'defend' their performance (see Chapter 12).

The review of the overall performance can be done in many ways:

- The corporate centre should challenge the way in which products and services are currently provided, and whether they are needed at all. This implies that the corporate centre has a good understanding of the different businesses.

- The corporate centre should consult with relevant stakeholders (subsidiary managers, employees, and customers) to explore and appraise options for improving performance, developing key performance indicators, and (when appropriate) setting performance-improvement targets.

- The corporate centre should review and compare performance of the different subsidiaries with competitors on the basis of the agreed key performance targets. Reviews will need to address the key aspects of performance which are important in the context of locally derived priorities. This enables the corporate centre to make an informed judgement about good or poor performance, and hence intervene when necessary to address the problem.

When the headquarter reviews the performance of subsidiaries, it should: challenge the way in which products and services are currently provided and whether they are needed at all; consult with relevant stakeholders (subsidiary managers, employees, and customers) to explore and appraise options for improving performance, developing key performance indicators, and when appropriate, setting performance improvement targets; and review and compare performance of the different subsidiaries with competitors on the basis of the agreed key performance targets. Reviews will need to address the key aspects of performance which are important in the context of locally derived priorities. This enables the corporate centre to make an informed judgement about good or poor performance, and hence intervene when necessary to address any problems.

9.5.2 The management of global portfolios

Several portfolio models have been proposed over the years to help firms manage their portfolios. However, most of these models were developed for firms operating in a single country, and are not therefore fully adequate to capture the complexity of diversified multinational firms. Diversified multinational firms cover multiple international markets, with multiple related or unrelated product lines. Few writers, however, have attempted to adapt well-known portfolio management tools to incorporate the multidimensional nature of diversified multinational firms. For example, the directional policy matrix—which was developed to assist managers to consider a portfolio of businesses in terms of the attractiveness of the industry within which the firm operates and the strength of the business units—was adapted by Harrell and Kiefer (1993) to develop a global market portfolio matrix as a way of considering a portfolio of businesses in different countries in terms of the country attractiveness and the company's compatibility with each country (see Exhibit 9.7).

The global market portfolio matrix positions subsidiaries in each country according to country attractiveness and competitive strength.

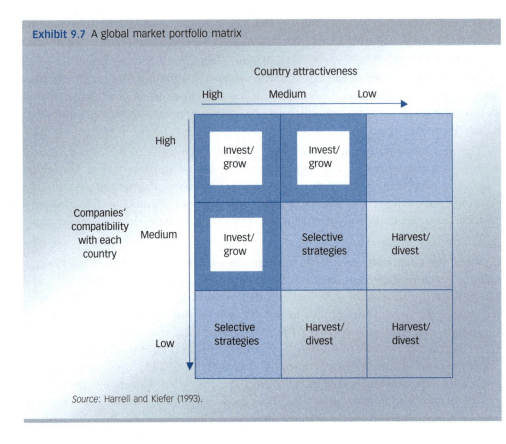

Exhibit 9.7 A global market portfolio matrix

Source: Harrell and Kiefer (1993).

Country attractiveness

How attractive is the relevant country in which the firm operates? Country attractiveness is measured by its market size—measured according to projected average annual sales in units—growth rate of its market, strength and number of competitors, workforce availability, legal business environment, economic indicators, and political risk and stability. The above factors should be weighted according to their relative importance (Harrell and Kiefer 1993). The weighting of the factors produces a single linear scale composed of the several factors. Below is an example of calculating country attractiveness proposed by Ford (Harrell and Kiefer 1993):

Country attractiveness = market size + 2 * market growth + 0.5 * price control/regulation + 0.25 * homologation requirements + 0.25 * local content and compensatory export requirements + 0.35 * inflation + 0.35 * trade balance + 0.3 * political factors.

The weights represent the relative importance of each variable to Ford's strategic planning efforts. The equation uses market size as a benchmark, and weights market growth as twice the weight of market size. That is, the importance of market growth for Ford is double that of market size. The weight of price-control regulation is half the weight of market size, and compensatory export requirements is one-fourth the weight of market size, and so on.

Competitive strength

How compatible is the company's strength with each country? The firm's competitive strength is measured by (1) relative market share, (2) product fit, (3) contribution margin, and (4) market support.

Relative market share Because market share tends to vary considerably from country to country, Harrell and Kiefer (1993) use market share as a benchmark factor. They argue that in domestic markets many industries have only three or four major competitors. Therefore the firm's relative market share is measured by its share of the market. In international markets, firms often have more than three or four competitors. Thus, rather than using market share as the single factor by which to measure the firm's relative market share, two market share factors are relevant to a multinational firm: the number of major competitors in the market and the firm's total market share.

Product fit Product fit represents an estimate of how closely the product fits a particular market need. In the tractor industry, for example, 'Ford defines this broadly in terms of horsepower classes and more specifically in terms of unique product features which may or may not match country needs' (Harrell and Kiefer 1993).

Contribution margin This is a measure of profit per unit and profit as a percentage of net dealer cost. Low contribution margins often reflect limited price scope because of competition or government controls. Harrell and Kiefer argue that while this measure should be reflected in the other three elements, it does serve as a measure of ability to gain profit, an important competitive strength.

Market support This includes availability of a high-quality workforce, and the firm's ability to attract the required number of employees to carry out parts service and technical support, and advertising and sales promotion capability within the country to acquire and enhance the company image there.

Ford used the above factors to compute a single linear scale reflecting a firm's competitive strength as follows (Harrell and Kiefer 1993):

Competitive strength = 0.5 ∗ absolute market share + 0.5 ∗ industry position + 2 ∗ product fit + 0.5 ∗ profit per unit + 0.5 ∗ profit percentage of net dealer cost + market support.

As with the country attractiveness, the weights reflect managers' subjective estimates of the relative importance of each variable in defining the competitive strength required to excel in international markets.

Each subsidiary is positioned within the 3 × 3 global market portfolio according to the above indicators of attractiveness and strength. The matrix thus helps managers consider appropriate corporate-level strategy, as shown in Exhibit 9.4. It suggests that the firm should invest and grow in markets with the highest attractiveness and the highest strength.

Markets in the invest/grow position require further commitment and resources by the corporate level to enable them to strengthen their presence and grow. This can involve such tactics as expanding existing plants, opening new plants, or both.

In contrast, the firm should harvest and divest from markets with the lowest attractiveness and the weakest strength. This can involve such tactics as closing or downsizing existing plants and selling off assets.

9.6 Summary

Most multinationals today have multiple businesses in different countries. The role of the headquarters or parent is to improve, or at least sustain, the value-creation capabilities of the subsidiaries and the multinational firm as a whole.

The corporate parent has three key roles. First, it must determine the overall strategic direction and structure of the firm as a whole. Second, it must clearly define the scope of the business in which the firm operates. Third, it must develop a basis for maintaining an overview of performance across all subsidiaries.

Headquarter-level or corporate parent strategy needs to be based on a clear view of how value can be added by the corporate parent (Goold and Campbell 2002: 221). The rule of thumb is that corporate parents should avoid intervening in businesses unless they have specific reasons for believing that their influence will be positive.

Effective strategic management at the headquarter or corporate level of the multinational firm requires a clear understanding both of the potential for strengthening the competitive position of the multinational through outsourcing and of the threats posed by outsourcing. Understanding the advantages and disadvantages of outsourcing helps corporate managers to decide whether or not to outsource, and to determine the optimal extent of outsourcing by the multinational firm.

Another fundamental task of the headquarters is to manage the multinational's growth strategy. Should the multinational operate in a single business, diversify into related businesses, diversify into unrelated businesses, diversify into geographically related countries, or diversify into geographically unrelated countries? When the multinational firm follows a diversified strategy, corporate managers at headquarters must be able to identify and create synergies among multiple subsidiaries or businesses. The parent must have sufficient skills and resources to implement strategies which take advantage of potential synergies. It should also play an active role, when required, in promoting, guiding, coordinating, and arbitrating between subsidiaries (Goold and Campbell 2002).

KEY READINGS

- Kotabe (1992) is a comprehensive book on global sourcing strategy.
- Goold et al. (1998) deals with the challenges of adding value at the corporate level.
- For an excellent review of the relationship between global diversification and firm value, see Denis et al. (2002), and Kim et al. (1989).

DISCUSSION QUESTIONS

1 Select a multinational company and discuss the advantages and disadvantages of pursuing (or not as the case may be) a vertically integrated strategy.

2 Multinational firms must outsource non-core activities to remain competitive. Discuss this statement, illustrating your answer with examples.

3 Critically examine the argument that firms in emerging economies should pursue a diversification strategy.

4 Refer to the closing case study and discuss the advantages and disadvantages of Lufthansa's diversification strategy.

5 Choose a multinational company and develop a Global Business Portfolio Matrix (refer to section 9.4).

Closing case study
Lufthansa's diversification strategy

The highly diversified Lufthansa group's business strategy has been under intense scrutiny following the announcement of massive losses accumulated by its non-core businesses. The German carrier, Europe's third-largest player behind Air France and British Airways, posted €980 million (US$1.22 billion) losses in March 2003, including an unexpected €700 million write-off covering LSG Sky Chefs. Moreover, the airline's operating profit plunged 96% to a weak €30 million.

Lufthansa maintains a broad portfolio of airline-related businesses such as catering (LSG Sky Chefs), tour operations (Thomas Cook), information technology (Lufthansa Systems), maintenance, repair and overhaul (Lufthansa Technic) and logistics (Lufthansa Cargo).

The diversification strategy was introduced by former chairman/CEO Juergen Weber, who spun off former business divisions into separate subsidiaries in the mid-late 1990s to boost third-party revenues. That way, Weber hoped, Lufthansa would become less dependent on economic cycles.

Two of the most ambitious projects appear to have failed. Under Weber's leadership, German retail giant KarstadtQuelle combined tour operator Neckermann and charter operator Condor Flugdienst into C&N Touristik. After acquiring British tour operator leader Thomas Cook, the company was renamed Thomas Cook. Now Europe's largest travel group, it has been plagued by falling market prices caused in part by travellers' increasing preference to book their own arrangements.

In the climate following September 11, 2001, US revenues of LSG Sky Chefs, the world's biggest airline caterer, suffered a dramatic decline. This deterioration has prompted a plan to put Chef Solutions, a division selling food to restaurants and supermarkets. According to JP Morgan's airline analyst, Chris Avery, Chef Solutions alone is losing as much as €100 million/year. According to HypoVereinsbank's Uwe Weinreich, the write-off for LSG Sky Chefs was €300 million above forecast.

Weber, who was succeeded by Wolfgang Mayrhuber, retains significant influence in the Lufthansa group and continues to serve as chairman of the board. In-house sources indicate that internal criticisms regarding current strategy are rife, although a fundamental shift is opposed at the very top management level.

Nevertheless, Lufthansa has begun to sell non-core assets, a policy that has generated since 2001 more than €1 billion in cash. The group sold its share in ground-services company Globeground for €370 million and a 25% stake in DHL International went for €610 million. Earlier this month, Lufthansa also sold its stake in Amadeus Global Travel. Despite losses, Lufthansa executives' predictions for 2004 remain optimistic, at least for the record.

Source: J. Flottau, 'German plunge: Lufthansa's 2003 results are writ in glaring red ink; non-core businesses, deteriorating markets fingered', *Aviation Week and Space Technology* 160(9) (1 Mar. 2004): 37.

Discussion questions

1 Was it wise for the former chairman/CEO Juergen Weber to enter new businesses in the mid-late 1990s?

2 Discuss Lufthansa's strategy in the period following September 11, 2001.

REFERENCES

Amihud, Y., and Lev, V. (1981). 'Risk reduction as a managerial motive for conglomerate mergers', *Bell Journal of Economics* 12: 605–17.

Amit, R., and Livnat, J. (1988). Diversification and the risk–return trade-off', *Academy of Management Journal* 31: 154–66.

Berger, G. P., and Ofek, E. (1995). 'Diversification's effect on firm value', *Journal of Financial Economics* 37: 39–65.

Buckley, P. J., and Casson, M. C. (1976). *The Future of the Multinational Enterprise* (London: Holmes & Meier).

Business Week (1986). 'The hollow corporation', *Business Week* (3 Mar.): 53–5.

Campbell, A., Goold, M., and Alexander, M. (1995). 'Corporate strategy: the quest for parenting advantage', *Harvard Business Review* 73(2): 120–32.

Christensen, M. C. (2001). 'The past and future of competitive advantage', *MIT Sloan Management Review* 42(2): 105–9.

Cohen, W. M., and Levinthal, A. D. (1990). 'Absorptive capacity: a new perspective on learning and innovation', *Administrative Science Quarterly* 35: 128–52.

Datta, D. K., Rajagopalan, N., and Rasheed, A. M. A. (1991). 'Diversification and performance: critical review and future directions', *Journal of Management Studies* 28: 529–58.

Davis, P. S., Robinson, R. B., Pearce, J. A., and Park, S. H. (1992). 'Business unit relatedness and performance: a look at the pulp and paper industry', *Strategic Management Journal* 13: 349–62.

Denis, J. D., Denis, K. D., and Sarin, A. (1997). 'Ownership structure and top executive turnover', *Journal of Financial Economics* 45(2): 193–221.

———— and Yost, K. (2002). 'Global diversification, industrial diversification, and firm value', *Journal of Finance*, 57(5): 1952–79.

Dun and Bradstreet (2000). 'Dun and Bradstreet sees 25 per cent growth for global outsourcing', www.businesswire.com (23 Feb.): 3–4.

Economist (2001). 'New Formula Coke' (3 Feb.).

Ghoshal, S., and Bartlett, A. C. (1988). 'Creation, adoption, and diffusion of innovation by subsidiaries of multinational corporations', *Journal of International Business Studies* 19: 365–88.

_____Korine, H., and Szulanski, G. (1994). 'Interunit communication in multinational corporations', *Management Science* 40(1): 96–110.

Gilley, K., and Rasheed, A. (2000). 'Making more by doing less: an analysis of outsourcing and its effects on firm performance', *Journal of Management* 26(4): 763–90.

Goold, M., and Campbell, A. (2000). 'Taking stock of synergy', *Long Range Planning* 33: 72–96.

_____ _____(2002). 'Parenting in complex structures', *Long Range Planning* 35: 219–43.

_____ _____and Alexander, M. (1998). 'Corporate strategy and parenting theory', *Long Range Planning* 31(2): 308–14.

Gupta, A. K., and Govindarajan, V. (1986). 'Resource sharing among SBUs: strategic antecedents and administrative implications', *Academy of Management Journal* 29: 695–714.

_____ _____(1991). 'Knowledge flows and the structure of control within multinational corporations', *Academy of Management Review* 16(4): 768–92.

Harrell, D. G., and Kiefer, O. R. (1993). 'Multinational market portfolios in global strategy development', *International Marketing Review* 10(1): 60–72.

Hitt, A. M., Hoskisson, E. R., and Kim, H. (1997). 'International diversification: effects on innovation and firm performance in product-diversified firms', *Academy of Management Journal* 40: 767–98.

Jensen, C. M. (1986). 'The agency costs of free cash flow: corporate finance and takeovers', *American Economic Review* 76(2): 223–9.

_____and Murphy, J. S. (1990). 'Performance pay and top management incentives', *Journal of Political Economy* 98(2): 225–64.

Khanna, T., and Palepu, K. (1997). 'Why focused strategies may be wrong for emerging markets', *Harvard Business Review* (July–Aug.): 41–51.

Kim, W. C., Hwang, P., and Burgers, P. W. (1989). 'Global diversification strategy and corporate profit performance', *Strategic Management Journal* 10: 45–57.

_____ _____ _____(1989). 'Global diversification strategy and corporate profit performance', *Strategic Management Journal* 10: 45–57.

Kotabe, M. (1992). *Global Sourcing Strategy* (New York: Qurom Books).

_____(1998). 'Efficiency vs. effectiveness orientation of global sourcing strategy: a comparison of U.S. and Japanese multinational companies', *Academy of Management Executive* 12(4): 107–19.

_____and Murray, Y. J. (2004). 'Global sourcing strategy and sustainable competitive advantage', *Industrial Marketing Management* 33(1): 7–14.

Lins, V. K., and Servaes, H. (2002). 'Is corporate diversification beneficial in emerging economies?', *Financial Management* 31(2): 5–32.

Oijen, A. van, and Douma, S. W. (2000). Diversification strategy and the roles of the centre', *Long Range Planning* 33: 560–78.

Osegowitsch, T., and Madhok, A. (2003). 'Vertical integration is dead, or is it?', *Business Horizon* 46(2): 24–35.

Szulanski, G. (1996). 'Exploring internal stickiness: impediments to the transfer of best practice within the firm', *Strategic Management Journal* 17: 27–44.

Tallman, S., and Li, J. (1996). 'Effects of international diversity and product diversity on the performance of multinational firms', *Academy of Management Journal* 39: 179–96.

Thompson, A. A. Jr., and Strickland, J. A. (2003). *Strategic Management: Concepts and Cases*, 13th edn. (New York: McGraw-Hill)

Vachani, S. (1991). 'Distinguishing between related and unrelated international geographic diversification: a comprehensive measure of global diversification', *Journal of International Business Studies* (second quarter): 307–22.

Zander, U., and Kogut, B. (1995). 'Knowledge and the speed of the transfer and imitation of organizational capabilities', *Organization Science* 6(1): 76–92.

It was the last week of March 2000. The President of ABB Flexible Automation (FA) was considering strategy options for the division, which had traditionally focused on the automotive industry. Ten years ago, over 60% of business went to automotive OEMs. The figure had now dropped to 40%.

The industry was changing rapidly. Automotive OEMs acted as designers and assemblers while other manufacturers supplied parts and components. Customers were buying differently. The new market environment called for a change in strategy.

TRW, the U.S.-based manufacturer for aerospace, information systems, and automotive components, had recently announced a $7 billion acquisition of British auto parts maker Lucas-Varity PLC. The deal would create an auto parts giant with revenue of $18.7 billion. It would also position TRW to offer complete modular packages for automobile front ends. In spite of widespread industry expectation that the TRW bid would go through, rival components manufacturer Federal-Mogul, previously rebuffed for its own offer of $6.44 billion in cash and stock to Lucas-Varity, had just announced plans to tender a revised bid.

In addition, U.S.-based Ford Motor Co., the No. 2 automaker worldwide, had finalized its purchase of Swedish auto manufacturer Volvo for $6.47 billion. The deal had been in negotiation for some months and was no surprise.

In late 1996, FA had signed a joint venture with Volvo AB of Sweden to supply automation equipment for automotive body assembly and press lines. The JV had become part of the flexible automation unit and included operations in Toronto, Detroit, and Sao Paulo, as well as at the Volvo site in Sweden. FA had retained a majority share and assumed management responsibility. Volvo had benefited by streamlining operations, and FA had increased its resources for serving the automotive industry. An FA executive reflected on how recent events might impact global buying patterns.

'Our customers are changing rapidly, especially in the automotive industry. The dividing line between the role of automotive OEMs and auto parts makers is in transition and will influence how we do business. New opportunities are opening in other markets as well. As we move into the 21st century, we must examine our competitive formula and see if it still applies. We face a multitude of options, but we cannot pursue them all.'

Goals of the Flexible Automation Business Area

The FA goal was to achieve $3 billion in orders by the year 2000 and sell 15,000 robots with 25% of sales from the general industry segment. These targets represented a big increase over 1996–1997 activity: $1.4 billion in orders, 8,500 robots sold, and 12% of sales to general industry. An executive stated:

This case was prepared by Martha Lanning, Research Associate, William F. Glavin Center for Global Management, based on research by Todd Zilinski, MBA candidate, under the direction of Jean-Pierre Jeannet, F. W. Olin Distinguished Professor of Global Business at Babson College. The case was written as a basis for class discussion rather than to illustrate either effective or ineffective handling of a business situation.

See cases *Asea Robotics AB (A)* and *Asea Robotics AB (B)*, and industry note *The Worldwide Robotics Industry 1987*. See also *ABB Flexible Automation (A): Global Strategy for the Millennium*, and *Note on the Robotics and Flexible Automation Industry (1999)*.

Our total orders increased through 1997, but the automotive industry worldwide has experienced slowing investment. General industry order volume has also increased, and we can expect it to continue in this positive direction. However, we may need to manage our activity so that we are less dependent on customers in automotive vehicle manufacturing.

FA faced critical issues. Profit margins were declining, the robot market was becoming commoditized, and customized systems development had begun to monopolize business. Margin decline resulted from downward price movements caused by stiff competition, robot commoditization, and global purchasing operations serving larger customers. In 1997, 71% of business was in systems including customized systems and function packages. The remaining 29% of business was robotics products (18%) and customer service (11%). The division planned to improve its numbers by focusing on three goals:

- Increase function package sales
- Globalize operations, processes, and products
- Diversify the industry mix

Strategic Options

Global customers expected high quality and uniform service in all locations. FA would need to offer a common business approach and product range worldwide. To maintain lead position in multiple markets and industry segments, it would be necessary to maximize advantages already in place and increase customer benefits. The following options were now under consideration, some in combination with one another:

1. Add new industry segments:

FA was examining entry into new industries making parts and products outside the automotive and auto parts-making segments, such as metal fabrication, rubber, plastics, aluminum foundries, and consumer packaging. It would be desirable if applications already in use could serve in new industries. For example, the automotive segment required shaping, forming, and welding, and FA possessed expertise in these areas. These applications could be adapted for use in other segments. (**Exhibit I**)

Metal fabrication would not require adding new applications, a positive factor in cost analysis. Sheet

Exhibit I New industry segments

Value added activities for a robotics press automation line project	Cost Components of a Bakery System	Percent of Total Cost
Design engineering	Conveyers	20%
Project management	End Effectors	20%
Other equipment/services	Robot	30%
Mechanical components/de-stacker	Engineering	15%
Grippers	Ancillary equipment	10%
Control system	Miscellaneous	5%
Installation/programming		

metal required forming, cutting, joining, and welding, all functions for which FA had already developed equipment, components, and applications. Aluminum foundries involved die-casting, deburring, and placing an object into a container. FA already produced many of these applications. Consumer goods packaging, particularly the food and beverage segment, required picking, packing, and palletizing. The new FlexPalletizer already in use was proving highly successful in these applications, and FA could expand the customer base. Rubber and plastics were new areas, and it would be necessary to explore the cost of adding activity in these segments. Expansion would mean strengthening capability to serve nonautomotive customers.

Adding segments meant either adding new applications or expanding applications already in use. Each option implied different requirements. A breakdown of applications used by the installed base of 60,000 units suggested process applications and assembly as the weakest areas. (Exhibit II) Two considerations would be whether market opportunity existed and whether the cost of a new segment would make adding it worthwhile. Cost depended on using applications already available vs developing new applications.

Building a new robot family meant developing peripherals, function package, and software. Software development was critical because software drove the operation of the cell. For example, to perform arc welding, it was necessary to optimize basic robot parameters such as movement for corners and curves, parts gripping and handling, speed, accuracy, and welding process requirements. For the cell to perform with the required precision, the robot needed 'vision' software which used lasers, cameras, fixtures, and parts grippers. (Exhibit III)

Adding a new robot family required 20 man-years (MYs) in engineering investment. Creating application software to make the robot work took 15 MYs, and developing the robot shape took five MYs. One MY cost $100,000. Ten people working for six months was equivalent to five MYs. FA now used 300 MYs annually. One-third of this figure was required to maintain the present line. Of the remaining 200 MYs, 150 were required to develop new projects. Developing a cell took 20 MYs per application segment, such as yogurt handling in consumer goods packaging. Assuming R&D expenditure of 5%, each robot cost $50 thousand. To break even, sales of $40 million or 800 units in two years were required. Given product life cycle of four to five years, planning required investment payback in two years.

Exhibit II Application base installed

Application	FA installed base	Worldwide installed base
Arc Welding	19%	13%
Spot Welding	32%	25%
Glueing/Sealing	3%	1%
Painting	11%	3%
Cutting/Deburring/Polishing	5%	2%
Picking/Packing/Palletizing	3%	3%
Foundry	9%	3%
Materials Handling		13%
Assembly		18%
Others	18% (including handling and assembly)	

Exhibit III **Flexible automation system: components and application costs**

COMPONENTS

Conveyers
Sensors
Fixtures/Jigs
Tools
Programmable logic controllers
PCs
Software
Hydraulics/pneumatics
Turntables
Actuators
Test/inspection equipment
Control panels
Fencing/safety equipment
Exhaust/environmental equipment
Magazines

APPLICATION COSTS (GENERAL MARKET AVERAGES)

Systems Application	Average Price per Robot	System Markup Factor per Robot	Average Cost per System (with 1 robot)
Arc Welding	$40,000	1.7–2.0	$74,000
Spot Welding	$50,000	2.0–2.3	$107,500
Materials Handling	$65,000	1.3–1.5	$91,000
Painting	$80,000	3.0–4.0	$280,000
Other	$55,000	1.0–1.7	$74,000

2. Increase total order volume:

By 1997, total order volume had reached $1.4 billion. FA had set a goal of $3 billion for the year 2000. Reaching this goal represented approximately doubling 1997-level activity and required increased volume in all sectors. (**Exhibit IV**) FA would need to enhance service to both global and local customers to capture additional business in fiercely competitive markets. FA would need to leverage scale advantages and global supply management, develop the Centers of Excellence, and advance the level of standardization for robot content in all systems. Advantages of scale and increased standardization could provide an edge over small and midsize systems integrators.

Expanding order volume might include some or all of the following:

Options for expanding order volume:	Considerations required:
1. Add market share.	Capture market share from competitors. Decide which segment(s) to pursue.
2. Add new products.	Analyze market opportunity.
3. Sell greater volume of current products.	To which customers? In which segments? Reduce prices? Increase services?
4. Acquisition, joint venture, or other agreements.	Which industry? Which segment? Where geographically?
5. Add new customers in new industries.	Cost of adding new applications. Which industry? Which segment? Where geographically?
6. Expand customer base in current industries.	By adding market share? Create new products. Capture customers from competitors.
7. Add new segments.	Which industry? New application vs. use application currently offered.

3. Reduce costs:

During the period 1991–1994, FA had successfully reduced the cost of robotics products by 30%. Global customers were managing supply globally with more bundling and standardization, putting pressure on prices. Reducing costs for robotics and body-in-white systems would be a priority in the extremely competitive climate.

One way to reduce costs was to increase standardization, especially for systems products. FA had used this strategy to standardize solutions and function packages for paint robots. Engineering and production time had dropped by 80% from 550 hours per robot in 1995 to 100 hours in 1997. The press automation cell was another successful example. During 1994 to 1998, average system costs had fallen by 30% from $650,000 to $450,000.

Body-in-white prices had dropped 25% to 30% in the last three years, and it would be desirable to reduce costs in this sector. Maximizing economies of scale to trim costs would answer global customer demand for price reduction and increase competitive edge over small and midsize local systems integrators. FA could benefit from the same factors that had provided advantage with robotics products:

- Centralized production and delivery
- Economies of scale
- Global standardization
- Global supply management

4. Change pricing policies:

A recent survey of European country managers ranked FA above rivals in most categories. Weakest scores were in pricing policies and pricing image. FA was often at a disadvantage. Small local systems houses

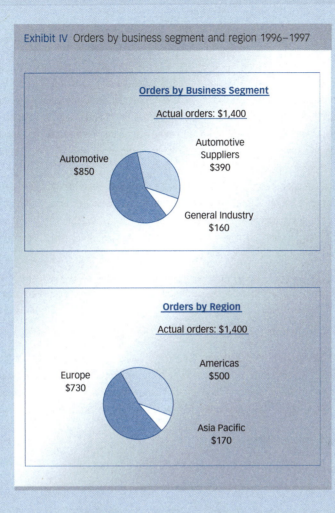

Exhibit IV Orders by business segment and region 1996–1997

Orders by Business Segment

Actual orders: $1,400

Automotive
$850

Automotive
Suppliers
$390

General Industry
$160

Orders by Region

Actual orders: $1,400

Europe
$730

Americas
$500

Asia Pacific
$170

used lower prices because of modest overhead, whereas FA as a global company supported larger overhead. It would be necessary to review pricing policies and determine where changes were needed to remain competitive.

5. Reshape the function package concept:

CoEs had begun to develop function packages and market them worldwide. FA had incorporated more standard equipment into these products, hoping for greater global economies of scale. The rationale had been to capture local business when purchasing decisions were based on price, thereby gaining ground over small local systems suppliers. Function packages brought higher margins. Naked robots were becoming commoditized, and robot makers that failed to integrate were being squeezed. Systems added value and generated most of the profit. Improving function package sales would raise profits. The question was how far to integrate in order to compete yet remain cost-effective.

The function package concept had been discussed as early as 1988. Over 50 potential function packages had been identified, but by 1997 only 12 had been developed. CoE engineers responsible for development found implementation difficult. One reason was their global mandate, which meant they developed and sold systems to customers around the world. CoEs were usually located near their main customers and the engineers were not accustomed to thinking globally. (**Exhibit V**) The control panel of a machine exemplified problems in developing a global function package. Specialized systems, developed in one country for one customer, could be equipped with a control panel outfitted with commands and signs common to the local spoken language. However, engineers now faced the task of designing a panel with universal symbols. This requirement was forcing engineers to think globally. A solution that might work in one country might not work in another, an undesirable situation for cost savings. Most CoEs could not sell enough function packages in their local countries to compensate for volume potentially lost because of single-country focus in design.

A second challenge appeared when CoEs tried to develop a solution for the general industry segment. FACs and CoEs realized they did not understand customer needs, unlike in the automotive segment. They had persisted in designing function packages they thought would be beneficial, but without adequate customer input. Many function packages developed had originally been conceived for the automotive industry. The President of FA Germany defined the problem:

'Function packages are taking longer than expected to implement at FA because of the organizational time requirements and the lack of knowledge about the market, especially for the general industry segment.'

6. Modify the FAC concept:

Running FACs worldwide now cost approximately 10% of sales. FACs operated as company-owned sales offices. FA was the only competitor to run such a worldwide operation. FACs had initially supplied products and service on a global level. It was now time to rethink the FAC concept. Phasing them out either partially or totally could reduce costs. New solutions could be devised to assure supply and service. (**Exhibit VI**)

7. Modularize the product line:

One way to become more efficient would be to modularize the product line.

Exhibit V Centers of excellence

Application	Location	Business unit
Spot welding	France, Sweden, Canada	Body-in-white systems
Die casting	Germany	Robotic systems
Powertrain assembly	Germany	Robotic systems
Sealing	Germany	Paint automation
Press brake tending	Italy	Robotic systems
Glazing/Power	Italy	Paint automation
Paint atomizers	Japan	Paint automation
Press automation, robot-based	Spain	Body-in-white systems
Press automation, doppin-based	Sweden	Body-in-white systems
Palletizing	Sweden	Robotic systems
Arc welding	Sweden	Robotic systems
Waterjet cutting	Sweden	Robotic systems
Deburring/grinding	Switzerland	Robotic systems
Trim & final assembly	U.S.	Robotic systems

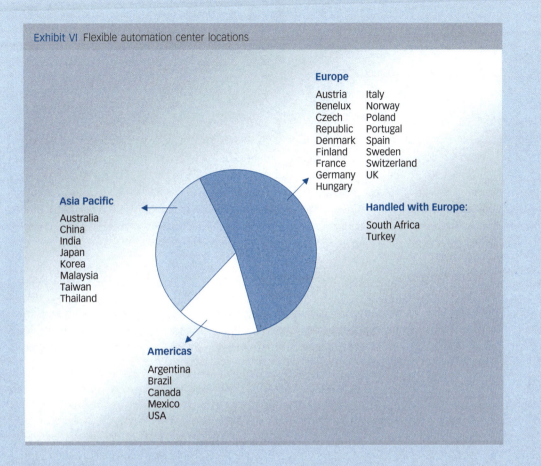

Exhibit VI Flexible automation center locations

Europe

Austria	Italy
Benelux	Norway
Czech	Poland
Republic	Portugal
Denmark	Spain
Finland	Sweden
France	Switzerland
Germany	UK
Hungary	

Handled with Europe:

South Africa
Turkey

Asia Pacific

Australia
China
India
Japan
Korea
Malaysia
Taiwan
Thailand

Americas

Argentina
Brazil
Canada
Mexico
USA

8. Enhance global key account management:

Global key account management was of critical importance. A key account was a large customer who purchased significant volume. One senior executive managed each key account. The executive oversaw consistency of service, tracked the customer's changing needs, and assured that all locations harmonized work on cross-border projects. FA was now considering how to enhance service to global customers, as well as how to win new customers among the select group of large global players. Global key accounts included GM, Ford, and Philips in North America, as well as Unilever, VW, Volvo, Reneault and others in Europe and Asia Pacific. The Vice President for Marketing Europe explained:

'We used to chase the 10 automotive firms we did business with around the world. But now there are 20 to 30 parts companies to consider. These firms are also playing globally. Our global account structure needs to change. We need to analyze what we are doing now and decide what to do differently.'

It would be necessary to understand each customer's strategy and to obtain or update corporate contacts, especially in central engineering departments. FA could position as a partner for the long-term and develop a complete strategy, drawing from ABB corporate services such as project financing. Quality and performance would be closely monitored. Further development of global competence would require increased investment, including management training and rotation. Service could be leveraged through:

- Global key account management
- Global product and service offering
- Promoting the global brand name
- Advantages of scale, standardization, and supply management
- Combining global strengths with local strengths

FA business structure was designed according to the ABB matrix: local in operation but global in strategy. The many decentralized profit centers ran their businesses differently. One customer exclaimed, 'If ABB Flexible Automation knew what ABB Flexible Automation knows, we would never go anywhere else.' Operations were already global because of automotive customers. This advantage needed to be used to greater effect. Most executives held more than one role in the matrix organization. For example, a country manager was responsible for business operations in the country and also for some strategic objective for the company. The matrix structure worked well at higher levels of management but became difficult at lower levels.

To take full advantage of FA global expertise, sales staff and engineers had to be able to communicate and share knowledge with each other. The official language of ABB was English, and most upper managers used it proficiently. Farther down in the organization, employees reverted to the local language. This meant that information had to be translated to English or another language for communication throughout the company. On a daily basis, lower level workers were concerned with local operations rather than strategy and activity in other countries.

9. Expand geographic segmentation:

ABB Group companies operated worldwide. FA would be able to rely on the corporate connection to set up activity quickly or expand product and service offerings in response to global customers and new market opportunity. Eastern Europe markets had already gained attention, particularly Hungary and Poland. Discussions had been held regarding Latin America, South Africa, China, and India. Centers of Excellence in North America, Europe, and Asia could be used as a springboard for expansion. (Exhibit VII)

10. Increase business with automotive parts makers:

At the close of 1996, the automotive vehicle manufacturing segment represented slightly over 65% of order volume. By 1998 the figure had dropped to approximately 30% to 40%, and 40% to 60% of robot manufacturing was going to auto parts manufacturers. Growth resulted largely from increased sales to parts manufacturers. Global customers in the parts manufacturing segment included: Bosch, Allied Signal, Rockwell, Valeo, Krupp-Thyssen, Klockner, Johnson Controls, and Lear Corporation.

In the early years, FA had dealt with approximately ten vehicle OEMs producing parts and components (GM, Ford). OEMs now relied more on manufacturing by parts and components suppliers to add economies of scale. Ford was now buying bumpers ready-made from component suppliers. Business to vehicle OEMs was likely to decrease.

Another factor influencing change was 'just-in-time' delivery. With OEMs using components from parts makers, the need for just-in-time delivery was causing parts makers to locate near OEM customers. When OEMs established new locations, this business requirement forced parts makers to set up operations nearby.

Exhibit VII Market share by geographic region

EUROPE

Company	Market Share by Rank Order
ABB	1
Kuka	2
Yaskawa	3
Fanuc	4
Others	

Europe accounted for 52% of ABB FA's 1996 orders. Companies ranked 1–4 accounted for 80% of the market in Europe.

AMERICAS

Company	Market Share by Rank Order
ABB	1
Fanuc	2
Kawasaki	3
Yaskawa	4
Others	

The Americas accounted for 36% of ABB FA's 1996 orders. Companies ranked 1–4 accounted for 95% of the market in the Americas.

ASIA PACIFIC

Company	Market Share by Rank Order
Yaskawa	1
Fanuc	2
Panasonic	3
Kawasaki	4
ABB	5
Others	

Asia Pacific accounted for 12% of ABB FA's 1996 orders. Companies ranked 1–4 (not including ABB No. 5) accounted for 65% of the market in Asia Pacific.

However, in light of the goal to increase order volume, automotive would need to expand while the business split percents changed. It would be necessary to decide what percent of sales should target parts makers. If more volume went to parts makers and less to automotive OEMs, the change would be felt at all levels of operation. It would impact FACs, globalization, CoEs, application development, and geographic segmentation.

Recent acquisitions and mergers in parts offered opportunity. TRW and Lucas Varity now formed a major parts manufacturer with worldwide operations and global purchasing. The Ford–Volvo alliance offered potential, given the joint venture already in place between FA and Volvo. Volvo planned to drop auto manufacturing and concentrate on trucks. In fact, in January 1999, Volvo had bought 12.85% of Swedish truck maker Scania and subsequently announced takeover plans, a move creating the largest truck maker in Europe. Volvo's merger bid had been deemed hostile. It remained to be seen how the deal would shake out. Meanwhile, it might be worthwhile to look at opportunities with Volvo's move into trucks.

11. Expand general industry:

In 1997, general industry was 12% of FA revenue. The goal was to increase business to 25% by the year 2000. This segment was an attractive target for two reasons. First, it reduced dependence on the automotive industry and its cyclical purchasing patterns which caused FA business to fluctuate. Second, it promised higher profits. Flexible automation in the automotive industry was mature, which depressed prices.

A report from the Robotic Industries Association showed that food and beverage in the U.S. accounted for 7% of robot units shipped in 1997 but 13% of money spent in the robotics industry. Automotive purchased 60% of units but accounted for only 45% of money spent. Cost averages were $65,000 for a robotics system in automotive and $150,000 for a system in food and beverage.

From the corporate level down, ABB was an engineering-based company. ABB did not have any consumer businesses. Bidding for projects occurred *after* a customer submitted a request for proposal. The marketing effort required to sell to such customers was insignificant, and ABB had not developed the marketing function. FA reflected this orientation and had not developed marketing expertise. Like other flexible automation companies with strong automotive industry ties, FA lacked experience with customers unfamiliar with robotics technology. FA lacked knowledge of the businesses and of general industry customer needs. This fact had slowed segment growth.

General industry customers were different from the typical flexible automation customer. In many cases, the businesses were much smaller. They did not seek robotics solutions when implementing a project, often due to short time and minimal engineering resources. They did not have the engineering know-how to specify a system, and they were preoccupied with day-to-day work. This meant that companies selling flexible automation solutions needed to take a different approach, a more aggressive mindset to seek out customers. Enhanced customer contact would help CoEs develop more effective solutions for function packages.

Typical end product areas included white goods, TV tubes, computer screens, off-road vehicles, and furniture. Manufacturing operations in these areas had traditionally favored hard automation, for example as used in assembly lines, over flexible automation. White goods such as refrigerators and dishwashers generally lasted a long time, and product design did not change frequently, unlike automotive design. Manufacturers could buy their own equipment and build a production line in a relatively cost-effective manner. Flexible automation did not offer major advantages.

FA had begun to address the problem. The Palletizing CoE was created to develop and market general industry function packages and solutions. The FlexPalletizer was launched as the solution for loading and unloading pallets. A branch office had opened in Wisconsin to differentiate general industry business from the auto industry located nearby in Michigan, but the office had experienced little success.

The food and beverage segment presented a demanding environment for flexible automation in cases where totally clean robot operation was required, for example to avoid contamination when comestible material touched the packaging or the equipment.

Large consumer goods operations such as Wal-Mart offered significant opportunity in customized shelving and assembly which required flexible automation.

FA management believed Japanese robotics firms had approximately twice as much volume as FA in the general industry segment.

Conclusion

FA management considered strategic options and reflected on the need for change. ABB Flexible Automation was recognized as the industry leader. It was critical to rethink the competitive formula. Were the goals proposed for the year 2000 reasonable? What was the best course to pursue, and what adjustments would be required?

PART IV
Global strategic implementation

10

Global structures and designs

Learning outcomes

After reading this chapter you should be able to:

- explain the contingency factors that determine the structure of multinational firms;

- list and explain the different ways in which a multinational firm can be structured;

- explain the strengths and weaknesses of each structure in the light of the strategy being adopted;

- list and discuss the different forms multinational firms adopt to balance the need for global integration with the pressure for local responsiveness;

- choose a structure that supports the different forms of multinational firm.

Al-Qaeda is a fundamentalist group established in the early 1980s and headed by Osama bin Laden. It is reported that its overall aim is to restore all Islamic lands to what they consider a pure form of Islam. In the early 2000s bin Laden operated from Afghanistan, sheltered by the Taliban regime then in power.

The events of 11 September 2001, when aircraft piloted by members allegedly linked to al-Qaeda were flown into the World Trade Center in New York, jolted the USA and other Western governments into further action against al-Qaeda. The USA declared war on the Taliban regime in Afghanistan, which had been harbouring bin Laden and his chief lieutenants, and succeeded in overthrowing it and installing a Western-friendly government. Some of bin Laden's senior associates were killed or captured, but he himself and some of his followers escaped, probably to the tribal lands on the Pakistan–Afghanistan border. With the overthrow of his protectors—the Taliban—it was thought that bin Laden was now isolated and powerless, and furthermore that al-Qaeda was broken because its leadership had been fragmented, its structure fractured, and much of its financial resources neutralized. The US army believed that by using precision air weapons, war against al-Qaeda could be won by selectively taking out the leaders of the organization, and by disrupting its communication systems and its economic infrastructure. They applied conventional war strategies by targeting the leaders directly, or what is known in war jargon as 'going for the head of the snake'. This strategy, it was believed, would result in killing enemy leaders, isolating them from their troops and affiliates, or making them vulnerable to overthrow by local groups in Afghanistan.

In 2003 and 2004, however, there were further terrorist attacks in Turkey, Spain, Saudi Arabia, and Iraq, and several Western countries were put on high alert from the perceived threat of attack.

To believe that the actions of the US and its allies in Afghanistan had defeated al-Qaeda was to misunderstand the nature of its organizational structure and design. It was assumed that al-Qaeda must be organized like any other organization operating in many countries, with a well-defined hierarchy that was able to coordinate and control the actions of its operatives in the field. However, it was more amoeba-like—a loose association of like-minded groups with the same overall vision.

The pattern emerging is of the remaining al-Qaeda leadership coordinating with these loosely connected affiliated organizations to carry out activities at suggested times and in suggested places, but leaving the details to the local organizations. Now, instead of fighting a terrorist organization with a recognized structure, the US and its allies are faced with dozens of small groups whose fighters have often been trained in al-Qaeda camps in Afghanistan. Rohan Gunaratna of the Institute of Defence and Strategic Studies in Singapore described these camps as a military training Disneyland, where you could meet anyone from any fundamentalist group. This mingling of members of different groups has resulted in similarities between the communications techniques that the groups use, and the way they use explosives. So 'the Base' (the translation of al-Qaeda) spreads best practice and inculcates a common vision.

10.1 **Introduction**

The success of any organisation depends on its structure and design. This chapter deals with the structures and designs of multinational firms. A firm's structure can be seen as the blueprint depicting the formal reporting relationships within the firm. It explains the manner in which the firm organizes its resources and capabilities into specific tasks and achieves coordination among these tasks.

The structure of the firm is often represented in the form of a diagram or chart. These are like maps of towns or countries, giving a diagrammatic representation of the reporting relationship within the firm. Such diagrams and charts must be simple—typically emphasizing, generalizing, and omitting certain features. In other words, while an organizational structure, as depicted in an organizational diagram or chart, can be seen as a mirror of the organization's reporting relationships, the content of the structure diagram or chart is intentionally reduced and selectively distilled to focus on one or two particular items, such as formal reporting relationships and responsibility over tasks.

Associated with structure is design—the way the major activities of an organization are carried out within the structure that provides the skeleton for control and coordination. Design includes such matters as where decisions are made, the form of the information systems used, how people are rewarded for their contributions, and how knowledge is transferred within the organization. Together, structure and design have been termed the 'internal architecture' of an organization (Kay 1993: 14).

Management scholars have approached structures and designs of multinational firms from two different perspectives. The first perspective, led by Stopford and Wells (1972), focused on the structural fit between multinational firms' expansion strategy and their organizational structure. This literature dominated structures and designs of multinational firms from the 1960s to the late 1980s. The second perspective, led by Bartlett and Ghosal (1989), generally known as the 'integration-responsiveness literature', changed the focus from the issue of structural fit to the question of trade-offs between pressure for global integration and pressure for local responsiveness. While the first perspective put more emphasis on structural control, the second put more emphasis on normative social control (Chi et al. 2004: 220). Before we explain these two perspectives, let us look at structures and designs of domestic firms or firms operating in a single country.

10.2 **Domestic organizational structures**

To begin the discussion of structures and design, we will first review the structures common to domestic operations—the operations of a firm before it goes international. We start here because, almost without exception, a firm begins in one country—its home country—and thus in any subsequent international expansion, the domestic structure is the one that is built on and extended.

Whilst a business consists of many functions, when considering organizational structures it is convenient to consider a business as being composed of four 'super' functions: operations (including procurement), marketing (including distribution, sales, and after-sales), support

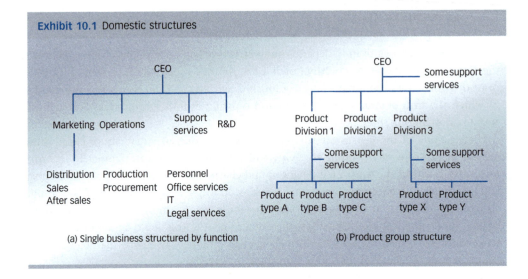

Exhibit 10.1 Domestic structures

(a) Single business structured by function

(b) Product group structure

services (functions such as personnel, finance, and IT), and research and development (R&D). The most common way in which a business is structured is by function, as shown in Exhibits 10.1a and 10.1b.

A modification of this organization is to split marketing into more than one area, depending on customer characteristics. For example, food manufacturers treat the supermarket chains as key accounts—giving them better treatment than other customers. Similarly, a particularly significant product may be handled by a special team outside the normal processes.

However, many organizations will have more than one strategic business unit in their portfolios: they are firms. A major consideration in organizational structure is how to group the businesses within a firm. As a general rule, groupings will depend on the degree of relatedness of the activities of the constituent units. Exhibit 10.1b illustrates product subdivision. The assumption is that the similarities of the activities in one product division are greater than between those of any other product division. Thus, for example, product types A, B, and C in product division 1 are more similar to each other than to products X and Y in product division 3.

10.3 Strategy and structure of multinationals

During the early 1960s Chandler (1962; 1966) mapped the growth of multi-product companies in the USA. He saw the small local firm move progressively to set up sales organizations in far-away cities; subsequently, production units would follow this expansion. Diversification into new products and services would follow. Each move led to a different organizational form. The appropriate form was such as to balance two divergent forces: that of specialization (or departmentalization), employed for the sake of efficiency, and coordination, so that all the units were contributing to the bigger whole. His research led him to enunciate the view that *structure follows strategy*, where structure can best be defined as the way in which an organization divides its labour into distinct tasks and then achieves coordination among them.

Stopford and Wells (1972) applied Chandler's contingency framework to analysing the structures of multinational firms. Using data from 187 large US multinationals, they suggested that *foreign product diversity*, measured by the number of products sold internationally, and *foreign sales as a percentage of total sales*, i.e. the importance of international sales to the company, determine the structure of the multinational firm.

Stopford and Wells (1972) suggested that multinational firms have four structures: international division, worldwide product division, area division, and matrix division. At the early stage of foreign expansion, foreign product diversity and foreign sales are both relatively low. Multinationals tend to support this small level of international expansion with an *international division structure*. Stopford and Wells observed that after the first stage some multinational firms expanded their sales abroad without significantly increasing foreign product diversity. These companies tended to adopt an *area division structure*. While some multinational firms expanded their sales without significantly increasing their product diversity, other multinationals increased foreign product diversity without expanding their percentage of foreign sales. These multinational firms supported their strategy with *worldwide product division structure*. This structure gives domestic product divisions a global responsibility for the performance of their product lines worldwide. Finally, when multinational firms expanded both their foreign product diversity and percentage of foreign sales, they tend to employ a *matrix structure*. A matrix structure is an overlap of the two above discussed structures—product division and area division structures.

KEY CONCEPT

Structure can best be defined as the way in which an organization divides its labour into distinct tasks and then achieves coordination among them. There are five basic types of structures for multinational firms: a functional structure, an international division structure, an area or geographic division structure, a product division structure and a matrix structure.

Several management scholars revised the model put forward by Stopford and Wells and added, deleted, or integrated different stages and structures (Egelhoff 1988). Chi et al (2004: 224) proposed a similar framework to that of Stopford and Wells, but replaced the international division structure with 'functional form'. Similarly, Egelhoff (1982) listed four forms: functional, international, geographical, and product. Thus we add functional structure to the four structures of Stopford and Wells. We will discuss the characteristics of the five types of structures below.

10.3.1 Functional structures

A grouping by functions is shown in Exhibit 10.2. Such a structure is likely to evolve as an expansion of a domestic functional configuration, possibly via an International Division

Exhibit 10.2 Functional structure

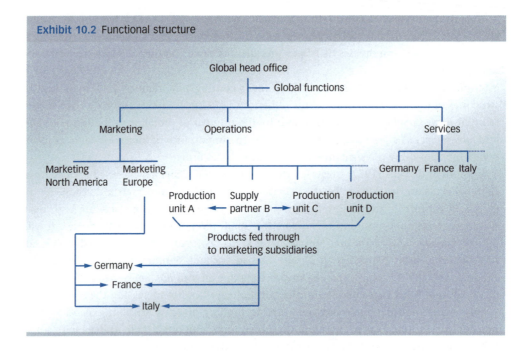

arrangement. Management control and coordination comes through functional authority, whilst the operation units themselves focus on specific product groups which are then sold through the mainstream established distribution and sales channels, which are controlled from the centre.

Grouping by function is suitable for a multinational firm with a clear separation in the activities undertaken by each of the foreign subsidiaries. Examples of this are where procurement is from one country and assembly is in another; and where a production unit is located in a low-cost country but the majority of sales are in Europe. Here it makes sense to organize functionally, with global operations responsible for product integration and efficiency. This sort of arrangement suits companies where the integration of manufacturing or service operations can achieve economies of scale. Thus it is a particularly good arrangement in the European Union at the turn of the twenty-first century, where there is a need to reduce duplication in national operations to match the continental scale required.

Grouping by function also makes sense when there is a need to coordinate marketing and sales efforts, especially where strong central control is required. This is the common practice with international brands such as McDonald's and Coca-Cola, whereby the global marketing function controls many of the marketing and sales features of a product that is sold internationally, although the product offering is likely to be tailored nationally. It also makes sense when there is a particular need to integrate financial activity; for example, where such matters as transfer pricing and national taxation regimes require a great deal of expertise to be available to the centre. Grouping by function is also applicable to small companies that cannot afford to duplicate support services, and need the centre to provide them.

A functional arrangement can be unfortunate, however, where one or two powerful units do not accept central authority. Is it likely, for example, that a head office in France can dictate personnel or IT policies in the USA or Japan if the units there are large? British American Tobacco has traditionally had difficulty getting its very powerful US and Brazilian companies to follow parental advice: they are too large and too profitable to be dictated to by the centre.

KEY CONCEPT

Grouping by function is suitable where the units are performing one pure task, e.g. only operations or only selling. It is a particularly good option where economies of scale in operations can be achieved and/or where there is a strong need to control global marketing. The major weaknesses of functional groupings are that national responsiveness is likely to be somewhat blunted, and the face of the organization in a country is somewhat diffused. However, functional expertise is likely to be maintained at a very high level.

10.3.2 International division structure

For the firm that is selling a large proportion of its output in its domestic market and a small quantity internationally, and has low foreign-product diversity, the most common form of organizational structure is the international division structure, as depicted in Exhibit 10.3. That is, the international division structure is appropriate when foreign operations are relatively small.

Historically, this form of structure is the way in which purely national players dipped their toes into international waters, since it is a low-risk method of servicing overseas markets. An example here is exporting firms. The exporting firm is firmly based in its home country, with any exporting likely to be on an opportunistic basis: certainly, international operations are likely to be secondary to the domestic. The exporting firm is not much concerned with international coordination because its international involvement is

Exhibit 10.3 International division structure

at arm's-length and any coordination takes place naturally within the home-based marketing function. Until the 1990s this split was very common amongst US firms, mainly because
of the enormous size of their home market. The academic publisher Addison-Wesley was a
case in point prior to its takeover by Pearson in 1998.

With an international division structure, all foreign subsidiaries report directly to an international division at the centre. The international division is separate from the domestic
operations of the multinational firms. As a result, foreign branches are given considerable
flexibility to design and implement strategies that fit their local conditions. As a result,
under the international division structure communication between domestic divisions and
international divisions is often poor.

Exhibit 10.3 illustrates the extended geographical groupings. Note that the areas are not
necessarily single nation-states: it may well be that some form of regionalization is preferred.

10.3.3 Area or geographical division structure

Multinationals following an area—or, as some call it, geographical—division structure divide the global market into geographical areas, each allocated its own headquarters responsible for all lines of products and businesses within that area. Subsidiaries in each geographical area coordinate their activities to optimize performance. However, coordination and
communication between geographical areas are usually poor. This would be the appropriate organization when country and/or regional considerations are more significant than the
standardization of the product. Multinationals with sufficiently large foreign operations and
a high percentage of foreign sales or manufacturing tend to adopt area or geographical division structure (see Exhibit 10.4).

Grouping nations into regional groupings that will work well together is not always easy.

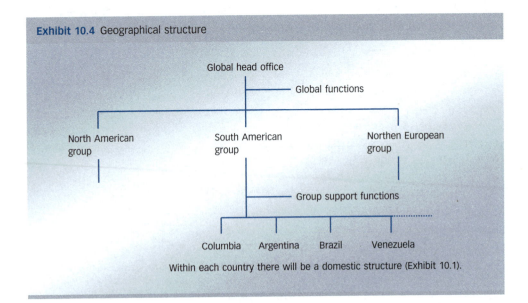

Exhibit 10.4 Geographical structure

This is evident from the moves made by firms in Europe to integrate national activities in regional centres. It is also evident where companies have lumped Japan alongside other East Asian operations. Structures must take into account the cultural, social, political, and economic differences amongst the nations. These will be particularly strong where units have 'done their own thing' for many years. Further, the area or geographical division structure is a high-cost structure, requiring large separate regional headquarters dealing with both product matters and country or regional issues.

KEY CONCEPT

Grouping by geography is suitable when regional economies of scale can be achieved (but there are few global economies). Another factor favouring a geographical grouping is if countries are culturally homogeneous and have similar consumer tastes. The major weaknesses of geographical groupings are that global economies of scale will not be fully realized, and that whilst national responsiveness is likely to be good, global initiatives are likely to be blunted.

10.3.4 Product division structure

A firm will be structured along geographical lines because the country-to-country linkages are stronger than those along other dimensions. A firm would move to organize itself by product group if it manufactures and sells a wide range of products and the core products are effectively standard across borders. This means that the core products themselves are central to the organization, with modifications to non-core features made market by market. The Ford Mondeo, as its name suggests, was Ford's first significant attempt to develop a world car—one that could be sold in all its major markets. An example of the same core offering in services is telecommunications.

A product structure based on the primacy of global operations will be organized to achieve economies of scale, often through vertical integration of procurement operations and distribution, utilizing sources of low-cost labour. With marketing activities tailored to the specifics of the market, these consequently tend to be less cost-effective. If the regions are large enough for production and procurement economies yet homogeneous enough to be considered one broad market, then the product structure will work, with the regional head office taking control of both operations and marketing.

Whilst global marketing is subservient to operations in this sort of organization, each product line has its own dedicated marketing staff, often with their own support services. A representation is shown in Exhibit 10.5. In such a grouping there appears to be a high degree of duplication: each product group has its own dedicated marketing staff. However, these are not unnecessary duplication if the product groups are distinct. For example, 3M has four major product groups: automotive and chemical, consumer and office, electronics and communications, and industrial. These groups have distinct characteristics, and their products are sold to very different customers. This means that in practice dedicated marketing staff can be much more knowledgeable than personnel who needed to cover a great range of products.

Exhibit 10.5 Product structure

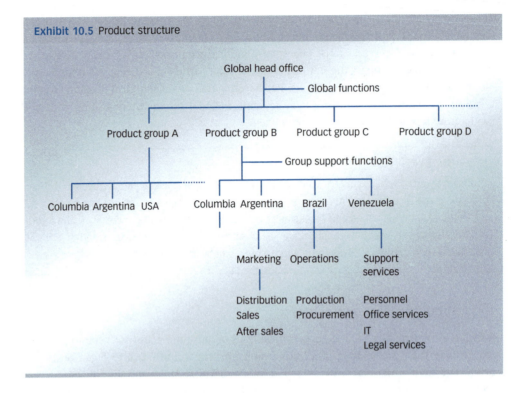

10.3.5 **The matrix structure**

Since the 1980s large multinational firms, as discussed in Chapter 9, have increased both their international sales and operations in foreign markets, and diversification across both products and geographical areas. According to the Stopford and Wells model, a high de-gree of diversification and foreign sales and operations should lead the multinational firm to adopt a matrix structure (Chi et al. 2004: 221). Further, each of the four arrangements discussed so far has strengths but also severe weaknesses. Giving primacy to the functions through functional grouping is likely to mean that national responsiveness is weak. Giving primacy to the nations or regions in a geographical grouping is likely to reduce the level of global integration. Giving primacy to operations in product groupings can easily lead to marketing and service duplication, and weaken the role of global marketing and service initiatives.

Given these weaknesses, it makes sense to combine authority over operations, marketing, and geography in some way. Such a combination attempts to coordinate matters so that the organization does not lose any economies of scale or the advantages of locally responsive marketing. The way this is done is to operate a matrix structure in which each operating unit in a region has responsibility for both marketing and the operations that are conducted there. This gives primacy to the geographical regions but with the head of each unit having two reporting lines at regional or global head office—to someone in operations and to someone else in marketing. A matrix structure is shown in Exhibit 10.6, which shows an arrangement whereby products in three product groups are sold in two geographical areas. Picked out is one unit and the responsibilities of the head of the unit: the geographical line of responsibility is to region 1, the functional line of responsibility is to operations, and the product line of responsibility to product group B.

The matrix structure has certain advantages—in theory at least. The sales force is likely to be more efficient, being able to offer a wider portfolio of offers than would be possible if it were working for only one product group. Brand management will be able to maintain the characteristics of the brand over all markets. The downside of this is that the sales force is likely to be less dedicated and less knowledgeable about the products—a significant disadvantage if the products are technically sophisticated. Small decisions can be made locally and large decisions will be more informed, with the decision-makers knowing all sides of the product–market situation, and knowing the bigger national or regional picture.

Exhibit 10.6 Matrix structure

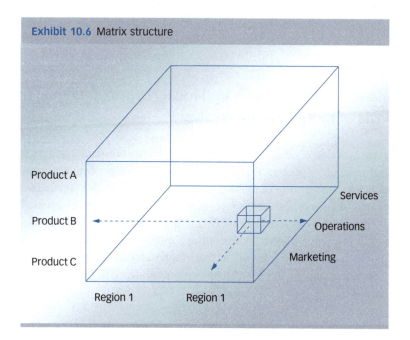

Having responsibility for both product and market and being mindful of the subsidiary's wider regional responsibilities should mean that managers develop into more general managers, but at the cost of the triple chains of responsibility leading to greater management stress levels. Planning and control are likely to be more complex within a matrix structure. Decisions are likely to take longer, as three chains of command are involved. Culture may be a significant feature. The introduction of matrix organizations, whereby an employee reports to two bosses (one responsible for the task, such as the launch of a new product, and one responsible for the function, such as accounts or marketing), has been a failure in Italy. This is because in Italy bosses are like fathers, and you cannot have two fathers (Trompenaars and Hampden-Turner 1997).

In general, the advantages that might come from adopting a matrix structure seem to be outweighed by the disadvantages—mainly the massive demands on managers, especially having to deal with multiple lines of command. Many companies have tried a matrix organization and abandoned it. For example, Texas Instruments found that the structure created too much ambiguity and too little coordination, and abandoned it in favour of product groupings with integrated functional support (Egelhof 1993: 182–210). However, others have successfully adopted a matrix structure—at least for many years. ABB (ASEA Brown Boveri) under Percy Barnevik in the late 1990s was a company that would appear to have an extensive matrix structure.

> **KEY CONCEPT**
>
> Matrix structures have many theoretical advantages, particularly the coordination between country, function, and products and the organizational learning that this can encourage. Operating in a matrix organization is demanding, with two or three bosses to consider. The matrix organization offers fast managerial development and informed, albeit slow, decision-making. Overall, however, such structures appear in practice to put a great strain on personnel.

10.4 Balancing integrations and local responsiveness: broad forms of international strategy

Firms will begin in one country, and almost invariably will initially have their production facilities and head office located there. They will almost always begin by supplying solely their home market. In wishing to move to supply foreign markets, there are two major and generally conflicting pressures. First, there is the pressure to become and remain responsive to the foreign markets—to satisfy the differing demands as they arise. Second, there is a pressure to use the scope offered by operating abroad—both economies of scale and the ability to tap into the differing expertise that resides abroad (Bartlett and Ghoshal 1989). These two pressures suggest the four broad configurations that are shown in Exhibit 10.7 (Finlay 2000: 539).

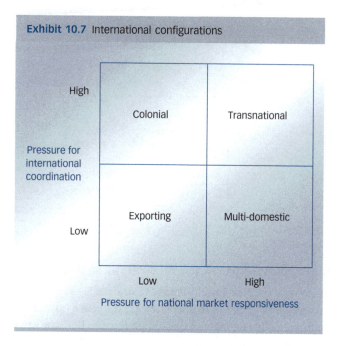

Exhibit 10.7 International configurations

10.4.1 **The export firm**

For the firm that is selling a large proportion of its output in its domestic market and a small quantity internationally, the most common form of organizational structure is the incorporation of an export section into the already-existing domestic marketing function, as depicted in Exhibit 10.8. Historically, this form of structure is the way in which purely national players experimented with foreign markets, since it is a low-risk method of servicing overseas markets. The marketing and sales functions would be split between 'domestic' and 'export', with the export section possibly organized along national or regional lines (e.g. grouping all European countries in one group and all South American countries in another). The setting up of an export section brings internationally experienced personnel together to handle such things as export documentation and foreign exchange interactions.

10.4.2 **The multi-domestic firm**

The multi-domestic firm consists of several businesses operating almost independently, each in a home base that is similar to a mother country—having its own production capacity and a country head office. Any concern for international cooperation tends to be muted, since almost all the products of each business are destined for their own home markets. Classic examples of this are retail banking, newspapers, and TV, where the local context is so important.

Exhibit 10.8 Export structure

CEO

Marketing   Operations   Support services

Domestic   Export

Organizational structures to support a multi-domestic strategy

The rationale for a firm to choose a multi-domestic strategy is that the nation—or some similar geographical grouping—has a particularly strong influence on activities. Such grouping would almost automatically come about and be preferred where the strategy had involved the acquisition of strong national businesses—as in Europe, especially after the EU was formed. Organizational groupings to fit this strategy will naturally be by geography.

The term 'multi-domestic' indicates what the organizational structure will be like. Within each country the structure will replicate the domestic arrangements discussed in section 10.3.3. For cases where there is just one product line in each country, the simple structure depicted in Exhibit 10.1a, or something very similar, will be implemented; where there are multi-products, the structure shown in Exhibit 10.1b would be appropriate. The reporting lines might be directly from country to head office, or there might be regional groupings as shown in Exhibit 10.3. The grouping shown in Exhibit 10.3 is appropriate where the businesses in each country are totally owned by the organization. However, many such holdings may not be wholly owned by the firm: indeed, alliances that give rise to partly owned joint ventures are a significant way in which firms expand globally. The extreme structural case is where the global head office acts as a holding company, having shareholdings in one or more separate companies. A holding company structure is shown in Exhibit 10.9.

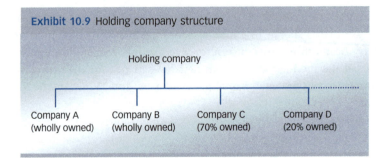

Exhibit 10.9 Holding company structure

Holding company

Company A (wholly owned)   Company B (wholly owned)   Company C (70% owned)   Company D (20% owned)

With a holding company structure, the linkages between the parent and its operating companies are kept to the minimum. Such an arrangement suits a diversified organization where the linkages between the businesses are effectively nonexistent. The parent restricts itself to providing very broad strategic direction, generally setting boundaries to the scope of the businesses and setting financial targets for them. The parent will have some financial and legal expertise, but these are unlikely to be offered to the businesses.

A significant weakness of the multi-domestic arrangement is duplication, particularly of support services, and the inability of the units to obtain economies of scale. A further deficiency is that organizational learning is likely to be hindered by the lack of contact between national operations.

KEY CONCEPT

A firm following a multi-domestic strategy has two possible structures that it can employ. Where it wholly owns all the businesses in its portfolio, it is most likely to support domestic arrangements in each country with reporting of business performance to the parent. Where ownership of some of its units is shared, the parent may wish to operate as a holding company. In many cases, the two structures may be adopted to run side by side.

Compared to the holding company, the divisionalized structure has high central overheads, because the parent carries out many more of the parenting functions. With such a slim head office, the holding company will put no effort into developing synergies or providing central services.

10.4.3 The colonial firm

The colonial strategy is similar to what we called throughout the book a global strategy. To be consistent with Finlay's (2000) typology, in this section we use the term 'colonial' rather than 'global'. The colonial firm has a presence in many countries to take advantage of favourable trading conditions (Porter 1985). A colonial firm is characterized as selling and/or producing a standard core product in many countries—examples are pharmaceuticals, aircraft, aero engines, and computers. The requirement to produce this standard core product drives international cooperation in operations—both in procurement and production—and this in turn demands highly specified outputs from each unit. The major car assemblers, such as General Motors and Ford, have many of the characteristics of a colonial firm.

Organizational structures to support a colonial strategy

The multinational firm, depending on its strategy, uses one of the structures discussed in section 10.3 to support the colonial strategy. Unlike the exporting and multi-domestic arrangements, a colonial strategy requires the parent to coordinate positively the activities of many units. These units are not just sales partners but also units involved in procurement and production. Thus, there can be many different types of unit within a colonial style strategy: they can range from distribution and sales partners, as in exporting structures, the businesses that are a feature of the multi-domestic arrangements, and include units involved with procurement and operations. There will often also be joint ventures, as established by General Motors and Toyota with their 50/50 New United Motor Manufacturing Inc. (NUMMI) operation. So not only is a colonial strategy concerned with a range of units, but the relationships with such units are diverse: partnerships with many suppliers and sales and distribution outlets, full ownership of others, and shared ownership in the case of joint ventures. Additionally, some of these units will have been built up from scratch, others acquired as going concerns through acquisition. Thus the cultures will also be diverse.

A shift to a colonial strategy from either an exporting or a multi-domestic one—and thus the move to new structural forms—is different from the moves from a domestic to an exporting or multi-domestic organization. These latter moves tend to be incremental, in the sense of the alterations made to operations and marketing: in contrast, the move to structures appropriate to a colonial strategy requires changes that are revolutionary.

KEY CONCEPT

The portfolio of a colonial organization is likely to be diverse, perhaps consisting of production, distribution, and marketing partners, units only involved with procurement and operations, and businesses. There are also diverse relationships: formal and informal partnerships, full ownership of some units, and shared ownership in the case of joint ventures. Such diverse elements lead to complex arrangements.

10.4.4 The transnational firm

Bartlett and Ghoshal (1989) consider that the transnational firm is the most effective configuration for organizations with many international operations. It shares with the colonial firm the advantages of scope that a company with global reach can have (e.g. being able to locate operations in countries with low labour costs), yet it shares with the multi-domestic firm the advantages of being locally responsive—responsive to the tastes and standards of the local market place (see Exhibit 10.10). Marketing is the least integrated function, since all the elements of the marketing mix—distribution channels, media, and outlets—can differ extensively across nations. It is only when these elements are little affected by local conditions that integration of marketing can make sense.

Transnational organizations are currently fairly rare: the engineering company ABB shows many transnational characteristics. The al-Qaeda case illustrates a structure that is a very good example of a transnational.

KEY CONCEPT

Organizational structure must match the strategy that the organization adopts. When operating internationally, the response to the two conflicting forces of integration and local responsiveness must be balanced. Integration will allow for efficiencies that will lead to cost competitiveness, whilst local responsiveness is effectively a call for local autonomy with freedom to adapt to customer requirements.

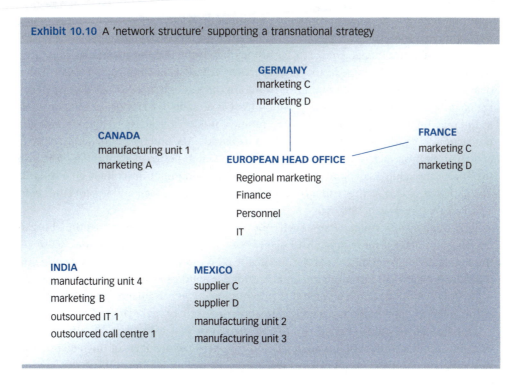

Exhibit 10.10 A 'network structure' supporting a transnational strategy

GERMANY
marketing C
marketing D

CANADA
manufacturing unit 1
marketing A

EUROPEAN HEAD OFFICE
Regional marketing
Finance
Personnel
IT

FRANCE
marketing C
marketing D

INDIA
manufacturing unit 4
marketing B
outsourced IT 1
outsourced call centre 1

MEXICO
supplier C
supplier D
manufacturing unit 2
manufacturing unit 3

Organizational structures to support a transnational strategy

Companies need periodically to realign structures as strategies and environmental conditions change. Realignment will often be evolutionary, but may sometimes be so great as to be revolutionary. A move to a transnational strategy would be one such move, revolutionary in the way in which lines of responsibility and command are delineated.

The matrix structure broke away from the most common characteristic of almost all structures—a single line of command/responsibility for all personnel. It replaced this with dual or triple lines—with a consequent almost unbearable strain on employees. In contrast, a transnational organization moves away from the single line of responsibility by downplaying the importance of hierarchy. A transnational firm is not dominated by hierarchies: hierarchies remain, but they play nowhere near as strong a role as in other arrangements.

Senior managers in transnational organizations must think in terms of managing a network of associates rather than operating within a hierarchy: a network of centres for each of research, development, component manufacture, assembly, distribution and sales, and marketing. The emphasis is on interdependence rather than independence or hierarchical subservience, and the ability to work with colleagues from many different cultures is important. In the ultimate, there would be no head office and no home country, although for legal reasons an office would have to be nominated as such. There would be a set of units that take the lead in an aspect of marketing, or of operations or some aspect of services. For example, part of Bombardier, the Canadian engineering firm specializing in railway and tram systems, now operates this sort of structure.

Advances in IT—through the internet and through video conferencing—support such developments. For example, the Taiwanese-based Giant bicycle company would appear to be acting as a transnational. One of its biggest markets is the EU, and it manufactures in the Netherlands so as to be close to this major market, as well as in China and Taiwan. Three-quarters of the bikes it sells around the world are the same, but the other quarter have a regional flavour. Bikes are as much a fashion item as a mode of transport in some markets: in the mid-1990s Giant introduced five to ten new models a year. As well as spreading its production, it has designers in Taiwan, China, Japan, the US, and the Netherlands. Chinese and Japanese customers seek commuting bikes, the Dutch designers contribute ideas from the European racing scene, and the US designers are working on mountain bike variants. The designers work together using computer-aided design facilities, and get together twice a year in Taiwan (Marsh 1997: 16).

Roles in a network structure are much more ambiguous than those in traditional organizations, and make it more difficult to define precise responsibilities and duties. However, this ambiguity makes it more important to define roles carefully, not just as a way of telling individuals what their responsibilities are, but for communicating with the rest of the network. Role definition should be such that it fosters loyalty to the alliance, not to the parent, as this helps to develop the focus and motivation necessary to make the network function.

Interpersonal relationships are key to the success of any network-based structure. Although it is not easy to establish good relationships between members of the network from very different business cultures, it is even harder to sustain it. Operational and cultural differences will emerge after collaboration is under way, and these dissimilarities require working out, with much more communication than anyone could have anticipated (Kanter 1994: 96–108).

A major role for all senior managers in a transnational structure is to manage the relationships between the units in the corporate portfolio. Although some cooperation between units will almost always be desirable, in a transnational organization the need to facilitate rather than dictate cooperation becomes paramount. There are several ways that units can usefully collaborate:

- Sharing best practice: by which the parent encourages groups of units to use each other as benchmarks and in this way spread best practice. This is spreading knowledge—of process and of technology. In the past, BAT Industries has grouped its worldwide tobacco operations into a set of triplets—for example, Brazil, Germany, and the UK—with each member of the triplet looking at the others' activities to see what they could find of benefit to themselves.

- Sharing skills: Linked somewhat to spreading best practice is the spreading skills. Skills are tacit knowledge that cannot be codified, and the only real way of spreading these is to move the people who have these skills. The parent has the role, through its personnel policies, of moving its personnel around the firm, inculcating others with the skills they have and learning new ones to pass on subsequently. Nestlé is a company that has acted in this way in its European operations for many years. Al-Qaeda is doing this through its training camps.

- Sharing data: It is useful, particularly in the financial services sector, to use customer data to cross-sell services. For example, someone with a mortgage will have their data available to the unit that is selling insurance. The availability of enterprise resource planning systems is an aid to this.

- Co-operation when dealing with stakeholders: It can be beneficial for units to share distribution channels or to combine when facing a powerful supplier. This allows start-up activities, or activities with low activation rates, to piggyback on the activities of others.

> **KEY CONCEPT**
>
> In contrast to other structures, a transnational organization is not dominated by hierarchies: hierarchies remain, but they play nowhere near as marked a role. Senior managers must think in terms of managing a network of associates, and must have the ability to work with colleagues from many different cultures. The emphasis is on interdependence rather than independence.

10.5 Summary

Organizational structure provides the skeleton on which the organization is designed. Structure has to match the strategy that the organization is following, in order to make best use of company resources. A company's resources have been considered to consist of four super functions: operations (including procurement), marketing (including distribution, sales, and after-sales), support services (functions such as personnel, finance, IT), and research and development (R&D). The first three functions are concerned with ongoing activities and the present, whereas R&D is concerned with the future. For ease of discussion, structures to support ongoing activities can be treated separately from those aimed at the future.

There is no one best structure. It is a case of horses for courses (Ghoshal and Nohria 1993). Different strategies require different structures, and different structures may require different strategies. All structures embody trade-offs. As a rule, strategy and structure must match. A mismatch between strategy and structure will ultimately lead to poor communication and coordination between departments, administrative problems, employee frustration, and poor customer satisfaction.

Stopford and Wells suggested that multinational companies adopt four structures: international division, worldwide product division, area division, and matrix division. Multinationals with an international division structure have a low level of foreign product diversity and low percentage of foreign sales. Multinational firms with worldwide product division structures have a higher level of foreign-product diversity than multinationals with international division or area division structures. Multinationals with area division structures have a greater percentage of foreign sales than multinationals with international division or product division structures. Multinationals with matrix structures have high levels of both foreign product sales and product diversity (Egelhoff 1988: 4).

The four broad types of international strategy—export, multi-domestic, colonial and transnational—give rise to several types of structure. A simple exporting strategy can usually be successfully managed through extending a domestic marketing organization to include an export marketing section. As the foreign activities become more complex, however, an international division may be set up containing people with all the requisite knowledge to support the international activity. A multi-domestic strategy can be supported by replicating domestic structures in each of the countries in which the organization is active.

Both the exporting and multi-domestic strategies can be carried out with structures that evolve out of the structure adopted in the mother country. If an organization moves to a co-lonial or transnational strategy, then something akin to a revolution in structure and design is required.

There are four broad organizational structures that a colonial firm might use to organize its activities: the functional, geographical, product, and matrix structures. The most appro-priate configuration will depend on industrial structures, and the gains that a company can get through giving primacy to one or other of function, product, or geography.

In contrast to all other organizational structures, a transnational organization is not dom-inated by hierarchies: hierarchies remain, but they play nowhere near as marked a role. Senior managers must think in terms of managing a network of associates and to have the ability to work with colleagues from many different cultures. The emphasis is on interde-pendence rather than independence.

KEY READINGS

- An old but still very useful book on the different structures of multinational firms is Stopford and Wells (1972).
- A very readable account of organizational forms, both national and international, is provided in Mintzberg (1979), and reproduced in H. Mintzberg and J. B. Quinn, *The Strategy Process: Concepts, Contexts, Cases* (New York: Prentice Hall, many editions).
- For further discussion of the phases of global strategy see Bartlett and Ghoshal (1989), or the later version of this book published by Century Business, in 1992.

DISCUSSION QUESTIONS

1 From your own experiences, or by looking on the internet, find two firms that fit into each of the four major organizational categories.

2 When discussing international strategies, is it reasonable to consider a business to be composed of four 'super' functions: operations, marketing, support services, and research and development (R&D)? Is it reasonable to make the distinction that the first three functions are concerned with ongoing activities and the present, whereas R&D is concerned with the future, and thus can be treated separately?

3 What are the advantages and disadvantages of the five structures (refer to section 10.3)?

4 What are the advantages and disadvantages of each of the possible organizational forms that support a colonial strategy?

Closing case study
Restructuring Sony

Established in Japan in 1946, Sony is a leading manufacturer of audio, video, communications, and IT products. By the early 1990s the Sony Group was organized into three sectors—electronics, entertainment (including music, television, computer entertainment, and motion pictures), and financial services (insurance and finance). The electronics sector was split into four product groups (video, audio, TV, and 'others'—mainly IT equipment and games).

Restructuring initiated in 1994

Around that time Sony's management felt that the group structure was inappropriate for the future, more dynamic business environment. In 1994 the product groups of the electronics sector were regrouped into eight divisional companies concerned with consumer audio and video products, recording media and energy, broadcast products, business and industrial systems, infocom products, mobile electronics, components, and semiconductors. This restructuring was aimed at improving the company's focus on high-potential products and making the company more responsive to changing market conditions.

Each divisional company had its own goals and was responsible for all its operations (production, sales, and finance). The presidents of the divisional companies were authorized to decide upon the investments to be made up to a prescribed limit. They could also take decisions regarding the human resource (HR) issues for all employees up to the level of divisional director. The number of layers in the decision-making process was reduced from six to four or fewer. Commenting on his responsibilities within the new structure, Norio Ohga, the group chairman and CEO, said, 'First of all, I would like the divisional presidents to run their companies as if they were reporting to shareholders once a year at a shareholders' meeting. My role will be to review their strategies, examine any points I feel should be questioned, and provide advice when and where necessary.'

Restructuring initiated in 1995

In 1995, after the implementation of the divisional company structure in the electronics sector, changes were made in the group management structure, with Sony led by a team that included Ohga, the group president and chief operating officer (COO), and the presidents of the divisional companies. In March 1995, Nobuyuki Idei was appointed the group president and COO.

Given Sony's poor financial performance at this time, the top management decided to integrate the group's various domestic and global business functions such as marketing, R&D, finance, and HR. Thus many of the functions of the divisional companies were brought under the direct supervision of headquarters. Idei also decided to strengthen the existing eight-company structure and to lay more emphasis on R&D in the IT field.

Accordingly, in January 1996 a new ten-company structure was announced for the electronics sector. Under the new structure, the previous consumer audio and video products company was split into three new companies—display, home audio-video, and personal audio-video. A new company—information technology—was created to focus on Sony's business interests in the PC and IT industries. Infocom products and mobile electronics were merged to create personal and mobile communications. The other companies formed were recording media and energy, and broadcast products. Business and industrial systems was renamed image and sound communications, and components was renamed components and computer peripherals. Semiconductors remained unchanged.

Further group changes

In order to devise and implement the corporate strategies of the Sony group, an executive board was created, chaired by Idei. The other members of the board included the chief HR officer, the chief production officer, the chief marketing officer, the chief communications officer, the chief technology officer, the chief financial officer, the executive deputy president and representative director, and the senior managing director.

In an attempt to consolidate the marketing operations of Sony, the marketing divisions that had belonged to the previous organizational setup were spun off to create three new marketing groups: the Japan Marketing Group (JMG), the International Marketing and Operations Group (IM&O) and the Electronic Components and Devices Marketing Group (ECDMG). The JMG was responsible for all marketing activities in Japan for five companies—display, home audio-video, IT, personal audio-video, and image and sound communications. The IM&O was responsible for supporting all overseas marketing efforts for these companies. The ECDMG oversaw the worldwide marketing operations for semiconductors and for components and computer peripherals.

To centralize all the R&D efforts of Sony's electronics sector, the previous R&D structure (in which each company had its own R&D unit) was revamped and three new corporate laboratories were established. The laboratories were the architecture laboratory (responsible for software, network, and IT-related technologies), the product development laboratory (audio and video), and the system laboratory (system design and the basic components of hardware products). In addition, a new D21 laboratory was established to conduct long-term R&D for future-oriented technology-intensive products.

Sony also gave emphasis to grooming young, talented people to take up top management positions. The company also introduced the concept of 'virtual companies'—temporary groups consisting of people from different divisions for launching hybrid products. Sony applied this idea when developing the latest generation of mini disk players.

Restructuring initiated in 1998

During early 1998, Sony formed Sony Online Entertainment in the US to focus on internet related projects. In May 1998, it changed the composition of its board of directors and established the new position of Co-chief executive officer (Co-CEO). Idei was appointed Co-CEO. The new organization separated individuals responsible for policy-making from those responsible for operations.

Under the new system, Idei was responsible for planning and designing Sony's strategies and supervising the growth of e-business. Along with Ohga, he had to supervise the performance of the entire Sony group. The chief financial officer was made responsible for the company's financial strategies and network businesses.

In the late 1990s Sony's management felt the need to establish a link between its electronics business (TVs, music systems, computers) and its content-related businesses (music, video games, movies, and financial services) by making use of the internet. It wanted to use the internet as a medium for selling its electronics products as well as its content (music, movies, and so on). In order to achieve this, Sony announced another reorganization of business operations—to the unified–dispersed management model.

Restructuring initiated in 1999

In April 1999 Sony's key electronics and entertainment interests were reorganized into network businesses. This involved reducing the ten divisional companies into five; three network companies, Sony Computer Entertainment (SCE), and Broadcasting and Professional Systems (B&PS). SCE was responsible for the Playstation business while the B&PS supplied video and audio equipment for business, broadcast, education, industrial, medical, and production-related markets. The restructuring aimed at achieving three objectives: strengthening the electronics business, privatizing three Sony subsidiaries, and strengthening management capabilities.

Strengthening the electronics business

The three network companies created were Home Network, Personal IT Network, and Core Technology Network. Each network company was governed by a network company management committee (NCMC) and a network committee board (NCB). The NCMC was responsible for developing management policies and strategies. Its members included the officers and presidents of the network company concerned. An NCB was responsible for managing the day-to-day operations of the network company while keeping in mind the overall Sony corporate strategy.

The new structure aimed at decentralizing the worldwide operations of the company. The corporate headquarters gave the network companies the authority to function as autonomous entities in their business areas. To facilitate more functional and operational autonomy, the corporate headquarters also transferred the required support functions and R&D laboratories to each network company.

Privatizing Sony's subsidiaries

As part of its strategy to promote functional and operational autonomy and to devote more attention to units which contributed significantly to its revenues and profits, Sony decided to convert three of its companies—Sony Music Entertainment (Japan), Sony Chemical Corporation (which manufactured printed circuit boards (PSBs), recording media, and had battery operations), and Sony Precision Technology (manufactured semiconductor inspection equipment and precision measuring devices)—into wholly owned subsidiaries of Sony. In addition, Sony converted SCE, jointly owned by Sony and Sony Music Entertainment (Japan), into a wholly owned subsidiary of Sony.

Strengthening the management capability

To strengthen the management capability, Sony clearly defined the roles of headquarters and the newly created network companies. In particular, a sharp distinction was made between the strategic and support functions. Sony's headquarters was split into two separate units: group headquarters and business unit support.

The role of group headquarters was to oversee group operations and expedite the allocation of resources within the group. The support functions, such as accounting, HR, and general affairs, were handled by the network companies so that they could enjoy more autonomy in their operations. Significant long-term R&D projects were directly supervised by headquarters, while immediate and short-term R&D projects were transferred to the network companies concerned.

Restructuring initiated in 2001

At the beginning of the 2000s Sony faced increased competition from domestic and foreign players (Korean companies like Samsung and LG) in its electronics and entertainment businesses. The domestic rivals Matsushita and NEC were able to capture a substantial market share in the internet-ready cellphone market. Analysts felt that the US-based software giants like Microsoft and Sun Microsystems and the networking major Cisco Systems posed a serious threat to Sony's home entertainment business.

Sony announced another round of organizational restructuring in March 2001. The company aimed at transforming itself into a personal broadband network solutions company by launching a wide range of broadband products and services for its customers across the world. Explaining the objective of the restructuring, Idei said, 'By capitalizing on this business structure and by having businesses cooperate with each other, we aim to become the leading media and technology company in the broadband era.' The restructuring involved designing a new headquarters to function as a hub for Sony's strategy, strengthening the electronics business, and facilitating network-based content distribution.

Sony's headquarters was revamped into a global hub centred on five key businesses—electronics, entertainment, games, financial services and internet/communication service. The primary role of the global hub (headed by the top management) was to devise the overall management strategy of the company.

Sony's management decided to integrate all the electronics business-related activities under the newly created electronic headquarters. In order to achieve the convergence of audio-video products with IT, Sony devised a unique strategy called the 'four-network gateway'. Under this strategy, the games and internet/communication service businesses were combined with the electronics hardware business so that innovative products could be developed and offered for the broadband market.

In order to provide support services for the entire group, a management platform was created which consisted of key support functions in diverse fields such as accounting, finance, legal, intellectual copyrights, HR, information systems, public relations, external affairs, and design. The management platform was later split into the engineering, management and customer service (EMCS) company and the sales platform (which comprised the regional sales companies and region-based internet direct marketing functions). The management platform was headed by the chief administrative officer, a newly created position.

Sony's management also converted the product-centric network companies into solution-oriented companies by regrouping them into seven companies. Group resources were allocated among the network companies on the basis of their growth potential.

For the first quarter, ending 30 June 2003, the Sony Corporation stunned the corporate world by reporting a decline in net profits of 98%. In the financial year 2002–3, Sony had spent a massive ¥100 billion on restructuring.* Moreover, in April 2003 the company had already announced its plans to spend another ¥1 trillion on a major restructuring initiative in the next three years.

Source: Based on K. Prashanth and V. Gupta, *Restructuring Sony* (case study, ICFAI Center for Management Research, Hyderabad, India, 2003–4).

Discussion questions

1 When discussing international strategies, businesses were considered to be composed of four 'super' functions: operations, marketing, support services, and R&D. Track the changes for each of these functions from 1994 onwards, together with the changes to the overall structure of the Sony group and its electronics sector.

2 Identify Sony's organizational structures in terms of the types described in the chapter.

REFERENCES

3M Company, Annual Report and Accounts 1996–2003.

Bartlett, C. A., and Ghoshal, S. (1989). *Managing across Borders: The Transnational Solution* (Boston, Mass.: Harvard Business School Press).

Chandler, A. D. (1962). *Strategy and Structure: Chapters in the History of the American Industrial Enterprise* (Cambridge, Mass.: MIT Press).

——(1966). *Strategy and Structure* (New York: Doubleday).

Chi, T., Nystrom, C. P., and Kircher, P. (2004). 'Knowledge-based resources as determinants of MNC structure: tests of an integrative model', *Journal of International Management* 10: 219–38.

Egelhof, W. G. (1982). 'Strategy and structure in multinational corporations: an information-processing approach', *Administrative Science Quarterly* 27: 435–58.

——(1988). 'Strategy and structure in multinational corporations: a revision of the Stopford and Wells model', *Strategic Management Journal* 9: 1–14.

——(1993). 'Information-processing theory and the multinational corporation', in S. Ghoshal and D. E. Westney (eds.), *Organization Theory and the Multinational Corporation* (New York: St. Martin's Press).

European Industrial Management Association (1987). *The Role and Organisation of Corporate R&D* (EIMA).

Finlay, P. N. (2000). *Strategic Management: An Introduction to Business and Corporate Strategy* (Harlow: FT Prentice Hall).

Ghoshal, S., and Nohria, N. (1993). 'Horses for courses: organizational forms for multinational corporations', *Sloan Management Review* 34(2): 23–36.

Kanter, R. M. (1994). 'Collaborative advantage: the art of alliances', *Harvard Business Review* (July–Aug.): 96–108.

Kay, J. (1993). *Foundations of Corporate Success: How Business Strategies Add Value* (Oxford: Oxford University Press).

Marsh, P. (1997). Interview with Antony Lo, CEO of Giant, *Financial Times* (1 Oct.): 16.

* As on 23 July 2003, €1 = ¥132; US$1 = ¥118.

Mintzberg, H. (1979). *The Structuring of Organizations* (New York: Prentice Hall).

Porter, M. E. (1985). *Competitive Advantage: Creating and Sustaining Superior Performance* (New York: Free Press).

Stopford, J. M., and Wells, L. T. Jr (1972). *Managing the Multinational Enterprise* (London: Longman).

Trompenaars, F., and Hampden-Turner, C. (1997). *Riding the Waves of Culture: Understanding Cultural Diversity in Business* (London: Brealey).

11

Global management of change

Learning outcomes

After reading this chapter you should be able to:

- describe the two types of strategic change and recognize where management and where leadership are required;

- explain the characteristics required of a change agent;

- recognize the three phases of the change process;

- empathize with people when their work processes are changed and thus be able to manage most appropriately the change process;

- select the change-management style that best fits the context under which change is taking place.

Opening case study
Minebea and Rose

The Minebea group of Japan is a global company specializing in the mass production of miniature ball bearings and electronic components. In 1988 Minebea acquired Rose Bearings, based in Lincolnshire, England, producing hi-tech bearings.

Minebea had a highly entrepreneurial focus. Its philosophy was to diversify—in terms both of products and of customers. The company was a sales-led organization, with the sales team charged with winning orders at the market price (i.e. the price needed to obtain the customer's order, with no consideration as to the actual manufacturing costs). Minebea's established manufacturing plants had no input to the marketing and sales strategies, but were sufficiently flexible and innovative to be able to cope with the demands placed upon them: they were exceptionally good at manufacturing innovation to provide good margins at the prices obtained. For example, the Japanese were continually improving their manufacturing methods through using faster machines, introducing robotics, and employing dedicated production lines that their high volumes could support.

After Minebea took over Rose, a similar spirit of entrepreneurship was injected, particularly into the sales team. The Minebea sales-led strategy was implemented within Rose, but with no consideration of the markets in which Rose was operating. The sales manager took over responsibility from the technical manager for applications engineering—designing bearings with and for specific customers. Responsibility for estimating the cost of these new products was transferred from production engineering to sales, and market pricing was used. Almost immediately the sales team were bringing in enquiries at a prodigious rate. These enquiries included products that were not within Rose's core capabilities.

The huge influx of orders caused absolute chaos in the production department. The sales department was taking orders using standard lead times. No consideration was given to the capacity within the factory, or to the lead time required to develop the engineering and manufacturing techniques required for the influx of new products. Rose did not have the capability to innovate within manufacturing that the Japanese had.

In 1989 new production and operations managers were appointed from outside Rose and the Minebea Group. Although turnover had increased by around 30% within one year, by 1990 the company was in severe trouble: Rose had gone from a modest profit to a loss of almost £1 million. Overheads had increased due to the financial costs associated with the investment in machine tools financed by Minebea. The reaction of the sales department was to inject even more orders, which crippled the factory and exacerbated the situation.

By this time Rose's customers were in despair. Within twelve months the company, which had previously held an enviable reputation for product quality and delivery reliability, had experienced production line stoppages and lengthened lead times.

Minebea had a European sales operation—NMB Minebea—with offices in Frankfurt, Milan, and Paris and in the UK (in Bracknell). In 1991 Minebea combined Rose's sales force with NMB Minebea. By the end of 1992 it was obvious that the combination was a disaster. Minebea was upsetting the customers: it was acting as a buffer between the customer and the technical expertise at Rose.

Source: Shore (2000: 625–33).

11.1 **Introduction**

All types of firm, multinationals or single-country, small or large, single-business or diversified, need constantly to undertake operational renewal in order to renew those parts of the organization that are ageing. However, as demonstrated in the opening case study, for change to succeed it must be coordinated throughout the firm. Piecemeal change, like that introduced by Minebea and Rose, may create new problems without solving the old ones.

Also, due to the inherent instability in the business environment today, firms often find themselves facing the need to undertake strategic renewal in order to pursue a change strategy and/or to adjust to changing environmental factors. Where environmental change is slow and/or small, organizational change is likely to be in small, incremental steps. The changes that the organization needs to undertake are likely to be larger, however, where the environmental changes are larger or because it wishes to change its strategy significantly, as did Minebea. Such changes are transformational.

Strategic change in multinationals is more complex than that in single-country firms. The more complex the environment within which change takes place, the more difficult it is to design and implement a coherent change strategy. Multinational firms operate across several countries, which creates a complex and sometimes chaotic *mélange* of management practices influenced by different national cultures and institutions. In addition, some subsidiaries are more aware of the competitive nature of the business environment and its dynamics, and as a result are less resistant to change. Others are oblivious to the nature of the business environment, perhaps because the subsidiary or the industry is protected or subsidized by the government, and hence may not fully understand the importance of change and may resist it. Further, people's attitudes towards change are also affected by a set of culture-specific factors, such as taken-for-granted behaviour, norms, and values, which adds another layer of complexity to change management in multinational firms. The different behaviours and attitudes of employees and management at subsidiary level towards change increase the potential for conflict between the centre and subsidiaries, and may hinder the success of the change strategy (Andrews and Chompusri 2001).

11.2 **Types of change**

Organizations have to be prepared to undertake both incremental change and transformational change.

11.2.1 **Incremental change**

By far the most frequent sort of change in organizations is incremental change. Incremental change alters behaviours in the organization, but generally leaves undisturbed the more deeply held organizational beliefs. Examples of incremental change aim to produce more of 'something' and/or do things better. The incorporation of an export department into the

Exhibit 11.1 Differences between incremental and transformational change

Incremental change	Transformational change
Management	Leadership
Doing things better or doing more of them	Doing things very differently or doing different things
Bottom-up	Top-down
Fundamental beliefs unaffected	Fundamental beliefs changed
Efficiency	Effectiveness

Source: Adapted from Stacey (1996).

existing domestic marketing function when a firm begins exporting (see Chapter 10) would probably be considered incremental, since no large-scale changes are involved.

Incremental change is a role for management. Managers deal with the physical resources of an organization—with its capital, raw materials, technology, and with the demonstrable skills of the workforce. They are concerned with efficiency and with mastering routines. They are the people who resolve issues as they arise: they do things right—working within defined policies. However, although incremental change may be sanctioned by managers, much incremental change is originated by the people most intimately connected with the organization's processes, its products/services, and its customers. If they are suitably empowered, they can bring about the required change themselves.

Incremental change is more associated with management rather than leadership, since management generally continues current activities with a concern for efficiency. Incremental change does not lead to a change in the implicit fundamental beliefs underpinning the organizational way of working. The characteristics of situations involving incremental change are summarized in the first column of Exhibit 11.1.

11.2.2 Transformational change

Transformational change involves changing one or more of the fundamental organizational beliefs, and with it the values of the organization. Examples of transformational change are the changes in the processes associated with doing things very differently, or with undertaking very different activities, as Minebea did moving Rose to market pricing. The changes that an organization makes to move to either a multi-domestic or a colonial strategy (see Chapter 10) are transformational. In such cases management alone generally is not sufficient—what is required is leadership.

Leaders are people who are concerned with effectiveness: they do the right things, they make policy. They act on the emotional and spiritual resources of the organization, dealing with its values, commitment, and aspirations (Bennis and Nanus 1985: 21). Leaders are also issue *finders*: they seek issues in their search for opportunities. Zaleznik (1992: 129, 131) distinguishes between managers and leaders: 'Managers aim to shift balances of power toward solutions acceptable as compromises amongst conflicting values … [while] leaders develop fresh ideas to long-standing problems and open issues to new options.'

But the way in which leadership is viewed differs between countries. Kay (1995: 15) makes an interesting contrast between US and UK views on leadership and those of the rest of Europe. In the US and UK (and to some extent in France) the chief executive is seen as the master of the organization, and business success becomes, in effect, realizing the chief executive's vision. In Japan and most of the rest of Europe, senior executives are seen as the servants of the organization, and success is seen as maximizing the value of an organization's distinctive capabilities.

The major differences between the situations appropriate for incremental management and those suitable for transformational leadership can be seen by comparing the two lists in Exhibit 11.1. In general, transformational change will be a top-down process, initiated and possibly imposed by the top team.

KEY CONCEPT

Two types of change can be recognized: *incremental change*, which takes place without disturbing fundamental organizational beliefs, and *transformational change*, which does change them. In general, carrying through incremental change requires mainly management skills, whilst carrying out transformational change involves considerable leadership skills. From this it can be seen that successfully effecting change requires senior managers not simply to manage but also to lead. Since the only constant in the business lives of managers will be change, the ability to handle strategic change is a fundamental skill for such people.

11.2.3 Types of change and national cultures

While all types of strategic change, small or large, incremental or radical, are to a varying degree difficult to manage, strategic change in multinational firms is much more difficult to manage than change in firms operating in a single country. This is because employees and management in different countries hold different managerial values and are used to different managerial practices. Harding's (1996: 111) study of strategic change of Lucas Car Braking Systems in Britain and Germany found that during the process of change, the British workforce were stuck in what he called the 'bad practice learning phase'; in contrast, the German workforce were more receptive to learning in the post shock phase. As a result, management used a different method of change in the two sites. In the case of the British workforce, Harding argues that to overcome the inherent resistance to change there is a need for a shock or transformational change. In contrast, the German workforce's acceptance of the need for change makes the gradual or incremental change strategy more appropriate. That is, compatibility between the type of change and the cultural values and management practices of the workforce is a necessary ingredient for the success of the change strategy.

11.3 People involved in the change process

There are likely to be several individuals or groups of individuals involved with any one change process—people who move in and out of important roles as the change progresses. Davenport (1993) has identified several players in the change process:

- the advocate, who proposes change;
- the sponsor, who legitimizes change;
- the targets, who are the people who undergo change;
- the change agents, who implement change;
- the process owner, who is typically the most senior member of the group targeted for change.

This chapter will mainly focus on change agents and targets. How change affects the people who undergo change will be considered in section 11.3.2.

11.3.1 The change agent

A change agent is the individual or group who has the specific role of implementing change in an organization. While one person is often the source of an idea or invention, a team is generally required to innovate, and thus the change agent very often leads a team. In many cases the change agent(s) are employees of the organization and are given special responsibilities. Often, however, external consultants may be recruited to effect change. In international operations the change agent may often be an expatriate. Sometimes the change agent is a consulting firm, such as the Canadian IT consultants SolCorp, who offer specialist and change-management skills in corporate financial services, employing a group of North American and British specialists who operate worldwide.

If the change agent is the chief executive, some of the problems with strategic change management will disappear, or be significantly reduced; for example, in many situations there should be less difficulty in obtaining the resources required to bring about change. However, many chief executives have not the time to be closely involved with any one specific change programme, and some have not the inclination; thus they delegate the task to others. Change agents need not be a member of the top management team (the main board directors at head office), but they are almost always managers. They have a particularly difficult task, because (to paraphrase Machiavelli 1993) the innovator may face a lot of resistance from those who have done well under old conditions and little support from those who may benefit under new conditions. The requirements of a change agent are set out in Exhibit 11.2.

11.3.2 The role of subordinate and subsidiary managers

Subordinate and subsidiary managers, particularly middle managers, play a very significant role in the management of change. Hampton-Turner and Trompenaars (1993a) make the point that in the US, the top team specifies the strategy in a very precise way: top

Exhibit 11.2 The requirement of a change agent

Relating to objectives

1. Sensitivity to the way changes in senior personnel, management perceptions, and business conditions affect the goals of the change programme.

2. Clarity in defining objectives.

3. Flexibility in responding to changing conditions.

Political awareness

1. Being aware of potential coalitions and understanding their significance.

2. Continually ensuring that more senior management are backing the team. Continuing senior management commitment and involvement is of overriding importance.

3. Balancing conflicting goals and perceptions.

4. Being aware of the extent of their own power.

Sensitivity

1. Being able to empathize with people undergoing a change process.

2. Sensitivity to the organizational context in terms of where the forces for change and inhibiting forces might come from, and to the style of change process that will be acceptable.

Communication and negotiation

1. Networking skills to establish and maintain the appropriate contacts within and outside the organization.

2. Communication skills to inform team members, superiors, and networkers of progress and needs.

3. Ability to enrol others in plans and ideas.

4. Negotiating with key individuals within the organization for resources.

Team-building and leadership

1. Team-building abilities, to identify key potential team members, enrol them, and motivate them to ensure they work as a team.

2. Team management, to define team members' responsibilities and delegate authority accordingly.

3. Team leadership, to provide a vision for the future.

Individual characteristics

1. Enthusiasm for change.

2. Tolerance of ambiguity: being able to work effectively and efficiently in an uncertain environment.

Source: Adapted from Buchanan and Boddy (1992: 92–3).

management knows, or thinks it knows, what is required. This way of operating is often carried over into the international sphere, with US head office stipulating what is required for their foreign subsidiary managers to carry out. In such a situation the foreign, subordinate managers are the implementers of closely specified change: their role is to make the resources available, make plans to implement the change, and control costs and resource usage. In such a situation subordinate managers are likely to be seen as inhibitors of change, especially as the precise specification of the change developed by the top team has probably been made without a full knowledge of their subsidiary's situation and capabilities.

In contrast, Japanese senior management take a less precise approach to strategy. Hampton-Turner and Trompenaars (1993a) illustrate this by contrasting the Japanese approach—where the senior managers would say to middle managers, 'We are going to make a microprocessor—what kind of microprocessor would you like the firm to make?'—with the US approach, in which senior managers would tell middle managers, 'This is the new microprocessor we want.'

Nonaka and Takeuchi (1995) describe the role of the middle manager in the more flexible Japanese situation. Such managers take the broad vision of top managers and combine it with the detailed, often tacit knowledge of front-line employees, such as salespeople and factory operatives, to make the vision a reality. The middle managers thus have a creative, pivotal role in modern business—much more than the downsizers and lean-management gurus would have us believe. However, it is not apparent that this domestic way of operating can be transplanted into production facilities in other countries, as the Minebea case shows.

One problem that middle managers have as the initiators of change is in obtaining the ear of top management to obtain the resources they need to support the changes. Another problem is that technical people have difficulty in finding ways to translate their technical ideas into a form that allows senior management to evaluate the idea (Hampden-Turner and Trompenaars 1993: 98). This problem is particularly acute if expatriate specialists have to liaise with nationals in a language in which they are not fluent.

KEY CONCEPT

A change agent is the individual or group who has the specific role of implementing change in an organization. A change agent very often leads a team. Middle managers have a pivotal role in the change process. In Japanese companies they take the broad vision of top managers and combine it with the detailed, often tacit knowledge of front-line employees, to make the vision a reality. In many Western firms, the middle manager is simply asked to implement detailed, centrally decided requirements.

11.4 **The change process**

11.4.1 **A model of the change process**

Change agents are concerned with initiating and implementing both incremental and transformational change. Both types of change process can be considered to involve three phases: unfreezing, adjustment, and refreezing (Schein 1947).

Unfreezing

The change process begins with a loosening of the hold of established behaviour and/or beliefs, because there is a feeling that change is needed and feasible. Three ingredients must be present to some degree for unfreezing to take place:

- serious discomfort, because there is evidence that does not support the current ways of thinking and/or doing;
- the connection of this discomforting information to important goals and ideals;
- enough 'psychological safety' to support action. It is important that a group is able to see the possibility of resolving the issue without the group having to be disbanded or dismembered.

If certain levels of profit and customer satisfaction are important organizational goals, two examples of discomforting information would be decreased profits and increased customer complaints. It is a common trick of politicians to invoke an external threat—real or not—to force changes in values and behaviours, and this device is available to managers. Nonaka and Takeuchi (1995) recount how senior Japanese managers put their middle managers under severe pressure by presenting them with very stiff challenges, in order to force change. A new leader with a new vision may be a catalyst for change, because he/she may see the major issues in a way that allows for their resolution: the new leader is providing the psychological safety net that the group will survive, keeping its integrity intact. However, without a period of prior discomfort it may well be that the visionary leader will not be listened to: people are only ready to listen when they feel something is wrong and/or they could do better. An expatriate transplant into an ailing subsidiary has a greater chance of success than one joining a successfully led operation, since in the former case the employees expect—and indeed may positively welcome—change.

Adjustment

Following unfreezing, adjustment can then take place. The deeper the cultural change being sought, the more difficult it is to bring about adjustment. However, the deeper the change, the more lasting and fundamental the adjustment is likely to be—and the more general are the consequences. If behavioural adjustment is coerced, the adjustment is unlikely to last when the coercion is removed, as shown by the inability of communism to survive the totalitarian regimes that coerced whole nations for fifty years.

As well as involving new types of behaviour by individuals, the adjustments made will generally include organizational changes, such as the implementation of new control systems and modifications to the way people are rewarded.

Refreezing

Following adjustment, the new ways of thought and behaviour need to be locked in place, in the process termed 'refreezing'. For refreezing to take place, confirmatory information needs to be provided to show that the new behaviours and/or beliefs more closely mirror the perceived reality. If such information is not forthcoming, then coping with the existing situation, together with a search for a new approach, will continue. The importance of confirmatory evidence means that the managers should ensure that it is provided. One way of doing this is to ensure that the change programme includes some quick hits, so that some success comes early in the programme, rather than there being an extended period of uncertainty when success is unclear. Once sufficient confirmatory information has been gained, then the situation will stabilize until further uncomfortable information triggers off the whole unfreezing–adjustment–refreezing process once more.

The unfreezing–adjustment–refreezing process can be observed in successful transformational change of various multinational firms. For instance, when Carlos Ghosn became the chief executive of Nissan in 1999, he purposely set out to unfreeze old practices. A key part of his approach was to use repeatedly the example of a recently failed Japanese bank to illustrate to Nissan's employees the dangers of not changing; he also made sure to communicate the difficult situation of the company to the employees in order to increase their willingness to change their behaviour. Adjustment took place, using methods such as performance evaluations and a restructuring of the organization. Finally, refreezing was helped through Ghosn's relatively quick success in returning Nissan to profitability, which demonstrated to the employees the value of the changes made.

> **KEY CONCEPT**
>
> Change management requires three phases: unfreezing, adjustment, and refreezing. The deeper the cultural change being sought, the more difficult it is to bring about adjustment. However, the deeper the change, the more lasting and fundamental the adjustment is likely to be. Winning hearts and minds is fundamental to deep and lasting change.

11.4.2 People's reaction to change

Almost everyone feels some sort of stress when facing and enacting change. An important requirement for the change agent is to be able to empathize with people who are undergoing change and to manage those individuals' self-esteem. Esteem will suffer in many cases because skills will be devalued before other skills are fully learned. Part of the empathy is to understand the phases that affect people who are undergoing the unfreezing–adjustment–refreezing process. *The coping cycle* (Carnall 2003: 242–7) describes how the people involved in change are affected (see Exhibit 11.3).

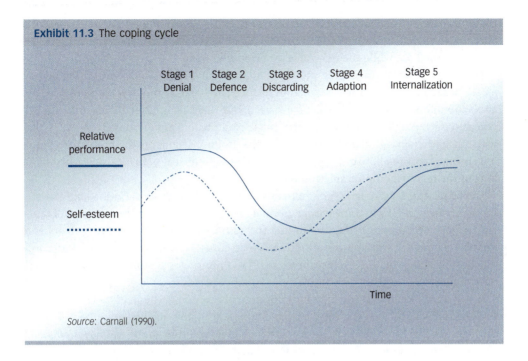

Exhibit 11.3 The coping cycle

	Stage 1	Stage 2	Stage 3	Stage 4	Stage 5
	Denial	Defence	Discarding	Adaption	Internalization

Relative performance

Self-esteem

Time

Source: Carnall (1990).

The first stage of the coping cycle is **denial**. The tendency to deny the validity of new ideas, at least initially, does seem to be a general reaction to the announcement of change. The responses are along the lines of 'Why fix it if it isn't broken?' and 'We've always done it that way'. Managing change in past-oriented cultures, typical of Asian societies, poses considerable challenges (Trompenaars and Hampden-Turner 1997: 133).

Paradoxically perhaps, self-esteem could rise during the period of denial as the advantages of the present job and the value of the group are emphasized. Performance levels relative to some 'normal' fiduciary level could go up or down due to the combination of this increased self-esteem and the energy expended in discussing the impending changes. If change occurs without warning, then the performance loss could be large.

The second stage of the coping cycle is **defence**, where the individuals have to come to terms with the fact that change is going to take place. This phase is often accompanied by a feeling of frustration and depression, as the individual doesn't know what to do. This can lead to defensive reactions. Both self-esteem and performance are likely to suffer significantly.

Defence and denial have focused on the past. In stage three of the coping process the focus is on **discarding** the past and looking forward. If possible, it is valuable to allow people to experiment or experience the future; through visits to organizations operating in the 'future' way, 'playing through' the possibilities by using a computer simulation, or, where a new or enhanced computer information system is to be installed, allowing staff to play around with it. In this way a positive attitude to change may develop, and the change may begin to be seen as inevitable and/or may begin to be seen as for the better. Self-esteem begins to recover as people begin to resolve problems and take the initiative, but perform-ance may continue to drop, not least because this is often the time when the old processes must be carried out while the new ones are being phased in.

The fourth stage of the coping process is **adaptation**. Here a process of testing and ad-aptation/adoption takes place: adaptation of the individual to the new working practices, and adoption of the practices as people learn about them. It is often a trial-and-error pro-cess, and the build-up of skill can be slow and frustrating. If a group is involved—as is likely with strategic change—then the strength of the group will support the individuals within it. It is important to allow people to have control over how the activities are carried out as long as the required outputs are achieved.

The final stage, **internalizing**, corresponds to the refreezing stage, as individuals internal-ize the changes as they become part of 'normal' behaviour. Relative performance will return to 'normal', although this could mean that the absolute output is much better than before the new method of working was introduced. The group has re-established itself as a well-functioning team, and has built team strength as a result of the problems it has faced and overcome.

It should be noted that the 'buy-in' to change often follows the marketing model, with first the innovators, then the early adopters, followed by the majority and then finally by the laggards. The innovators are the leaders of change, and thus in the early days of change the manager should seek out such people and make sure that their acceptance of change is noticed by others, particularly by the early adopters, who will be looking to the innovators to see what is happening. As time progresses, the next group that the manager should focus on are the early adopters, and later the majority and the laggards.

KEY CONCEPT

People facing change often go through five phases as they discard the old and internalize the new: denial, defence, discarding, adaptation, and internalizing. It is important for the change agent to recognize the stage that an individual has reached and to empathize with the diffi-culties they may be having. The buy-in to change often follows the marketing model: first the innovators, then the early adopters, then the majority and then the laggards.

11.5 Appropriate styles of change management

In general, organizations will act differently when facing the same environmental change because they will have different resources and different cultures and are likely to be posi-tioned in strategically different ways. The specific manner in which they react to change will be contingent on the position they find themselves in.

The approaches of Nonaka and Takeuchi (1995) and Simons (1994: 69–189), and that described in the last section, might have suggested that a considerable level of particip-ation is appropriate in all change situations. But this is not the case, as different change

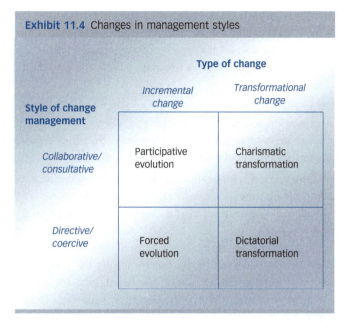

Exhibit 11.4 Changes in management styles

	Type of change	
Style of change management	*Incremental change*	*Transformational change*
Collaborative/ consultative	Participative evolution	Charismatic transformation
Directive/ coercive	Forced evolution	Dictatorial transformation

situations require different styles of change management. The appropriate style of change management depends on four factors:

- the magnitude of the change, and whether it is incremental or transformational;
- the fit of the organization to its environment;
- the time available for discussion;
- the support for change within the organization.

Depending on the above four factors, a firm may select a specific style of change management. Styles of change management differ considerably. Dunphy and Stace (1993: 905–20) have identified four such styles: participative evolution, forced evolution, charismatic transformation, and dictatorial transformation. These four styles are shown in Exhibit 11.4.

- **Participative evolution** is most appropriate for incremental change when an organization broadly matches its environment and only minor adjustments are required. It is also the appropriate response when there is a relatively poor strategic fit between the organization and its external business environment but when time is available for people to participate, and key individuals and groups favour change. The appropriate management style is collaborative or consultative. The **collaborative style** is one in which there is full input from all members of the group to the change required. A smaller level of participation occurs with the **consultative style**, where the people involved and affected by the proposed changes are asked for their views.

- **Forced evolution** is most appropriate for incremental change under similar conditions of organizational–environmental fit and time availability as for participative evolution.

However, this is the appropriate approach when key interests oppose change. The appropriate management style is directive or coercive. A **directive style** is one whereby people are told what they are to do and they are reasonably happy with the changes, whilst a **coercive style** is one where people are not happy with the proposed changes and resist them.

- **Charismatic transformation** is most appropriate when there is a substantial mismatch between an organization and its environment, and when there is little time for extensive participation but there is support for radical change within the organization. The appropriate management style is collaborative or consultative.

- **Dictatorial transformation** is most appropriate when an organization does not match its environment, there is no time for extensive participation, and there is little or no support for radical change, but when radical change is vital for organizational wellbeing. When an organization is performing so badly that the chief executive is sacked, the new chief executive is often appointed to carry out a dictatorial transformation. The autocrat needs a clear vision of the organizational goals, but should let the people in the organization who know the operational details decide on the means of achieving it. The situation is like a ship in a storm: the captain knows the port they want to shelter in, but uses the expertise of the first mate to take the most appropriate course. The appropriate management style is directive or coercive.

KEY CONCEPT

Different styles of change management are likely to be appropriate at different times in an organization's existence, and the appropriate approach will not necessarily be the same for all parts of an organization.

11.6 Implementing change

Implementing change is never easy, because of the inherent resistance to change within most organizations. But implementing change can be assisted through project teams, and through moving people within the multinational firm.

11.6.1 Project teams

A project can be considered to be a set of processes aimed at achieving a firm objective within a specified timescale. Thus the building of a new car production line would be a project; running that line would not. Project teams can play a key role in the management of change. For instance, project teams played a key role in Lufthansa's transformation from a state-owned airline on the verge of bankruptcy in 1992 to one of the most profitable airlines ten years later. This transformation was made possible by the use of project teams, which reported directly to Lufthansa's chief executive and led the implementation of change strategies such as Programm 15 (to reduce the cost target for transporting one aircraft seat from 17.7 pfennig per kilometre to 15 pfennig between 1996–2001) and D-Check (another cost-cutting exercise from 2001).

Project management has long been recognized as a specialist field; indeed, there are project-management qualifications and professional project-management organizations. Traditionally, the term has been associated with large and lengthy civil engineering projects such as the construction of the Channel Tunnel between France and the UK. However, the concern for rapid response has led to the demand for organizations to be flexible, able to cope with complexity, and be at ease with innovating and initiating change. Many years ago, Bennis (1969: 34) argued that one of the key descriptive terms for a flexible, organic organizational structure is that it is temporary. He claims: 'these structures will be adaptive, rapidly-changing temporary systems. They will be project teams organized around problems to be solved by groups of relative strangers with diverse professional skills.' Very often, therefore, the project team will only exist for the duration of the project, being disbanded once the project is completed.

The use of project teams to tackle complex issues is widespread throughout business (Buchanan 1994; Bennis 1969: 34), so much so that there is the view that management has become very much project-based management—at least for all managers when they are involved in change. This widespread use of project teams means that skill in project management has become one of the key requirements for managers.

One complication for project managers is the requirement to work with colleagues over whom they have no direct authority. This is particularly apparent when working internationally, when a project team is set up with people from several countries and/or involving several agencies. Another complication lies in the inclusion of individuals in the project team from units which have not empowered them to act on behalf of their unit, and which require them to report back before anything can be agreed. This is a particular problem with some Asian cultures. There are individuals who expect to be consulted fully before others take action and introduce changes that will affect them. The need for the project manager to be aware of the power they themselves have, and to use it appropriately, is crucial in these situations.

11.6.2 Moving people

One of the best ways of spreading ideas—and, by extension, best head office practice—is by moving people. Moving people through the organization in a structured way is common in Germany and Japan, where an individual's career is framed by the firm rather than by professional qualifications (Lam 1998). When a person becomes a manager they have a very wide knowledge of many aspects of the company and share a common mindset with other managers. Similarly, the composition of project teams can be designed so that the tacit knowledge generated and spread through team discussions will automatically be spread throughout the organization when the team members go back to their 'home' units and discuss what they have been doing.

Moving people can be a key part of a change strategy. For instance, Nissan's transformation from an unprofitable to a profitable multinational firm between 1999 and 2000 was greatly aided by moving people. One problem that Nissan faced in 1999 was that Japanese employees in functional departments failed to challenge existing work practices. So Nissan set up nine cross-functional teams, each with line managers from different departments, to allow managers to see beyond functional responsibilities and to see how the success of their own department depended on cooperating with other departments. Learning about their business from a bird's-eye perspective allowed managers to be much more engaged in Nissan's change strategy.

11.6.3 Expatriates

One extreme variant of moving people is the use of expatriates—who will be defined here as professional or managerial personnel employed outside their home country on secondment to another part of the organization. This definition thus includes not only the common relocation from a parent organization to one of its subsidiaries but also the reverse move, and moves between subsidiaries. Thus expatriates would include a French national seconded from the Paris head office to work in Vietnam, a Vietnamese seconded to Paris, and a Vietnamese sent to work in an affiliate in Algeria.

There are many reasons for employing expatriates. The most obvious is that they are able to bring sophisticated technology or managerial practice to a less-developed country. There is also the feeling of the parent that it will only be able to exercise appropriate control over its foreign subsidiaries if they are headed by someone whose first loyalty is to the firm rather than to the host country and host nationals. In this respect the expatriates are carriers of organizational culture. This sort of thinking has certainly been prevalent in the initial stages of internationalization where, in addition to the control issue, head office wished to learn about its foreign operations. Research suggests that staffing strategy is affected by an organization's stage in the internationalization process, the country of origin (with Japanese using more expatriates than others), the cultural divide between the head office and subsidiaries, and task complexity (Thomas 2002: 219).

There is a considerable downside to the use of expatriates. The cost of employing them can be considerable, especially if their transfer also means relocation of their family. Expatriates typically cost two or three times as much as the equivalent person in the parent country, and often very much more than a local person. The expatriate may be seen as simply a controller, and resentment can build up. Being an expatriate is a difficult job, operating as they do at the interface between head office and the host organization. This requires them to be sensitive to other ways of working, and to be able to adapt to other social environments.

There are indications that the number of European expatriates sent overseas by European firms is diminishing. Part of this is due to cost, part is due to spouses not wishing to relocate. Part is due to the heightened fear of terrorist activity. But this does not mean that the overall flow of expatriates is lessening. Standard Chartered, one of the oldest British banks operating overseas, has been sending executives to run subsidiaries in India and China since

1853. Today, the bank's top 3,000 managers are drawn from seventy different nationalities and there are more overseas expatriates in its London head office than Britons abroad (Roberts 2003: 13).

KEY CONCEPT

Implementing change can be assisted through project teams and through moving people within the multinational firm. A project team can be defined as a set of processes aimed at achieving a firm's objectives within a specified timescale.

11.7 Communication issues

11.7.1 Difficulties in discussing issues linked to change

It is generally important for the people who are affected by the change to discuss what the change means for them. The difficulty in discussing and debating change issues depends on the circumstances.

People are much more ready to debate and discuss some things than others. This hinges on which ring of the cultural onion is being worked upon. Bowman (1995: 4–12) has described these as 'zones of debate'. People are reasonably happy discussing norms of behaviour but less so discussing values. Values may be discussed, but generally this would be outside formal meetings, as values often concern vested interests and personal reputations. But to make major progress there is a need to 'surface' the fundamental organizational beliefs and challenge them in order to build a shared vision (Senge 1990: 7–23). In general, however, the fundamental organizational beliefs are not discussed, often because they are never surfaced. The greater the feeling of crisis, however, the more people may feel that they must challenge some of the fundamental organizational beliefs, since these beliefs are failing them.

11.7.2 The role of language

The difficulties that people have in talking about change is made worse if individuals have different verbal fluency, and obviously this is particularly marked if one or more parties must use a language other than their mother tongue. Feely (2003: 206–35) describes the problems, from misunderstandings through to loss of face in group discussions and loss of power and authority. Neal (1998) interviewed 174 foreign managers working in the UK, and found that working with their UK colleagues in English was frustrating to them and that the language barrier made them feel like outsiders.

Exhibit 11.5 Global influence index

Rank	Language	Index
1	English	100
2	German	42
3	French	33
4	Japanese	32
5	Spanish	31
6	Chinese	22
7	Arabic	8
8	Portuguese	5
9	Malay	4
10	Russian	3

Although the number of active languages is shrinking rapidly, there are approximately 5,000 languages in the world (Hearn and Button 1994). Thus an organization operating in many parts of the globe will have to accommodate many languages. Microsoft has adopted a policy of offering its software in about eighty languages.

The 100 most widely spoken languages are spoken by 95% of the world's inhabitants. The ten most influential languages are listed in Exhibit 11.5.

Whilst English is firmly established as the most popular language for business (some firms, such as the Swedish-Swiss engineering company ABB, use it as their corporate language), its continuing ascendancy is not assured. Feely (2003: 206–35) takes the view that the dying out of many languages will benefit regional languages rather than English. He points out that the primacy of English in the second part of the twentieth century was due in large measure to technology: people needed to learn English to use computing and telecommunications and to enjoy TV and films. Technology has now advanced, so that low-cost translations are possible, and so people can use their own language and lose much less. He believes that the number of people learning English as a second language will peak within the next ten years and then start to fall.

Thus in many parts of the world in future English will no longer be the obvious language of business. Multinational managers may well have to be multilingual.

11.7.3 Business implications

The lack of fluency in one language has serious implications for conducting international business. It will make it harder to communicate between subsidiaries and the centre. This is likely to mean that head office centralizes decision-making, but with well-defined local autonomy. It will also mean that it will be harder to establish global sourcing.

As early as 1975, Johanson and Wiedersheim-Paul (1975: 411–32) found that firms preferred to establish their first foreign subsidiaries in countries that were 'linguistically close'. This finding is reflected in the fact that UK companies have established subsidiaries in countries such as Australia and New Zealand, physically located far from the mother country, rather than in the much nearer Continental Europe.

The mode of entry used to establish a subsidiary also varies with the 'linguistic closeness' of the two countries involved. Kogat and Singh (1988: 411–32) found that the entry mode into the US favoured by overseas companies differed depending on this. UK and Canadian firms strongly preferred acquisition to joint ventures, as did the Netherlands and Germany, which both have a strong English-language orientation. In contrast, France and Japan, not noted for their English-language skills, preferred to enter through joint ventures.

11.7.4 Overcoming language problems

If an audit of an organization's language capability indicates a lack of competence, one obvious approach is to employ professional translators and interpreters. Whilst this can go some way to overcoming language problems it can only go so far—it is really only of value in more formal situations, and tends to be expensive. More radical solutions are to establish customized training programmes for affected staff—as Volkswagen has done—but these involve a long-term commitment. An alternative is to adopt a single corporate language. The Swedish firm Electrolux, the German firm Siemens, the German-US firm DaimlerChrysler, and the Italian firm Olivetti have all selected English as the language for formal communication. Nestlé has settled on two corporate languages—French and English. Using a corporate language does have the advantage of easing the maintenance of technical literature, helping with informal communications across national boundaries, and helping to diffuse a corporate ethos.

Adopting a corporate language will do little to ease the language barriers with outside parties, however—with buyers, suppliers and government agencies. Where such interaction is subtle and important, it may well be that managers with the appropriate language skills will be recruited. However, such personnel are in short supply, and therefore difficult to recruit. Those that are recruited are then special creatures—and become very powerful 'gatekeepers'. Staff will be tempted to bypass a formal chain of command if by doing so they can get access to the people they want to.

KEY CONCEPT

Difficulty in discussing and debating change issues depends on the circumstances. People are reasonably happy discussing norms of behaviour, but less so discussing values. Only in exceptional circumstances are fundamental organizational beliefs likely to be discussed. Fluency of language is an important aspect of successful communication between people, especially during stressful periods such as when change is being discussed and implemented. Language training and the adoption of a single corporate language are means of reducing the barrier that imperfect language skills can present to communication.

11.8 Negotiation with outside parties

A change strategy calls for considerable negotiation with people and groups within the organization, a very important area for negotiation is that with external bodies—customers, suppliers, and government agencies.

Management must pay attention to the fact that individuals from different cultures tend to adopt different conflict resolution strategies. Members of collectivist cultures, for instance, perceive and manage conflict differently from those in individualistic cultures. While people in collectivist cultures tend to avoid open conflict, people in individualistic countries tend to face it head-on. And when conflict does emerge after all efforts have been exhausted to avoid it, people in collectivist countries tend to resolve it in inner circles before it becomes serious enough to justify public involvement. Only when repeated efforts within the inner circle fail to resolve the conflict is the conflict likely to be resolved by top management in a top-down fashion (Ting-Toomey 1988).

Despite cultural differences, some negotiation frameworks are generic and can be used across cultures. One such framework that takes culture into consideration is Graham's (1985) five-step negotiation process.

1. Preparation. At this stage the managers should learn as much as feasible about the people with whom they will be negotiating—their cultural background and what this means for negotiation, their negotiating style and what they wish to achieve at the end of the process.

2. 'Getting to know you'. This stage is where the parties learn about the personalities involved prior to getting down to the negotiation. It is relationship-building. The so-called 'low-context countries', such as those of northern Europe, the US, and Canada, tend to abbreviate this stage and proceed straight to stage 3—the real business. In 'high-context' cultures, such as most Asian, Latin American, and Arabic countries, it is considered very important to build up personal relationships and trust. It is no use people from low-context cultures trying to abbreviate this stage: people from high-context cultures are doing business with an individual rather than with an organization.

3. Task-related exchange of information. This is the stage where the parties concerned state their positions, providing the information to support their case. Negotiators from some cultures—particularly Chinese, Russians, and Latin Americans—state an extreme initial position. North Americans tend to open negotiations with a position fairly close to what they will be happy with.

   Negotiators from low-context cultures will see this stage as a free flow of information, asking questions and giving answers readily. The Chinese tend to ask a lot of very detailed and specific questions, but in a rather vague way. The Russians tend to be very well prepared in the technical details, and pose questions to elicit technical details. At the end of this stage all parties should know the fundamentals of the proposition being put before them.

4. Persuasion. In this stage the fundamentals of the proposition are further explored, with the aim of changing initial positions. This stage has both formal and informal sides.

The context is quite important, with each party deploying tactics to persuade the other parties to accede. Tactics that might be employed are calculated delays, expressions of time constraints, the presence of other partners in the proposal who could replace one of the parties, and so on. In such situations, body language provides important clues to the experienced negotiator.

5. Agreement. In this stage, it is likely that both parties give ground somewhat. The American and North European style is to move incrementally towards an agreement, finalizing a portion of the proposal and then moving on to the next piece. In contrast, Asians and Latin Americans are more holistic negotiators, going back and forth over the ground and only agreeing the full deal at the end of negotiations.

11.9 Summary

Change is a journey, not an event, and on this journey organizations face two types of strategic change—incremental and transformational. In general, incremental change is a managerial issue, while transformational change involves leadership. The general change process of unfreezing–adjustment–freezing is the same for both types of change, but the part of the culture that is changed is likely to differ. Three 'zones of debate' are recognized, each differing in the ease with which they are open to discussion.

People facing change often go through five phases as they discard the old and internalize the new: denial, defence, discarding, adaptation, and internalizing. It is important for the change agent to recognize the stages that an individual has reached and to empathize with the difficulties he or she may be having. The appropriate style of change management depends on four factors: the magnitude of the change, the fit of the organization to its environment, the time available for discussion, and the support for change within the organization.

The role of the change agent is a demanding one, with special emphasis on interpersonal and political skills. In particular, they must be adept at recognizing blocking tactics used by people who are resistant to change. Whilst it is possible within an organization to operate by diktat, negotiation is a fundamental part of any change process involving outside people and agencies. To understand the different ways in which people negotiate is thus vital for success. Communication between individuals and groups is vitally important in the change process, and in that process, language fluency is very significant.

KEY READINGS

- J. P. Kotter, *Leading Change* (Cambridge, Mass.: Harvard Business School, 1996) and Dave Buchanan and Dave Boddy, *The Expertise of the Change Agent: Public Performance and Backstage Activity* (Harlow: Prentice Hall, 1992) cover most of the ground concerning the roles of leader-managers in the change programmes. Kotter's book is written for managers, and is practical rather than academic in emphasis.

- Chapters 4 and 5 of Ikujiro Nonaka and Hirotaka Takeuchi, *The Knowledge-Creating Company:*

How Japanese Companies Create the Dynamics of Innovation (Oxford: Oxford University Press, 1995) describe knowledge creation through project teams in Japanese companies.

● Colin Carnall covers fully the way in which people react to the stresses and opportunities of change in C. A. Carnall, *Managing Change in Organizations,* 4th edn. (Harlow: FT Prentice Hall, 2003).

DISCUSSION QUESTIONS

1 The strategic management environment may be characterized as chaotic, complex, dynamic, and turbulent—all generally increasing the level of uncertainty facing managers. How might changes in environmental characteristics affect the approach taken to global strategic change management?

2 How do you think the attributes of a change agent would differ across cultures?

3 One of the key challenges of strategic change across cultures is creating and managing global teams to design and manage teams. List and discuss the key attributes of a successful global team.

4 Multinational firms cannot use a 'one size fits all' approach when managing change in different countries. Discuss this statement.

Closing case study
ARM Ltd

ARM designs high-performance, low-cost, power-efficient microchips and related software, and licenses them to chip manufacturers and application software developers. It is not engaged in manufacturing.

Many end products, such as a mobile phone, an air bag for a car or a computer games console will have microchips embedded within them. These will be made by a chip manufacturer such as Texas Instruments. To be effective the microchips need to be allied to software, from such firms as ARM and Symbian (the joint venture of Psion with the mobile phone manufacturers Nokia, Ericsson, and Motorola) and the chip manufacturers themselves.

The world of chips is not straightforward. Intel appears as likely to be an ARM customer as a competitor. In May 1998 Intel acquired Digital, and with it Digital's licence to use ARM technology. Intel has subsequently increased the designs it licensed from ARM, although it has retained its own chip design team. Motorola is a shareholder in ARM licensee Symbian.

Robin Saxby, the CEO, explains the reasons why the chip industry is changing:

● Everything is getting so complicated—with 10 million transistors on a chip—that no single engineer or small group of engineers can get their heads round all of them.

● The cost of manufacturing in the semiconductor industry is now horrendous: a manufacturing plant will now cost at least $3 billion. To keep the factories full, you need to be able to make chips for many customers.

● Software is becoming a bigger and bigger proportion of the cost of the product. In the past, integrated chip companies could do everything themselves; now, time-to-market and the greater complexity strongly suggest that collaboration with specialists is appropriate.

As a result, the industry is now more willing to outsource and to collaborate. According to Saxby,

> In the past people like Texas Instruments, Intel, Alcatel, Sharp, and Sony would each design their own proprietary standards and the architectures for their own embedded products. What we are saying is, don't design your own thing, come to ARM as a standard and we will license the technology to you. You can add your own differentiated technology on top of what we do to make more successful products for you. In joining the ARM community you get software, design tools, and so on. My key customers are my semiconductor partners, my key competitors are semiconductor companies, and ARM is saying, why do you want to compete? Why not collaborate?

This is the rationale underlying the partnering arrangements that ARM is fostering.

Partnering: the ARM community

ARM's vision is to establish its microchip architecture as the standard for embedded microprocessors. To accelerate the acceptance of its architecture and the products that use its designs, it has created a network of partners in what it terms the ARM community. This community comprises three main groups of companies:

- microchip manufacturers, including such companies as Hewlett-Packard, Hyundai, IBM, Intel, LG Semiconductor, Matsushita, OKI, Philips, Texas Instruments; and the Toshiba Corporation;
- software systems partners, including Microsoft, Sun Microsystems, and Symbian;
- design and tools partners, including Sirius Communications, Cadence, Mentor, and Hewlett-Packard.

The flexibility offered by an open ARM architecture enables semiconductor and software partners to design applications rapidly, and facilitates ongoing design and maintenance. The combined ARM chip design, compatible software, and associated development tools assure the end-product manufacturers (such as Nokia for mobile phones and Bosch for air bags) that microchips will be available from multiple sources, and that the architecture will provide a well-defined evolutionary route.

Potential partners are now knocking at ARM's door. ARM has limited resources, and has to prioritize who it will work with, because partnerships involving technology transfer take time and effort to achieve. ARM agrees a strategy statement with each new partner in which the partner commits itself to contribute to the ARM community. So ARM is asking for more than just money from a partnership. Partners are part of the project in all design development: they influence the technology, bring engineering resources, provide test sites, and engage in joint project development. However, licensees are not exclusively ARM licensees: they still have their own design teams, and also often license technology that competes with ARM's.

Management structure

ARM is a globally oriented organization with European offices in Cambridge, Maidenhead, Munich, and Paris, East Asian offices in Seoul and Tokyo, and US offices in Austin, Texas, Los Gatos, California, Seattle, Washington, and Boston. The CEO, financial director, and chief operating officer are not co-located. Shares in the company are traded in both London and New York.

Good dialogue is vital to sustain the ARM partnership, and one feature of the ARM community is a high level of electronic communication—through email and video conferencing. But in Robin Saxby's view, you also need face-to-face interaction and critical mass. Clusters are important, especially intellectual clusters.

Exhibit C The ARM culture

The culture and value norms which evolve within an organization and which ultimately pervade all individual and organizational activities are fundamental components of the motivational climate of that organization, and ultimately relate directly to individual job satisfaction and job performance. Recognizing this as fundamental, ARM has sought consistently, since its formation in 1990 and throughout its years of growth into a public company, to build and sustain a culture that reflects and supports a set of core values which all members of the company can endorse and which they feel are appropriate for ARM—a culture which attracts people to ARM.

Whilst any concept as intangible as culture is difficult to explain, the following phrases have frequently been used to demonstrate an attitude or value which represents a desirable component of 'the ARM culture'.

- portraying a 'can do' approach to any request or challenge;
- treating time as a valuable and scarce resource—every deadline is urgent;
- seeking understanding of customer and partner perceptions and perspectives;
- respecting and appreciating colleagues' contributions;
- developing team-working and peer relationships;
- contributing to change in the interests of organizational growth;
- sharing knowledge openly whilst respecting confidences;
- developing mutual trust with colleagues, partners, and customers;
- striving for continuous improvement in performance standards and delivery;
- promoting creativity and innovation;
- investing personal time and effort in self-development and betterment;
- fulfilling leadership roles in relation to tasks, teams, and individuals;
- being proactive and taking initiatives;
- building re-usable working methodologies and processes;
- promoting and exploiting ARM's progressive and leading-edge market position;
- nurturing and propagating ARM's greatest asset—its people and their ideas;
- respecting, valuing, and exploiting ARM's geographical and cultural diversity;
- balancing hard work and fun.

Through these, ARM seeks to be a premier global company, respected throughout the world for the calibre and status of its people, the efficacy of its business model, the uniqueness of its partner and customer relationships, the innovativeness and usefulness of its progressive, leading-edge technologies, and for having ARM technology everywhere.

'A large part of our world is still Silicon Valley—Intel, LSI Logica have head offices there and many other industry opinion leaders are there. That's why Reynette [vice-president, worldwide marketing] is there. Our design team in Austin focuses on high-performance design. In Silicon Valley it's software porting work. In Seattle we're near to Microsoft, and Texas Instruments is in Houston. We are where our partners are. So you have critical mass but this doesn't mean that everyone needs to be in the same room. If you stay in the same room you become inward-looking. I'm a member of the electronic community in Silicon Valley just as I am in Cambridge.'

Once a year ARM holds a partner meeting in the vacation period at a Cambridge college. Typically about 300 people will attend. ARM has close links with universities, especially Cambridge, with its research expertise and its supply of students, and also Manchester, Harvard, and Stanford universities—wherever the best work is going on.

Although the quality of ARM's relationships with its partners is vital to its success, so too are its internal relationships. One of the challenges with a fast-growing company is that people forget the strategy and forget to check the direction they're going in. ARM runs around six global operations conferences annually. These are two-day off-site meetings involving a series of workshops to discuss strategy and such matters as how to exploit ARM's success, its intellectual property, and its new software. It is at these workshops that new staff are taught the ARM culture and older members are reacquainted with it.

Everyone in ARM is responsible for their own education. There is a performance appraisal review process, but the culture is that if anyone wants training, and it makes sense in the light of ARM's vision and strategy, then ARM will pay for it. For example, when one of ARM's lawyers in the UK wanted to take the American Bar exams, ARM paid the air fare. Several people are studying part-time for master's degrees. All staff attend at least one major company learning event each year. There is the two-day globalization conference for all staff, the ARM partners' meeting is attended by many staff, and there is an annual global sales conference held at different locations worldwide.

The leadership style is described as 'Come on, we can do it'. All developments apparently come from below the top team. As Robin Saxby puts it, 'All we say is "The industry is going this way, have you thought of this?" We set direction, we hire people, and we set up the mechanism for them to get approval for resources. Anyone in the company can put a proposal to the board.' Share arrangements have allowed ARM to attract and retain very high-quality staff, and bonuses are paid when patents are achieved.

Source: Finlay (2000: 654–64).

Discussion questions

1 What is the ARM community model, and how well does it allow for change to be enthusiastically embraced?

2 Are ARM's internal organization structure and design suitable for a fast-changing, high-technology environment?

REFERENCES

Andrews, T. G., and Chompusri, N. (2001). 'Lessons in crossvergence: restructuring the Thai subsidiary corporation', *Journal of International Business Studies* 32(1): 77–93.

Bennis, W. G. (1969). *Organizational Development: Its Nature, Origins, and Prospects* (New York: Addison-Wesley).

——and Nanus, B. (1985). *Leaders: The Strategies for Taking Charge* (New York: Harper & Row).

Bowman, C. (1995). 'Strategy workshops and top team commitment to strategic change', *Journal of Managerial Psychology* 10(8): 42–50.

Buchanan, D. (1994). *Theories of Change* (Loughborough University Business School Research Series, paper 5).

——and Boddy, D. (1992). *The Expertise of the Change Agent: Public Performance and Backstage Activity* (New York: Prentice Hall).

Carnall, C. A. (2003). *Managing Change in Organizations*, 4th edn. (Harlow: FT Prentice Hall).

Davenport, T. H. (1993). *Process Innovation: Re-engineering Work through IT* (Boston: Harvard Business School Press).

Dunphy, D., and Stace, D. (1993). 'The strategic management of corporate change', *Human Relations* 46(8): 905–20.

Feely, A. (2003). 'Communication across language boundaries', in M. Tayeb (ed.), *International Management Theories and Practices* (Harlow: FT Prentice Hall).

Finlay, Paul (ed.), (2000). *Strategic Management: An Introduction to Business and Corporate Strategy* (Harlow: FT Prentice Hall).

Graham, J. L. (1985). 'The influence of culture on the process of business negotiations: an exploratory study', *Journal of International Business Studies* 16(1): 81–95.

Hampden-Turner, C., and Trompenaars, F. (1993). *The Seven Cultures of Capitalism: Value Systems for Creating Wealth in the United States, Britain, Japan, Germany, France, Sweden, and the Netherlands* (New York: Doubleday).

Harding, R. (1996). 'Implementing strategic change: a survey of British and German workers', *Technovation* 16(3): 101–13.

Hearn, P., and Button, D. (1994). *Languages Industries Atlas* (Amsterdam: IOS Press).

Johanson, J., and Wiedersheim-Paul, F. (1975). 'The internationalisation of the firm: four Swedish cases', *Journal of Management Studies* 19(3): 305–22.

Kay, J. (1995). *Foundations of Corporate Success: How Business Strategies Add Value* (Oxford: Oxford University Press).

Kogat, B., and Singh, H. (1988). 'The effect of national culture on the choice of entry mode', *Journal of International Business Studies* 19(3): 411–32.

Lam, A. (1998). 'Tacit knowledge, organisational learning and innovation: a societal perspective', paper presented at the British Academy of Management Conference, Nottingham, 14–16 Sept.

Machiavelli, N. (1993). *The Prince* (Hertfordshire: Wordsworth Editions).

Neal, M. (1998). *The Culture Factor: Cross-National Management and the Foreign Venture* (London: Macmillan).

Nonaka, I., and Takeuchi, H. (1995). *The Knowledge-Creating Company: How Japanese Companies Create the Dynamics of Innovation* (Oxford: Oxford University Press).

Petersen, D. F., and Scannell, T. (2000). 'An empirical study of global sourcing strategy effectiveness', *Journal of Supply Chain Management* 36(2): 29–38.

Roberts, D. (2003). 'Sun setting on expatriate life', *Financial Times* (22 and 23 Nov.).

Schein, E. H. (1947). *Organizational Culture and Leadership*, 2nd edn. (San Francisco, Calif.: Jossey-Bass), chs. 15 and 16 developing the original theory of K. Lewin, 'Group decision and social change', in T. N. Newcombe and E. L. Hartley (eds.), *Readings in Social Psychology* (New York: Holt, Rinehart & Winston, 1947).

Senge, P. M. (1990). 'The leader's new work: building learning organisations', *Sloan Management Review* 32(1): 7–23.

Shore, D. (2000). 'Rose Bearings', in Finlay (2000), *Strategic Management: An Introduction to Business and Corporate Strategy* (Harlow: FT Prentice Hall).

Simons, R. (1994). 'How top managers use control systems as levers of strategic renewal', *Strategic Management Journal* 15(3): 169–89.

Stacey, R. D. (1996). *Strategic Management and Organisational Dynamics*, 2nd edn. (London: Pitman).

Thomas, D. C. (2002). *Essentials of International Management: A Cross-Cultural Perspective* (Thousand Oaks, Calif.: Sage).

Ting-Toomey, S. (1988). 'Intercultural conflict styles: a face-negotiation theory', in Y. Kim and W. Gudykunst (eds.), *Theories in Intercultural Communication* (Newbury Park, Calif.: Sage).

Trompenaars, F., and Hampden-Turner, C. (1997). *Riding the Waves of Culture: Understanding Cultural Diversity in Business* (London: Brealey).

Zaleznik, A. (1992). 'Managers and leaders: are they different?', *Harvard Business Review* (Mar.–Apr.).

12

Global strategic control

Learning outcomes

After reading this chapter you should be able to:

- list and characterize the six forms of strategic control system that global organizations need to use;

- characterize the three broad methods of control—of inputs, processes, and outputs;

- understand when and where each of the broad methods are likely to be useful;

- understand the role of culture in deciding on the relevant control system to use;

- understand the potential difficulties with control systems utilized in a global context;

- be able to design an appropriate control system for use to support a chosen strategy.

Samsung and GoldStar are the two foremost electronics firms in Korea. They are part of the Samsung and Lucky–GoldStar groups which themselves are part of a large group of companies in a *chaebol* (a large group of complementary businesses). During the 1980s and 1990s they were faced with the same environmental changes and altered their strategies to fit the new environment in similar ways. However, their performance over this period differed markedly, with Samsung clearly outperforming its rival. It would appear that the difference in performance is the result of the different forms of control used in the two organizations.

In the late 1980s Samsung strengthened its already famous environmental scanning system by appointing monitors of information in every business section, and by introducing a management information system for collecting and disseminating information. The head office was boosted to include 200 elite managers, and this strengthened its supervisory role over the subsidiary units. The major control tool was the annual budget, with rebudgeting every six months. At roughly the same time GoldStar changed to giving greater autonomy to its sub-units, defining the head office role as coordinator and supporter rather than controller. Its strategic planning horizon became three years.

Samsung operates a highly formalized feedback control system. Reporting is comprehensive, with subsidiary units reporting fifteen or sixteen times a month to head office. Evaluation is tough and the reward and punishment system is based on well-established rules—and it is harsh; for example, the bonus payments are zero-sum: when some members are paid extra, others are paid less. By contrast, GoldStar's reporting system is less formalized and is based to some extent on the strong involvement of members of the founding families. This involvement makes it difficult to implement the reward and punishment system objectively.

Samsung depends on the Samsung group's recruitment system for new managers, except for some specialists such as R&D staff. Since Samsung's own recruitment focuses on qualifications and skills while the group's recruitment emphasizes the commitment, attitude, and personality of applicants, this shift in recruitment policy is weakening the socialization of new staff. Samsung has a well-developed education and training scheme, with company career paths leading to generalists with some special knowledge. GoldStar recruits about half its managers itself, with the Lucky–GoldStar group recruiting the rest. Its rigorous education and training system is geared to providing different career paths for general managers, R&D staff, and shopfloor managers. In Samsung informal communication is not strong and sub-group formation is frowned upon. By contrast, in GoldStar informal communication and sub-group formation are welcomed.

In short, Samsung has strengthened its strategic planning while reducing emphasis on its recruitment process as a control mechanism. It has strengthened two integrative mechanisms—centralization and formalization—whilst reducing socialization amongst employees. On the other hand, GoldStar has strengthened central control of socialization, whilst decentralizing strategic planning and budgeting.

Source: Y.-K. Kim and N. Campbell, 'Strategic control in Korean MNCs', *Management International Review* 35(1) (1995): 95–9.

12.1 **Introduction**

As demonstrated by the Samsung and GoldStar case study, the control system employed has a strong impact on the firm's performance. Samsung and GoldStar operated within the same external business environment but employed different control systems. Their performance differed markedly, with Samsung outperforming GoldStar. This difference in performance is attributed, at least in part, to the different control systems used.

Control can be considered as the process of keeping something within prescribed limits. The purpose of all forms of strategic control is to identify whether the multinational firm should continue with its current strategy or modify it in the light of changed circumstances. Controls can take many forms: those that apply after the event and those that aim to anticipate events; those that are internal and those imposed from outside; those that rely on formal quantitative objectives and those that rely on looser mechanisms; those that are planned and those that are reactions to crises.

Controls bring out tensions in multinationals; between the ongoing and the future, coercion and motivation, efficiency and freedom, rewards and punishments, and the mandatory and the suggested. Unless appropriately applied, controls can easily lead to counterproductive behaviour, so it is vital that managers understand the advantages and disadvantages of different forms of control and strike the appropriate balance between them. The striking of this balance is particularly problematic for multinational firms. In addition to all the normal difficulties, there are the issues posed by a more extensive organization, those resulting from physical and cultural separation, and the balance that needs to be struck between local responsiveness and global integration and coordination.

This chapter discusses the six types of control systems, the fundamentals of all control systems, methods of control and characteristics of strategic control objectives. The *chapter is aimed at the advanced student* who wishes to deepen his/her understanding of the nature of operational systems for the successful implementation of multinational strategies. The discussed concepts are very complex and it is not recommended for the student to read this chapter on a stand-alone basis. The chapter is intended to complement a taught course.

KEY CONCEPT

Control is the process of keeping something within prescribed limits. The purpose of all forms of strategic control is to identify whether the multinational firm should continue with its current strategy or modify it in the light of changed circumstances.

12.2 **Types of strategic control system**

Effective strategic control is concerned both with controlling the present processes and with preparing for the future. It combines the reactive (i.e. changing things after a deficiency has been detected) with the proactive (i.e. preparing for things that are likely to occur in the

Exhibit 12.1 Types of strategic control system

Type of control		Description
• Assumption	Proactive	Focused environmental monitoring of the assumptions under which strategy has been selected
• Surveillance		Unfocused environmental monitoring in order to provide early warning of changes in the business environment
• Climate		Aimed at establishing and maintaining a favourable business environment
• Implementation		Focused on the implementation of strategic change
• Operational	Reactive	Internally focused on making the present processes more effective and efficient
• Crisis		Managing potentially damaging, rapidly arising issues

future). To do this appropriately, organizations need to ensure that the six types of strategic control listed in Exhibit 12.1 are employed. The types are ordered broadly according to their degree of proactivity, with assumption control considered the most proactive and operational control the least, with crisis control showing both proactive and reactive features.

12.2.1 Assumption control

Forecasting is the traditional way in which views of the future are derived. All forecasting methods depend on assumptions about the future, and as we take a long-term look into the future our ability to feel confident about our predictions gets less and less. Forecasting is not appropriate for the longer term, and another way of 'picturing the future' is needed. This is through the development of scenarios (see Chapter 2 for a fuller discussion).

Checking on the continuing suitability of a strategy requires monitoring the assumptions that have been made about the value of the variables used in these scenarios. This monitoring provides assumption control, which concentrates on strategic uncertainties (Simons 1994).

As an example of assumption control, suppose a European multinational is experiencing increasing demand for its products in the USA. One proposal to cater for this is to continue with its exporting strategy and to continue to export from its home base in Europe. The second proposal is to move to a colonial strategy and open a new factory in the US. Two important factors in any scenarios that might be developed are the level of protectionism that the US government might impose against foreign manufacturers and the euro–dollar exchange rate. Six scenarios might be developed, resulting from considering three levels of protectionism and two values for the exchange rate, as illustrated in Exhibit 12.1. Thus

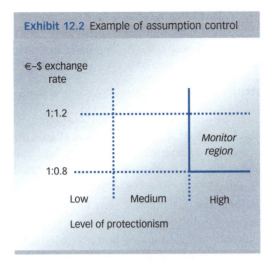

Exhibit 12.2 Example of assumption control

€–$ exchange rate

1:1.2

Monitor region

1:0.8

Low   Medium   High

Level of protectionism

scenario A is that the exchange rate will be 1:1.12 one (i.e. €1 will be worth US$1.2) and protectionism will be low; scenario B is that the exchange rate will be 1:0.8 and protectionism will be medium.

Suppose that the strategy to open the factory in the US would appear to be the better option as long as the euro–dollar exchange rate stayed above 1:0.8 and if the threatened level of protectionism stayed high. Then the company would monitor to see if the predictions of the level of protectionism and the euro–dollar rate continued to remain within the monitor region shown in Exhibit 12.2. If it looked as though these bounds were going to be broken, then the decision to open the factory in the US would need to be reconsidered.

As discussed in Chapter 2, scenario-writing and the associated assumption control is particularly important where the environment is highly unpredictable. This can be especially so where government can make arbitrary decisions. There is also the problem of data availability in many developing countries, which increases uncertainty about the values of scenario variables.

12.2.2 Surveillance control

Even though the scenario planning will have helped to consider events of low probability but of potentially high impact, assumption control is a very focused form of control. In contrast, surveillance control is 'early warning control', akin to the picking up of a blob on a radar screen. Surveillance control is a broad search, and its diffuseness means that it is not a job that can be left to a single individual or group. Many people in the organization should be involved in scanning both the external and internal environments. This will often occur quite naturally—for example, salespersons meeting with their customers and finding out about competitors, specialists reading their specialist journals, and many of the workforce watching news and current affairs programmes on TV. The problem is with channelling this knowledge to the places where it can be appropriately interpreted and acted upon. People in the subsidiaries must be able to feed back to the centre, and must know what is potentially important to the centre. This is likely to be of concern unless an effort is made to design the appropriate channels. Establishing a business intelligence unit is one way of doing this, although this formal approach is only really open to large multinationals.

12.2.3 Climate control

Climate control is concerned with establishing and maintaining a climate that is benevolent to the organization's interest. Much of climate control goes under the name of 'public relations', aimed at achieving understanding and support, and at influencing opinion and behaviour. Sometimes public relations is a long-term effort and not targeted at any particular issue, such as that conducted over many years by trade associations such as the Tobacco Manufacturers' Association. On other occasions the focus is much sharper, as it has been for the many organizations attempting to establish a first-mover advantage in the Chinese market by influencing political decision-makers and public opinion. Another example is attempts by US multinationals to stop, or at least weaken, the boycott of US goods in some parts of the world.

It is often important to use public relations consultants when framing the public relations campaign. They are helpful in marshalling arguments and determining the best channels of communication to use. They often have personal contacts with people in high places. It is also helpful to use experts, who have the authority which comes from being an expert and which allows the organization, through them, to communicate with lesser experts and so on, cascading information through to the stakeholders. Obviously it is very important to use local people to 'front' any such public relations exercises, and extremely important to know fully the context into which the messages are to be placed. For example, to project a local image and develop and sustain political capital in China, Shanghai Volkswagen always had Chinese managers in key positions.

12.2.4 Implementation control

Implementation control is concerned with the implementation of strategic change and thus with whether a new strategy remains on track. When implementing new ventures, Western cultures see a need to establish a set of objectives with a well-defined chronology on the way to implementation. Such a breakdown into milestones is very much contrary to Asian decision-making, however, where, according to Graham (2001: 522), 'all the issues are discussed at once, in no apparent order, and concessions are made on all issues at the end of the discussion'.

The Western way of carrying through new ventures is invariably to use a project team, and control will be exercised through the associated formal project planning and control systems. In Japan, however, the J-form organization described by Aoki (1998) and by Lam (1998) is prevalent, and differs markedly in the way in which knowledge is created and embedded in the organization, rather than residing with individuals.

The dominant forms of knowledge in the J-form organization is that which is embedded in its operating routines and shared culture. Firms that have this form have been termed knowledge-creating companies by Nonaka and Takeuchi (1995: 5). A primary feature of J-form organizations is that non-hierarchical project teams, consisting of people from various functions, operate in parallel with the formal hierarchical structure. This allows members of the project teams, who will be engaged in the new activities, to feed back and embed their new knowledge into the 'normal' organizational structure and thus link the new with the old. The stability and efficiency of the organization is married to the flexibility of the project teams. Nonaka and Takeuchi use the term 'hypertext organization', a term borrowed from computer science, to describe the easy and dynamic way in which people can interact with the different layers in their organization.

12.2.5 Operational control

Although ongoing operational control is not a parental responsibility, it is the responsibility of the parent to ensure that appropriate operational control systems are in place within the subsidiaries.

A good operational control system needs to assist the organization to be both efficient and effective. To do this it needs to be both attention-conserving and attention-enhancing. It needs to be an attention-conserving device to allow the unit to operate without constant monitoring. It allows leader-managers to be freed from the mundane and 'in-control' areas by the staff professionals (e.g. accountants and sales administrators) who keep the system working smoothly. Staff professionals are the gatekeepers for diagnostic control systems, safeguarding the integrity of data input and preventing reports from being distorted. For an operational control system to operate effectively, therefore, strong ethical and professional codes are needed.

However, a good control system needs to be more than a diagnostic system. It needs to be an insightful one that supports learning. For this to occur the control system needs to be an attention-enhancer, in contrast to the diagnostic system, which is attention-conserving. Attention is greatly enhanced if the information system is interactive, whereby causes and effects can be explored.

12.2.6 Crisis control

A crisis may be defined as an event that occurs without specific warning and to which the organization has to react. Crisis control relies on both proactive and reactive control. It is proactive in that, although the precise form of the crisis will be unknown, broad elements of many crisis situations will be known, and these can be planned for through what is termed 'contingency planning'. Crisis control is also reactive, in that the specifics of the situations must be dealt with as they unfold.

One special form of control is rumour control. A rumour is a proposition that is unverified and in general circulation (Rosnow and Fine 1976). Being unverified does not mean that a rumour is untrue, only that it is not known whether it is or not. Allport and Postman (1947) developed a formula linking the amount of rumour in circulation with the importance/interest attached to it by the people transmitting the rumour, and the ambiguity of

Exhibit 12.3 Characteristics of strategic control

	Assumption	Surveillance	Climate	Implementation	Operational	Crisis
Purpose	To ensure that planned strategy remains appropriate Proactive	To pick up weak signals quickly Proactive	To generate and maintain a receptive climate for the business Proactive	To keep strategy on track Diagnosis Reactive	To ensure efficient ongoing operations Very often reactive	To limit the damage to the business—its reputation and the claims against it Reactive and proactive
People involved	Top management	Top management People in contact with all stakeholders	Public relations	Project management Middle management	Operating core	Designated central control
Focus	Narrow	Diffuse	Narrow	Narrow	Narrow	Narrow
Information sources	Predetermined groups or individuals—internal and external	Varied and not prescribed except for business information systems	People in the know and influential external stakeholders	Project management	Internal	The proactive element could be benchmarking. The reactive portion from outside stakeholders, particularly the media
Form of information acquisition	Monitoring	External to the organization		Internal to the organization	Monitoring internal operations	Rumour
Process periodicity	Periodically and triggered	Triggered		Milestones Project management	Ongoing with some periodicity	Episodic

the evidence about the topic. Thus if the rumour is not interesting it will not be transmitted. Similarly, ambiguity indicates that a situation is unclear; if a situation is unambiguous, then any rumour will die away.

An ambiguous situation can arise when there is more than one source providing information that differs, thus creating confusion. Censorship and conspiracy are other conditions giving rise to ambiguous situations. A way to avoid rumour, therefore, is for there to be one and only one source for official information, and for this source to be as open as possible.

An interesting account of many rumours is given by Koenig (1985), who has analysed a great many rumours in the US. These range from worms in McDonald's beefburgers and the poprocks sweets that 'made kids' stomachs explode' to Ray Kroc, the president of Mc-Donald's allegedly supporting the Church of Satan, and Procter & Gamble's 'man on the moon' charge.

KEY CONCEPT

Effective strategic control requires the use of six types of control. Assumption control is narrowly focused on the values of the key variables on which the strategy is based. Surveillance control is weakly focused: it scans the environment in order to identify emergent issues. Climate control is concerned with establishing and maintaining a climate that is benevolent to the organization's interest. All three are forms of proactive control.

Implementation control is concerned with controlling strategic change, whilst operational control involves control of present, ongoing processes. Both rely primarily on reactive control. Crisis control is concerned with managing suddenly emerging issues, and is both proactive and reactive.

12.3 A model of control

The major characteristics of the six types of strategic control system are set out in Exhibit 12.3, which highlights the differences between the types. All systems, however, share several fundamental features. These common features are best seen through examining a model of control. Such a model then allows the *methods* of control appropriate for each of the organizational structures described in Chapter 10 to be explored.

12.3.1 A simple model of control

The common features of control can perhaps be most easily illustrated by first considering the operation of a budgetary control system of the type almost universally used in organizations. A model of such a system is shown in the lower portion of Exhibit 12.4 (by unbroken full lines) where, to give an example, a set of processes associated with a sales function is considered. This function has two broad types of input: environmental inputs that cannot be controlled (e.g. economic conditions) and controllable inputs (e.g. a product specification) that *can* be controlled. The outputs from the process (such as revenue) are measured

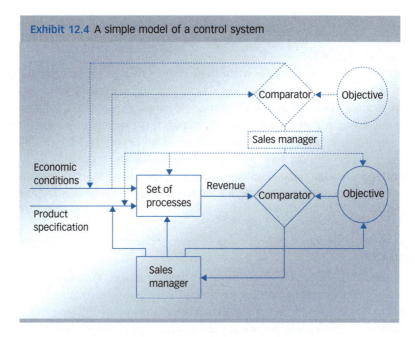

Exhibit 12.4 A simple model of a control system

and compared in the comparator (typically, monthly variance reports) with a preset, desired value (an objective). If the measured output differs from the objective in what is considered to be an undesirable way (e.g. revenues are lower than desired), then a signal is sent to the actuator (the sales manager). The sales manager may alter an input (the product specification) or the operation of one or more of the processes undertaken by the function (e.g. tightening up on quality control), or may recognize that the required output is unattainable and should be changed (e.g. by lowering the target revenue for the next period).

The control system described above provides only half the control that is needed: it only provides reactive control—and thus it only models implementation, operational and part of crisis control. To model assumption, surveillance, and climate control as well, Exhibit 12.4 needs to be augmented with proactive features—as shown in the upper portion of Exhibit 12.4 by dotted lines. Here information about the future environment is assessed and action taken to allow for the new situation before it occurs. For example, if economic conditions appeared likely to change in the coming year—say, a severe reduction in disposable income—then this view would probably result in a change in one or more elements of the control system.

12.3.2 A fuller model of control

Whatever the organizational structure, the parent needs to intervene in order to secure the necessary level of subsidiary performance and effect the required global integration. Thus the situation described above and shown in Exhibit 12.4 is deficient in providing a model of control for multi-unit organizations, since it does not indicate the hierarchy of control that exists in a multinational firm. This situation is shown in Exhibit 12.5, in which the subsidiary is shown with its own control system embedded within the parental system. Generally, of course, a parent would be responsible not just for one subsidiary but for several—often many.

Effective strategic control has to combine controls that apply after the event (reactive) and those that try to anticipate events (proactive). It also requires the sharing of responsibility and authority between the parent and the subordinate units. These considerations lead to a fuller definition of control: the process of keeping something within prescribed limits through the continuous critical evaluation of plans, inputs, processes, and outputs to provide information for future action (after Schreyögg and Steinmann 1987).

The simple budgetary control system described earlier would not allow the sales manager to reach the revenue objective if national conditions prevailed which severely limited the output of the associated production unit. Meeting the target would only be possible if the parent allowed products for sale to be brought in from outside. This illustrates a very important concept: a system can only be controlled if the control variables are at least as effective in altering the system outputs as are the environmental variables whose effects are to be countered. This, in slightly simplified form, is the law of requisite variety. Ross-Ashby (1970) enunciated the law of requisite variety: for a system to be able to maintain itself it must have at least as much variety as the environment in which it is operating. 'Requisite variety' is Ross-Ashby's way of describing the required power to change things—the power that the controller requires so that they can counter the variation in the environment and thus effect the required level of control. Many subsidiaries are likely to be subject to government fiat (such as the rule that any board of directors must include a majority of host country nationals), making control very difficult or even impossible.

KEY CONCEPT

A difficulty in all forms of control is for the right people to have the power to effect change. Without sufficient control variables, the controller is given responsibility without power: the two need to be balanced. The difficulty in achieving this balance is particularly acute with the hierarchy involved in the parent–subsidiary relationship, where the split of control functions must be such as to balance cost and flexibility.

12.4 Methods of control

With the model of control shown in Exhibit 12.5, we will consider the sort of parental interventions that will be necessary to produce the appropriate level of integration between the activities of subsidiaries whilst ensuring that those subsidiaries are locally responsive.

Three methods of control are recognized, based on the type of intervention that the parent makes in the activities of the subsidiary: output-based, process-based, and input-based. Output-based systems are concerned with results, with the parent having little concern for how these are achieved. Process-based systems focus on work processes, with the parent involved in deciding how these processes are carried out. Input-based systems focus on the

Exhibit 12.5 A model of a parent–subsidiary control system

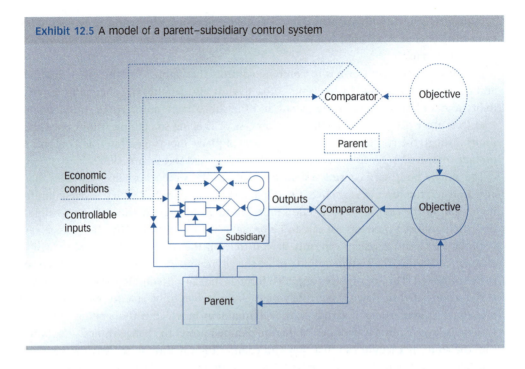

Exhibit 12.6 Characteristics of the three control methods

Output-based	Process-based	Input-based
Focuses on *what* has happened or was required, defined by objectives such as: • sales growth, revenues • advertising reach • labour costs • wastage rates • output per person-hour	Focuses on *how* things are to be done, by defining processes such as: • the marketing planning system • how decisions are made • information flows	Focuses on the 'internal climate'—with getting the conditions right for activities—through: • the recruitment of staff • internal promotion of staff with desirable attributes • moving managers internationally • continuous reinforcement of the organization's vision, mission, and goals

way in which the conditions are set up to achieve the required subsidiary performance, and here the parent is concerned with the 'internal climate' within which the subsidiary is operating. Exhibit 12.6 summarizes the characteristics of each of these three methods. Although every parent will need to exercise some of its control through outputs, as we shall see, this does not mean that output control will necessarily always be the only or even the major method of control.

Exhibit 12.7 Characteristics of financial control and strategic planning styles

Financial control	Strategic planning
• Subsidiary managers are responsible for strategy development. • The parent exerts influence through short-term budgetary controls. • Few potential synergies are realized. • There is a bias against investments with long lead times and paybacks. • Good at developing executives with a 'winner psychology'. • Subsidiaries will tend to be risk-averse, having to meet the monthly/quarterly financial targets. • Can be responsive to changing market conditions. • Shakes managers loose from bad strategies.	• The parent is deeply involved in subsidiary strategy development. • The subsidiaries are isolated from short-term financial pressures. • Synergies between subsidiaries can be exploited. • Fosters the creation of ambitious strategies. • A wide variety of views may be put forward. • The subsidiaries will be less risk-averse. • Subsidiary managers may have motivational problems, as there may be little ownership of strategy. • A diminished flexibility to respond quickly to changing markets. • The firm may persist with losing strategies for too long.

In their dealings with subordinates, not all parents act in the same way. Goold and Campbell (1987) and Goold et al. (1993a) identified three types of parent, depending on the influence the parent had on planning the activities of the subsidiaries and on the way in which control was exercised. Later research (Goold et al. 1993b) suggested that one of the styles—the strategic control style—was falling out of use, and thus it is appropriate to consider just the two other styles—financial control and strategic planning. Their characteristics are summarized in Exhibit 12.7. From these characteristics it is evident that financial control is a form of output control, with parental control revolving around the financial results achieved. Strategic planning is a mix of input and process control.

An extreme form of financial control is the 'hands-off' parent who is involved in determining the organization's portfolio of subsidiaries, and then lets the managers in each subsidiary run it in almost any way they think fit as long as well-specified financial targets are met. In such financially controlled companies the parent plays little part in developing strategy. Such parents have been termed 'corporate catalysts' (Hofstede 1968: 154–5).

12.4.1 Control through outputs

As its name suggests, control through outputs means that the parent exercises control through comparing the output that the subsidiary has achieved with the objective that has been agreed upon. It is up to the subsidiary to change itself through altering inputs and its processes—or through negotiating with its parent for objectives to be changed. Samsung would appear to operate a very full and formalized version of output control.

Exhibit 12.8 Characteristics of a good objective: REMIT

Relevant   Directly related to the overall task/mission of the organization

Energizing   Presents an achievable and stretching target and thus is motivating

Measurable   Allows achievement to be recognized

Insightful   Improves learning

Timed   Defines when performance should have been achieved

The characteristics of a good strategic objective

To effect control through outputs, the most important consideration is that appropriate objectives can be devised and can be stated precisely. However, a good objective needs to do more—it needs to provide a suitable REMIT for managers to support what they are trying to achieve for their organizations. The characteristics of a good objective are summarized in Exhibit 12.8.

What is **relevant** is particularly significant when a subsidiary or the people in it have different objectives from those of the organization. Whilst organizations do not have objectives—only individuals do—what pass for organizational objectives are those of the dominant individual or coalition (Perrow 1970: 134). Not surprisingly, it is not to be expected that all individuals in an organization will have the same objectives. There is likely to be alignment on central issues, otherwise an individual would not remain in the organization. However, there might be opposition to other organizational objectives—for example, sales to a country governed by what is considered to be a reprehensible regime.

Not only may individual objectives not align with those of the organization, but the norms of a group may also not align. This is of particular concern when different cultures and allegences are involved. As Hofstede (1991) and Trompenaars and Hampden-Turner (1997) have found, there are very different views of where loyalty lies. In the US, the UK, and the rest of north-western Europe, individuals are expected to look after themselves; in much of Continental Europe a communitarian view is taken; and in much of East Asia harmonious relationships are valued above individual gains.

Additionally, many employees belong to professional and other organizations, such as national trade unions, law societies, and accounting bodies. These organizations have rules and regulations—and indeed inculcate an ethos—covering their members' conduct. This is particularly evident in what Mintzberg (1991) has termed 'professional firms'. Such a situation may give rise to individual or group objectives that may differ from the organizational objectives, and thus can have a significant effect on control as well as on strategy. This problem may be particularly evident in the current quest of law firms to provide global legal services to their global clients (see opening case study of Chapter 7).

A good objective is **energizing** in that it is stretching. Left to their own devices, managers will choose highly achievable 'official' objectives for themselves, to improve the predictability of their forecasts and to ensure that there are only a few poor outcomes for their superiors to focus on. This sort of behaviour clearly poses a problem for the parent who does not understand the details of a unit's operations and position. However, the associated organizational slack will allow the unit the resources for experimentation—generally no bad thing.

There is also a need to incentivize the attainment of objectives through giving and withholding rewards. Here a major concern is the tension between rewarding the individual and rewarding the group. If it is the group that is rewarded, then there is the problem of defining the group. Again, there are significant differences across cultures in this dimension (Hofstede 1991).

An outcome may be **measurable**, but it may be difficult to link any difference from the objective to the actions of subsidiary managers. For example, where there is a measure of integration between subsidiaries, then the performance of the subsidiary is likely to be modified as it contributes to the good of the whole organization. If a subsidiary sets up simply to sell the company's products is then called upon to host a regional office, it becomes more difficult to assign appropriate costs to the subsidiary. If a subsidiary is carrying out some of the R&D required by the company as a whole, then the costs associated with this will need to be separated out in order to determine those associated with its other activities.

An objective should be chosen so that any deviation between the value achieved and the objective will initiate thinking that leads to **insights** concerning how the unit operates and its relationships with its environment. The objective should also be **timed**—have a duration attached: it is no good setting an objective of doubling turnover, for example, if there is no limit to the time that can be taken in its achievement. Obviously, the time-scale should be both relevant and realistic.

KEY CONCEPT

A goal is a general statement of intent whilst an objective is a well-defined commitment to achieve. A good objective provides a manager with a REMIT; it has the characteristics of being relevant, energizing, measurable, insightful, and timed.

Output control would tend to be the primary form of parental control where the activities of the subsidiary are clear-cut and objectives clearly match these activities. This would generally apply where a subsidiary is simply a sales outlet or where it is simply a production unit producing to a well-defined specification. Thus it would be appropriate for a colonial strategy. It would also be the primary form of control used by a parent operating a multi-domestic strategy. With a trans-national strategy, the complexities of the interactions between units would diminish the power of output controls.

Output control is also appropriate as the major form of control when the parent lacks knowledge of the context in which the subsidiary is operating—such as the country's economic systems and political climate. This would occur when the subsidiary is first set up in a new country, and where conditions are very different from those experienced by the parent.

> **KEY CONCEPT**
>
> Whilst output control will almost always be needed, it may not always be the major form of control. Output control requires appropriate and precise objectives to be devised. This can only occur if there is a clear understanding of the relationship between cause and effect, and the causes can be identified and understood. This is likely to be the case where the subsidiary is carrying out a simple and usually stand-alone task. Such situations will arise with the sales and marketing agencies used by exporting firms, and with the subsidiaries within a multi-domestic strategy. It will also arise with stand-alone units within colonial firms which are feeding their output into other subsidiaries.

12.4.2 Control through process

Process-based control focuses on the processes that the subsidiary uses to carry out the tasks it has been assigned. Processes can be split into two types (Dermer 1977). The first is structured processes, defined as stable, repetitive activities or procedures that can be systematized, such as clerical or assembly-line tasks. The second type is unstructured processes, which are novel activities requiring judgement. Examples of unstructured activities are those associated with the leadership roles of managers, one-off projects, and many of the activities of knowledge workers—in R&D and in legal and public relations practices.

Sometimes it is straightforward to establish objectives associated with unstructured activities; at other times it can be very difficult. Although some of the outputs of a personnel department can be precisely defined, such as the number of employees recruited or the number of wrongful dismissal cases brought against the company, the outputs of its many other roles, such as responsibility for employee development and training, are much more difficult to specify. Such difficulties appear with most unstructured activities.

Unstructured activities are those that have a considerable element of judgement and uniqueness. In such cases direct feedback of information is not possible, as exactly the same activities are never repeated: rather, indirect feedback takes place through the accumulation of knowledge of how similar activities might be performed in the future. Such a link between past and ongoing activities is a far cry from the direct feedback implicit in Exhibit 12.5. Because the variance is likely to be complex in unstructured situations, there is the distinct possibility that communication of it could be flawed. Difficulties in communication could be further exacerbated by differences in language. This is not usually the obvious differences in language between two people, since an interpreter can usually be found. Rather, as Graham (2001: 515) points out, it is the non-verbal behaviours that affect—often in a subconscious way—the way people relate to each other. Thus all aspects of a unit's activities need to be considered, including how decisions are made, the reward systems it uses, information flows, internal organizational form, and the unit's links to outside agencies.

In the strategic planning style identified by Goold and Campbell (1987) (see Exhibit 12.4) the parent and each subsidiary work together to formulate the subsidiary strategy. When adopting a strategic planning style, the parent is adopting process control.

The joint approach of the strategic planning style allows the parent to expose potential synergies between subsidiaries and where competencies could be used. In a global company, the differences in the way different cultures negotiate (see e.g. Cateora and Graham 2000) may mean that this style of management control needs a great deal of effort to make it successful.

Process control would be an appropriate adjunct to output control when the parent has acquired knowledge of 'how things are done' in the country in which the subsidiary is operating. The parent will be able to gauge the impact of marketing campaigns and what influences governmental thinking. So it will be able to suggest or even impose appropriate operating procedures, information systems, and media policies.

> **KEY CONCEPT**
>
> Process-based control focuses on the processes that the subsidiary uses to carry out the tasks it has been assigned. The strategic planning style of parent–subsidiary interaction is a form of process control, with the parent influencing the processes that the subsidiary adopts.

12.4.3 Control through inputs

Input-based control systems focus on setting up appropriate conditions for the subsidiary to perform as the parent wishes. It is thus a form of proactive control. The emphasis is on the knowledge and skills of employees in the subsidiary, their values and motives. These values and motives are intimately bound up with the culture and with the major role it plays in organizational health. It is through understanding culture that the very important less formal controls exercised by individuals themselves, and particularly by a group, can be exercised. The value of understanding organizational culture has been well expressed by Schein (1986: 46): 'If we give culture its due, if we take an inquiring attitude toward the deciphering of culture, if we respect what culture is and what functions it serves, we will find that it is a potentially friendly animal that can be tamed and made to work for us.'

The role of culture

There are many definitions of 'culture' (Schall 1983; Schein 1985). Some address the bases of culture and some the manifestations of it. A good brief definition is that culture is the shared norms of behaviour, values, and assumptions that knit a community together. It has been described as 'collective mental programming' (Hofstede 1980). Culture is the property of a group, not of an individual, although it will be individuals who will 'carry it around'. Culture will determine how the person sees the world.

It is very useful and illuminating to explore the different facets of culture. Culture can be likened to an onion with three layers. In the outer ring of the cultural onion are those aspects of culture that are readily apparent—the norms of behaviour. Norms are the acceptable behaviour by members of a group.

The second ring of the cultural onion involves values. These are of two sorts. There is the ethical stance that is taken about what is good and just: for example, 'Last in first out' when redundancies are under consideration. They are also the organization's general goals and ideals—such as 'It is best to promote from within' and 'It is vital to be number one in every market'. Values are about how the group aspires to behave, with its processes, and what the group aspires to achieve, with its results. Values are more general than norms and usually provide the basis for several norms. Two examples should make the distinction between values and norms clear. Japanese will generally bow when meeting superiors. If they do this because it is conventional behaviour, then bowing is simply a norm. If they do it out of respect for the superior, it would reflect a value that would also show itself in other norms—such as genuinely agreeing with their superiors' views and seeking their advice. Managers working long hours because it is expected of them are meeting a norm: if they did it because they wanted to do a good job and an extended business day was necessary to achieve this, then long-hour working would be an expression of values.

At the core of the onion are the basic or implicit assumptions that members of an organization 'unconsciously carry round with them'. The fashionable term for this shared mindset is 'paradigm'. Following Kuhn (1970), a paradigm may be defined as a constellation of concepts and perceptions shared by a group that determines how the group views the world. A paradigm therefore acts as the lens through which the group looks at the world, and it therefore determines what the members of the group perceive. Culture has been described as the learnt product of group experience (Schein 1985).

Without setting formal rules, therefore, in any subsidiary there will be levels of general conformity to the established norms—for example, managers conforming to a dress code, or the level of socializing outside the workplace. Not surprisingly, multinational firms will have difficulty in inculcating a parental or common culture sometimes referred to as the 'global mindset', since much of culture is very deep-seated, and the subtle meaning of overt cultural signs need to be interpreted in terms of values. The work of Hofstede (1991) is particularly relevant, since his findings relate to the employees in the multinational IBM. He found that, although the subjects of his research were all in the same organization dealing with the same sort of products and services, the differences between nationalities were marked. To promote organizational learning—one of the major assets of a multinational firm—cultural differences need to be well understood or they will block learning. Frequent transfer of managers between subsidiaries helps to break down cultural misunderstandings as well as inculcating the parent's ethos. Many European companies—for example, Nestlé and Ford—have a policy of moving managers within Europe so that they learn to think and act as Europeans rather than as any specific nationality.

Perhaps the most obvious form of control through inputs is through recruitment of key personnel. The opening case illustrated the different ways in which Samsung and Gold-Star went about this. The role of the expatriate can be a significant form of 'recruitment', although there are considerable costs in using expatriate managers, since the expense of sending an executive to another country—possibly with family—can be considerable. There is also the need to have managers who are familiar with the culture and the commercial environment in the foreign country, and they may not always be available; training costs can be high. Even if these two considerations are met, however, there may still be reluctance on the part of host countries to accept foreigners—especially if they are members of the top management team.

Visions and missions

A vision, sometimes termed a 'strategic intent', is a future reality (Snyder et al. 1994: 18). Rolls-Royce states its strategic intent as follows: 'to make Rolls-Royce the world's leading high-integrity power systems company for the next century.' Bill Gates had as the vision for Microsoft 'to put a PC on every desk'. On the announcement of Ford's takeover of the Volvo car interests in 1999, William Clay Ford Jr. is quoted as saying: 'Our twenty-first-century vision is to become the world's leading consumer company for automotive products' (Ford 1999: 19).

Whilst a vision is meant to inspire, it is not very helpful in the shorter term. Top management in many organizations now understand that their employees need to know what the organization stands for and why they should give it their loyalty. What is required is a 'road map', and this is very often articulated in a mission statement, which sets out actions and behaviour for the present and for the immediate future. A mission statement has three major components; purpose, strategy and values (Peters and Waterman, 1982).

> **KEY CONCEPT**
>
> A vision or strategic intent is a view of a future reality that the organization seeks. A mission statement is a declaration of the broad directions that the organization wishes to follow—a 'road map' for employees.

Purpose   The purpose of an organization is its 'reason for being'—its overarching strategic aim. The value of setting out the organization's purpose is that it indicates the business areas the organization is in (or seeks to enter), and thus lets employees know the boundaries and limitations it is placing on its intended actions. This is particularly useful for subordinate units, as it sets the bounds within which they are allowed to operate. The purpose of Matsushita Electric is perhaps an extreme one from a Western perspective (see Exhibit 12.9).

Strategy   Formally writing down the purpose of an organization is helpful, in that it sets out the scope of the organization's operations. The strategic goals are likely to have far-reaching consequences for many employees, and thus it is useful to indicate the organization's products, services, and customers. An important point is that goals are about priorities: a list of goals would probably be the same for most organizations in the same industry, but the emphasis given to each would be expected to differ. It is also important to provide guidance as to how the organization means to attain its strategic goals. An organization might specify that it will proceed through internal development rather than outsourcing—an important consideration to employees thinking of spending a significant part of their working lives within that organization.

Standards and values   Many mission statements include a statement of the standards of the organization: what the outside world can expect of the organization as a whole and what

> **Exhibit 12.9 Mission statement of Matsushita Electric**
>
> The purpose of a firm is to contribute to society by supplying goods of high quality at low prices in ample quantity. The happiness of man is built on mental stability and material affluence. To serve the foundation of happiness, through making man's life affluent with an inexpensive and inexhaustible supply of life's necessities like water, is the duty of a manufacturer. The purpose of the enterprise is to materialize the duty and consequently contribute to society.
>
> *Source*: www.matsushita.co.jp.

is expected of employees in their dealings both with external stakeholders and within the organization—in short, organizational policies and individual behaviour.

A further feature of many mission statements is an affirmation of the organization's values. Values are what the organization considers important in its dealings with its stakeholders—its customers, employees, etc. The statement of values expresses the organization's ethical stance. As with goals, values are about priorities: a list of values would probably be the same for most organizations in the same industry, but the priorities would be different.

Values represent boundaries on behaviour, similar to the boundaries on strategic activity. They are most needed when there is a lack of trust in the organization—perhaps because of a lack of shared experience, or low homogeneity amongst employees, or loosely coupled organizations where shared values cannot be assumed (Kanter 1977: 49–55).

> **KEY CONCEPT**
>
> Input-based control systems focus on setting up the appropriate conditions for the subsidiary to perform as the parent wishes. Thus it is a form of proactive control. The culture of the firm will be significant, and expatriates can be very useful in helping to inculcate the corporate culture. Another important way in which to set the conditions right for a subsidiary is to have an appropriate and well-articulated mission statement for each unit.

12.5 Summary

Strategic control is the continuous critical evaluation of plans, inputs, processes, and outputs to provide information for future action. The difficulties surrounding all forms of control revolve around setting appropriate objectives, with communicating information to the right people at the right time, and for those people to have the power to effect change. All these difficulties are likely to be exacerbated in multinational firms due to physical distance, national peculiarities, and cultural diversity.

Reactive control is invoked only in response to an undesirable state of affairs: it involves feeding information back from the output to the process and/or its inputs. Proactive control is a way of preparing the organization for environmental change; it involves feeding forward information from the environment to the process and/or its inputs. For most organizations, both methods of control will be used.

The model of control appropriate for a parent involves a hierarchy of control systems, with both proactive and reactive characteristics. Six forms of strategic control have been identified. In a broad progression from fully proactive to reactive, these are assumption, surveillance, climate, implementation, and operational. Crisis control is a hybrid of proactive and reactive control.

Objectives are commitments to achieve, and these commitments should have the characteristics of being relevant, energizing, measurable, insightful, and timed. Multiple objectives are a particular concern, especially the tensions between individual and group objectives and those of the organization. Organizational culture will play a significant role in the selection of appropriate objectives.

Three methods of control are recognized, based on the type of intervention that the parent makes in the activities of the subsidiary. Output-based systems are concerned with results, process-based systems focus on work processes, and input-based systems focus on the way in which the conditions are set up to achieve the required performance.

In practice, two broad styles of formal parental control are significant: strategic planning, where the emphasis is on process and input control, and financial control, where the emphasis is on controlling the outputs. Overlaying these formal controls are the more informal controls exercised by individuals themselves and by the group through its culture.

KEY READINGS

- Many aspects of control in large organizations are discussed in the book by Goold et al. (1994).
- A very readable account of financial control systems in everyday use is given by Frank Wood and Alan Sangster in *Frank Wood's Business Accounting 2*, 8th edn. (London: Financial Times Management, 1999).
- A short and very interesting and amusing account of rumours and how they are generated and their consequences is Koenig (1985).
- Management of product recalls is described in N. Craig Smith, Robert J. Thomas, and John A. Quelch, 'A strategic approach to managing product recalls', *Harvard Business Review* (Sept.–Oct. 1996): 102–12.

DISCUSSION QUESTIONS

1 To operate efficiently and effectively, an organization needs to establish six types of strategic control. What might be required organizationally to establish each type?

2 What is the link between the four types of international configuration described in Chapter 10 and the types and strength of the control that is to be exercised?

3 You are posted to India to run the national sales office. You find that the only control system you have is a budgetary control system that allows accountants to provide you with cost and revenue variances. How would you go about improving control?

4 You are working at the head office of a multinational firm. You have been asked to review the strategic control mechanisms associated with subsidiaries. What general features about strategic control objectives would you stress in your dealings with personnel in the subsidiaries?

5 It has been rumoured in the USA that one of your products is defective: it is suggested that an ill-constructed electrical component in a popular hairdryer could lead to electrocution. The particular accusation first appeared on the internet and has now been picked up by the mainstream media in several other countries. How would you deal with this issue?

6 Assumption and surveillance control are two types of strategic control. What is their relationship to scenarios and scenario-building?

7 The global environment can be characterized as chaotic, complex, dynamic, and turbulent—all generally increasing the level of uncertainty facing senior managers. How might these environmental characteristics affect the way control is exercised in a multinational firm?

Closing case study
Sappron

Sappron International is a successful marketer of premium grade motor lubricants, with 10,000 people supplying the product worldwide through 80 subsidiaries and a further 50 agents. Sappron is well established in East Asia with business units in China, Malaysia, Singapore, Vietnam, Indonesia, and Thailand. In spite of the recent economic turmoil the region remains a 'key plank' of the company's forward corporate strategy, evidenced by the relocation of Sappron regional headquarters from the UK to Hong Kong at the end of 1998.

The Thai unit began operations as an agency some thirty years before the formation of a wholly owned Sappron subsidiary (Sappron Thailand) in 1986. The long-serving British CEO employed a 'laissez-faire' management style and the organizational culture and working practices became steadily more 'Asian' in flavour as day-to-day power was gradually taken over by the six Thai directors of the executive committee.

Powerful networks form the crux of Thai commercial activity, supported by a set of social values condemned as 'cronyism, collusion, corruption and complacency'. Managers seek to do business only with people they know and trust. Loyalty is expected between group members—as within a family—because they are considered to share the same world-views and communicate more efficiently in routine situations. Patronage loyalties tend to determine inter-departmental relationships within a business unit where bureaucratic norms would prevail in the West. In this cultural context, acceptance of the need for externally imposed change programs is invariably construed as a 'loss of face' by senior local executives who have grown up with the traditional top-down management system.

Sappron (Thailand) Ltd.

The divergence in business practices and values between Sappron UK headquarters and its Thai subsidiary was highlighted in a 1996 survey. The survey appeared to demonstrate that whereas head office personnel are overwhelmingly 'results-driven', 'serious', 'assertive', 'punctual', 'self-disciplined', 'diligent' and 'meticulous', their Thai counterparts display a set of business characteristics depicted as 'process-oriented', 'relationship-driven', 'soft-mannered', 'relaxed', 'informal' and 'respectful'. Corporate staff expressed concern with the perceived lack of forward planning by the local management, the emphasis on 'form and procedure' over outcomes and a 'mysterious' emphasis on non-verbal cues to impart opinion and feeling.

Thailand began to be viewed with increasing concern by UK headquarters toward the end of 1996, particularly in the wake of deteriorating productivity levels and a spiralling staff headcount. David Lloyd was installed as the new CEO in January 1997, the first major change at the top of the Thai unit for almost twenty years. Touted as a Sappron marketing specialist, Lloyd was quick to criticise the existing set-up for its lack of a 'cohesive strategy', held to be behind the decline in local market share.

'Project Delta': The restructuring of Sappron Thailand

The main focus in Project Delta concerned the restructuring imposed by head office upon the Thai marketing department in November 1997. Under the ten-year direction of Mr. Somkid, the department had encompassed both marketing and sales functions but with a marked emphasis on sales, as evidenced by a Bangkok based senior sales manager—Mr. Chokiat—effectively doubling as the department's 'strategist' and second-in-command. Between them Somkid and Chokiat drafted all necessary planning and strategy documents, including those for departmental advertising and promotion campaigns. Departmental power resided with the eight senior sales managers, half of whom controlled the 'two-wheel' market, the other half dealing with cars, trucks and agri-vehicles.

This organizational structure was highly idiosyncratic for a Sappron marketing division, and a major thrust of Lloyd's mandate was to bring the unit 'back into line' with regional corporate guidelines. Lloyd set about strengthening the marketing function by creating a new 'consumer marketing' unit, separate from sales and placed under the control of a new, hand-picked managerial recruit. This half-Thai, half-English newcomer—Mr. Dongchai-James—was then charged with recruiting three new managers, two of whom he selected externally. With the remaining half of his old department Somkid was allowed to keep his sales 'directorship', although he was clearly seen to suffer a demotion in status. The product divisions were restructured in line with the three Sappron corporate norms of 'motorcycle', 'automotive' and 'agri-trucks'. Each new 'senior' sales manager was to be held responsible for one division spanning the entire country, thus effectively reducing their number from eight to three, each with a 'product counterpart' to be drawn from the three new consumer marketing managers selected by Dongchai-James.

The challenge ahead for Sappron was not so much this re-drawing of structural boundaries, but successfully operationalizing the long-term adoption of change. The key areas of corporate change are considered below.

Sappron corporate values

Traditionally, newly recruited sales representatives were trained solely in 'marketing process', rather than taking the corporate-oriented induction course: with an emphasis on hands-on experience, corporate philosophy was deemed unnecessary and kept to a minimum. Part of the post-restructuring changes involved an insistence by Lloyd that both sales and marketing departments should acquire more awareness of corporate ideology through attendance at the corporate course, in line with other Sappron regional units. The concession to Somkid—agreed with Dongchai-James—was that the two departments would provide additional training programs in conjunction with Human Resources.

Product–territory reorganization

The aim of the product–territory split was to give precedence to product groupings. Practically, this effectively shifted resources away from a 'Central Bangkok' focus to a more balanced nationwide approach. Senior sales management resented what they viewed as interference from headquarters and attempted to dissuade Lloyd by emphasizing the primacy of the Bangkok area. Their argument was supported by the fact that Thailand has the highest 'primary-index'—the difference between first and second cities—in the world. A refusal by Lloyd and 'new-marketing' to rethink the structure—on the long-term conviction that Thailand would be more successful if run the 'Sappron-way'—led Somkid and Chokiat to work around the organization chart by keeping to the traditional links behind the scenes. The so-called 'bamboo-network' formed among favoured suppliers, clients and departmental employees allowed sales management to keep an informal but highly effective grip upon their former territories to the extent that individual marketing assistants, co-ordinators and finally managers had little alternative but to heed traditional working practice. Some months following the imposed changes a compromise was reached whereby corporate product divisions were incorporated at senior management level but with the former geographic structure kept intact under 'area sales controllers'—four for each product division.

Sappron downsizing

All staff were assessed by means of a company-wide input/output process matrix. A handful of individual 'casualties' were identified for each department. Somkid was presented with the names of two female executives deemed redundant. Somkid resisted their redundancy on the grounds of 'Thai managerial values'. The younger of the two ladies was the daughter of an ex-senior sales manager who had been tragically killed in a road accident; the elder had given over twenty years of service. Appealing to local 'paternalistic' responsibilities, Somkid argued to keep the younger member. The notion that the elder was under-performing was also rejected on the grounds that performance appraisal in the Western sense of the term was inappropriate for a Thai Sales department. Somkid pointed instead to the lady's loyalty and integrity of character as being far more important. The Thai concept of 'kreng jai'—whereby an individual seeks to avoid potentially traumatic or discomforting situations even where his or her own interests may be compromised—was also alluded to. A compromise was reached that allowed Somkid to keep the younger staff member while the elder was presented with a special severance package, personalized for reward of service.

Marketing planning

Dongchai-James's office as new consumer marketing director doubled as the departmental library for corporate plans. This apparent desire on the part of a senior manager to be bound by plans was considered by sales to be a mark of inflexibility and naivety. Instinctive decision-making was the traditionally considered pre-requisite for marketing success in Thailand.

Impressive long-term sales growth coupled with an apparent lack of any written direction gave corporate headquarters reason to let Somkid be shielded at key annual budget meetings by the ex-CEO. Twelve months into Project Delta both Lloyd and Dongchai-James increasingly came to accept the difficulties of trend prediction in a culture where planning seemed almost non-existent. Although charged with satisfying head office that corporate guidelines were being followed, substantially less written material was now issued by Dongchai-James's marketing department than at its inception.

Product imaging

Consumer marketing quickly voiced their dissatisfaction with the locally conceived flagship product *Si-Flow*, sold exclusively in Thailand since its launch in 1995. Marginal sales figures, a racy, 'sexist' packaging and doubts over quality had also begun to trigger unease at head office. The plan to replace *Si-Flow* with an international alternative was all but quashed however, by a sales-prompted conspiracy between company reps, key Bangkok customers and a sympathetic accounts receivables team. Wild swings in *Si-Flow* sales from one week to the next effectively warned Lloyd and Dongchai-James against tampering with what they came to view as a 'sensitive case'. A compromise was reached with a rebranded, *New Si-Flow* and a heavily promoted re-launch campaign.

Price formulation

Corporate dissatisfaction with Somkid's 'gut-feeling' approach to product pricing—apparently drawn from vague notions of competitor activity and premium branding—led to Dongchai-James's being charged with constructing a line-by-line audit as to how local prices were determined. Largely unassisted by a resentful sales management team, Dongchai-James was unable to do so. Corporate attention to rational structure and analysis had once again come up against the Thai emphasis on instinct, flexibility and secrecy. With each product priced independently and with no written record of methodology, Lloyd and Dongchai-James largely surrendered control. Still with nominal responsibility for pricing, consumer marketing gradually built a systematic formula but only once senior sales approval had been obtained.

Promotion campaigns

A major sales promotion was the targeted supply of 'gold' coins in special packs. Corporate concern for these measures was not merely about their 'corruption' but also with the ad-hoc and unmonitored tracking of results and trends. The compromise adopted allowed consumer sales to keep charge of targeting while holding marketing responsible for the post-campaign analysis.

Distribution

Sappron Thailand channels product through the seven major outlets defined as spare-parts shops, independent petrol stations, company 'service stops', automotive dealerships (franchised and non-franchised), department stores and wholesalers. In practical terms the latter category accounted for almost 80% of product distribution. Corporate criticism of existing distribution control was the unsystematic hand-out of 'support'—trade discounts and promotions across the seven channels, with the relative revenue generated by an individual dealer rarely proportionate to resource expenditure. In terms of 'Thai-style' business practice the sales team held that the long-standing relations developed between reps and dealers was non-quantifiable and unique in every case. The argument for local flexibility was then bolstered by a rare admission of the profound nepotism that appeared to regulate case-by-case assistance (senior managers were even equity holders in some favoured establishments). Non-familial links were bound by the Thai cultural concept of 'bunkhun' which involves the twin elements of gratitude and indebtedness on the one hand and kindness on the other, reciprocated in an ongoing cycle which ensures bilateral trust and respect. Content with an agreement from sales to provide 'transparent' and regular updates on distribution support, Lloyd decided, for the 'good of the business', to leave the traditional, albeit idiosyncratic, network largely as it stood.

Source: Andrews and Chompusri (2001: 77–94).

Discussion questions

1 What successes and what failures did Lloyd and Dongchai-James have with Project Delta? What was the reason for their successes and failures?

2 If you were placed in the position of Lloyd, how would you have gone about handling the change process?

REFERENCES

Allport, G., and Postman, L. J. (1947). *The Psychology of Rumor* (New York: Holt).

Aoki, M. (1998). *Information, Incentives and Bargaining in the Japanese Economy* (Cambridge: Cambridge University Press).

Cateora, P. R., and Graham, J. L. (2000). *International Marketing* (New York: Irwin/McGraw-Hill).

Dermer, J. (1977). *Management Planning and Control Systems: Advanced Concepts and Cases* (Homewood, Ill.: Irwin).

Ford, W. C. Jr (1999), quoted in the *Guardian* (29 Jan.), 19.

Goold, M., and Campbell, A. (1987). *Strategies and Styles: The Role of the Centre in Managing Diversified Corporations* (Oxford: Blackwell).

_____ and Alexander, M. (1994). *Corporate-Level Strategy: Creating Value in the Multibusiness Company* (New York: Wiley).

_____ and Luchs, K. (1993a). 'Strategies and styles revisited: strategic planning and financial control', *Long Range Planning* 26(5): 49–60.

_____ (1993b). 'Strategies and styles revisited: "strategic control" is it tenable?', *Long Range Planning* 26(6): 54–61.

Graham, J. L. (2001). 'Culture and human resources management', in A. M. Rugman and T. L. Brewer (eds.), *The Oxford Handbook of International Business* (Oxford: Oxford University Press).

Hofstede, G. (1968). *The Game of Budget Control* (London: Tavistock).

_____ (1980). *Culture's Consequences* (Beverley Hills, Calif.: Sage).

_____ (1991). *Cultures and Organizations: Software of the Mind* (New York: McGraw-Hill).

Kanter, R. M. (1977). *Men and Women of the Corporation* (New York: Basic Books).

Kim, Y.-K., and Campbell, N. (1995). 'Strategic control in Korean MNCs', *Management International Review* 35(1): 95–9.

Koenig, F. (1985). *Rumor in the Marketplace: The Social Psychology of Commercial Hearsay* (Dover, Mass.: Auburn House).

Kuhn, T. S. (1970). *The Structure of Scientific Revolutions* (Chicago: University of Chicago Press).

Lam, A. (1998). *Tacit Knowledge, Organisational Learning and Innovation: A Societal Perspective*, (Danish Research Unit for Industrial Dynamics, DRUID Working Paper no. 98-22, Aalborg University).

Mintzberg, H. (1991). '*The structuring of organizations*', in H. Mintzberg and J. B. Quinn (eds.), *The Strategy Process: Concepts, Contexts, Cases*, 2nd edn. (New York: Prentice Hall International).

Nonaka, I., and Takeuchi, T. (1995). *The Knowledge-Creating Company: How Japanese Companies Create the Dynamics of Innovation* (Oxford: Oxford University Press).

Perrow, C. (1970). *Organisational Analysis: A Sociological View* (London: Tavistock).

Peters, T. J., and Waterman, R. H. Jr (1982). *In Search of Excellence: Lessons from America's Best-Run Companies* (New York: Harper & Row).

Rosnow, R., and Fine, G. (1976). *Rumor and Gossip* (New York: Elsevier).

Ross-Ashby, W. (1970). *An Introduction to Cybernetics* (New York: University Paperbacks).

Schall, M. S. (1983). 'A communication-rules approach to organizational culture', *Administrative Science Quarterly* 28: 557–81.

Schein, E. (1985). *Organizational Culture and Leadership: A Dynamic View* (San Francisco, Calif.: Jossey-Bass).

——(1986). '*How Culture Forms, Develops, and Changes*', in R. H. Kilmann, M. J. Saxton, R. Serpa et al., *Gaining Control of the Corporate Culture* (San Francisco, Calif.: Jossey-Bass).

Schreyögg, G., and Steinmann, H. (1987). 'Strategic control: a new perspective', *Academy of Management Review* 12(1): 91–103.

Simons, R. (1994). 'How top managers use control systems as levers of strategic renewal', *Strategic Management Journal* 15(3): 169–89.

Snyder, N. H., Dowd, J. J. Jr, and Houghton, M. D. (1994). *Vision, Values and Courage: Leadership for Quality Management* (New York: Free Press).

Trompenaars, F., and Hampden-Turner, C. (1997). *Riding the Waves of Culture: Understanding Cultural Diversity in Business* (London: Brealey).

It (Path to Growth Strategy) is all about how we can reshape ourselves for faster growth and expanded margins.

Niall FitzGerald, Co-Chairman, Unilever Group, in February 2000[1]

A troubled giant

In September 1999, Unilever, one of the largest consumer goods companies in the world, announced plans to restructure its brand portfolio by the end of 2004. The plan involved cutting down on its unwieldy portfolio of 1,600 brands and focusing on the top 400 brands. This move was read by the market as an indication that the company was unable to manage its brands and so was scaling back growth plans. This development, coupled with the fact that the growing popularity of internet and telecom stocks was luring investors away from old economy stocks, resulted in Unilever finding itself in deep trouble—its stock price plummeted rapidly during 1999.

According to reports, Unilever's market capitalization of about £51 billion ($82 billion) in June 1999 shrank by almost £20 billion by January 2000. As a result, the company lagged far behind its competitors like Nestlé and Procter & Gamble (P&G) in market capitalization.

The fact that Unilever had failed to meet its performance expectations for 1999 added to its problems. Analysts attributed this failure to the sluggish growth of its top line brands. They said that the company's existing brand strategy framework had lost its focus. They also criticized Unilever for investing less in strengthening its leading brands during the 1990s (as a majority of its investments went into business restructuring and acquisitions). Meanwhile, the competitors had begun eating into Unilever's market share in a major way.

Unilever realized that it had to restructure its brand portfolio and operations to meet the challenges brought about by the changing market conditions. In February 2000, the company announced a €5 billion five-year growth strategy, aimed at bringing about a significant improvement in its performance. The initiative was named the 'Path to Growth' Strategy (PGS). The exercise involved a comprehensive restructuring of operations and businesses. While many industry observers welcomed the move, some were skeptical about the slow-moving old economy giant's ability to regain its momentum in time to meet the intensifying competition.

Background note

Unilever (called the Unilever Group) functioned as the operational arm of Unilever NV (Netherlands), and Unilever Plc., (UK), its two parent companies. Though the parent companies operated as separate legal

---

[1]'Shrinking to Grow', Economist, 26 February, 2000.

entities (with separate stock exchange listings), they functioned as a single business, with a single set of financials and a common board of directors (See Exhibit I for the group's structure).

Unilever was formed in 1930 when a Dutch margarine company, Margarine Unie, and a British soap company, Lever Brothers merged (See Exhibit III for a brief timeline of Unilever). While Margarine Unie had been formed by merging many margarine companies during the 1920s and was a leading global player in the business, Lever Brothers was a name worth reckoning with in the worldwide soap market and had soap factories across the world. Lever Brothers diversified into many other businesses (primarily related to foods). At the time of the merger, Margarine Unie and Lever Brothers, together, had operations in over 40 countries.

In the 1930s and 1940s, Unilever strengthened its presence in the US by acquiring Thomas J. Lipton (1937) and Pepsodent (1944). While the company's competitive position was adversely hit when its arch rival P&G launched Tide, a synthetic detergent, in 1946, it continued to prosper in Europe. This was because of the post-war boom in the demand for consumer goods, the growing popularity of margarine and personal care products, and the new detergent technologies.

During the 1960s and 1970s, Unilever rapidly expanded its operations through vertical and horizontal integration, emerging as a diversified conglomerate by the early 1980s. Diversification into different businesses was prompted in one way or the other by the existing business lines. For instance, oilseeds crushed for use in the margarine and soap businesses, yielded a by-product called 'cattle cake', and this led the company into the animal feeds business.

Likewise, by-products such as glycerine and fatty acids, formed from processing oil for use in margarine and soap production, prompted its entry into the chemicals business. The company operated 24 packaging plants (for its consumer products) in six European countries, from where goods were distributed worldwide. This activity made the company one of the largest truckers in Britain and one of the largest shipping company owners.

By 1980, soaps and edible fats accounted for only 40% of the company's total turnover as against 90% in 1930. At this point, frozen foods, ice creams, packaged soups, tea and personal products accounted for a significant share of the turnover. The net profit contribution of Unilever's non-European operations increased to 40% as against 20% in 1930. This was because the company had focused on expanding its operations in South America, Africa and Asia.

During the 1980s, Unilever decided to adopt a more focused approach towards business, referring to this as its 'core strategy'. As part of this, the company decided to focus on the following four industries—Foods, Personal Care, Home Care and Specialty Chemicals.

The decision to focus on these industries involved acquisition and divestiture of brands and companies as well. In 1984, Unilever acquired Brooke Bond, a leading tea brand, to strengthen its presence in Europe's tea market. In 1985, the company sold Palm Line, its shipping company. In 1987, it acquired Chesebrough-Pond's Inc., to establish itself strongly in the US personal products market and strengthen its position in the world skin care market.

As a result of these initiatives, Unilever built up an extensive range of product categories under each business segment. However, the company reportedly did not take steps to streamline its business processes as it increased in size. Gradually, it found itself becoming inflexible to change due to its cumbersome operations and other related inefficiencies. Some industry observers even referred to Unilever (of the late 1980s) as a 'sleeping giant'.

To come out of this mess, the company decided to restructure its operations in the early 1990s. The task involved reducing the number of product categories from 50 to 13, and focusing only on the core categories under each business segment. As a part of this strategy, the company made numerous acquisitions and divestitures. Between 1992 and 1996, Unilever made around 100 acquisitions. More than half of these were in the foods business, while the remaining related to detergents and personal care products. During 1995 alone, Unilever acquired 38 companies.

The company also decided to target emerging economies and began focusing more on Central and Eastern Europe, South East Asia, Latin America, China and India through the mid-1990s. This strategy yielded encouraging results in the late 1990s, as sales increased in these regions.

However, the recession in the food business in Western Europe (the company's largest food market accounting for 68% of its food sales) and the US severely affected Unilever's performance during the 1990s and it had to shut down or sell many food companies. To increase food sales, the company devised a new strategy—focusing on different product segments in different countries based on their sales potential. Thus, it focused on ice cream and margarine in South-East Asia, Southern Latin America and China, rather than giving an equally strong push to ice cream products all over the world. On account of this strategy, ice cream sales doubled as the reach increased to 45 countries (as against 20 countries previously).

Unilever exited from various businesses such as plant breeding and other agricultural products, packaging and professional cleaning products as well in the 1990s. In 1997, it exited from the chemicals business to focus better on the other core businesses. In October 1999, the company acquired Kibon (Brazil) and consolidated its position as the leading ice cream maker in the world.

In 1999, Unilever owned over 1,600 global, regional and local brands in the foods and home and personal care markets worldwide. The business was divided across five geographical segments—Europe, North America, Africa and the Middle East, Asia and Pacific, and Latin America. On account of the restructuring thrust, between 1985 and 1999, the company succeeded in improving its operating margins from less than 6% to over 11% and its return on capital from less than 11% to over 22%. The average earnings per share (EPS) increased by over 9% during this period. The company became the second largest packaged consumer goods company (after P&G) and the third largest food firm (after Nestlé and Kraft Foods) in the world.

The negative developments with respect to the financial performance and the stock price during 1999 put a major dampener on Unilever's prospects. According to industry watchers, given these circumstances, the decision to launch the PGS initiative was inevitable. At the time of announcing the PGS, Antony Burgmans and Niall FitzGerald, Unilever's Co-Chairmen, said, 'We see our future in a portfolio of strong brands with international and local scale. These will increasingly reach the consumer via a diversity of channels and a variety of communications media. That is at the heart of what we are announcing.'[2]

Unilever committed itself to achieving the following objectives by 2004—annual top line growth of 5%–6%; operating margins of 16% (as against 11% in 1999); and continued low double digit earnings per share growth. The market reacted positively to the announcement—the company's stock price increased by 4% in the European markets and investment banks such as Barings and Warburg Dillon Read upgraded the company's stock from hold to buy. Unilever sources were reportedly happy to see the initiative get off to a positive start.

What 'PGS' is all about

To achieve the objectives of the PGS, Unilever decided to concentrate on the following areas—modify the existing organizational structure, focus on leading brands, support these leading brands with strong

[2] 'Unilever Undertakes Massive Restructuring', Chemical Market Reporter, 28 February, 2000.

innovation and focused marketing strategies; rationalize the supply chain; simplify business processes; and restructure or weed-out under-performing businesses and brands (See Exhibit IV for the key drivers of value creation in the PGS).

Unilever expected the PGS to result in annual cost savings of €1.5 billion by 2004. An additional €1.6 billion in savings was to come from global procurement by the end of 2002. Apart from this, the PGS was to involve laying off over 25,000 employees (approximately 10% of the employee base) by 2004, on account of divestments or site closures, and restructuring and simplification of processes. The company announced that though the restructuring would be worldwide, it would mainly focus on the US and Europe.

Organizational restructuring

Unilever was split into two, separate global units: Foods, and Home and Personal Care (HPC). These two global divisions were headed by Unilever's two Executive Directors, Patrick Cescau (Foods) and Keki Dadiseth (HPC). Previously, these businesses functioned as a single entity, with a board of directors managing them in different geographical regions.

According to Unilever, separately managing the foods and HPC businesses was expected to help the company improve its focus on foods and HPC operations at the global as well as regional levels. The company also expected this new structure to help it make faster decisions and to strengthen its capacity for innovation by more effective integration of research into the divisional structure. Unilever's over 300 operating companies across the world were placed under ten regional groups (See Exhibit I for Unilever's regional groups).

Unilever also appointed regional Presidents for both the Foods and HPC divisions, and they reported to their respective divisional Executive Directors. Apart from these two global divisions, the company also operated a non-divisional group in the African region, which covered the area south of the Sahara. In this region, the company operated foods and HPC as a combined business.

Unilever decentralized the control of its subsidiaries too, with the corporate headquarters (in London and the Netherlands) monitoring profit levels. The headquarters also ensured that the subsidiaries were empowered enough to manage their operations and they were held responsible for their performance.

Exhibit I Unilever—regional groups

Division	Regional Groups
Foods	Foods North Africa, Middle East and Turkey. Unilever Bestfoods Asia. Unilever Bestfoods Latin America. Unilever Bestfoods North America & Slim-Fast worldwide. Unilever Bestfoods, Europe.
Home & Personal Care	Home and Personal Care, Asia. Home and Personal Care, Europe. Home and Personal Care, North America. HPC North Africa, Middle East & Turkey. HPC Division, Latin America.

Source: www.unilever.com.

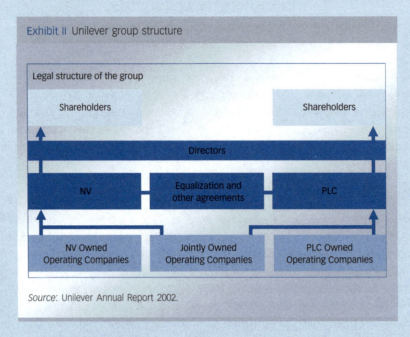

Exhibit II Unilever group structure

Source: Unilever Annual Report 2002.

Unilever also decided to significantly downsize the brands/businesses that were not contributing much to the profits. This decrease in businesses/brands was expected to make nearly 100 manufacturing plants redundant, and the company decided to close these down. The slashing of brands, closure of manufacturing plants and exit from businesses was expected to result in about 25,000 job cuts [nearly 10% of Unilever's employee base (246,000 in 2000)] by the end of 2004.

Apart from this, in the early 21st century, Unilever, under the leadership of FitzGerald committed itself to promoting a new crop of younger executives, who were willing to take risks, unlike its previous generation of conservative and rational executives, who averted risks. According to FitzGerald, over 40 of the company's top 100 executives were new to the company's ranks between 2000 and 2002. Commenting on the rationale for this, he said, 'Unilever has traditionally been a very cerebral company. What you need is a bit of action.'[3]

Brand restructuring

As part of the PGS, Unilever decided to slash its wide product portfolio of 1,600 brands to concentrate on the 400 leading brands such as Snuggle, Vaseline, Close-up, Ponds, Dove, Persil, Bird's Eye, Knorr, Sunsilk, Calvin Klein, Lipton, Magnum and Omo (See Exhibit V for some major Unilever brands) through focused product innovation and brands development efforts.

The decision was also propelled by the fact that over 1,000 brands of the company's total brand portfolio of 1,600 brands accounted for a mere 8% of the turnover. So, Unilever felt that by pruning the poorly performing brands, it could drastically reduce fragmentation of resources, and these could then be re-routed to support the leading brands. Unilever expected its leading brands to account for over 95% of its total turnover as against 75% in 1999.

[3] 'Unilever Restocks', BusinessWeek, 6 August, 2001.

Exhibit III Timeline of Unilever

1885	Lever Brothers founded by William Hesketh Lever.
1917	Lever diversifies into foods.
1920s	Association formed with Thomas Lipton's tea company.
1927	Margarine Unie formed by merger of Jurgens and Van Den Bergh.
1929	Unilever formed when the Dutch margarine company Margarine Unie merged with British soapmaker Lever Brothers.
1930s	Soaps and edible fats account for 90% of business.
1940s/50s	Extensive investment in new technology and research facilities.
1970s	Expansion through acquisitions in chemicals and packaging.
1980	Frozen foods, ice cream, packaged soups, tea and personal products account for 60% of business.
1980s	Acquisition of Faberge/Elizabeth Arden and Calvin Klein fragrance businesses acquired.
1987	Acquisition of Chesebrough-Pond's in the US.
1990s	Ancillary businesses, including packaging companies, agribusiness interests and speciality chemicals are sold.
1999	Acquisition of Amora Maille.
2000	Acquisition of Slim-Fast, Ben & Jerry's and Bestfoods.
2000	Company is restructured to reflect the split between the Unilever Bestfoods (Foods) and Home and Personal Care divisions.

Source: www.unilever.com.

Exhibit IV Key drivers of value creation in PBS

- Growth of the leading brands.
- Exit from the tail brands and businesses in a value creating way.
- Delivery of EPS growth in a quality way with increased gross operating margins, partly re-invested to support leading brands.
- Restructuring proceeding according to plan.
- Under-performing businesses being pruned.
- Organization restructured, to execute the PBS with a real passion for winning.

Source: www.unilever.com.

Exhibit V Unilever—a list of major brands (partial)

FOOD BRANDS		HOME & PERSONAL CARE BRANDS	
• Bertolli	• Findus	• Axe	• Domestos
• Heart	• Iglo	• Lux	• Radiant
• Knorr	• Healthy Heart	• Rexona	• Surf
• Birdseye	• Amora	• Cif	• Dove
• Hellmann's	• Floral/Becel Pro.Activ	• Omo	• Skip
• Lipton	• Magnum	• Signal	• Snuggle
• Slim-Fast	• Cornetto	• Comfort	• Calvin Klein
• IBF Brand	• Family Brand	• Pond's	• Close Up
• UBF Food Solutions		• Sunsilk	• Vaseline

Source: www.unilever.com.

The company called its brand focus strategy 'nourishing the core' as it felt that limiting its resources to 400 leading brands would enable more effective innovations and faster rollout of new products. According to Unilever sources, with a more powerful and focused portfolio of brands, the company could expect to increase its share in various markets across the globe. Some of the major categories the company was focusing on as part of the PGS were tea and beverages, ice cream, culinary dishes, margarines and spreads, and health and wellness.

The major components of the brand strategy under PGS included—exploiting brands within the existing product categories but outside their scope (for instance, Dove in Hair and Knorr in Frozen foods); extending brands outside their existing geography/category; extending brands to adjacent segments (for instance, Cornetto into the Soft Ice market, Lipton into the soft drinks market with Ready-to-Drink Tea, and Sunsilk into hair colorants); moving brands into new channels (mainly in the food business) and expanding brands into new markets, specifically in the fast growing, developing and emerging markets.

FitzGerald also revealed plans to embark on an acquisition spree to strengthen Unilever's position in the food and HPC markets worldwide. As part of its acquisition strategy, the company mainly focused on acquiring American food companies and brands, as the valuations of these companies were low during that period, owing to the prevailing recession.

Beginning early 2000, Unilever acquired many companies to strengthen its presence in various product categories across various markets. The company's major acquisitions since 2000 included Bestfoods (US, Foods), Groupo Cressida Central America Foods Corporation (Central America, HPC), Amora Maille (France, Culinary Products), Jaboneria NA (Ecuadaor, Foods and HPC), Ben & Jerry's (US, Ice Cream), Cressida (Honduras, Foods, Soaps and Detergents), Codepar/SPCD (Tunisia, HPC), Slim-Fast (USA, Slimming Products).

According to analysts, Bestfoods (acquired for $24 billion, in June 2000), which owned popular food brands such as Knorr, Hellmann's mayonnaise, Mazola oil, Pot Noodle and Bovril, was an excellent fit in Unilever's food business. Commenting on the rationale for buying Bestfoods, FitzGerald said that there were very few global brands in food and by acquiring Bestfoods, Unilever had gained two of its top three

Exhibit VI Growth in Unilever's operating margin, sales and earnings per share under PGS

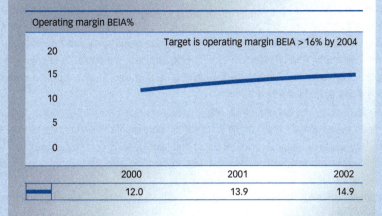

Operating margin BEIA%

Target is operating margin BEIA >16% by 2004

	2000	2001	2002
	12.0	13.9	14.9

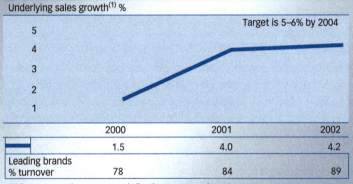

Underlying sales growth[1] %

Target is 5–6% by 2004

	2000	2001	2002
	1.5	4.0	4.2
Leading brands % turnover	78	84	89

(1) Turnover growth per annum excluding the year-on-year impact of acquisitions and disposals in all years.

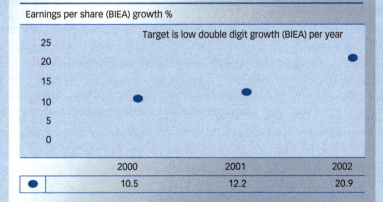

Earnings per share (BIEA) growth %

Target is low double digit growth (BIEA) per year

	2000	2001	2002
	10.5	12.2	20.9

Source: Unilever Annual Report 2002.

biggest food brands, Knorr and Hellmann's (the third brand being Bachelors', which comprised dried food products). Apart from this, the integration of Bestfoods was expected to result in annual cost savings of about €0.8 billion to Unilever.

The acquisition of Slim-Fast Foods Co., (for $2.3 billion, in April 2000), a diet supplement manufacturer and Ben & Jerry's Homemade Inc. (for $223 million, in April 2000), a leading ice cream maker, was expected to strengthen Unilever's presence in the US and provide it with products and brands that could be expanded internationally. Analysts felt that by acquiring Slim-Fast, the company strengthened its position in the fast growing 'functional foods'[4] market while it consolidated its position as a leading ice cream maker in the world by acquiring Ben & Jerry's.

In the same manner, the acquisition of Amora Malie, a French culinary products company, in early 2000, increased the company's share of the European culinary product market from 9% to 12%. The major products of Amora Malie included French mustards and sauces, salad dressing and ketchup. According to Unilever sources, the acquisition of all the above food companies filled the gaps in the company's product portfolios and helped to strengthen the company itself.

Next, Unilever decided to dispose about 1,200 brands to streamline its businesses and generate cost savings. According to company sources, a majority of these brands belonged to the foods segment. This was because the food business, comprising over 1,000 brands, had many under-performing brands. In 1999, sales in the fats and frozen-food businesses (excluding the ice cream and drinks businesses) declined by 4.6% to $9.2 billion.

The company first decided to improve the performance of its under-performing businesses such as the Elizabeth Arden range of fragrances and skin care products, and the European baking business. Businesses/brands that failed to improve their performance even after such attempts were marked for disposal. The company sold many food businesses and brands through 2000, and these included the European Bakery business, Benedicta, a France-based culinary business and Bestfoods Baking Co. which owned popular brands such as Thomas' English muffins, Boboli Italian pizza crusts and Entenmann's baked goods. In 2000, Unilever disposed of 27 businesses and brands, netting $642 million.

These moves resulted in the company's decision to dispose a significant number of its manufacturing plants which had become surplus after brand divestitures. As part of this move, Unilever decided to re-arrange its manufacturing operations around a base of 150 key manufacturing plants (from the total base of 388 manufacturing plants), and to close or dispose of around 100 manufacturing plants. According to reports, the closure of these plants was expected to cost the company about €2.3 billion.

According to reports, the expenditure on marketing support for the brands was expected to increase from 13% of sales in 1999 to 15% of sales by 2004. Thus in 2000, the company said that it would invest £1 billion in additional marketing support to its leading brands over the next five years.

The next task was the creation of new distribution channels. A major part of Unilever's distribution activity was carried out through grocery channels. However, in the early 21st century, consumer trends were changing radically and a significant percentage of food consumption was being done outside of homes (in the US, this percentage was estimated to be 50%). This made the company realize that it needed to move beyond the grocery channels route. So, Unilever created new distribution channels to widen its reach. For example, it launched the Lipton Soup Bar, a soup station for fast service and supermarket food

---

[4]Functional foods can be described as the food products that are formulated with naturally occurring chemicals found in vegetables, herbs, fruits, grains and spices, to provide health benefits beyond basic nutrition to the consumers.

service operators. Similarly in Turkey, the company appointed a sales team that used a fleet of boats with ice-cream freezers to sell ice-creams to consumers on yachts in the bays.

Unilever also decided to reinforce its advertising strategies to strengthen its leading brands such as Bird's Eye, Hellmann's and Ben & Jerry's. As part of this decision, the company in May 2002, struck a 4-year advertising deal worth €500 million with Carlton Communications and Granada Plc., major broadcasting companies in the UK, which controlled ITV, the biggest commercial television network in the UK. As part of the deal, considered to be the biggest advertising contract of its kind, Unilever earned the rights to promote its leading brands on ITV. During the same time, the company also closed a 5-year advertising deal with France-based JCDecaux, the biggest billboards (poster) company in Europe. Under this deal, JCDecaux was to handle the poster advertising of Unilever, in over 22 European countries.

As part of its marketing initiatives to strengthen its leading brands in Europe, Unilever entered into an online advertising contract with Microsoft for three years. This deal was for developing interactive and online marketing strategies for the company's leading brands in France, the UK and Germany. The contract was an extension of the company's online advertising contract (formed in 1998) with Microsoft to promote Unilever brands on its MSN.com portal in the US.

Under its online advertising contract in Europe, Unilever was the prime sponsor of the Womencentral channel on MSN.com. Apart from this, Unilever placed banners and advertisements on MSN.com (Europe) and had dedicated websites and interactive displays in France, UK and Germany. Commenting on the contract with Microsoft, Christoph Michalski, Director, Interactive Brand and Customer Center (Amsterdam), Unilever, said, 'We are very pleased with the extension of this relationship into Europe. This is a great opportunity for many of our key brands to experiment with this medium in Europe and to develop original content and interactive marketing and communications strategies.'[5]

Apart from such marketing strategies, Unilever also focused on innovations to support its leading brands. The decision to de-emphasize about 1,200 brands enabled the company to focus its innovations (through increased resources) on strengthening the leading brands.

Simplification of processes

As part of simplifying processes, the company decided to use the latest information technology (IT) tools and the internet. According to Unilever, the use of the latest technology was expected to drastically bring down overhead costs and help the company to streamline its corporate centre and operations. The installation and integration of such knowledge and information systems into the company's processes was expected to cost €2.0 billion.

Until 2000, Unilever had a decentralized IT infrastructure with multiple IT environments—it was using many legacy systems and enterprise resource planning (ERP) applications from different companies (like SAP, BPCS, MFG Pro and Fourth Shift). In 2000, the company realized that it needed a global information network that would provide all its employees easy and fast access to actionable information (on both a regional and global basis).

Though Unilever had a well established intranet, which linked about 70,000 computers and helped company executives, throughout Unilever facilities worldwide, access and share knowledge, it felt that this infrastructure might not support the quick information transfer needed for meeting the PGS objectives. So, in late 2000, the company launched the Unilever Information Program (UIP). The UIP's major goal

[5]'Unilever Extends Online Advertising with Microsoft into Europe,' www.unilever.com, 20 February, 2000.

was to harness the mass of data from various information sources that included seven regional business groups and over 300 operating units, which were supported by numerous IT environments.

The company's first priority under the UIP was to develop a quick data integration solution so that employees could gain access to numerous data sources simultaneously, enabling an in-depth analysis of the issue at hand. The UIP team embarked on the task of developing an infrastructure with the corporate data warehouse at its core.

The global data warehouse offered unified access to financial, brand, customer and supply chain information to over 100,000 users throughout Unilever. Standardizing the data and making it easily accessible to global management teams at the company under the UIP was expected to help identify global trends and opportunities quickly.[6]

During the same period, Unilever also realized that it needed to change its strategies to survive in the highly competitive market. So it decided to invest in e-commerce in a major way to meet the changing market needs and dynamics. According to reports, the company planned to invest about £130 million ($208 million) in e-commerce. The company decided to use the internet to improve its brand communication, marketing and online-selling activities and to simplify business-to-business transactions across its supply chain. It entered into deals with technology and B2B companies such as IBM, Microsoft, Compaq, Ariba Inc., Excite@Home and WOWGO to enable faster identification and implementation of e-commerce opportunities.

In February 2000, Unilever entered into a $200 million joint venture with iVillage, an American portal, targeting women in the age group of 25–54 years, who were prime consumers of personal care products. In 2001, Unilever closed a deal, dubbed Global Infrastructure Organization (GIO) E-Services, with Syntegra, an e-Solutions firm. As part of the deal, Syntegra would lend its web hosting capabilities to Unilever's 2,700 websites. GIO E-Services was expected to help Unilever maintain the security standards it desired on its websites by consolidating the infrastructure required to host all its websites. During that period, the company was also contemplating multiple web hosting agreements with different companies.

The majority of Unilever's websites offered product and brand specific information to customers worldwide. Apart from these, the company also maintained a number of intranet sites that enabled Unilever employees across the world, to communicate and share information among themselves. According to Martin Armitage, head of GIO and senior vice president, Unilever, the partnership with Syntegra would largely help in the future development of the company's leading brands via internet.

Supply chain restructuring

Restructuring the supply chain was one of the six major components of the 'PGS'. This initiative was expected to save €1.75 billion in supply chain costs. The company's decision to cut down its brand portfolio was expected to help improve supply chain efficiencies. According to FitzGerald, 'The consequence is that the tail brands (under performing brands) will fall away in due course and we will be able to simplify and make major improvements to the supply chain and to the way in which we do business generally.'[7]

Unilever decided to make significant changes to its supply chain of 388 manufacturing plants across the world, by focusing on 150 key plants. The major thrust areas of supply chain restructuring were: implementing executive purchasing; attracting, developing and retaining world class supply management

[6]A detailed description of the UIP initiative is covered in the ICMR case study, 'Unilever Restructures its Supply Chain Management Practices'.
[7]'Unilever to Shed 10% of Workforce in Global Restructuring,' www.wsws.org, 1 March, 2000.

executives; professionalizing the purchase of non-production items; enabling e-sourcing in all worldwide facilities; accelerating and leveraging simplification of supply chain; and driving information and management.

As part of its supply chain restructuring Unilever restructured its supply chain organization. It established a supply chain division that was led by two vice presidents (one each from the Foods and Home & Personal Care businesses). In addition, the company also set up a supply chain steering team to lead the supply chain restructuring process. This steering team and the supply chain division managed the supply chain initiatives and ensured the delivery of expected results.[8]

The company also realized that having an efficient and committed supplier base was important for the success of its supply chain initiatives. It therefore focused on fostering healthy relationships with its supplier base. To motivate suppliers to commit themselves to the 'PGS', the company rewarded them on the basis of their ability to help in innovations (under key brands) and to improve their processes to reduce costs.

Unilever also laid high emphasis on supply management for non-production items. It established a non-production item supply management division, led by a global vice president, who was made responsible for the entire non-production item purchasing set up. The non-production items purchase strategy was mainly based on cross-business control. So, the regional supply management divisions purchased non-production items for the Foods as well as Home & Personal Care divisions.

The company also emphasized on e-procurement after identifying many supply chain redundancies in its procurement model. In March 2000, it partnered with Ariba to use the Ariba B2B eCommerce platform. This was done to create global economies of scale and achieve supply chain efficiencies through web-based transactions. Unilever planned to reduce procurement costs by streamlining worldwide purchases from its large supplier base.

With the help of the Ariba solution, Unilever piloted an e-auction program in the US, whereby it procured the required materials through conducting reverse auctions on the internet. Unilever expanded its e-procurement activity to other regions as well by 2002. However, initially e-auctions were restricted to the purchase of goods such as packaging materials, which did not have huge quality differences even when sourced from different suppliers. The company estimated that 20% of its overall procurement activities would become web-based by the end of 2003.

As part of restructuring its distribution network, Unilever combined all its warehouses and chose one warehouse in each region to consolidate its products. This drastically reduced the number of warehouses and simplified the process of warehouse management. In 2002, Unilever announced that it would build five regional mega distribution centres (of 1 million sq.ft each), which would have special arrangements for storing both its product lines. According to company sources, these centres were expected to reduce freight and warehousing costs by 10%–20% and enable the company to transport orders to the customer within 24 hours.

Apart from removing redundancies in warehousing, Unilever also focused on eliminating inefficiencies in its shipping processes. The company decided to combine shipping processes of its home and personal care products, the idea being that a single customer (retailer) received all home and personal care products by one truck. According to company sources, this unification of shipping processes was expected to considerably reduce transportation costs.

---

[8] A detailed description of the supply chain management restructuring undertaken by Unilever is covered in the ICMR case study, 'Unilever Restructures its Supply Chain Management Practices'.

Results of PGS (Till 2003)

In 2000, the company witnessed a dramatic increase in its turnover with sales increasing by 16% to €47.6 billion. This was mainly attributed to the acquisition of the Bestfoods, Slim-Fast, Ben & Jerry's and Amora Maille businesses. Since the announcement of the PGS, Unilever's share price had recovered by 30% to $59 in August 2001, and this seemed to highlight the positive results of its restructuring exercise.

By July 2002, Unilever's 400 leading brands accounted for 88% of the sales, up from 75% in 1999. By then, over 30,000 employees had been laid-off. Commenting on the positive results of the PGS in mid-2002, FitzGerald said, 'We have now reached the mid-point in the PGS and we continue to be confident about delivering our program. Brand focus continues apace with 88% of our turnover now attributable to leading brands. These brands are showing great resilience in a tough economic environment and will drive accelerating top line growth.'[9]

In fiscal 2002, Unilever's operating margin increased to 14.9%, a 1% and 3.8% increase over its margins in 2001 and 1999 respectively (See Exhibit VI). Analysts largely attributed this to the savings achieved on account of the restructuring initiatives. By this time, the company had exited from about 100 businesses and closed over 122 manufacturing plants. According to reports, the net debt of the company had reduced from €23.20 billion to €16.97 billion in 2002, and this was mainly attributed to strong operating cash flow, proceeds from the sale of businesses/brands.

By mid-2003, the company had achieved over €1 billion in restructuring savings and exceeded its Bestfoods integration savings target of €0.8 billion. It exceeded its €1.6 billion in savings targets from its SCM and procurement initiatives as well by the end of 2002. The company further raised its 2003 savings estimated from these activities from €450 million to €600 million. The capital efficiency of Unilever too improved (on account of reduction in fixed assets and working capital) by 8% of sales to 21%.

On account of enhanced product portfolio (under key brands), increased operating margins and enhanced capital efficiency, Unilever also achieved a significant increase in annual free cash flow, which increased by €1 billion as compared to the 1999 figure of €3 billion. During this period, the company's cash flow from operations was €7.9 billion and its annual EPS growth rate was 21% (See Exhibit VII).

By mid-2003, Unilever had reduced its brand portfolio to 635 brands and was fast closing in on its target of 400 brands. The top 400 brands accounted for 90% of the company's turnover and had increased their sales by 3.2% and 3.1% during the first two quarters of 2003—HPC brands grew at 3% and the Foods brands by 3.3% during the first half of the year (See Exhibit VII).

The company's focused promotional and distribution initiatives in developing markets, reportedly, also contributed to the growth in the sales of leading brands. Apart from this, the focused innovation strategy helped the company extend many of its leading brands to different categories. For instance, Dove soap was extended into the shampoo and deodorants categories in across 80 countries. As a result of this, the brand grew by 25% by the end of 2002 (since early 2000s).

Other major innovation successes during the early 21st century were new Axe/Lynx fragrances, Magnum 7 Deadly Sins in Europe, Hellmann's Dippin' sauces and Lipton Asian side dishes in North America, Lipton Sparkle in Japan, Brooke Bond boilable tea bags launch in India, Becel Pro.Activ in Brazil, Knorr bouillon launch in China and Knorr noodle cups in Mexico.

[9] 'Anglo-Dutch Giant Unilever Raises Full-Year Outlook,' Eurofood, 15 August, 2002.

Exhibit VII Unilever financials (in € million)

BY GROUP

	1998	1999	2000	2001	2002
Group Turnover	40,437	40,977	47,582	51,514	48,270
Group Operating Profit:					
Group Operating Profit BEIA	4,293	4,595	5,729	7,149	7,165
Exceptional Items	125	(269)	(2,113)	(588)	(879)
Amortization of Goodwill and Intangibles	(8)	(23)	(435)	(1,387)	(1,245)
Total Gross Operating Profit	4,410	4,303	3,181	5,174	5,041
Income from Fixed Investments	37	52	53	96	111
Interest	156	(14)	(632)	(1,646)	(1,173)
Profit on Ordinary Activities before Taxation	4,603	4,341	2,602	3,624	3,979
Profit on Ordinary Activities after Taxation	3,088	2,972	1,320	2,077	2,441
Net Profit	2,944	2,771	1,105	1,838	2,129

BY GEOGRAPHIC REGION

GEOGRAPHIC REGION	1998	1999	2000	2001	2002
Group Turnover					
Europe	18,165	18,040	18,967	20,119	19,573
North America	8,417	8,838	11,631	13,767	12,446
Africa, Middle East and Turkey	3,034	3,048	3,296	3,191	3,139
Asia and Pacific	5,803	6,723	8,038	7,846	7,679
Latin America	5,018	4,328	5,650	6,591	5,433
Total	40,437	40,977	47,582	51,514	48,270
Group Operating Profit					
Europe	2,254	2,131	1,693	2,689	1,750
North America	942	847	48	1,092	1,435
Africa, Middle East and Turkey	268	302	321	203	286
Asia and Pacific	457	642	776	862	1,077
Latin America	489	381	343	328	493
Total	4,410	4,303	3,181	5,174	5,041

BY OPERATIONS

OPERATION	1998	1999	2000	2001	2002
Group Turnover					
Foods	20,919	20,339	23,898	28,155	26,937
Home & Personal Care	18,783	19,781	22,825	22,739	20,801
Other Operations	735	857	859	620	532
	40,437	40,977	47,582	51,514	48,270
Group Operating Profits					
Foods	1,801	1,788	1,735	2,303	2,185
Home & Personal Care	2,093	2,361	1,415	2,823	2,814
Other Operations	516	154	31	48	42
Total	4,410	4,303	3,181	5,174	5,041

Source: Unilever Annual Report 2002.

Unilever's future prospects

In August 2003, Unilever announced its half-yearly results for the year—sales dropped by 15% and profits fell by 13%. During this time, the company reduced its growth forecasts to 4% from the 5%–6%, it had promised its investors in the early 2003, stating that it was struggling with a more challenging business environment—poor sales in the dietary and food service markets, and the sluggish growth in the retail market on account of slower economic growth, worldwide.

In October 2003, Unilever's share price fell by 7% (to 487 pence) on the London Stock Exchange, immediately after it announced that it was lowering its growth forecasts for its leading brands to below 3% for 2003. The company attributed this move to the waning popularity of its famous fragrance and dieting products (including Calvin Klein, Eternity, Prestige and Slim-Fast), and the poor performance of its other health and wellness products. This was the second time in 2003, that the company had reduced its growth forecasts for its leading brands.

FitzGerald blamed himself for the fall in the company's share price, after the announcement of reduced growth rates. According to him, the market had misunderstood Unilever's growth forecasts previously as the company had failed to communicate them clearly to its investors. He said, 'I blame myself here. Perhaps we did not communicate this as sharply as we should have. We promised 5%–6% by the end of 2004.'[10]

Despite lowered growth rates for 2003, Unilever claimed to be well on its way to achieving the PGS targets. FitzGerald said, 'In every respect, other than the top line sales number, we are not only on course but we are ahead of plan.'[11] Commenting on the ongoing PGS initiatives, he added, 'We planned to cut our product range from 1,600 brands to 400 by the end of 2004 and we are already at about 600. We wanted to focus the portfolio on global brands. We had four at the start of 2000 with sales of more than 1 billion [£700 million] and we now have 14.'[12]

FitzGerald announced that by February 2004, Unilever's sales would be back on track and the company would then reveal its Path to Growth Strategy II, to build on the results achieved in the first phase, now referred to as PGS I.

Some analysts feared that it might be hard for Unilever to achieve the growth targets for its leading brands, as many of the markets for these brands, especially in the foods and detergent category, were nearing saturation. However, many others felt that considering Unilever's greater presence (than any other company except Nestlé) in the emerging markets, where the purchasing power was drastically rising, it would not be impossible for the company to sustain a 5%–6% growth rate (for the leading brands) in the near future.

In 2003, Unilever's profits from developing markets grew on an average by 11% a year, as compared to an average of 8% a year in developed countries. The developing markets accounted for a third of the company's total sales. According to reports, the purchasing power of developing markets was expected to exceed that of the developed markets by 2006. In the light of this, analysts commented that Unilever might even achieve higher than expected growth rates, if it continued to strengthen its operations in developing markets.

[10]'An Unwelcome Loss of Weight for Unilever', www.telegraph.co.uk, 3 August, 2003.
[11]'An Unwelcome Loss of Weight for Unilever', www.telegraph.co.uk, 3 August, 2003.
[12]'An Unwelcome Loss of Weight for Unilever,' www.telegraph.co.uk, 3 August, 2003.

ADDITIONAL READING AND REFERENCES

1. **Munching on Change**, Economist, 6 January, 1996.

2. Unilever to Create 'Power Brands', http://news.bbc.co.uk, 21 September, 1999.

3. Rohan Mike, **Refocused Unilever on Global Acquisition Spree**, www.itsfood.com, 4 January, 2000.

4. **Unilever Changes Tack**, http://news.bbc.co.uk, 22 February, 2000.

5. **Unilever to Axe 25,000 Jobs in Cost Overhaul**, Many Food Brands to Go, www.industrysearch.com.au, 23 February, 2000.

6. **Shrinking to Grow**, Economist, 26 February, 2000.

7. Harvilicz Helen, **Unilever Undertakes Massive Restructuring**, Chemical Market Reporter, 28 February, 2000.

8. Stevens Robert, **Unilever to Shed 10 Percent of Workforce in Global Restructuring**, www.wsws.org, 1 March, 2000.

9. **Unilever to Slash 25,000 Jobs**, Eurofood, 2 March, 2000.

10. **Fat and Thin**, Economist, 15 April, 2000.

11. Lee Allen Robin, **Unilever Scoops Ben & Jerry's,** Ices Changes, Nation's Restaurant News, 24 April, 2000.

12. **Food Fights**, Economist, 6 May, 2000.

13. **Unilever Sells its European Bakery Supplies Business**, Eurofood, 20 July, 2000.

14. Armitage Jim, **Unilever Reveals Global Shake-Up**, www.thisismoney.com, 4 August, 2000.

15. **Unilever Announces Rise in Sales Following Restructuring**, www.netlondon.com, 4 August, 2000.

16. **Unilever on Target**, Eurofood, 23 November, 2000.

17. **Unilever Pares Down to Leading Brands**, Mergers & Acquisitions, April 2001.

18. **Unilever Axes 8,000 Jobs**, http://money.cnn.com, 27 April, 2001.

19. Boulton Clint, **Unilever Taps Syntegra to Manage its Web Presence**, www.internetnews.com, 14 May, 2001.

20. **Unilever Embarks on Global Strategy**, www.computing.co.uk, 1 August, 2001.

21. **Unilever Restocks**, www.businessweek.com, 6 August, 2001.

22. **Unilever**, www.corporatewatch.org.uk, 25 September, 2001.

23. Hicks Matt, **Inside E-Procurement**, www.eweek.com, 7 January, 2002.

24. S. Nash Kim, **Unilever's Supply-Chain Diet**, www.baselinemag.com, 15 June, 2002.

25. **Anglo-Dutch Giant Unilever Raises Full-Year Outlook**, Eurofood, 15 August, 2002.

26. **Bold not Bland for Unilever**, Sinclair Lara, 23 September, 2002.

27. Hawkes Steve, **Unilever Cuts Forecasts in Growth Blow**, www.thisislondon.com, 23 June, 2003.

28. **An Unwelcome Loss of Weight for Unilever**, www.telegraph.co.uk, 3 August, 2003.

29. **Eurostocks Static, Unilever Slumps on Outlook**, www.forbes.com, 20 October, 2003.

30. **Unilever Shares Fall on Dim Outlook**, www.theage.com.au, 21 October, 2003.

31. Bawden Tom, **Unilever Shares Fall 7% After New Sales Warning**, www.timesonline.co.uk, 21 October, 2003.

32. www.unilever.com.

33. http://uk.biz.yahoo.com.

34. http://news.bbc.co.uk.

35. http://www.corporatewatch.org.uk.

36. www.newint.org.

INDEX